GLOBAL ETHICS

GLOBAL ETHICS

edited by
Wyatt Galusky
Andrew Garnar
Harlan Miller
Jean Miller

Virginia Tech

KENDALL/HUNT PUBLISHING COMPANY
4050 Westmark Drive   Dubuque, Iowa 52002

Copyright © 2002 by Kendall/Hunt Publishing Company

ISBN 0-7872-9839-5

All rights reserved. No part of this publication may be reproduced, stored in a retrieval system, or transmitted, in any form or by any means, electronic, mechanical, photocopying, recording, or otherwise, without the prior written permission of the copyright owner.

Printed in the United States of America
10   9   8   7   6   5   4   3   2

TABLE OF CONTENTS

Preface   ix

Universals

Introduction	3
The Biological Basis of Ethics	16
Peter Singer	
United Nations Universal Declaration of Human Rights	32
Introduction to the Principles of Morals and Legislation	37
Jeremy Bentham	
Utilitarianism	43
John Stuart Mill	
The Limits of Neopragmatism	48
Cornel West	

Instantiation$_1$ Intervention and Responsibility

Introduction	55
The Singer Solution to World Poverty	57
Peter Singer	
On the Obligation to Keep Informed about Distant Atrocities	62
Carlo Filice	
Globalization and September 11	74
Michael Mann	

Instantiation$_2$ The Development Question

Introduction	93
Development, Ecology and Women	96
Vandana Shiva	
Excerpt from Excess-ive Bodies	105
Theresa Ebert	
Globalization and Its Discontents	108
Herman Daly	
An Anniversary of Consequence and Relevance	113
David Harvey	
Consumption as a Theme in the North-South Dialogue	122
Luis Camacho	
The African Context of Human Rights	126
Claude Ake	

Instantiation₃ Environment

Introduction	135
Nature versus the Environment	137
Mark Sagoff	
"Let them Eat Pollution": Capitalism and the World Environment	142
John Bellemy Foster	
The Consistency Argument for Ethical Vegetarianism: Why YOU Are Committed to the Immorality of Eating Meat and Other Animal Products	149
Mylan Engel, Jr.	
Post-Modernism and the Environmental Crisis	170
Leo Marx	

Instantiation₄ Force and Resistance

Introduction	175
Nations, Identity and Conflict	186
Jonathan Glover	
Defining a Just War	201
Richard Falk	
Humanitarian Military Intervention	207
Jules Lobel and Michael Ratner	

Instantiation₅ Technologies

Introduction	215
Information Rich, Information Poor	218
William Wresch	
What Makes Mainstream Media Mainstream	234
Noam Chomsky	
The Biotech Century: Playing Ecological Roulette with Mother Nature's Designs	242
Jeremy Rifkin	
Animals as Inventions: Biotechnology and Intellectual Property Rights	249
Mark Sagoff	
Gandhi on Machinery	256
Monhandas Karamchana Gandhi	

Universals' A Coda...

A Note on the Value of Gender-Identification	263
Christine M. Korsgaard	

Permissions   267

PREFACE

This book is primarily a collection of readings, with stage settings, bridges, and suggestions from the editors. It is designed for use in a course called 'Global Ethics' at Virginia Tech, but we hope that it will be useful elsewhere. In fact some of us plan to use it elsewhere.

What follows is organized into six sections. The first and longest—Universals—is concerned with ethics in at least four senses of the word 'ethics'. It sketches out the origins of ethical behavior and the structure of ethical theory.

The next five sections—Instantiations—are concerned with issues or groups of issues of international ethical significance right now—at the start of the twenty-first century. These sections concern global responsibility and intervention, development, the environment, force and resistance, and technology.

Both because interests vary and because these areas overlap in many ways, these six sections can be read in many different orders and one may well jump from section to section and back again. Your instructor (or you) may assign readings in absolutely any order.

These issues are ethical in that they concern right and wrong and good and bad. They are global in that they essentially involve relations between different populations. A problem may be universal without being global. Spousal abuse is in one way a universal problem. But when cultures collide and what one considers proper and normal treatment of a wife seems to the other to be outrageous abuse, or when transnational forces disrupt a traditional economy and exacerbate abuse, the matter takes on a global aspect. Disease is certainly a universal and timeless human problem. But if a poor society suffers from a seriously debilitating disease that could easily be eliminated with the resources of a much wealthier society, then the matter becomes a global one.

This book contains only a tiny selection of the available information on these and many other global issues. A special supporting web site is at http://www.phil.vt.edu/Global/. Here you will find links to many sources of information and argument. To suggest additions, to report dead links, or to make comments, send email to the address on the first page of the site.

We hope that you will learn from, and be moved by, some of the readings that follow. We certainly hope that you will not enjoy all of them.

Wyatt Galusky
Andrew Garnar
Harlan B. Miller
Jean A. Miller

Blacksburg, Virginia, July, 2002

UNIVERSALS

INTRODUCTION

Ethics and Ethics and Ethics and Ethics

There are at least four different things that may be referred to by the term 'ethics'. Some people, sometimes, mark some of these distinctions by contrasting 'ethics' with 'morals' or 'morality'. We will use these terms interchangeably. 'Ethics' is derived from Greek, and 'morals' from the equivalent word in Latin. 'Morals' has a negative and oppressive connotation for many people, probably because of the time, not so very long ago, when it generally meant following a very specific set of rules for sexual behavior. In that sense a woman who refused to accept the double standard was said to have 'loose morals' even if she was the most honest and decent person imaginable.

There are, of course, ethical questions about sex, as there are about parking, but there are many more about truthfulness, power, and money.

In the simplest sense, ethics is a matter of patterns of behavior. All social animals have ways of interacting in sharing food, claiming mates, recognizing rank, and so on. In social insects these may be hard-wired, but in social mammals they appear to be learned. Violations are punished. These are sometimes fairly complicated systems, but, as far as we know, in nonhuman animals they never become consciously recognized and stated rules.

Every human society on record, in contrast, not only has acceptable and unacceptable behaviors, but has explicit sets of rules (often incomplete) that are taught and by which actions and people are judged. Some things are done and some are not done and properly brought-up people know which are which. The second sense of 'ethics' is a recognized body of rules governing a group. The study of ethics in this sense lies within the domain of sociology, anthropology, and psychology.

With the third sense of 'ethics' we reach the domain of moral philosophy. Ethics in this sense is the normative study of right and wrong and good and bad. 'Normative' here contrasts with 'descriptive.' An anthropologist may describe the moral beliefs of a culture, what members of that group in fact take to be right and wrong. But a philosophical ethics, on the other hand, concerns what IS right and wrong—what ought and what ought not be done. It argues for some basic ethical principles and from them and the facts of the world draws conclusions about what we must do and what we must not do.

There are many practical studies. Dairy science examines what one must do if one wishes to produce milk efficiently. Auto mechanics examines what one must do if one wants to keep automobiles running well. Civil engineering examines what one must do to build and maintain bridges and highways and sewer systems. Ethics in this sense is the most general practical study. It attempts to determine what we must do no matter what we want. A complete ethical theory would give us a general theory of right and wrong (or good and bad—these are alternative approaches). It is this third sense of 'ethics' with which we are concerned here. Ethics is the study of right and wrong at the most basic level.

The fourth sense of 'ethics' is what philosophers call 'metaethics.' Metaethics is the study of ethical systems (i.e. of competing ethical theories in the third sense). We will be doing some metaethics, especially in this section, whenever we compare one theory to another or describe the strengths and weaknesses of theories. But other metaethical questions, such as the nature of ethical truth, the correct analysis of ethical judgments, and whether or not one can accept an ethical judgment but just not care about it, are simply not on the menu here.

The Evolution of Ethics

We can only do the sorts of things we can do, and understand the sorts of things we can understand, because we are the sorts of animals we are. This is actually a very trivial truth. If we did not have the minds we have we could not understand mathematics. No one concludes that therefore arithmetic is true only for us, or that we don't really know that 9 + 2 is 11. But people do draw such conclusions about ethics. Of course ethical behavior developed as our distant ancestors developed. But nothing follows about how we *should* behave. The natural is not necessarily the desirable. Rape, racism, smallpox and syphilis are all quite natural.

For a discussion of the genesis and development of moral behavior and a critique of too-simple sociobiological accounts read the first selection below. This is the first of two selections by the Australian philosopher Peter Singer.

As Singer emphasizes, to explain how something originated is neither to justify it nor to undermine it. Justification of ethical rules and judgments is the task of normative ethical systems.

Systems of Normative Ethics

Ethics and Religion

Some normative ethical systems originate in religion. Confucianism, in a way, just is a system with a bit of religious baggage. Although Buddhism is now as diverse as Christianity, it may be argued that the Buddha's essential insight is at once metaphysical and ethical. In the Abramic religions (Judaism, Christianity, and Islam) the relations between ethics and belief are more tangled.

There are two wrong views about the relation between ethics and religion, one just wrong and the other wrong if simple. The 'just wrong' view is that God is (or the gods are) very powerful and vengeful (and all-knowing) so obeying divine commands is right because otherwise you'll fry. Essentially all philosophers and the overwhelming majority of Christian and Jewish theologians reject this view. If a powerful being (perhaps a thug with a shotgun) orders you to do something, that is a reason to do it, but not a moral reason. If a god commands you to torture kittens and threatens everlasting torments if you disobey, that certainly provides you with a prudential reason for torturing kittens. But there is no moral reason for the torture, and couldn't be. One probably should be forgiven for giving in, but the truly noble course would be to spit in the S.O.B.'s eye and suffer everlasting torments.

The wrong-if-simple view is the divine command theory—the view that what makes right things right and good things good is the command of God. In its simple forms this has been conclusively refuted since Plato's dialogue *Euthyphro*. Socrates' key question is a simple one. Is it good because the gods approve it, or do the gods approve it because it is good? In an Abramic culture we could ask this question. If God commanded us to torture kittens, would that make it right? Some will reply, "Yes, but God could never command that" and others just "God could never command that." After all, God is good, and torturing kittens is obviously not good.

But if 'good' just means 'approved by God' then to say that God is good is just to say that God approves of himself. This is certainly not what Jews, Christians, and Muslims mean when they say that God is good. (Hitler, after all, approved of himself.) The simple form of the divine command theory subverts ethics, but it does even more damage to theology.

It is of course true that religious beliefs shape one's views of oneself and of the world and therefore of one's duties. It is also true that much of the good done in the world, and much of the valuable moral teaching, is and has been done in the name of religion. And of course much of the evil, and of the vicious moral teaching, is and has been done in the name of religion.

Religion is often morally important, but it is not the source of morality. This is, in fact, the doctrine of the Roman Catholic Church.

Ethics and Science

Ethics and natural science are often wrongly contrasted. There is certainly disagreement within ethics. But the same is true of science. There is argument about what arguments are good, and about what evidence is relevant and what it establishes. Ethical arguments often produce emotion, but so do scientific arguments. Nothing is worth studying unless it concerns something we care about. In fact, we would claim, ethics is the science of right and wrong.

Consider the field of nutrition. Almost everyone has opinions about what one should and should not eat, and why. A few of these opinions, and many of the reasons behind them, are nonsense. But there is no doubt that there are facts of the matter about what humans can and cannot live on. And in fact every theory with the least plausibility has to account for a large body of established truths. There are areas of disagreement, but they are dwarfed by the areas of agreement. (See below on areas of agreement and disagreement in ethics.)

Deontology and Consequentialism

It is now time to classify normative ethical theories. This is not a simple matter. There is one basic distinction which is in principle both exclusive and exhaustive. That is, every theory must be one or the other, and none can be both. But as we shall see, there are many attempts to blur this distinction and gather elements from both sides of the divide.

The basic distinction is between deontology and consequentialism. Consequentialism holds that, given a choice, the right choice is the one that promises the best consequences. Deontology holds that the right act is the one of the right nature, or in accordance with the right rule, no matter what the consequences.

All of us can feel the pull of both sorts of theory. Consider telling the truth. Suppose that no one else knows what really happened and I have the choice between telling the truth, which puts me in a somewhat bad light, and telling the truth, which favors a now-dead friend. Surely I should tell the truth. Truth-telling is right, and I'm a deontologist. But suppose that Aunt Matilda, on her deathbed, asks if I liked the apple pies of which she was so proud. And suppose that, in fact, Aunt Matilda's apple pies always had the taste and consistency of low-grade cardboard. Should I tell the truth? Of course not. Any decent person would lie. So I'm a consequentialist.

Deontology: Natural Law

Natural law theories hold that our nature and/or the nature of the universe determine what is good for us and what is good. Because we are a certain kind of thing we need to live a certain kind of life and it follows that some things are right and some things are wrong. This is the official doctrine of the Catholic Church, from Aristotle via St. Thomas Aquinas, and it also seems to underlie the positions of thinkers as diverse as Immanuel Kant, John Dewey, and most U.S. state legislatures. Natural law principles are evident in the United States Declaration of Independence and the United Nations Declaration of Human Rights (a reading in this section). Even if it makes everyone concerned happy and has no bad consequences, an act of incest is wrong. Even if hundreds perish, promise-keeping is right. Masturbation is always wrong because it perverts nature's (or God's) will. Abortion is permissible because it respects the inherent autonomy of the woman. Obviously not all believers in natural law believe in the same natural laws.

Deontology: Divine Command

As we saw above, simple divine command theories come close to self-refutation. But some such theories are much more sophisticated. Some are essentially equivalent to natural law theories. God created everything and gave everything its nature. And the nature of a thing determines what is right and wrong in relation to that thing. So God creates, and God's commands reflect, what is right and wrong.

This certainly follows from both divine creation and natural law, but is not morally different from natural law.

Another variant is even less persuasive. God knows all, and thus God knows the nature of every being and God can determine what is right or wrong in any situation. So God's commands are always right. But this sets up God as an expert on right or wrong (and on tall or short, light or dark, acid or alkali), but not as determining right or wrong. A human with perfect color vision would be an authority on colors but not what made colors the colors that they are.

Deontology: Kantian Theories

Immanuel Kant (1724-1804) was one of the most influential philosophers in history. In his ethical writings he claims to prove, starting merely from the concept of a rational agent, the fundamental principle of ethics: the Categorical Imperative. Two of Kant's formulations of the Categorical Imperative are:

1) Always treat yourself and all other rational agents as ends and never just as means.
2) Always act in a way that you would want everyone else always to act in the same circumstances.

The first of these is echoed in ordinary life when we object to someone or some action as just using people. The second is a close relative of the Golden Rule.

The moral rules that Kant derived from the Categorical Imperative were often very harsh. It is never acceptable to commit suicide, to fail to develop one's natural gifts, or to lie, even to protect someone from a murderous maniac (Kant's example). Modern Kantians accept the Categorical Imperative but generally find Kant's specific derivations unconvincing. One of the most impressive of modern Kantians is Onora O'Neill.

Deontology: Libertarianism, Natural Rights

Libertarian and other natural rights theories are in one sense versions of natural law. On these theories humans, just because they are humans, have certain rights. For libertarians the most important (and perhaps the only) such rights are the right to be left alone and to be restricted in one's actions only by the rights of others to be left alone. There are no positive rights to assistance or anything else. From each as each chooses, to each as others choose. Other natural rights theorists, including the authors of the United Nations Declaration on Human Rights, ascribe to everyone some positive natural rights, including rights to minimal food, shelter, and companionship, as well as (and often in conflict with) the negative rights of the libertarians.

Deontology: Contractarianism

Traditional contract theories can be seen as special forms of natural law. There is just one natural law—that promises be kept, and we have all, explicitly and implicitly, made lots of promises by entering into stated or understood agreements with our family members, neighbors, fellow citizens, and perhaps others. I am obliged not to steal or kill because, by living in society and deriving benefits from doing so, I have implicitly agreed to play by the rules.

In some contexts there is some truth in this sort of contract view. Politically they explain why someone who has participated in a state, derived benefits from doing so, and had the opportunity to leave or opt out, has at least a *prima facie* obligation to work within that state's system. Plainly such an obligation would be a matter of degree. The longer one hangs around (after 16 or so) and the more fully one is engaged in the state, the stronger the obligation.

But as a general account of morality such contract theories are not very persuasive. None of us ever explicitly contracted in. In fact, of course, we were completely indoctrinated and enmeshed in our culture's moral system long before we were old enough to consider any alternatives (or even to consider that there might be alternatives).

Many modern contractarian (or 'contractualist') theories are quite different. They use the idea of a contract not as an argument for obligation to play by the rules, but as a device to determine and to justify the correct set of rules. The correct rules are those that we would all agree to if we were not self-interested, confused, stupid, brain-washed, obsessed, or otherwise impaired. So imagine a group of agents perfectly reasonable and well-informed (with the exceptions in the next sentence) who are deciding the rules for a society of which they will be members. None of these planners knows anything about who or what they will be in the society. They might be male or female, poor or rich, smart or dumb, weak or strong, beautiful or ugly, etc. They thus cannot be influenced by any morally irrelevant factors. The rules such beings would agree to are *ipso facto* reasonable rules, and we should all accept them.

Consequentialism

In contrast to deontological views, on which duty is primary and one must always do one's duty no matter what, consequentialism theories hold that the right choice is the one with (as far as one can tell) the best consequences. What differentiates one sort of consequentialist theory from another is what counts as good and bad consequences.

Consequentialism: Divine Satisfaction

Judaism, Christianity and Islam (the Abramic religions) hold that God is good, so whatever God commands is good. What goodness is, however, is determined by natural law or something else. For some other religions, though, the situation is quite different. The Olympian gods of classical Greece, for example, certainly were not, as a rule, good. They were petty and childish and vindictive and often fought among themselves. For states and individuals the most important thing was to keep them happy and not irritate them. We can state a corresponding consequentialist moral theory. Of the actions available choose that one most like to satisfy the gods (or God). It is not easy to take this seriously as a self-standing theory however. Such behavior would keep one from suffering, perhaps, but if it is right it is because of some deeper theory, perhaps egoism or utilitarianism.

Consequentialism: Egoism

Egoism is the theory that the correct action is the one that has best results for me. It cannot consistently hold that everyone should do whatever has the best results for themselves. Such a theory is inconsistent. If there is just one beer left and two of us, it cannot be true that we both ought to grab it. If I am an egoist, I must believe that it is right for me to have it and you go thirsty. If you take it, I must hold that your behavior is wrong. The right thing is what benefits ME.

In its simplest form egoism is an exceptionally unattractive theory. It produces both endless conflict and a life without love or trust. But in fact egoism has grounded some very important positions. Egoism underlies some contractarian and libertarian theories, and versions of 'free enterprise' thinking. We're all selfish, and that's fine. We just need to work out some rules for cooperating and staying out of each other's way for our mutual benefit. No one really needs to care about the welfare of anyone else. This can in fact be a workable plan, and some people live by it. But a life without love and the risks love entails is hardly an attractive life.

Some people think that ethical egoism (I should care only about myself) is necessary because psychological egoism (everyone, necessarily, cares only about themselves) is true. Psychological egoism is a factual claim. It is the claim that no one does (or ever could) act for anything other than selfish reasons. It is a popular view, which is odd since it is so obviously false. Every day millions of people do unselfish things. They let strangers change lanes. They pick up trash. They buy life insurance. They refrain from undetectable thefts. They contribute (often anonymously) to charities. They build schools and conserve resources for unrelated children not yet born. "But they only do it because they want to do it!" True, and they want to do it because they care about others.

Consequentialism: Utilitarianism

Utilitarianism, hedonic consequentialism, is certainly the dominant consequentialist moral theory today. It has played such a central role in moral and political thinking in the last couple of centuries that in effect it now defines the theories that oppose it. There is almost a formula: "Because utilitarianism has the horrible consequence that X, we must reject it and instead adopt theory Y."

Roughly, the theory is this: That act, among those open to us, is the right one if and only if it maximizes the utility (or minimizes the disutility) of all those affected. Utility is pleasure or satisfaction or welfare or happiness. Disutility is pain or frustration or misery or suffering. Those affected are every being the utility of which can be affected by the action.

It is almost impossible to exaggerate the influence and importance of utilitarianism. There are sketches of the theory in the ancient Greeks, but it received its full exposition in the late Eighteenth and early-to-late Nineteenth Century by Jeremy Bentham (1748-1832), his pupil John Stuart Mill (1806-1873), and Henry Sidgwick (1838-1900). Readings from Bentham and from Mill are provided in this section.

There are very many variations and complications even in classical one-level utilitarianism. Are we concerned with actual utility or expected utility? Should we decide on the basis of total utility or average utility (if total then a very large just barely happy population is better than a small but very happy one). Just what is utility? Is it pleasant sensations, healthy functioning, or what? How can we handle the difficulty that in many situations it is just not possible to compute all the relevant consequences of an action? Should we maximize what is good for people, or what they want? (The two are obviously sometimes quite different.) There are scholarly journals and societies dedicated to working out and/or criticizing utilitarian theories.

Some of the most interesting recent moral theories have been what are sometimes called 'two-level utilitarianism.' At the upper level, detached, cool, and contemplative, we decide, on a purely utilitarian basis, what the rules are by which people should live, and we attempt to make sure that people are brought up to internalize these rules and to set up social structures to reinforce them. At the lower level we operate by the rules, and criticize those who break them. It is important that the rules are really built into us. We find lying and stealing abhorrent. As with

Aristotle, on this theory the honest person does not have to resist the temptation to steal. She never feels that temptation in the first place. But sometimes the temptation, or the need, is very powerful indeed. And then, although still quite reluctant, the reflective person may have to move to the upper level and ask whether or not the consequences of theft might be so great and so certain as to justify an exception.

No human operates on the upper level for more than 1% or 2% of their lives, and many humans never do. But legislators and constitution drafters do (or at least should), and any of us, in very unusual circumstances, might be called upon to do so. It isn't easy, and shouldn't be.

Consequentialism: Eco-holism

In principle there could be an indefinitely large number of consequentialist theories. But few have any plausibility. One that, unfortunately, sometimes does is embodied in some forms of fanaticism. Any action whatever is justified if it is believed to contribute to the establishment of the True Doctrine. In sharp contrast, Buddhism can be seen as consequentialist and in fact utilitarian (a very pessimistic utilitarianism). A central insight of the Buddha was that the world is overwhelmingly a world of suffering. Our duty is, first, not to contribute to that suffering and, second, to do what we can to end it.

A very different form of consequentialism is manifested in the various theories we will call 'eco-holisms.' Utilitarianism considers the welfare of all sentient beings (many utilitarians manage to forget this, but the Buddha never did). To eco-holists this just shows an unfounded preference for experiencers. We should act, on these theories, to maximize the good of something bigger and more important than any mere individual animal. The good to be maximized is the "beauty, integrity, and stability" of ecosystems, or the preservation of species or uninterrupted natural processes, or the health of Gaia, or some other whole that transcends the interests of members of any species. We will return to such theories in the section on the environment.

Consequentialism: Ideal Utilitarianism

Early in the Twentieth Century G. E. Moore (1873-1958) promoted a theory, sometimes called 'ideal utilitarianism' that holds that we ought to maximize a number of things, pleasure among them, but also knowledge, satisfaction, beauty, and love. The attractions of such a theory are apparent, but of course conflicts would show up immediately. Knowledge and satisfaction are notoriously likely to interfere with one another. No plausible way of ranking the goals has been produced.

Mixed Theories

In one way it is impossible to combine consequentialist and deontological theories. Either the consequences matter or they don't. But in fact some of the most promising alternatives today are in effect mixed theories. Two-level utilitarianism of the sort propounded by Richard M. Hare (1919-2002) are effectively mixed theories, deriving deontological rules from utilitarian principles. Some contractarian moral systems have been based on egoism, and others on utilitarianism. A system of rights may be based on utilitarianism. If people are to be able to lead happy lives they must be granted certain rights even though sometimes the exercises of such rights will not maximize utility.

Virtue Ethics

Very roughly one can distinguish virtue ethics from deontological theories and from consequentialist theories, which are action ethics. The first question, for virtue ethics, is not "what should I do?" but "what should I be?". I should be a virtuous person. The action questions are secondary. I should act as a virtuous person would act.

But how do I know what a virtuous person would do? Or how do I know which are the virtuous people? Aristotle is generally credited with founding virtue ethics. How did he identify the virtues and the virtuous? He relied upon what any right-thinking upper class Greek male of his time would believe. Aristotle's ethical works are among the most valuable ever written. His is a mind of amazing power and subtlety. But his table of virtues rests on the racist, sexist, class-ist, world view of the wealthy men of Athens in the Fourth Century B.C. If Aristotle could not transcend the rules and conventions of his own society, then we are surely not going to be able to do so, either.

If virtues are basic, and we take our virtues from our traditions, the resulting theory can only be quite conservative. And in fact, at the very start of the Twenty-first Century, talk of 'virtue' is generally heard from the right end of the political spectrum. In the United States that includes William Bennett and Lynne Cheney.

If we could identify the ideal human character, then of course we could infer the ideal virtues. But it was just this that Aristotle took himself to be doing. In fact, however, virtue cannot be basic. All (or almost all) ethical theories recognize virtues. The virtues are the dispositions that make a person a good person. But the nature of a good person is either determined by natural law, or (according to Hume) by our natural sentiments of approval and disapproval, or by being the sort of person whose actions will lead to the best consequences.

There is an aspect of modern virtue ethics that escapes this criticism and has certainly had a healthy influence on the contemporary literature. Attention to specific virtues provides 'thick' characterizations of actions and people, unlike the 'thin' notions of right and wrong, good and bad. Honesty and dishonesty, cruelty and kindness, loyalty and betrayal, courage and cowardice are what really matter in ordinary life.

Feminist Theories

It is very dangerous to try to provide a brief account of feminism in general and feminist ethics in particular. In the last four decades of the Twentieth Century (and before) and in the early years of the Twenty First, a baffling range of feminist positions have been staked out and a large number of competing and cross-cutting distinctions have been offered: first-, second-, and third-stage feminism; liberal vs. radical feminism, difference feminism vs. equality feminism, etc. We make no attempt here to discuss or even enumerate the varieties. To be feminist a theory must, as a minimum, assert two claims.

> (1) That Western (and all or most non-Western) culture systematically undervalues and marginalizes women in social structures.
>
> (2) That the theories developed by these cultures not only disregard and/or stereotype women, but are quite significantly distorted as a result.

Claim (1) can hardly be denied. It is claim (2) that makes a position genuinely feminist. At least most feminist theories are optimistic enough to assert a third claim:

> (3) Once we free ourselves from the sexist bias built into existing intellectual structures, we can construct superior theories retaining the strengths of the old ones and correcting at least some of their defects.

A feminist ethical theory must be anti-libertarian and at least generally anti-contractarian. These theories rest on the assumption of separated individuals with no inherent connection to anyone else. But no human can be such. We are born into families. We are not born with a set of economic rights and an ordered list of desires. Instead we all become who we are, and we could not do so without those who feed and protect and guide us. To consider an individual stripped of concerns and obligations is to picture an individual either impossible or pathetic.

Some feminists have urged us to base ethics on care for and sympathy with others. (Some have seen David Hume (1711-1776) as a feminist thinker before his time.) We are not simply dropped here by aliens to negotiate with strangers. We are situated beings already and necessarily bound to others.

Central to our interests here is the continuing conversation among feminists of the so-called First and Third Worlds. A number of relevant sites are linked to the www.phil.vt.edu/Global/ web site.

Pragmatic Ethics

All ethics worthy of the name is concerned with practice and in that sense is pragmatic. By 'pragmatic' or 'neo-pragmatist' ethics today is meant an ethical theory inspired by the great American pragmatist philosophers: Charles Sanders Peirce (1839-1914), William James (1842-1910), George Herbert Mead (1863-1931), and above all John Dewey (1859-1952).

The prospects for, and the obstacles to, a neopragmatist revival are discussed by Cornel West in Reading 6 below, the last in this section.

Areas of Agreement and Disagreement

This may look like a wild jumble of theories but in fact they (almost) all agree over very wide areas of human life. Among those theories that have any significant followers among moral philosophers, the areas of agreement are much more extensive than the areas of disagreement. Just as Aristotelian, Newtonian, and Einsteinian theories of mechanics give almost exactly the same predictions about middle-sized bodies near the surface of the Earth, which is what we are all most concerned with, so utilitarian, libertarian, contractarian, natural, pragmatic, and even feminist theories usually classify the same acts as right and wrong in the sorts of situations in which we generally find ourselves. They are far more likely to differ at, and about, the boundaries of moral community than within a moral community. Just where the borders of moral community lie, and the status of those within the community, are central questions of global ethics.

Moral Community

The moral community is the collection of all moral agents and moral patients. A moral agent is a being whose acts can be evaluated morally. A moral patient is a being with a welfare that is of moral significance (i.e. a being the treatment of which can be evaluated morally). Normal adult humans are both moral agents and moral patients. Perhaps God is, too, or perhaps God cannot be helped or hurt. If so, God is a moral agent but not a moral patient. Perhaps the same is true of Enron, or the United States of America, or the Roman Catholic Church. (Of course individual members of these organizations are both moral agents and moral patients, but the organizations themselves can surely act and surely not suffer.) Infants and the comatose and the irreversibly senile are moral patients but not moral agents. It matters how we treat them, but we cannot properly evaluate their acts (if they have any). On almost all theories sentient[1] (i.e. capable of experience) nonhuman animals are moral patients but not moral agents. Eco-holist theories add one or more non-sentient beings to the list of moral patients.

Within the (almost) uncontested heartland of moral community, relations among normal adult humans, all the plausible moral theories are likely to agree. All encourage courage and honesty, and all prohibit murder, torture for fun, rape, theft, malicious humiliation, and so on.

There are some conflicts. Utilitarians are likely to favor strong welfare programs and libertarians to oppose them, with natural law theorists, Kantians, and contract supporters in the middle or on both sides. Only strict Kantians think that lying is never permissible. Libertarians are likely to think suicide a fundamental right, and natural law theorists to find it always impermissible. Almost all theories hold that cruelty to animals is wrong, but they differ enormously on why it is wrong.

The Borders of Moral Community

Where the theories differ, and differ in ways directly relevant to global ethics, is about the borders of the moral community. For some natural law theorists, for Kant, and for strict contractarians and libertarians, the defining property is rationality and all genuine moral patients are moral agents. For other natural law theorists and for utilitarians the border is sentience—all and only conscious beings matter morally.

---

[1] 'Sentient' is a long-standing technical term in philosophy and psychology. It means being 'sensitive', i.e. capable of some sort of experience. Recently an unfortunate use of 'sentient' has emerged in science fiction, especially on television. Here 'sentient' means being self-conscious and capable of reason and communication (i.e. being a person).

For eco-holists humans are clearly moral agents, but perhaps not moral patients (i.e. the welfare of an individual of any species may just not matter).

No one worth listening to today adjusts the borders of moral community by sex or gender or race. But feminists argue that we have not freed ourselves from racism or sexism. We still read and revere Aristotle. See the quote from Sidgwick, a profoundly liberal and benevolent man of his day, at the start of the Singer reading just below. We no longer believe such things, but they were part of the groundwork of theories we still accept.

On the other hand, there is substantial support for drawing morally significant lines along the borders of nationality, actuality, and species.

I am an American. Does the moral community of which I am a part include all humanity or just Americans? Utilitarians are likely to hold that distance and nationality are irrelevant. If I can, I am under the same obligation to help a starving resident of Chad as I am to help a starving person next door. Some contractarians disagree. If I send funds to Chad that may be admirable, but toward my neighbor I have an obligation.

In rich countries utilitarians and some natural law theorists are more likely to have guilty consciences than are libertarians or contractarians.

By 'actuality' is meant the distinction between presently existing beings, former beings now departed, and future beings. Most theories recognize some very limited obligations toward the dead. There is wide variation on obligations to future generations. (Any contractarian can ask "What has the future ever done for me?".) Obligations to non-sentient former persons and, especially, to organisms that could become persons, are notoriously controversial. Some contractarians and some natural law theorists think that the answers are straightforward (but differ sharply on what the answers are). Almost no other theorists even think the answers straightforward.

There is very substantial disagreement about the moral significance of the species boundary. Are any nonhuman animals members of the moral community? If so, which ones and what is their status? Here the theories differ very sharply, but no respectable moral theory bases membership in the moral community on species membership alone. We will return to these matters in the section on the environment.

The 'hottest' and most contentious areas in moral theory, both scholarly and political, are questions of the boundaries of moral community. Many of these are central to global ethics. Obligations of the rich to the poor, both within and across nations, euthanasia, abortion, the status of nonhumans—all these concern who counts and how much.

Relativism

Relativism in its many varieties is a serious obstacle to clear thinking in ethics. It is very widespread due especially to mis-education in the social sciences and to a confused notion of tolerance.

Subjectivism is the most extreme version of relativism. The subjectivist holds that whatever a person thinks is right *is* right for that person. It is not uncommon for otherwise intelligent people to express this view, but they quickly abandon it once they see that it means that Hitler's and Osama bin Laden's actions were right as long as they were sincere. Subjectivists must agree that it is right for non-subjectivists to flunk or otherwise penalize them just because they are subjectivists.

As a moral view subjectivism is hopeless. Some people maintain it by abandoning morality. It then becomes a theory of what people 'really' mean when they make ethical claims. This sort of amoral cynicism has, on its own terms, no moral weight, but it's depressing.

Cultural Relativism

The view that what is right is whatever one's culture says is right is more promising than subjectivism. In fact there's some truth in it. But not much.

The analogy to nutritional theory is useful here. There are a wide variety of different diets that can support a flourishing human life. Just what nutrients you need, and when you need them, depends on your environment, your activity, your history, and probably just luck. But you can't get by without some protein and some carbohydrates, and you can't last a week without water.

In Arab cultures it is wrong to present the soles of your feet to strangers, but in most European and American cultures it isn't. That is because in Arab, but not European, cultures, presenting the soles of the feet is a very insulting gesture, and in all cultures it is wrong to be gratuitously insulting. Even in the very same culture it may be perfectly appropriate for you to ignore a hitchhiker, but obligatory for me to pick her up, if I have promised to do so, and you have not. In France it is wicked to drive on the left side of the road. In England it is wicked not to.

So in some ways what's right or wrong depends on who you are, where you are, and what's expected of you. Thus there is a small but significant way in which morality is relative.

On a larger scale, however, morality isn't relative to culture at all. We can and often do criticize cultural norms as immoral. The culturally and legally sanctioned segregation of the southern states in the 1940s and 1950s was wrong. The slave-holding culture of many of our ancestors and Founding Fathers was wrong. The treatment of women by the Taliban, and in current Saudi society, is intolerable. One may disagree with any of these claims, but obviously they are not just stupidly incoherent, as they would be if cultural relativism were correct.

For a convinced cultural relativist, reformers are always wrong, since by definition they oppose the dominant view of their society. Jesus was wrong, the Buddha was wrong, Susan B. Anthony and those other uppity women were wrong, Martin Luther King Jr. was wrong, and so on. For that matter political revolutionaries are always wrong (until they win) so Washington and Jefferson were wrong, too.

The so-called 'tolerance' of cultural relativism is a delusion. A view that ranks Hitler's Germany and the Taliban's Afghanistan as morally equivalent to contemporary Norway isn't tolerant. It's idiotic.

The following readings are, of course, a very tiny selection from the literature. Please see the web site at http://www.phil.vt.edu/Global/ for more.

THE BIOLOGICAL BASIS OF ETHICS
PETER SINGER

We should all agree that each of us is bound to show kindness to his parents and spouse and children, and to other kinsmen in a less degree; and to those who have rendered services to him, and any others whom he may have admitted to his intimacy and called friends; and to neighbours and to fellow-countrymen more than others; and perhaps we may say to those of our own race more than to black or yellow men, and generally to human beings in proportion to their affinity to ourselves.

-HENRY SIDGWICK, *The Methods of Ethics*

Every human society has some code of behavior for its members. This is true of nomads and city-dwellers, of hunter-gatherers and of industrial civilizations, of Eskimos in Greenland and Bushmen in Africa, of a tribe of twenty Australian aborigines and of the billion people that make up China. Ethics is part of the natural human condition.

That ethics is natural to human beings has been denied. More than three hundred years ago Thomas Hobbes wrote in his *Leviathan*:

> During the time men live without a common Power to keep them all in awe they are in that condition called War; and such a war, as is of every man against every other man.... To this war of every man against every man, this also is consequent; that nothing can be Unjust. The notions of Right and Wrong, Justice and Injustice have there no place.

Hobbes's guess about human life in the state of nature was no better than Rousseau's idea that we were naturally solitary. It is not the force of the state that persuades us to act ethically. The state, or some other form of social power, may reinforce our tendency to observe an ethical code, but that tendency exists before the social power is established. The primary role Hobbes gave to the state was always suspect on philosophical grounds, for it invites the question why, having agreed to set up a power to enforce the law, human beings would trust each other long enough to make the agreement work. Now we also have biological grounds for rejecting Hobbes's theory.

Occasionally there are claims that a group of human beings totally lacking any ethical code has been discovered. The Ik, a northern Uganda tribe described by Colin Turnbull in *The Mountain People*, is the most recent example. The biologist Garrett Hardin has even claimed that the Ik are an incarnation of Hobbes's natural man, living in a state of war of every Ik against every other Ik. The Ik certainly were, at the time of Turnbull's visit, a most unfortunate people. Originally nomadic hunters and gatherers, their hunting ground was turned into a national park. They were forced to become farmers in an arid mountain area in which they had difficulty supporting themselves; a prolonged drought and consequent famine was the final blow. As a result, according to Turnbull, Ik society collapsed. Parents turned their three-year-old children out to fend for themselves, the strong took food from the mouths of the weak, the sufferings of the old and sick were a source of laughter, and anyone who helped another was considered a fool. The Ik, Turnbull says, abandoned family, cooperation, social life, love, religion, and everything else except the pursuit of self-interest. They teach us that our much vaunted human values are, in Turnbull's words, "luxuries that can be dispensed with."

The idea of a people without human values holds a certain repugnant fascination. *The Mountain People* achieved a rare degree of fame for a work of anthropology. It was reviewed in *Life*, talked about over cocktails, and turned into a stage play by the noted director Peter Brook. It was also severely criticized by some anthropologists. They pointed out the subjective nature of many of Turnbull's observations, the vagueness of his data, contradictions between *The Mountain People* and an earlier report Turnbull had published (in which he described the Ik as fun-loving, helpful, and "great family people"), and contradictions within *The Mountain People* itself. In reply Turnbull admitted that "the data in the book are inadequate for anything approaching proof" and recognized the existence of evidence pointing toward a different picture of Ik life.

Even if we take the picture of Ik life in *The Mountain People* at face value, there is still ample evidence that Ik society has an ethical code. Turnbull refers to disputes over the theft of berries which reveal that, although stealing takes place, the Ik retain notions of private property and the wrongness of theft. Turnbull mentions the Ik's attachment to the mountains and the reverence with which they speak of Mount Morungole, which seems to be a sacred place for them. He observes that the Ik like to sit together in groups and insist on living together in villages. He describes a code that has to be followed by an Ik husband who intends to beat his wife, a code that gives the wife a chance to leave first. He reports that the obligations of a pact of mutual assistance known as *nyot* are invariably carried out. He tells us that there is a strict prohibition on Ik killing each other or even drawing blood. The Ik may let each other starve, but they apparently do not think of other Ik as they think of any non-human animals they find--that is, as potential food. A normal well-fed reader will take the prohibition of cannibalism for granted, but under the circumstances in which the Ik were living human flesh would have been a great boost to the diets of stronger Ik; that they refrain from this source of food is an example of the continuing strength of their ethical code despite the crumbling of almost everything that had made their lives worth living.

Under extreme conditions like those of the Ik during famine, the individual's need to survive becomes so dominant that it may seem as if all other values have ceased to matter, when in fact they continue to exercise an influence. If any conditions can be worse than those the Ik endured, they were the conditions of the inmates of Soviet labor camps and, more horrible still, the Nazi death camps. Here too, it has been said that "the doomed devoured each other," that "all trace of human solidarity vanished," that all values were erased and every man fought for himself. Nor should it be surprising if this were so, for the camps deliberately and systematically dehumanized their inmates, stripping them naked, shaving their hair, assigning them numbers, forcing them to soil their clothing with excrement, letting them know in a hundred ways that their lives were of no account, beating them, torturing them, and starving them. The astonishing thing is that despite all this, life in the camps was *not* every man for himself. Again and again, survivors' reports show that prisoners helped each other. In Auschwitz prisoners risked their lives to pick up strangers who had fallen in the snow at roll call; they built a radio and disseminated news to keep up morale; though they were starving, they shared food with those still more needy. There were also ethical rules in the camps. Though theft occurred, stealing from one's fellow prisoners was strongly condemned and those caught stealing were punished by the prisoners themselves. As Terrence Des Pres observes in *The Survivor*, a book based on reports by those who survived the camps: "The assumption that there was no moral or social order in the camps is wrong.... Through innumerable small acts of humanness, most of them covert but everywhere in evidence, survivors were able to maintain societal structures workable enough to keep themselves alive and morally sane."

The core of ethics runs deep in our species and is common to human beings everywhere. It survives the most appalling hardships and the most ruthless attempts to deprive human beings of their humanity. Nevertheless, some people resist the idea that this core has a biological basis which we have inherited from our pre-human ancestors. One ground for resistance is that we like to think of our own actions as radically different from the behavior of animals, no matter how altruistic those animals may be. Animals act instinctively; humans are rational, self-conscious beings. We can reflect on the rightness or wrongness of our actions. Animals cannot. We can follow moral rules. We can see what is good, and choose it. Animals cannot. Or so many people think.

Attempts to draw sharp lines between ourselves and other animals have always failed. We thought we were the only beings capable of language, until we discovered that chimpanzees and gorillas can learn more than a hundred words in sign language, and use them in combinations of their own devising. Scientists are now laboriously discovering what many dog owners have long accepted; we are not the only animals that reason. As Darwin wrote in *The Descent of Man*: "The difference in mind between man and the higher animals, great as it is, certainly is one of degree and not of kind." It is a mistake to think of all animals as doing by blind instinct what we do by conscious deliberation. Both human and nonhuman animals have innate tendencies toward behaving in particular ways. Some of these tendencies rigidly prescribe a particular kind of behavior--like the fly, so set on going in one direction that it buzzes repeatedly into the glass, instead of trying different directions until it comes to the part of the window that is open. Other innate tendencies merely set a goal which leaves room for a diversity of strategies--like the fox that "instinctively" wants a hen and, as those who keep hens learn to their cost, can think of dozens of different ways to get it. The "instincts" of the social mammals are mostly of this more open sort. In this sense human beings have "instincts" too: think about how hard it is for parents to hear their baby cry without picking it up, or for adolescent and older humans to avoid taking an interest in sex.

Another ground for resisting the idea that ethics has a biological basis is that ethics is widely regarded as a cultural phenomenon, taking radically different forms in different societies. As our knowledge of remoter parts of the globe increased, so too did our awareness of the variety of human ethical codes. Edward Westermarck's *The*

Origin and Development of the Moral Ideas, published in 1906-8, consists of two large volumes, a total of more than 1,500 pages, comparing differences among societies on such matters as the wrongness of killing (including killing in warfare, euthanasia, suicide, infanticide, abortion, human sacrifices, and duels); whose duty it is to support children, or the aged, or the poor; the position of women, and the forms of sexual relations permitted; the holding of slaves, the right to property in general, and what constitutes theft; the duty to tell the truth; dietary restrictions; concern for nonhuman animals; duties to the dead, and to the gods; and so on. The overwhelming impression we get from Westermarck's book, and from most anthropological literature, is of an immense diversity in ethics, a diversity which must be of cultural rather than biological origin. Edward O. Wilson has conceded: "The evidence is strong that almost all differences between human societies are based on learning and social conditioning, rather than heredity." So it may seem that if we want to discuss human ethics we must shift our attention from biological theories of human nature to particular cultures and the factors that have led them to develop their own particular ethical codes. Yet while the diversity of ethics is indisputable, there are common elements underlying this diversity. Moreover, some of these common elements are so closely parallel to the forms of altruism observable in other social animals that they render implausible attempts to deny that human ethics has its origin in evolved patterns of behavior among social animals. I shall start with the ethical form of kin altruism.

Kin Selection in Human Ethics

The Methods of Ethics, from which I have taken the quotation at the beginning of this chapter, is a philosophical treatise on ethics written by the Cambridge philosopher Henry Sidgwick and first published in 1874. The passage quoted is a description of the principles regulating the duty of benevolence, as this duty was generally understood at that time, rather than a statement of Sidgwick's own views. It gives a graduated list of those to whom we should be kind which fits neatly with sociobiological theories. First place goes to kin altruism; then come reciprocal and group altruism. In this respect late Victorian England was not unusual. As Westermarck notes in *The Origin and Development of the Moral Ideas*, a mother's duty to look after her children has seemed so obvious that most anthropological accounts scarcely bother to mention it. The duty of a married man to support and protect his family is, Westermarck says, equally widespread, and he backs up his claim with a score of examples. His account of the duties almost universally accepted among human beings parallels Sidgwick's list in placing duties to parents alongside duties to children and wives, with duties to aid brothers and sisters closely following, and those toward more distant relatives more variable, but still prominent in most societies. Benevolence to other members of the tribe or group comes next in importance, with benevolence to outsiders often lacking entirely. The universal importance of kinship in human societies has been recognized by one of sociobiology's strongest critics, the anthropologist Marshall Sahlins. In The *Use and Abuse of Biology* Sahlins has written: "Kinship is the dominant structure of many of the peoples anthropologists have studied, the prevailing code not only in the domestic sphere but generally of economic, political and ritual action."

Sahlins goes on to deny that this has a biological basis, pointing out that who is recognized as "kin" in different cultures often fails to correspond to strict degrees of blood relationship. Sahlins, however, takes the sociobiological thesis too narrowly. His examples show that there is generally a considerable correlation between blood relationship and acceptance of someone as "kin." There is no need for a sociobiologist to demand more. Any reasonable sociobiologist will admit that culture plays a role in the structure of human societies, and biological forces therefore cannot always take the shortest and simplest route.

Today the unconcealed racial distinction referred to in Sidgwick's final sentence strikes a discordant note; but the reality of Sidgwick's account of the degrees of benevolence holds remarkably well, considering how many other elements of Victorian morality have changed in the past century. We still think first of our immediate family, then of friends, neighbors, and more distant relatives, next of our fellow citizens generally, and last of all of those who have nothing in common with us except that they are human beings. Think of our reaction to news of a famine in Africa. Those of us who care at all may send a donation to one of the agencies trying to help: ten dollars, or fifty dollars, or perhaps even a hundred dollars. Any more would be a rare act of generosity by the standards of our society. Yet those of us fortunate enough to live in Western Europe, North America, Australia, or Japan regularly spend as much or more on holidays, new clothes, or presents for our children. If we cared about the lives and welfare of strangers in Africa as we do about our own welfare and that of our children, would we spend money on these nonessential items for ourselves instead of using it to save lives? Of course, we have lots of excuses for not sending money to Africa: we say that our contribution could only be a drop in the ocean, or that the agencies waste the money they receive, or that food handouts are no good--what is needed is development, or a social revolution, or population control. In our more honest moments, though, we recognize that these are excuses. My contribution cannot end a famine, but it can save the lives of several people who might otherwise starve. While we seize on every newspaper report of relief efforts being wasted as a justification for not giving, how many of us bother to look at the overall efficiency of aid organizations, which is, in the case of voluntary organizations, actually very high by the standards of large corporations? And if we think that not food aid, but development, or revolution, or population control is the real answer to the famine problem, why aren't we contributing to groups promoting these solutions?

I have written and lectured on the subject of overseas aid, arguing that our affluence puts us under an obligation to do much more than we are now doing to help people in real need. At the popular level, the most frequent response is that we should look after our own poor first. Among philosophers, essentially similar replies are put in a more sophisticated manner. For instance, I have been told that while we should certainly do more to prevent poverty, we ought to do nothing inconsistent with our obligation to do the best for our children--an obligation which, it turns out, includes sending them to expensive private schools and buying them ten-speed bicycles. The proposal that we might risk lessening the happiness or prospects of our own children, to however slight a degree, in order to save strangers from starvation strikes many people as not merely idealistic but positively wrong.

The preference for "our own" is understandable in terms of our evolutionary history. It is an instance of the kin altruism we observed in other animals, with an element of group altruism added. This does not mean that a society must encourage its members to act in accordance with this preference. There have recently been concerted attempts to eliminate certain forms of preference for members of one's own group. In a multiracial society, preferences for members of one's own race or ethnic group often lead to strife, and in many countries it is now considered wrong to prefer those of one's own race or ethnic group in employment, education, or housing. Sanctions are invoked against those who do it. These efforts toward racial equality meet strong resistance, as one would expect from any attempt to counter a deep-seated bias, but they have generally been successful in changing people's attitudes, as well as their actions, toward fellow citizens of different races and ethnic backgrounds.

It has long been the dream of social reformers to carry out a similar equalizing process in respect of the family, so that members of a community no longer automatically prefer the interests of members of their family to those of the community. Like so many other perennial ideas, this goes back to Plato. In the *Republic*, Plato argues that unity is the greatest good in a community, and unity occurs "where all the citizens are glad or grieved on the same occasions of joy and sorrow." To bring this about, at least among the Guardians who are the rulers of Plato's ideal state, he suggests that there should be no separate households or marriages, but a form of communal marriage. Thus instead of "each man dragging any acquisition which he has made into a separate house of his own, where he has a separate wife and children and private pleasures and pains," we will have a situation in which the Guardians "are all of one opinion about what is near and dear to them, and therefore they all tend towards a common end." In his estimate of the divisive effect of the family within a strongly collective community, Plato was right.

Yonina Talmon unconsciously echoes Plato in her sociological study of Jewish collective settlements, *Family and Community in the Kibbutz*. Referring to the early pioneering days of these settlements, when the need for unity was strongest, Talmon says:

> Family ties are based on an exclusive and discriminating loyalty which sets the members of one's family more or less apart from others. Families may easily become competing foci of emotional involvement that can infringe on loyalty to the collective. Deep attachment to one's spouse and children . . . may gain precedence over the more ideological and more task-oriented relations with comrades.

But Plato's optimism over the prospects of doing away with the family has not been borne out by subsequent experiments. For the reasons Talmon gives, the kibbutz movement began by strongly discouraging family attachments. Children lived together in communal houses, apart from their parents. From infancy the kibbutz provided nurses and teachers, freeing both parents for work. Meals were taken in a communal dining room, not in family units, and entertainment was communal. Children were encouraged to call their parents by their names, rather than "father" or "mother." There was a ban on couples working in the same place, and husbands and wives who spent most of their time together were viewed with scorn. Upheld by deep ideological commitment to socialism and to Jewish settlement in what was then Palestine, these extreme limits on family relations were accepted as part of the settlement's struggle against an external environment that was hostile both in respect of the difficulties of growing food and in respect of the surrounding Palestinian population. In humans as well as other animals, an external threat leads a group to be more cohesive than usual. (Compare the sacrifices readily made by all sections of the British population during the Second World War, when there was a real external threat, with the lack of response to appeals by successive British Prime Ministers for a return to "the spirit of Dunkirk" to halt Britain's economic decline.) When the survival of the entire group is at stake, our concern with our own interests is subordinated to the need to ensure that the group survives; but in more normal times, individual interests return. Perhaps groups not able thus to mobilize resources in emergencies did not survive; while individuals who did not press their own interests when the emergency was over passed on fewer descendants.

In any case, for whatever reason, once the kibbutzim became established, and the twin dangers of starvation and Arab attack receded, the ideal of unity proved insufficient to maintain the original intensity of communal feeling. The kibbutzim have survived, but they have had to come to terms with the family. Couples spend more time in their apartments, often taking their meals there; children are with their parents for much of their free time, and often sleep in the family apartment rather than the children's house; it is no longer frowned upon for couples to sit next to each other on all public occasions; children once again call their parents "father" and "mother."

The experience of the kibbutz movement parallels that of other attempts to make the community, instead of the family, the basic unit of concern. After the Bolshevik Revolution, attempts were made in the Soviet Union to carry out the call of the *Communist Manifesto* for the abolition of the family. Within twenty years Soviet policy swung around completely, and began to encourage family life. (The *Manifesto* itself, incidentally, is equivocal about abolishing the family; not surprisingly, since Marx was as devoted to his family as any father.) Some religious communities have begun by bringing up children collectively; but the family has bounced back as soon as the bloom of spiritual enthusiasm fades. Monastic settlements have achieved a more permanent suppression of the family, but a community based on strict celibacy is hardly viable on its own.

A bias toward the interests of our own family, rather than those of the community in general, is a persistent tendency in human behavior, for good biological reasons. Not every persistent human tendency, however, is universally regarded as a virtue. (Compare attitudes toward another persistent human tendency, which probably also has a biological basis, the tendency to have sexual relations with more than one partner.) Why is it that in almost every human society concern for one's family is a mark of moral excellence? Why do societies not merely tolerate but go out of their way to praise parents who put the interests of their children ahead of the interests of other members of the community? The answer may lie, not just in the universality and strength of family feeling, but also in the benefits to society as a whole that come from families taking care of themselves. When families see that the children are fed, kept clean and sheltered, that the sick are nursed and the elderly cared for, they are led by bonds of natural affection to do what would otherwise fall on the community itself and either would not be done at all or would require labor unmotivated by natural impulses. (In a large modern community, it would require an expensive and impersonal bureaucracy.) Given the much greater intensity of family feeling compared with the degree of concern we have for the welfare of strangers, ethical rules which accept a degree of partiality toward the interests of one's own family may be the best means of promoting the welfare of all families and thus of the entire community.

Reciprocal Altruism and Human Ethics

Though kinship is the most basic and widespread bond between human beings, the bond of reciprocity is almost as universal. In his description of the Victorian moral view, Sidgwick lists a person's duty to show kindness "to those who have rendered services to him" immediately after the duty to be kind to kinsmen. Among the Ik, the mutual-assistance pact known as *nyot* survived when the family itself was breaking up. Westermarck says: "To requite a benefit, or to be grateful to him who bestows it, is probably everywhere, at least under certain circumstances, regarded as a duty." Since Westermarck wrote, anthropologists from Marcel Mauss to Claude Levi-Strauss have continued to stress the importance of reciprocity in human life. Howard Becker, author of *Man in Reciprocity*, finds our tendency for reciprocity so universal that he has proposed renaming our species *Homo reciprocus*. After surveying these and other recent studies, the sociologist Alvin Gouldner has concluded: "Contrary to some cultural relativists, it can be hypothesized that a norm of reciprocity is universal."

It is surprising how many features of human ethics could have grown out of simple reciprocal practices like the mutual removal of parasites from awkward places that one cannot oneself reach. Suppose I want to have the lice in my hair picked out. To obtain this I am willing to pick out someone else's lice. I must, however, be discriminating in selecting whom to groom. If I help everyone indiscriminately I shall find myself grooming others who do not groom me back. To avoid this waste of time and effort I distinguish between those who repay me for my assistance and those who do not. In other words, I separate those who deal fairly with me from those who cheat. Those who do not repay me I shall mark out to avoid; indeed, I may go further still, reacting with anger and hostility. Conceivably it will benefit me and other reciprocating altruists in my group if we make sure that the worst "cheats" are unable to take advantage of any of us again; killing them or driving them away would be effective ways of doing this. For those who do all that I hope they will do, on the other hand, I will have a positive feeling that increases the likelihood of my doing my part to preserve and develop a mutually advantageous relationship.

Let us take individually these outgrowths of reciprocal altruism. The first and most crucial is the distinction between those it is worth my while to assist and those it is not. Of course, if we all wait for each other to begin, we shall never get going. Initially someone has to remove someone else's parasites without knowing if there will be a return. After a bit of this, however, the track record of each member of the group will become clear. Then I can stop helping those who have not helped me. This requires a sense of what amounts to sufficient repayment for the help I have given. If I take an hour meticulously removing every louse from someone else's head, and she refuses even to look at my head, the verdict is clear; but what if she hurries over my head in ten minutes, leaving at least some of my lice in place? No doubt the practice of reciprocal altruism can tolerate rough justice at this point, but we would expect that as human powers of reasoning and communicating increased, decisions as to what is or is not an equitable exchange would become more precise. They would begin to take into account variations in circumstances: If, for instance, I can remove your few lice in ten minutes, should I demand that you spend the hour it would take to get rid of the multitude on my scalp? In answering this kind of question we would begin to develop a concept of fairness. More than two thousand years ago the Greek historian Polybius observed:

> . . . when a man who has been helped when in danger by another does not show gratitude to his preserver, but even goes to the length of attempting to do him injury, it is clear that those who become aware of it will naturally be displeased and offended by such conduct, sharing the resentment of their injured neighbor and imagining themselves in the same situation.

From all this there arises in everyone a notion of the meaning and theory of duty, which is the beginning and end of justice.

To say that the duty to repay benefits is the beginning and end of justice is an overstatement; but that it is the beginning is plausible. To "repay benefits" we should add the converse, "revenge injuries"; for the two are closely parallel and generally seen as going together. In tribal ethics the duties of gratitude and revenge often have a prominence they lack in our culture today. (I am not saying that they are not important motives in our society. They are; but we are less likely now to praise vengefulness as a virtue, and even gratitude no longer ranks as high among the virtues as it used to.)

Many tribal societies have elaborate rituals of gift-giving, always with the understanding that the recipient must repay. Often the repayment has to be superior to the original gift. Sometimes this escalation rises to such heights that people try at all costs to avoid receiving the gift, or try to pay it back immediately in order to be free of any obligation.

In the Western ethical tradition, too, gratitude and revenge have had a leading place. The investigation of justice undertaken in Plato's *Republic* gets under way by dissecting the popular view that justice consists in doing good to one's friends and harm to one's enemies. Cicero wrote that it is "the first demand of duty" that we do most for him that loves us most; "no duty is more imperative," he added, than that of proving one's gratitude. This is also the attitude to which Jesus referred in the Sermon on the Mount, when he said: "Ye have heard that it hath been said, thou shalt love thy neighbor and hate thine enemy." (Jesus proposed that we love our enemies instead of hating them, but even he found it necessary to hold out the prospect of a reward from God for doing more than publicans and sinners do.)

From our positive feelings for those who help us spring the bonds of friendship and the loyalty that we feel we owe to friends; from our negative feelings for those who do not reciprocate we get moral indignation and the desire to punish. If reciprocal altruism played a significant role in human evolution, an aversion to being cheated would be a distinct advantage. Humans have this aversion; indeed, we have it to such an extent that it often seems counterproductive. People who could not be induced to work an hour's overtime for ten dollars will spend an hour taking back defective goods worth five dollars. Nor is this lack of proportion unique to our culture. Anthropologists observing many different societies report bloody fights arising from apparently trivial causes. "It isn't the five dollars," we say in defense of our conduct, "it's the principle of the thing." No doubt the San "Bushmen" of the Kalahari say much the same when they fight over the distribution of the spoils of a hunt. But why do we care so much about the principle? One possible explanation is that while the cost of being cheated in a single incident may be very slight, over the long run constantly being cheated is much more costly. Hence it is worth going to some lengths to identify cheaters and make a complete break with them.

Personal resentment becomes moral indignation when it is shared by other members of a group and brought under a general principle. Polybius, in the passage quoted above, refers to others imagining themselves in the same situation, with the same feeling of resentment, as the victim of ingratitude. Because we can imagine ourselves in the position of others, and we can formulate general rules which deal with these cases, our personal feelings of resentment may solidify into a group code, with socially accepted standards of what constitutes adequate return for a service, and what should be done to those who cheat. Though vengeance in tribal societies is often left up to the injured party and his or her kin, there are obvious disadvantages in this system, since both sides will often see themselves as having been wronged, and the feud may continue to everyone's loss. To avoid this, in most societies blood feuds have been replaced by settled community procedures for hearing evidence in disputes, and pronouncing an authoritative verdict that all parties must obey.

Reciprocal altruism may be especially important within a group of beings who can reason and communicate as humans can, for then it can spread from a bilateral to a multilateral relationship. If I help you, but you do not help me, I can of course cease to help you in the future. If I can talk, however, I can do more. I can tell everyone else in the group what sort of a person you are. They may then also be less likely to help you in future. Conversely, the fact that someone is a reliable reciprocator may also become generally known, and make others readier to help that person. "Having a reputation" is only meaningful among creatures who communicate in a sophisticated manner; but when it develops, it immensely increases the usefulness of reciprocal altruism. If I have once saved a person from drowning, and am later in need of rescue myself, I will be lucky indeed if the very person I rescued is within earshot. So if my heroic deed is known only to the person I saved, it is unlikely to have future benefits. If, on the other hand, my saving someone increases the likelihood of any member of the community coming to my assistance, the chances of my altruism rebounding to my own advantage are much better.

That the practice of reciprocal altruism should be the source of many of our attitudes of moral approval and disapproval, including our ideas of fairness, cheating, gratitude, and retribution, would be easier to accept if it were not that this explanation seems to put these attitudes and ideas on too self-interested a footing. Reciprocal altruism seems not really altruism at all; it could more accurately be described as enlightened self-interest. One might be a fully reciprocating partner in this practice without having the slightest concern for the welfare of the person one helps. Concern for one's own interests, plus the knowledge that exchanges of assistance are likely to be in the long-term interests of both partners, is all that is needed. Our moral attitudes, however, demand something very different. If I am drowning in a raging surf and a stranger plunges in and rescues me, I shall be very grateful; but my gratitude will diminish if I learn that my rescuer first calculated the probability of receiving a sizable reward for saving my life, and took the plunge only because the prospects for the reward looked good. Nor is it only gratitude that diminishes when self-interested motives are revealed; moral approval is always warmest for acts which show either spontaneous concern for the welfare of others or else a conscientious desire to do what is right. Proof that an action we have praised had a self-interested motive almost always leads us to withdraw or qualify our praise.

Early in the previous chapter, we accepted a definition of altruism in terms of behavior--"altruistic behavior is behavior which benefits others at some cost to oneself"--without inquiring into motivation. Now we must note that when people talk of altruism they are normally thinking not simply of behavior but also of motivation. To be faithful to the generally accepted meaning of the term, we should redefine altruistic behavior as behavior which benefits others at some initial cost to oneself, and is motivated by the desire to benefit others. To what extent human beings are altruistically motivated is a question I shall consider in a later chapter. Meanwhile we should note that according to the common meaning of the term, which I shall use from now on, an act may in fact benefit me in the long run, and yet--perhaps because I didn't foresee that the act would rebound to my advantage-- still be altruistic because my intention was to benefit someone else.

Robert Trivers has offered a sociobiological explanation for our moral preference for altruistic motivation. People who are altruistically motivated will make more reliable partners than those motivated by self-interest.

After all, one day the calculations of self-interest may turn out differently. Looking at the shabby clothes I have left on the beach, a self-interested potential rescuer may decide that the prospects of a sizable reward are dim. In an exchange in which cheating is difficult to detect, a self-interested partner is more likely to cheat than a partner with real concern for my welfare. Evolution would therefore favor people who could distinguish self-interested from altruistic motivation in others, and then select only the altruistic as beneficiaries of their gifts or services.

Psychologists have experimented with the circumstances that lead people to behave altruistically, and their results show that we are more ready to act altruistically toward those we regard as genuinely altruistic than to those we think have ulterior motives for their apparently altruistic acts. As one review of the literature concludes: "When the legitimacy of the apparent altruism is questioned, reciprocity is less likely to prevail." Another experiment proved something most of us know from our own attitudes: we find genuine altruism a more attractive character trait than a pretense of altruism covering self-interested motives.

Here an intriguing and important point emerges; if there are advantages in being a partner in a reciprocal exchange, and if one is more likely to be selected as a partner if one has genuine concern for others, there is an evolutionary advantage in having genuine concern for others. (This assumes, of course, that potential partners can see through a pretense of altruism by those who are really self-interested-- something that is not always easy, but which we spend a lot of time trying to do, and often can do. Evolutionary theory would predict that we would get better at detecting pretense, but at the same time the performance of the pretenders would improve, so the task would never become a simple one.)

This conclusion is highly significant for understanding ethics, because it cuts across the tendency of sociobiological reasoning to explain behavior in terms of self-interest or the interests of one's kin. Properly understood, sociobiology does not imply that behavior is actually motivated by the desire to further one's own interests or those of one's kin. Sociobiology says nothing about motivation, for it remains on the level of the objective consequences of types of behavior. That a piece of behavior in fact benefits oneself does not mean that the behavior is motivated by self-interest, for one might be quite unaware of the benefits to oneself the behavior will bring. Nevertheless, it is a common assumption that sociobiology implies that we are motivated by self-interest, not by genuine altruism. This assumption gains credibility from some of the things sociobiologists write. We can now see that sociobiology itself can explain the existence of genuinely altruistic motivation. The implications of this I shall take up in a later chapter, but it may be useful to make the underlying mechanism more explicit. This can be done by reference to a puzzle known as the Prisoner's Dilemma.

In the cells of the Ruritanian secret police are two political prisoners. The police are trying to persuade them to confess to membership in an illegal opposition party. The prisoners know that if neither of them confesses, the police will not be able to make the charge stick, but they will be interrogated in the cells for another three months before the police give up and let them go. If one of them confesses, implicating the other, the one who confesses will be released immediately but the other will be sentenced to eight years in jail. If both of them confess, their helpfulness will be taken into account and they will get five years in jail. Since the prisoners are interrogated separately, neither can know if the other has confessed or not.

The dilemma is, of course, whether to confess. The point of the story is that circumstances have been so arranged that if either prisoner reasons from the point of view of self-interest, she will find it to her advantage to confess; whereas taking the interests of the two prisoners together, it is obviously in their interests if neither confesses. Thus the first prisoner's self-interested calculations go like this: "If the other prisoner confesses, it will be better for me if I have also confessed, for then I will get five years instead of eight; and if the other prisoner does not confess, it will still be better for me if I confess, for then I will be released immediately, instead of being interrogated for another three months. Since we are interrogated separately, whether the other prisoner confesses has nothing to do with whether I confess--our choices are entirely independent of each other. So whatever happens, it will be better for me if I confess." The second prisoner's self-interested reasoning will, of course, follow exactly the same route as the first prisoner's, and will come to the same conclusion. As a result, both prisoners, if self-interested, will confess, and both will spend the next five years in prison. There was a way for them both to be out in three months, but because they were locked into purely self-interested calculations, they could not take that route.

What would have to be changed in our assumptions about the prisoners to make it rational for them both to refuse to confess? One way of achieving this would be for the prisoners to make an agreement that would bind them both to silence. But how could each prisoner be confident that the other would keep the agreement? If one prisoner breaks the agreement, the other will be in prison for a long time, unable to punish the cheater in any way. So each prisoner will reason: "If the other one breaks the agreement, it will be better for me if I break it too; and if the other one keeps the agreement, I will still be better off if I break it. So I will break the agreement."

Without sanctions to back it up, an agreement is unable to bring two self-interested individuals to the outcome that is best for both of them, taking their interests together. What has to be changed to reach this result is the assumption that the prisoners are motivated by self-interest alone. If, for instance, they are altruistic to the extent of caring as much for the interests of their fellow prisoner as they care for their own interests, they will reason thus: "If the other prisoner does not confess it will be better for us both if I do not confess, for then between us we will be in prison for a total of six months, whereas if I do confess the total will be eight years; and if the other prisoner does confess it will still be better if I do not confess, for then the total served will be eight years, instead of ten. So whatever happens, taking our interests together, it will be better if I don't confess." A pair of altruistic prisoners will therefore come out of this situation better than a pair of self-interested prisoners, *even from the point of view of self-interest*.

Altruistic motivation is not the only way to achieve a happier solution. Another possibility is that the prisoners are conscientious, regarding it as morally wrong to inform on a fellow prisoner; or if they are able to make an agreement, they might believe they have a duty to keep their promises. In either case, each will be able to rely on the other not confessing and they will be free in three months. The Prisoner's Dilemma shows that, paradoxical as it may seem, we will sometimes be better off if we are not self-interested. Two or more people motivated by self-interest alone may not be able to promote their interests as well as they could if they were more altruistic or more conscientious.

The Prisoner's Dilemma explains why there could be an evolutionary advantage in being genuinely altruistic instead of making reciprocal exchanges on the basis of calculated self-interest. Prisons and confessions may not have played a substantial role in early human evolution, but other forms of cooperation surely did. Suppose two early humans are attacked by a sabertooth cat. If both flee, one will be picked off by the cat; if both stand their ground, there is a very good chance that they can fight the cat off; if one flees and the other stands and fights, the fugitive will escape and the fighter will be killed. Here the odds are sufficiently like those in the Prisoner's Dilemma to produce a similar result. From a self-interested point of view, if your partner flees your chances of survival are better if you flee too (you have a 50 percent chance rather than none at all) and if your partner stands and fights you still do better to run (you are sure of escape if you flee, whereas it is only probable, not certain, that together you and your partner can overcome the cat). So two purely self-interested early humans would flee, and one of them would die. Two early humans who cared for each other, however, would stand and fight, and most likely neither would die. Let us say, just to be able to put a figure on it, that two humans cooperating can defeat a sabertooth cat on nine out of every ten occasions and on the tenth occasion the cat kills one of them. Let us also say that when a sabertooth cat pursues two fleeing humans it always catches one of them, and which one it catches is entirely random, since differences in human running speed are negligible in comparison to the speed of the cat. Then one of a pair of purely self-interested humans would not, on average, last more than a single encounter with a sabertooth cat; but one of a pair of altruistic humans would on average survive ten such encounters.

If situations analogous to this imaginary sabertooth cat attack were common, early humans would do better hunting with altruistic comrades than with self-interested partners. Of course, an egoist who could find an altruist to go hunting with him would do better still; but altruists who could not detect--and refuse to assist--purely self-interested partners would be selected against. Evolution would therefore favor those who are genuinely altruistic to other genuine altruists, but are not altruistic to those who seek to take advantage of their altruism. We can add, again, that the same goal could be achieved if, instead of being altruistic, early humans were moved by something like a sense that it is wrong to desert a partner in the face of danger.

Group Altruism and Human Ethics

In the previous chapter we saw that most sociobiologists believe kin selection and reciprocity to have been more significant forces in evolution than group selection; nevertheless, we found some grounds for believing that group selection might have played a role. Whether or not group selection has been significant among non-human animals, when we look at human ethical systems the case for group selection is much stronger, although in view of the clear interest each society has in promoting devotion to the group, it is here even harder than in other cases to disentangle biological and cultural influences. What can be said for the biological side is that early humans lived in small groups, and these groups were at least sometimes reproductively isolated from each other by geography or mutual hostility; thus the conditions necessary for selection on a group basis existed. Cultural influences probably enhanced the tendency toward group altruism, by punishing those who put their own interests too far ahead of the interests of the group, and rewarding those who make sacrifices for the group.

In placing group altruism after kin and reciprocal altruism we are following, once more, Sidgwick's hierarchy of the degrees of benevolence. He reports the morality of his day as placing the duty to be benevolent "to neighbours and to fellow-countrymen" immediately after the duty to be benevolent to friends, and before the duty to be benevolent to members of our own race. That we have a duty to assist the poor of our own neighborhood or nation before we assist the poor of another neighborhood or country is still a popular sentiment. It is part of the common belief that we should look after "our own" before we make efforts to help the starving overseas. I have already mentioned this view in connection with the ties of kinship, but once the obligations of kinship are fulfilled the boundaries of "our own" expand to the next largest community with which we identify, whether this be a local or regional grouping, or an affiliation based not on living in the same area but on a shared characteristic like ethnic or class background, or religious belief. Beyond this priority of concern for the welfare of members of our particular group, there is also a loyalty to the group as a whole which is distinct from loyalty to individual members of the group. We tend to identify with a group, and see its fortunes as to some degree our fortunes. The distinction is easily seen at the national level, where "patriotism" describes a loyalty to one's nation that has little to do with helping individual fellow citizens.

Like kin altruism and reciprocal altruism, group altruism is a strong and pervasive feature of human life. When people live in small kinship groups, kin altruism and group altruism overlap; but the ethical codes of larger societies almost always contain elements of distinctively group altruism. It is very common for tribal societies to combine a high degree of altruism within the tribe with overt hostility to members of neighboring tribes. Similarly strong feelings of loyalty to one's group have been reported by anthropologists from many different cultures. The ancient Greeks particularly praised devotion to one's city-state, and we have seen how Plato thought that state loyalty should take precedence over family loyalty, at least among his Guardians. Cicero, in a characteristic piece of Roman rhetoric, wrote: Parents are dear; dear are children, relatives, friends; but one's native land embraces all our loves; and who that is true would hesitate to give his life for her, if by his death he could render her a service?

The persistence of group loyalty in modern times was only too clearly demonstrated by Hitler's success in arousing the nationalistic feelings of the German people, and Stalin's need to appeal to "Mother Russia" rather than the defense of Communism to rally the citizens of the Soviet Union to the war effort. In a less sinister way we can witness the appeal of group loyalty every weekend by watching the behavior of the crowds at football games.

Our ethical codes reflect our group feelings in two ways, corresponding to the difference between group altruism manifested as a preference for altruism directed toward individual members of one's own group, and group altruism manifested as loyalty to the group as a whole. We have seen the group bias of our ethics in respect to the first of these-the widespread and socially approved attitude that the obligation to assist people in other countries is much weaker than the obligation to assist our fellow citizens. The group bias of our ethics in respect to loyalty to the group as a whole shows itself in the high praise we give to patriotism.

Why is it that "my country, right or wrong!" can be taken seriously? Why do we regard patriotism as a virtue at all? We disapprove of selfish behavior, but we encourage group selfishness, and gild it with the name "patriotism." We erect statues to those who fought and died for our country, irrespective of the merits of the war in which they fought. (One of the reasons why Robert E. Lee, leader of the Confederate Army in the Civil War, is such an admired figure in American history is that he put his loyalty to his native Virginia above his publicly stated moral doubts about slavery.)

Patriotism has had its critics, among them many of the most enlightened and progressive thinkers. Diogenes the Cynic declared himself to be the citizen not of one country but of the whole world. Stoic philosophers like Seneca and Marcus Aurelius also argued that our loyalty should be to the world community, not to the state in which we happen to be born. Voltaire, Goethe, and Schiller espoused similar ideals of world, rather than national, citizenship. Yet patriotism has proved difficult to dislodge from its high place among the conventionally accepted virtues. The explanation for this could be that patriotism rests, at least in part, on a biological basis; but the explanation could also be cultural. Culture can itself be a factor in the evolutionary process, those cultures prevailing which enhance the group's prospect of survival. The prevalence of patriotism could easily be explained in this manner.

That cultural and biological factors interact is something that should be borne in mind throughout our discussion of the biological basis of ethics. Biological and cultural explanations of human behavior are not inconsistent unless, foolishly, we try to insist that one of these two is the sole cause of a complex piece of behavior. With certain exceptions, that is unlikely. Culture may intensify, soften, or perhaps under special conditions altogether suppress genetically based tendencies. Earlier in this chapter I referred to the extent to which practices based on racial and ethnic group feeling have been softened or eliminated by changes in attitudes. Here we have a clear example of something that may well have some biological basis—but also contains a strong cultural component-being altered by a cultural change. In a multiracial society, strong racial feelings are a disadvantage; strong patriotic feelings, however, are not.

One other cautionary note before I bring this chapter to a close: Up to this point our discussion has been purely descriptive. I have been speculating about the origins of human ethics. No ethical conclusions flow from these speculations. In particular, the suggestion that an aspect of human ethics is universal, or nearly so, in no way justifies that aspect of human ethics. Nor does the suggestion that a particular aspect of human ethics has a biological basis do anything to justify it. Because there is so much misunderstanding of the connection between biological theories about ethics and ethical conclusions themselves, the task of examining claims about this connection needs a chapter to itself.

Universal Declaration of Human Rights

Adopted and proclaimed by General Assembly resolution 217 A (III) of 10 December, 1948.

On December 10, 1948 the General Assembly of the United Nations adopted and proclaimed the Universal Declaration of Human Rights the full text of which appears in the following pages. Following this historic act the Assembly called upon all Member countries to publicize the text of the Declaration and "to cause it to be disseminated, displayed, read and expounded principally in schools and other educational institutions, without distinction based on the political status of countries or territories."

Preamble

Whereas recognition of the inherent dignity and of the equal and inalienable rights of all members of the human family is the foundation of freedom, justice and peace in the world,

Whereas disregard and contempt for human rights have resulted in barbarous acts which have outraged the conscience of mankind, and the advent of a world in which human beings shall enjoy freedom of speech and belief and freedom from fear and want has been proclaimed as the highest aspiration of the common people,

Whereas it is essential, if man is not to be compelled to have recourse, as a last resort, to rebellion against tyranny and oppression, that human rights should be protected by the rule of law,

Whereas it is essential to promote the development of friendly relations between nations,

Whereas the peoples of the United Nations have in the Charter reaffirmed their faith in fundamental human rights, in the dignity and worth of the human person and in the equal rights of men and women and have determined to promote social progress and better standards of life in larger freedom,

Whereas Member States have pledged themselves to achieve, in co-operation with the United Nations, the promotion of universal respect for and observance of human rights and fundamental freedoms,

Whereas a common understanding of these rights and freedoms is of the greatest importance for the full realization of this pledge,

Now, Therefore THE GENERAL ASSEMBLY proclaims THIS UNIVERSAL DECLARATION OF HUMAN RIGHTS as a common standard of achievement for all peoples and all nations, to the end that every individual and every organ of society, keeping this Declaration constantly in mind, shall strive by teaching and education to promote respect for these rights and freedoms and by progressive measures, national and international, to secure their universal and effective recognition and observance, both among the peoples of Member States themselves and among the peoples of territories under their jurisdiction.

Article 1.
All human beings are born free and equal in dignity and rights. They are endowed with reason and conscience and should act towards one another in a spirit of brotherhood.

Article 2.
Everyone is entitled to all the rights and freedoms set forth in this Declaration, without distinction of any kind, such as race, colour, sex, language, religion, political or other opinion, national or social origin, property, birth or other status. Furthermore, no distinction shall be made on the basis of the political, jurisdictional or international status of the country or territory to which a person belongs, whether it be independent, trust, non-self-governing or under any other limitation of sovereignty.

Article 3.
Everyone has the right to life, liberty and security of person.

Article 4.
No one shall be held in slavery or servitude; slavery and the slave trade shall be prohibited in all their forms.

Article 5.
No one shall be subjected to torture or to cruel, inhuman or degrading treatment or punishment.

Article 6.
Everyone has the right to recognition everywhere as a person before the law.

Article 7.
All are equal before the law and are entitled without any discrimination to equal protection of the law. All are entitled to equal protection against any discrimination in violation of this Declaration and against any incitement to such discrimination.

Article 8.
Everyone has the right to an effective remedy by the competent national tribunals for acts violating the fundamental rights granted him by the constitution or by law.

Article 9.
No one shall be subjected to arbitrary arrest, detention or exile.

Article 10.
Everyone is entitled in full equality to a fair and public hearing by an independent and impartial tribunal, in the determination of his rights and obligations and of any criminal charge against him.

Article 11.
(1) Everyone charged with a penal offence has the right to be presumed innocent until proved guilty according to law in a public trial at which he has had all the guarantees necessary for his defence.
(2) No one shall be held guilty of any penal offence on account of any act or omission which did not constitute a penal offence, under national or international law, at the time when it was committed. Nor shall a heavier penalty be imposed than the one that was applicable at the time the penal offence was committed.

Article 12.
No one shall be subjected to arbitrary interference with his privacy, family, home or correspondence, nor to attacks upon his honour and reputation. Everyone has the right to the protection of the law against such interference or attacks.

Article 13.
(1) Everyone has the right to freedom of movement and residence within the borders of each state.
(2) Everyone has the right to leave any country, including his own, and to return to his country.

Article 14.
(1) Everyone has the right to seek and to enjoy in other countries asylum from persecution.
(2) This right may not be invoked in the case of prosecutions genuinely arising from non-political crimes or from acts contrary to the purposes and principles of the United Nations.

Article 15.
(1) Everyone has the right to a nationality.
(2) No one shall be arbitrarily deprived of his nationality nor denied the right to change his nationality.

Article 16.
(1) Men and women of full age, without any limitation due to race, nationality or religion, have the right to marry and to found a family. They are entitled to equal rights as to marriage, during marriage and at its dissolution.
(2) Marriage shall be entered into only with the free and full consent of the intending spouses.
(3) The family is the natural and fundamental group unit of society and is entitled to protection by society and the State.

Article 17.
(1) Everyone has the right to own property alone as well as in association with others.
(2) No one shall be arbitrarily deprived of his property.

Article 18.
Everyone has the right to freedom of thought, conscience and religion; this right includes freedom to change his religion or belief, and freedom, either alone or in community with others and in public or private, to manifest his religion or belief in teaching, practice, worship and observance.

Article 19.
Everyone has the right to freedom of opinion and expression; this right includes freedom to hold opinions without interference and to seek, receive and impart information and ideas through any media and regardless of frontiers.

Article 20.
(1) Everyone has the right to freedom of peaceful assembly and association.
(2) No one may be compelled to belong to an association.

Article 21.
(1) Everyone has the right to take part in the government of his country, directly or through freely chosen representatives.
(2) Everyone has the right of equal access to public service in his country.
(3) The will of the people shall be the basis of the authority of government; this will shall be expressed in periodic and genuine elections which shall be by universal and equal suffrage and shall be held by secret vote or by equivalent free voting procedures.

Article 22.
Everyone, as a member of society, has the right to social security and is entitled to realization, through national effort and international co-operation and in accordance with the organization and resources of each State, of the economic, social and cultural rights indispensable for his dignity and the free development of his personality.

Article 23.
(1) Everyone has the right to work, to free choice of employment, to just and favourable conditions of work and to protection against unemployment.
(2) Everyone, without any discrimination, has the right to equal pay for equal work.
(3) Everyone who works has the right to just and favourable remuneration ensuring for himself and his family an existence worthy of human dignity, and supplemented, if necessary, by other means of social protection.
(4) Everyone has the right to form and to join trade unions for the protection of his interests.

Article 24.
Everyone has the right to rest and leisure, including reasonable limitation of working hours and periodic holidays with pay.

Article 25.
(1) Everyone has the right to a standard of living adequate for the health and well-being of himself and of his family, including food, clothing, housing and medical care

and necessary social services, and the right to security in the event of unemployment, sickness, disability, widowhood, old age or other lack of livelihood in circumstances beyond his control.
(2) Motherhood and childhood are entitled to special care and assistance. All children, whether born in or out of wedlock, shall enjoy the same social protection.

Article 26.
(1) Everyone has the right to education. Education shall be free, at least in the elementary and fundamental stages. Elementary education shall be compulsory. Technical and professional education shall be made generally available and higher education shall be equally accessible to all on the basis of merit.
(2) Education shall be directed to the full development of the human personality and to the strengthening of respect for human rights and fundamental freedoms. It shall promote understanding, tolerance and friendship among all nations, racial or religious groups, and shall further the activities of the United Nations for the maintenance of peace.
(3) Parents have a prior right to choose the kind of education that shall be given to their children.

Article 27.
(1) Everyone has the right freely to participate in the cultural life of the community, to enjoy the arts and to share in scientific advancement and its benefits.
(2) Everyone has the right to the protection of the moral and material interests resulting from any scientific, literary or artistic production of which he is the author.

Article 28.
Everyone is entitled to a social and international order in which the rights and freedoms set forth in this Declaration can be fully realized.

Article 29.
(1) Everyone has duties to the community in which alone the free and full development of his personality is possible.
(2) In the exercise of his rights and freedoms, everyone shall be subject only to such limitations as are determined by law solely for the purpose of securing due recognition and respect for the rights and freedoms of others and of meeting the just requirements of morality, public order and the general welfare in a democratic society.
(3) These rights and freedoms may in no case be exercised contrary to the purposes and principles of the United Nations.

Article 30.
Nothing in this Declaration may be interpreted as implying for any State, group or person any right to engage in any activity or to perform any act aimed at the destruction of any of the rights and freedoms set forth herein.

Introduction to the Principles of Morals and Legislation
Jeremy Bentham

Chapter 1
Of the Principle of Utility

I. Nature has placed mankind under the governance of two sovereign masters, pain and pleasure. It is for them alone to point out what we ought to do, as well as to determine what we shall do. On the one hand the standard of right and wrong, on the other the chain of causes and effects, are fastened to their throne. They govern us in all we do, in all we say, in all we think: every effort we can make to throw off our subjection, will serve but to demonstrate and confirm it. In words a man may pretend to abjure their empire: but in reality he will remain subject to it all the while. The principle of utility recognizes this subjection, and assumes it for the foundation of that system, the object of which is to rear the fabric of felicity by the hands of reason and of law. Systems which attempt to question it, deal in sounds instead of sense, in caprice instead of reason, in darkness instead of light.

But enough of metaphor and declamation: it is not by such means that moral science is to be improved.

II. The principle of utility is the foundation of the present work: it will be proper therefore at the outset to give an explicit and determinate account of what is meant by it. By the principle of utility is meant that principle which approves or disapproves of every action whatsoever according to the tendency it appears to have to augment or diminish the happiness of the party whose interest is in question: or, what is the same thing in other words to promote or to oppose that happiness. I say of every action whatsoever, and therefore not only of every action of a private individual, but of every measure of government.

III. By utility is meant that property in any object, whereby it tends to produce benefit, advantage, pleasure, good, or happiness, (all this in the present case comes to the same thing) or (what comes again to the same thing) to prevent the happening of mischief, pain, evil, or unhappiness to the party whose interest is considered: if that party be the community in general, then the happiness of the community: if a particular individual, then the happiness of that individual.

IV. The interest of the community is one of the most general expressions that can occur in the phraseology of morals: no wonder that the meaning of it is often lost. When it has a meaning, it is this. The community is a fictitious body, composed of the individual persons who are considered as constituting as it were its members. The interest of the community then is, what is it?—the sum of the interests of the several members who compose it.

V. It is in vain to talk of the interest of the community, without understanding what is the interest of the individual. A thing is said to promote the interest, or to be for the interest, of an individual, when it tends to add to the sum total of his pleasures: or, what comes to the same thing, to diminish the sum total of his pains.

VI. An action then may be said to be conformable to the principle of utility, or, for shortness sake, to utility, (meaning with respect to the community at large) when the tendency it has to augment the happiness of the community is greater than any it has to diminish it.

VII. A measure of government (which is but a particular kind of action, performed by a particular person or persons) may be said to be conformable to or dictated by the principle of utility, when in like manner the tendency which it has to augment the happiness of the community is greater than any which it has to diminish it.

VIII. When an action, or in particular a measure of government, is supposed by a man to be conformable to the principle of utility, it may be convenient, for the purposes of discourse, to imagine a kind of law or dictate, called a law or dictate of utility: and to speak of the action in question, as being conformable to such law to apply it, or on account of some prejudice or other which they were conformable to such law or dictate.

IX. A man may be said to be a partizan of the principle of utility, when the approbation or disapprobation he annexes to any action, or to any measure, is determined by and proportioned to the tendency which he conceives it to have to augment or to diminish the happiness of the community: or in other words, to its conformity or unconformity to the laws or dictates of utility.

X. Of an action that is conformable to the principle of utility one may always say either that it is one that ought to be done, or at least that it is not one that ought not to be done. One may say also, that it is right it should be done; at least that it is not wrong it should be done: that it is a right action; at least that it is not a wrong action. When thus interpreted, the words ought, and right and wrong and others of that stamp, have a meaning: when otherwise, they have none.

XI. Has the rectitude of this principle been ever formally contested? It should seem that it had, by those who have not known what they have been meaning. Is it susceptible of any direct proof? It should seem not: for that which is used to prove everything else, cannot itself be proved: a chain of proofs must have their commencement somewhere. To give such proof is as impossible as it is needless.

XII. Not that there is or ever has been that human creature at breathing, however stupid or perverse, who has not on many, perhaps on most occasions of his life, deferred to it. By the natural constitution of the human frame, on most occasions of their lives men in general embrace this principle, without thinking of it: if not for the ordering of their own actions, yet for the trying of their own actions, as well as of those of other men. There have been, at the same time, not many perhaps, even of the most intelligent, who have been disposed to embrace it purely and without reserve. There are even few who have not taken some occasion or other to quarrel with it, either on account of their not understanding always it to examine into, or could not bear to part with. For such is the stuff that man is made of: in principle and in practice, in a right track and in a wrong one, the rarest of all human qualities is consistency.

XIII. When a man attempts to combat the principle of utility, it is with reasons drawn, without his being aware of it, from that very principle itself. His arguments, if they prove anything, prove not that the principle is wrong, but that, according to the applications he supposes to be made of it, it is misapplied. Is it possible for a man to move the earth? Yes; but he must first find out another earth to stand upon.

XIV. To disprove the propriety of it by arguments is impossible; but, from the causes that have been mentioned, or from some confused or partial view of it, a man may happen to be disposed not to relish it. Where this is the case, if he thinks the settling of his opinions on such a subject worth the trouble, let him take the following steps, and at length, perhaps, he may come to reconcile himself to it.

> 1. Let him settle with himself, whether he would wish to discard this principle altogether; if so, let him consider what it is that all his reasonings (in matters of politics especially) can amount to?
> 2. If he would, let him settle with himself, whether he would judge and act without any principle, or whether there is any other he would judge an act by?
> 3. If there be, let him examine and satisfy himself whether the principle he thinks he has found is really any separate intelligible principle; or whether it be not a mere principle in words, a kind of phrase, which at bottom expresses neither more nor less than the mere averment of his own unfounded sentiments; that is, what in another person he might be apt to call caprice?
> 4. If he is inclined to think that his own approbation or disapprobation, annexed to the idea of an act, without any regard to its consequences, is a sufficient foundation for him to judge and act upon, let him ask himself whether his sentiment is to be a standard of right and wrong, with respect to every other man, or whether every man's sentiment has the same privilege of being a standard to itself?
> 5. In the first case, let him ask himself whether his principle is not despotical, and hostile to all the rest of human race?
> 6. In the second case, whether it is not anarchial, and whether at this rate there are not as many different standards of right and wrong as there are men? And whether even to the same man, the same thing, which is right to-day, may not (without the least change in its nature) be wrong tomorrow? And whether the same thing is not right and wrong in the same place at the

same time? And in either case, whether all argument is not at an end? and whether, when two men have said, "I like this", and "I don't like it", they can (upon such a principle) have any thing more to say?

7. If he should have said to himself, No: for that the sentiment which he proposes as a standard must be grounded on reflection, let him say on what particulars the reflection is to turn? If on particulars having relation to the utility of the act, then let him say whether this is not deserting his own principle, and borrowing assistance from that very one in opposition to which he sets it up: or if not on those particulars, on what other particulars?

8. If he should be for compounding the matter, and adopting his own principle in part, and the principle of utility in part, let him say how far he will adopt it?

9. When he has settled with himself where he will stop, then let him ask himself how he justifies to himself the adopting it so far? And why he will not adopt it any farther?

10. Admitting any other principle than the principle of utility to be a right principle, a principle that it is right for a man to pursue; admitting (what is not true) that the word right can have a meaning without reference to utility, let him say whether there is any such thing as a motive that a man can have to pursue the dictates of it: if there is, let him say what that motive is, and how it is to be distinguished from those which enforce the dictates of utility: if not, then lastly let him say what it is this other principle can be good for?

Chapter IV
Value of a Lot of Pleasure or Pain, How to be Measured

I. Pleasures then, and the avoidance of pains, are the ends that the legislator has in view; it behooves him therefore to understand their value. Pleasures and pains are the instruments he has to work with: it behooves him therefore to understand their force, which is again, in other words, their value.

II. To a person considered by himself, the value of a pleasure or pain considered by itself, will be greater or less, according to the four following circumstances:

    1. Its intensity.
    2. Its duration.
    3. Its certainty or uncertainty.
    4. Its propinquity or remoteness.

III. These are the circumstances which are to be considered in estimating a pleasure or a pain considered each of them by itself. But when the value of any pleasure or pain is considered for the purpose of estimating the tendency of any act by which it is produced, there are two other circumstances to be taken into the account; these are,

    5. Its fecundity, or the chance it has of being followed by sensations of the same kind: that is, pleasures, if it be a pleasure: pains, if it be a pain.

6. Its purity, or the chance it has of not being followed by sensations of the opposite kind: that is, pains, if it be a pleasure: pleasures, if it be a pain.

These two last, however, are in strictness scarcely to be deemed properties of the pleasure or the pain itself; they are not, therefore, in strictness to be taken into the account of the value of that pleasure or that pain. They are in strictness to be deemed properties only of the act, or other event, by which such pleasure or pain has been produced; and accordingly are only to be taken into the account of the tendency of such act or such event.

IV. To a number of persons, with reference to each of whom to the value of a pleasure or a pain is considered, it will be greater or less, according to seven circumstances: to wit, the six preceding ones; viz.
1. Its intensity.
2. Its duration.
3. Its certainty or uncertainty.
4. Its propinquity or remoteness.
5. Its fecundity.
6. Its purity.

And one other; to wit:
7. Its extent; that is, the number of persons to whom it extends; or (in other words) who are affected by it.

V. To take an exact account then of the general tendency of any act, by which the interests of a community are affected, proceed as follows. Begin with any one person of those whose interests seem most immediately to be affected by it: and take an account,

1. Of the value of each distinguishable pleasure which appears to be produced by it in the first instance.
2. Of the value of each pain which appears to be produced by it in the first instance.
3. Of the value of each pleasure which appears to be produced by it after the first. This constitutes the fecundity of the first pleasure and the impurity of the first pain.
4. Of the value of each pain which appears to be produced by it after the first. This constitutes the fecundity of the first pain, and the impurity of the first pleasure.
5. Sum up all the values of all the pleasures on the one side, and those of all the pains on the other. The balance, if it be on the side of pleasure, will give the good tendency of the act upon the whole, with respect to the interests of that individual person; if on the side of pain, the bad tendency of it upon the whole.
6. Take an account of the number of persons whose interests appear to be concerned; and repeat the above process with respect to each. Sum up the numbers expressive of the degrees of good tendency, which the act has, with respect to each individual, in regard to whom the tendency of it is good upon the whole: do this again with respect to each individual, in regard to whom

the tendency of it is good upon the whole: do this again with respect to each individual, in regard to whom the tendency of it is bad upon the whole. Take the balance which if on the side of pleasure, will give the general good tendency of the act, with respect to the total number or community of individuals concerned; if on the side of pain, the general evil tendency, with respect to the same community.

VI. It is not to be expected that this process should be strictly pursued previously to every moral judgment, or to every legislative or judicial operation. It may, however, be always kept in view: and as near as the process actually pursued on these occasions approaches to it, so near will such process approach to the character of an exact one.

VII. The same process is alike applicable to pleasure and pain, in whatever shape they appear: and by whatever denomination they are distinguished: to pleasure, whether it be called good (which is properly the cause or instrument of pleasure) or profit (which is distant pleasure, or the cause or instrument of, distant pleasure,) or convenience, or advantage, benefit, emolument, happiness, and so forth: to pain, whether it be called evil, (which corresponds to good) or mischief, or inconvenience or disadvantage, or loss, or unhappiness, and so forth.

VIII. Nor is this a novel and unwarranted, any more than it is a useless theory. In all this there is nothing but what the practice of mankind, wheresoever they have a clear view of their own interest, is perfectly conformable to. An article of property, an estate in land, for instance, is valuable, on what account? On account of the pleasures of all kinds which it enables a man to produce, and what comes to the same thing the pains of all kinds which it enables him to avert. But the value of such an article of property is universally understood to rise or fall according to the length or shortness of the time which a man has in it: the certainty or uncertainty of its coming into possession: and the nearness or remoteness of the time at which, if at all, it is to come into possession. As to the intensity of the pleasures which a man may derive from it, this is never thought of, because it depends upon the use which each particular person may come to make of it; which cannot be estimated till the particular pleasures he may come to derive from it, or the particular pains he may come to exclude by means of it, are brought to view. For the same reason, neither does he think of the fecundity or purity of those pleasures.

Thus much for pleasure and pain, happiness and unhappiness, in general. We come now to consider the several particular kinds of pain and pleasure.

UTILITARIANISM
JOHN STUART MILL

From Chapter 5
"On the Connection Between Justice and Utility"

Having thus endeavoured to determine the distinctive elements which enter into the composition of the idea of justice, we are ready to enter on the inquiry, whether the feeling, which accompanies the idea, is attached to it by a special dispensation of nature, or whether it could have grown up, by any known laws, out of the idea itself; and in particular, whether it can have originated in considerations of general expediency.

I conceive that the sentiment itself does not arise from anything which would commonly, or correctly, be termed an idea of expediency; but that though the sentiment does not, whatever is moral in it does.

We have seen that the two essential ingredients in the sentiment of justice are, the desire to punish a person who has done harm, and the knowledge or belief that there is some definite individual or individuals to whom harm has been done.

Now it appears to me, that the desire to punish a person who has done harm to some individual is a spontaneous outgrowth from two sentiments, both in the highest degree natural, and which either are or resemble instincts; the impulse of self-defence, and the feeling of sympathy.

It is natural to resent, and to repel or retaliate, any harm done or attempted against ourselves, or against those with whom we sympathise. The origin of this sentiment it is not necessary here to discuss. Whether it be an instinct or a result of intelligence, it is, we know, common to all animal nature; for every animal tries to hurt those who have hurt, or who it thinks are about to hurt, itself or its young. Human beings, on this point, only differ from other animals in two particulars. First, in being capable of sympathising, not solely with their offspring, or, like some of the more noble animals, with some superior animal who is kind to them, but with all human, and even with all sentient, beings. Secondly, in having a more developed intelligence, which gives a wider range to the whole of their sentiments, whether self-regarding or sympathetic. By virtue of his superior intelligence, even apart from his superior range of sympathy, a human being is capable of apprehending a community of interest between himself and the human society of which he forms a part, such that any conduct which threatens the security of the society generally, is threatening to his own, and calls forth his instinct (if instinct it be) of self-defence. The same superiority of intelligence joined to the power of sympathising with human beings generally, enables him to attach himself to the collective idea of his tribe, his country, or mankind, in such a manner that any act hurtful to them, raises his instinct of sympathy, and urges him to resistance.

The sentiment of justice, in that one of its elements which consists of the desire to punish, is thus, I conceive, the natural feeling of retaliation or vengeance, rendered by intellect and sympathy applicable to those injuries, that is, to those hurts, which wound us through, or in common with, society at large. This sentiment, in itself, has nothing moral in it; what is moral is, the exclusive subordination of it to the social sympathies, so as to wait on and obey their call. For the natural feeling would make us resent indiscriminately whatever any one does that is disagreeable to us; but when moralised by the social feeling, it only acts in the directions conformable to the general good: just persons resenting a hurt to society, though not otherwise a hurt to themselves, and not resenting a hurt to themselves, however painful, unless it be of the kind which society has a common interest with them in the repression of.

It is no objection against this doctrine to say, that when we feel our sentiment of justice outraged, we are not thinking of society at large, or of any collective interest, but only of the individual case. It is common enough certainly, though the reverse of commendable, to feel resentment merely because we have suffered pain; but a person whose resentment is really a moral feeling, that is, who considers whether an act is blamable before he allows himself to resent it- such a person, though he may not say expressly to himself that he is standing up for the interest of society, certainly does feel that he is asserting a rule which is for the benefit of others as well as for his own. If he is not feeling this- if he is regarding the act solely as it affects him individually- he is not consciously just; he is not concerning himself about the justice of his actions. This is admitted even by anti-utilitarian moralists. When Kant (as before remarked) propounds as the fundamental principle of morals, "So act, that thy rule of conduct might be adopted as a law by all rational beings," he virtually acknowledges that the interest of mankind collectively, or at least of mankind indiscriminately, must be in the mind of the agent when conscientiously deciding on the morality of the act. Otherwise he uses words without a meaning: for, that a rule even of utter selfishness could not *possibly* be adopted by all rational beings- that there is any insuperable obstacle in the nature of things to its adoption- cannot be even plausibly maintained. To give any meaning to Kant's principle, the sense put upon it must be, that we ought to shape our conduct by a rule which all rational beings might adopt *with benefit to their collective interest.*

To recapitulate: the idea of justice supposes two things; a rule of conduct, and a sentiment which sanctions the rule. The first must be supposed common to all mankind, and intended for their good. The other (the sentiment) is a desire that punishment may be suffered by those who infringe the rule. There is involved, in addition, the conception of some definite person who suffers by the infringement; whose rights (to use the expression appropriated to the case) are violated by it. And the sentiment of justice appears to me to be, the animal desire to repel or retaliate a hurt or damage to oneself, or to those with whom one sympathises, widened so as to include all persons, by the human capacity of enlarged sympathy, and the human conception of intelligent self-interest. From the latter elements, the feeling derives its morality; from the former, its peculiar impressiveness, and energy of self-assertion.

I have, throughout, treated the idea of a *right* residing in the injured person, and violated by the injury, not as a separate element in the composition of the idea and sentiment, but as one of the forms in which the other two elements clothe themselves. These elements are, a hurt to some assignable person or persons on the one hand, and a demand for punishment on the other. An examination of our own minds, I think, will show, that these two things include all that we mean when we speak of violation of a right. When we call anything a person's right, we mean that he has a valid claim on society to protect him in the possession of it, either by the force of law, or by that of education and opinion. If he has what we consider a sufficient claim, on whatever account, to have something guaranteed to him by society, we say that he has a right to it. If we desire to prove that anything does not belong to him by right, we think this done as soon as it is admitted that society ought not to take measures for securing it to him, but should leave him to chance, or to his own exertions. Thus, a person is said to have a right to what he can earn in fair professional competition; because society ought not to allow any other person to hinder him from endeavouring to earn in that manner as much as he can. But he has not a right to three hundred a-year, though he may happen to be earning it; because society is not called on to provide that he shall earn that sum. On the contrary, if he owns ten thousand pounds three per cent stock, he *has* a right to three hundred a-year; because society has come under an obligation to provide him with an income of that amount.

To have a right, then, is, I conceive, to have something which society ought to defend me in the possession of. If the objector goes on to ask, why it ought? I can give him no other reason than general utility. If that expression does not seem to convey a sufficient feeling of the strength of the obligation, nor to account for the peculiar energy of the feeling, it is because there goes to the composition of the sentiment, not a rational only, but also an animal element, the thirst for retaliation; and this thirst derives its intensity, as well as its moral justification, from the extraordinarily important and impressive kind of utility which is concerned. The interest involved is that of security, to every one's feelings the most vital of all interests. All other earthly benefits are needed by one person, not needed by another; and many of them can, if necessary, be cheerfully foregone, or replaced by something else; but security no human being can possibly do without on it we depend for all our immunity from evil, and for the whole value of all and every good, beyond the passing moment; since nothing but the gratification of the instant could be of any worth to us, if we could be deprived of anything the next instant by whoever was momentarily stronger than ourselves. Now this most indispensable of all necessaries, after physical nutriment, cannot be had, unless the machinery for providing it is kept unintermittedly in active play. Our notion, therefore, of the claim we have on our fellow-creatures to join in making safe for us the very groundwork of our existence, gathers feelings around it so much more intense than those concerned in any of the more common cases of utility, that the difference in degree (as is often the case in psychology) becomes a real difference in kind. The claim assumes that character of absoluteness, that apparent infinity, and incommensurability with all other considerations, which constitute the distinction between the feeling of right and wrong and that of ordinary expediency and inexpediency. The feelings concerned are so powerful, and we count so positively on finding a responsive feeling in others (all being alike interested), that *ought* and *should* grow into *must*, and recognised indispensability becomes a moral necessity, analogous to physical, and often not inferior to it in binding force....

Is, then the difference between the just and the Expedient a merely imaginary distinction? Have mankind been under a delusion in thinking that justice is a more sacred thing than policy, and that the latter ought only to be listened to after the former has been satisfied? By no means. The exposition we have given of the nature and origin of the sentiment, recognises a real distinction; and no one of those who profess the most sublime contempt for the consequences of actions as an element in their morality, attaches more importance to the distinction than I do. While I dispute the pretensions of any theory which sets up an imaginary standard of justice not grounded on utility, I account the justice which is grounded on utility to be the chief part, and incomparably the most sacred and binding part, of all morality. justice is a name for certain classes of moral rules, which concern the essentials of human well-being more nearly, and are therefore of more absolute obligation, than any other rules for the guidance of life; and the notion which we have found to be of the essence of the idea of justice, that of a right residing in an individual implies and testifies to this more binding obligation. The moral rules which forbid mankind to hurt one another (in which we must never forget to include wrongful interference with each other's freedom) are more vital to human well-being than any maxims, however important, which only point out the best mode of managing some department of human affairs. They have also the peculiarity, that they are the main element in determining the whole of the social feelings of mankind. It is their observance which alone preserves peace among human beings: if obedience to them were not the rule, and disobedience the exception, every one would see in every one else an enemy, against whom he must be perpetually guarding himself. What is hardly less important, these are the precepts which mankind have the strongest and the most direct inducements for impressing upon one another. By merely giving to each other prudential instruction or exhortation, they may gain, or think they gain, nothing: in inculcating on each other the duty of positive beneficence they have an unmistakable interest, but far less in degree: a person may possibly not need the benefits of others; but he always needs that they should not do him hurt. Thus the moralities which protect every individual from being harmed by others, either directly or by being hindered in his freedom of pursuing his own good, are at once those which he himself has most at heart, and those which he has the strongest interest in publishing and enforcing by word and deed. It is by a person's observance of these that his fitness to exist as one of the fellowship of human beings is tested and decided; for on that depends his being a nuisance or not to those with whom he is in contact. Now it is these moralities primarily which compose the obligations of justice. The most marked cases of injustice, and those which give the tone to the feeling of repugnance which characterises the sentiment, are acts of wrongful aggression, or wrongful exercise of power over some one; the next are those which consist in wrongfully withholding from him something which is his due; in both cases, inflicting on him a positive hurt, either in the form of direct suffering, or of the privation of some good which he had reasonable ground, either of a physical or of a social kind, for counting upon.

    The same powerful motives which command the observance of these primary moralities, enjoin the punishment of those who violate them; and as the impulses of self-defence, of defence of others, and of vengeance, are all called forth against such persons, retribution, or evil for evil, becomes closely connected with the sentiment of justice, and is universally included in the idea. Good for good is also one of the dictates of justice; and this, though its social utility is evident, and though it carries with it a natural human feeling, has not at first sight that obvious connection with hurt or injury, which, existing in the most elementary cases of just and unjust, is the source of the characteristic intensity of the sentiment. But the connection, though less obvious, is not less real. He who accepts benefits, and denies a return of them when needed, inflicts a real hurt, by disappointing one of the most natural and reasonable of expectations, and one which he must at least tacitly have encouraged, otherwise the benefits would seldom have been conferred. The important rank, among human evils and wrongs, of the disappointment of expectation, is shown in the fact that it constitutes the principal criminality of two such highly immoral acts as a breach of friendship and a breach of promise. Few hurts which human beings can sustain are greater, and none wound more, than when that on which they habitually and with full assurance relied, fails them in the hour of need; and few wrongs are greater than this mere withholding of good; none excite more resentment, either in the person suffering, or in a sympathising spectator. The principle, therefore, of giving to each what they deserve, that is, good for good as well as evil for evil, is not only included within the idea of justice as we have defined it, but is a proper object of that intensity of sentiment, which places the just, in human estimation, above the simply Expedient....

The considerations which have now been adduced resolve, I conceive, the only real difficulty in the utilitarian theory of morals. It has always been evident that all cases of justice are also cases of expediency: the difference is in the peculiar sentiment which attaches to the former, as contradistinguished from the latter. If this characteristic sentiment has been sufficiently accounted for; if there is no necessity to assume for it any peculiarity of origin; if it is simply the natural feeling of resentment, moralised by being made coextensive with the demands of social good; and if this feeling not only does but ought to exist in all the classes of cases to which the idea of justice corresponds; that idea no longer presents itself as a stumbling-block to the utilitarian ethics.

Justice remains the appropriate name for certain social utilities which are vastly more important, and therefore more absolute and imperative, than any others are as a class (though not more so than others may be in particular cases); and which, therefore, ought to be, as well as naturally are, guarded by a sentiment not only different in degree, but also in kind; distinguished from the milder feeling which attaches to the mere idea of promoting human pleasure or convenience, at once by the more definite nature of its commands, and by the sterner character of its sanctions.

THE LIMITS OF NEOPRAGMATISM
Cornel West

The renaissance of pragmatism in philosophy, literary criticism and legal thought in the past few years is a salutary development. It is part of a more general turn toward historicist approaches to truth and knowledge. I am delighted to see intellectual interest rekindled in Peirce, James, and especially Dewey. Yet I suspect that the new pragmatism may repeat and reproduce some of the blindness and silences of the old pragmatism--most important, an inadequate grasp of the complex operations of power, principally owing to a reluctance to take traditions of historical sociology and social theory seriously. In this essay, my strategy shall be as follows. First, I shall briefly map the different kinds of neopragmatisms in relation to perspectives regarding epistemology, theory and politics. Second, I shall suggest that neopragmatic viewpoints usually fail to situate their own projects in terms of present-day crises-including the crisis of purpose and vocation now raging in the professions. Third, I will try to show how my conception of prophetic pragmatism may provide what is needed to better illuminate and respond to these crises.

Much of the excitement about neopragmatism has to do with the antifoundationalist epistemic claims it puts forward. The idea that there are no self-justifying, intrinsically credible or ahistorical courts of appeal to terminate chains of epistemic justification calls into question positivistic and formalistic notions of objectivity; necessity and transcendentality. In this sense, all neopragmatists are antifoundationalists; that is, the validation of knowledge claims rests on practical judgments constituted by, and constructed in, dynamic social practices. For neopragmatists, we mortal creatures achieve and acquire knowledge by means of self-critical and self-correcting social procedures rooted in a variety of human processes.

Yet all neopragmatists are not antirealists. For example, Peircean pragmatists are intent on sidestepping any idealist or relativist traps and they therefore link a social conception of knowledge to a regulative ideal of truth. This viewpoint attempts to reject metaphysical conceptions of reality *and* skeptical reductions of truth-talk to knowledge-talk. In contrast, Deweyan pragmatists tend to be less concerned with charges of idealism or relativism, owing to a more insouciant attitude toward truth. In fact, some Deweyan pragmatists--similar to some sociologists of knowledge and idealists--wrongly collapse truth claims into warranted assertability claims or rational acceptability claims. Such moves provide fodder for the cannons of not only Peircean pragmatists, but also old style realists and foundationalists. To put it crudely, truth at the moment cannot be the truth about things, yet warranted assertable claims are the only truths we can get. To miss the subtle distinction between dynamic knowledge and regulative truth is to open the door to metaphysics or to slide down the slippery slope of sophomoric relativism. Yet the antifoundationalist claims put forward by neopragmatists are often construed such that many open such doors or slide down such slopes. In short; epistemic pluralism degenerates into an epistemic promiscuity that encourages epistemic policing by realists and foundationalists.

Neopragmatists disagree even more sharply in regarding the role of theory (explanatory accounts of the past and present). All neopragmatists shun grand theory because it smacks of metaphysical posturing. Yet this shunning often shades into a distrust of theory per se-hence a distancing from revisable social theories, provisional cultural theories or heuristic historical theories. This distrust may encourage an ostrichlike, piecemeal incrementalism that reeks of a vulgar antitheoreticism. On this view, neopragmatism amounts to crude practicalism. The grand pragmatism of Dewey and especially C. Wright Mills rejects such a view. Instead, it subtly incorporates an experimental temper within theory-laden descriptions of problematic situations (for instance, social and cultural crises). Unfortunately, the pragmatist tradition is widely associated with a distrust of theory that curtails its ability to fully grasp the operations of power within the personal, social and historical contexts of human activities.

It is no accident that the dominant form of politics in the pragmatist tradition accents the pedagogical and the dialogical. Such a noble liberalism assumes that vast disparities in resources, enormous polarizations in perceptions or intense conflicts of interests can be overcome by means of proper education and civil conversation. If persuasive historical sociological claims show that such disparities, polarizations and conflicts often produce improper agitation and uncivil confrontation, the dominant form of politics in the pragmatist tradition is paralyzed, or at least rendered more impotent than it is commonly believed. One crucial theme or subtext in my genealogy of pragmatism is the persistence of the sense of impotence of liberal intellectuals in American culture and society, primarily because of unattended class and regional disparities, unacknowledged racial and sexual polarization, and untheorized cultural and personal conflicts that permeate and pervade our past and present. My view neither downplays nor devalues education and conversation; it simply highlights the structural background conditions of pedagogical efforts and dialogical events.

This leads me to my second concern, namely, the relative absence of pragmatist accounts of why pragmatism surfaces now in the ways and forms that it does. Such an account must situate the nature of pragmatist intellectual interventions--their intended effects and unintended consequences--in the present historical moment in American society and culture. I suspect that part of the renaissance of neopragmatism can be attributed to the crisis of purpose and vocation in humanistic studies and professional schools. On this view, the recent hunger for interdisciplinary studies--or the erosion of disciplinary boundaries--promoted by neopragmatisms, poststructuralisms, Marxisms and feminisms is not only motivated by a quest for truth, but also activated by power struggles over what kinds of knowledge should be given status, be rewarded and be passed on to young, informed citizens in the next century. These power struggles are not simply over positions and curriculums, but also over ideals of what it means to be humanistic intellectuals in a declining empire--in a first-rate military power., a near-rescinding economic power, and a culture in decay. As Henry Adams suggests, the example of a turn toward history is most evident in American culture when decline is perceived to be undeniable and intellectuals feel most removed from the action. Furthermore, pragmatism at its best, in James and Dewey, provided a sense of purpose and vocation for intellectuals who believed they could make a difference in the public life of the nation. And it is not surprising that the first perceivable consequence of the renaissance of neopragmatism led by Richard Rorty echoed James's attack on professionalization and specialization. In this sense, Rorty's *Philosophy and the Mirror of Nature (1979)* not only told the first major and influential story of analytic philosophy, but was also a challenging narrative of how contemporary intellectuals have come to be contained within professional and specialized social spaces, with little outreach to a larger public and hence little visibility in, and minimal effect on, the larger society. Needless to say, Rorty's revival of Jamesian antiprofessionalism--not to be confused with anti-intellectualism or even antiacademicism--has increased intellectuals interest in public journalism and intensified the tension between journalists and academics.

The crisis of purpose and vocation in humanistic studies and professional schools is compounded by the impact of the class and regional disparities, racial and sexual polarizations, and cultural and personal conflicts that can no longer be ignored. This impact not only unsettles our paradigms in the production of knowledge, but also forces us to interrogate and examine our standards, criteria, styles and forms in which knowledge is assessed, legitimated and expressed. At its worst, pragmatism in the academy permits us to embrace this impact without attending to the implications of power. At its best, pragmatism behooves us to critically scrutinize this impact as we promote the democratization of American intellectual life without vulgar leveling or symbolic tokenism.

But what is this "pragmatism at its best"? What form does it take? What are its constitutive features or fundamental components? These questions bring me to my third point--the idea of a prophetic pragmatist perspective and praxis. I use the adjective "prophetic" in order to harken back to the rich, though flawed, traditions of Judaism and Christianity that promote courageous resistance against, and relentless critiques of, injustice and social misery. These traditions are rich in that they help keep alive collective memories, of moral (that is anti-idolatrous) struggle and nonmarket values (that is love for others, loyalty to an ethical ideal and social freedom) in a more and more historically amnesiac society and market-saturated culture. These traditions are flawed because they tend toward dogmatic pronouncements (that is "Thus saith the Lord") to homogeneous constituencies. Prophetic pragmatism gives courageous resistance and relentless critique a self-critical character and democratic content; that is it analyzes the social causes of unnecessary forms of social misery, promotes moral outrage against them, organizes different constituencies to alleviate them, yet does so with an openness to its own blindnesses and shortcomings.

Prophetic pragmatism is pragmatism at its best because it promotes a critical temper and democratic faith without making criticism a fetish or democracy an idol. The fetishization of criticism yields a sophisticated ironic consciousness of parody and paralysis, just as the idolization of democracy produces mob rule. As Peirce, James and Dewey noted, criticism always presupposes something in place--be it a set of beliefs or a tradition. Criticism yields results or makes a difference when something significant is antecedent to it such as rich, sustaining collective memories of moral struggle. Similarly, democracy assumes certain conditions for its flourishing--like a constitutional background. Such conditions for democracy are not subject to public veto.

Critical temper as a way of struggle and democratic faith as a way of life are the twin pillars of prophetic pragmatism. The major foes to be contested are despair, dogmatism and oppression. The critical temper promotes a full-fledged experimental disposition that highlights the provisional, tentative and revisable character of our visions, analyses and actions. Democratic faith consists of a Pascalian wager (hence underdetermined by the evidence) on the abilities and capacities of ordinary people to participate in decision-making procedures of institutions that fundamentally regulate their lives. The critical temper motivated by democratic faith yields all-embracing moral and/or religious visions that project credible ameliorative possibilities grounded in present realities in light of systemic structural analyses of the causes of social misery (without reducing all misery to historical causes). Such analyses must appeal to traditions of social theory and historical sociology just as visions must proceed from traditions of moral and/or religious communities. The forms of prophetic praxis depend on the insights of the social theories and the potency of the moral and/or religious communities. In order for these analyses and visions to combat despair, dogmatism and oppression, the existential, communal and political dimensions of prophetic pragmatism must be accented. The existential dimension is guided by the value of love--a risk-ridden affirmation of the distinct humanity of others that, at its best, holds despair at bay. The communal dimension is regulated by *loyalty*--a profound devotion to the critical temper and democratic faith that eschews dogmatism. The political dimension is guided by *freedom*--a perennial quest for self-realization and self-development that resists all forms of oppression.

The tradition of pragmatism is in need of a mode of cultural criticism that keeps track of social misery, solicits and channels moral outrage to alleviate it, and projects a future in which the potentialities of ordinary people flourish and flower. The first wave of pragmatism foundered on the rocks of cultural conservatism and corporate liberalism. Its defeat was tragic. Let us not permit the second wave of pragmatism to end as farce.

Instantiation[1]

Intervention and Responsibility

INTRODUCTION

Obligations to Intervene through Aid

One of the most basic questions in ethics involves the duty a person has to aid other people. Attempts to answer this question necessarily involve secondary questions, including: whom do we aid, when do we aid, what form should that aid take (and who decides), how do we distinguish between a moral obligation and an act of charity, etc. Approaches to answering these questions vary widely. Some attempt to establish a boundary of basic human need, with anyone (irrespective of relationship or location) falling below that line deserving of aid from those above it. Others introduce a sort of hierarchical or ordinal element of responsibility and concern, radiating out from the individual to the family, then the community, all the way to the entire human race (and even to animals and the environment – see Instantiation$_3$). Still others stop at the individual, indicating that no people have a moral claim to the personal acquisitions of any other person – acts of charity can be voluntarily performed, but not made obligatory. Global ethics tends to emphasize particular elements within this spectrum of questions and proposals: geographical distance and interconnectedness.

Geographical distance often can help to mitigate the responsibility one feels toward others. While one may feel at least minimally obligated to help someone in close proximity, what of the individual thousands of miles away who cannot be helped directly? This form of distance is more than just spatial. Included within that space are cultural differences and mediators who promise to help in one's name. There are also elements of empathy, regarding how real one finds the suffering of an individual far away. The question becomes determining which difficulties are ethically relevant in considering obligations to aid: cultural boundaries, commonality of experience, likelihood of effectiveness, connections to the event in question. Underlying all of these matters is the issue of why certain incidents get deemed newsworthy, and by extension ethically relevant, and others do not (see also Instantiation$_5$).

Interconnectedness also has an important part to play in global ethics discussions. With the development of, or at least current emphasis on, globalization, real dilemmas arise regarding how isolated an individual is from the rest of the world. Even if events or tragedies happen to people in places geographically far removed, can the modern individual claim no connection to those happenings? This question deals with more than just the ability of a person to view those events and empathize; it also focuses on global networks and flows of economic, informational, and political power. People from different continents and different cultures may be reachable now within days, hours, seconds. Their presence may also be felt in your breakfast and on your back. In a world where money and products and people circumnavigate the globe constantly, where history has sanctioned certain flows and not others, any person pursuing an ethical place in that world must confront issues of interconnectedness.

The following essays provide the individual with varying approaches and arguments regarding either one's specific ethical responsibilities to others in the world[1] or how interconnected people and plights are across cultures.

Peter Singer is Ira W. DeCamp Professor of bioethics in the University Center for Human Values at Princeton University. In "The Singer Solution to World Poverty," he argues that affluent individuals (relative to those suffering from poverty and related ills) are obligated to aid those less fortunate. He attempts to show that many behaviors which most people would find morally reprehensible are analogous to the actions those same people take on a daily basis: choosing material luxuries over the well-being of humans. For Singer, the key component in deciding this ethical dilemma is not the rights of individuals nor the relationship or proximity each person has to the other. Rather, the most basic and important consideration is whether people are suffering. An individual is obligated to help those suffering, provided the help does not cause comparable suffering in the giver.

Carlo Filice is a professor of philosophy at State University of New York at Geneseo. He uses a position similar to Singer's as a point of departure in "On the Obligation to Keep Informed about Distant Atrocities." Filice contends that such an obligation to ease suffering entails an equal obligation to be aware about possible atrocities that are occurring but which might not be newsworthy. Half ethical argument, half media critique, the essay connects right behavior in the world with a savvy, media-literate awareness of the world. To act, one must know. To know means more than being told. Relying too heavily on the media (see Instantiation$_5$) may ensure that certain atrocities will continue unchallenged internationally. Filice contends that lack of widespread international information about certain events does not make them less wrong. The ethical individual must be aware and seek out information as a prelude to acting.

In the final essay in this section, Michael Mann, professor of sociology at UCLA, explores some of the pressing issues surrounding the events of September 11th through the lens of globalization. In "Globalization and September 11," he details the four expressions of power (economic, military, political, ideological) that have historically guided the impetus toward globalization. The trajectories globalization has taken, however, have been far from uniform. As a result, these multiple trends can simultaneously illuminate commonalities and exacerbate differences. Mann contends that amidst these contradictions, the search for one world is premature at best.

How, then, might one's obligation to others be defined? Who are other people and how are we to understand our relationship to them? How much, or what, must I give to help others in need? These are open questions.

---

[1] See http://www.phil.vt.edu/global, the website accompaniment to the book for a link to the Richard Rorty essay, "Moral Universalism and Economic Triage." In it, he poses the question "who are we?" as a means of highlighting the importance of seriously considering the meaning of one's moral community in an international setting.

THE SINGER SOLUTION TO WORLD POVERTY[1]
PETER SINGER

In the Brazilian film "Central Station," Dora is a retired schoolteacher who makes ends meet by sitting at the station writing letters for illiterate people. Suddenly she has an opportunity to pocket $1,000. All she has to do is persuade a homeless 9-year-old boy to follow her to an address she has been given. (She is told he will be adopted by wealthy foreigners.) She delivers the boy, gets the money, spends some of it on a television set and settles down to enjoy her new acquisition. Her neighbor spoils the fun, however, by telling her that the boy was too old to be adopted — he will be killed and his organs sold for transplantation. Perhaps Dora knew this all along, but after her neighbor's plain speaking, she spends a troubled night. In the morning Dora resolves to take the boy back.

Suppose Dora had told her neighbor that it is a tough world, other people have nice new TV's too, and if selling the kid is the only way she can get one, well, he was only a street kid. She would then have become, in the eyes of the audience, a monster. She redeems herself only by being prepared to bear considerable risks to save the boy.

At the end of the movie, in cinemas in the affluent nations of the world, people who would have been quick to condemn Dora if she had not rescued the boy go home to places far more comfortable than her apartment. In fact, the average family in the United States spends almost one-third of its income on things that are no more necessary to them than Dora's new TV was to her. Going out to nice restaurants, buying new clothes because the old ones are no longer stylish, vacationing at beach resorts — so much of our income is spent on things not essential to the preservation of our lives and health. Donated to one of a number of charitable agencies, that money could mean the difference between life and death for children in need.

All of which raises a question: In the end, what is the ethical distinction between a Brazilian who sells a homeless child to organ peddlers and an American who already has a TV and upgrades to a better one — knowing that the money could be donated to an organization that would use it to save the lives of kids in need?

Of course, there are several differences between the two situations that could support different moral judgments about them. For one thing, to be able to consign a child to death when he is standing right in front of you takes a chilling kind of heartlessness; it is much easier to ignore an appeal for money to help children you will never meet. Yet for a utilitarian philosopher like myself — that is, one who judges whether acts are right or wrong by their consequences — if the upshot of the American's failure to donate the money is that one more kid dies on the streets of a Brazilian city, then it is, in some sense, just as bad as selling the kid to the organ peddlers. But one doesn't need to embrace my utilitarian ethic to see that, at the very

---

[1] Copyright © 1999 by The New York Times Co. Reprinted with permission.

least, there is a troubling incongruity in being so quick to condemn Dora for taking the child to the organ peddlers while, at the same time, not regarding the American consumer's behavior as raising a serious moral issue.

In his 1996 book, "Living High and Letting Die," the New York University philosopher Peter Unger presented an ingenious series of imaginary examples designed to probe our intuitions about whether it is wrong to live well without giving substantial amounts of money to help people who are hungry, malnourished or dying from easily treatable illnesses like diarrhea. Here's my paraphrase of one of these examples:

> Bob is close to retirement. He has invested most of his savings in a very rare and valuable old car, a Bugatti, which he has not been able to insure. The Bugatti is his pride and joy. In addition to the pleasure he gets from driving and caring for his car, Bob knows that its rising market value means that he will always be able to sell it and live comfortably after retirement. One day when Bob is out for a drive, he parks the Bugatti near the end of a railway siding and goes for a walk up the track. As he does so, he sees that a runaway train, with no one aboard, is running down the railway track. Looking farther down the track, he sees the small figure of a child very likely to be killed by the runaway train. He can't stop the train and the child is too far away to warn of the danger, but he can throw a switch that will divert the train down the siding where his Bugatti is parked. Then nobody will be killed -- but the train will destroy his Bugatti. Thinking of his joy in owning the car and the financial security it represents, Bob decides not to throw the switch. The child is killed. For many years to come, Bob enjoys owning his Bugatti and the financial security it represents.

Bob's conduct, most of us will immediately respond, was gravely wrong. Unger agrees. But then he reminds us that we, too, have opportunities to save the lives of children. We can give to organizations like Unicef or Oxfam America. How much would we have to give one of these organizations to have a high probability of saving the life of a child threatened by easily preventable diseases? (I do not believe that children are more worth saving than adults, but since no one can argue that children have brought their poverty on themselves, focusing on them simplifies the issues.) Unger called up some experts and used the information they provided to offer some plausible estimates that include the cost of raising money, administrative expenses and the cost of delivering aid where it is most needed. By his calculation, $200 in donations would help a sickly 2-year-old transform into a healthy 6-year-old — offering safe passage through childhood's most dangerous years. To show how practical philosophical argument can be, Unger even tells his readers that they can easily donate funds by using their credit card and calling one of these toll-free numbers: (800) 367-5437 for Unicef; (800) 693-2687 for Oxfam America.

Now you, too, have the information you need to save a child's life. How should you judge yourself if you don't do it? Think again about Bob and his Bugatti. Unlike Dora, Bob did not have to look into the eyes of the child he was sacrificing for his own material comfort. The child was a complete stranger to him and too far away to relate to in an intimate, personal way. Unlike Dora, too, he did not mislead the child or initiate the chain of events imperiling him. In all these respects, Bob's situation resembles that of people able but unwilling to donate to overseas aid and differs from Dora's situation.

If you still think that it was very wrong of Bob not to throw the switch that would have diverted the train and saved the child's life, then it is hard to see how you could deny that it is also very wrong not to send money to one of the organizations listed above. Unless, that is, there is some morally important difference between the two situations that I have overlooked.

Is it the practical uncertainties about whether aid will really reach the people who need it? Nobody who knows the world of overseas aid can doubt that such uncertainties exist. But Unger's figure of $200 to save a child's life was reached after he had made conservative assumptions about the proportion of the money donated that will actually reach its target.

One genuine difference between Bob and those who can afford to donate to overseas aid organizations but don't is that only Bob can save the child on the tracks, whereas there are hundreds of millions of people who can give $200 to overseas aid organizations. The problem is that most of them aren't doing it. Does this mean that it is all right for you not to do it?

Suppose that there were more owners of priceless vintage cars — Carol, Dave, Emma, Fred and so on, down to Ziggy — all in exactly the same situation as Bob, with their own siding and their own switch, all sacrificing the child in order to preserve their own cherished car. Would that make it all right for Bob to do the same? To answer this question affirmatively is to endorse follow-the-crowd ethics — the kind of ethics that led many Germans to look away when the Nazi atrocities were being committed. We do not excuse them because others were behaving no better.

We seem to lack a sound basis for drawing a clear moral line between Bob's situation and that of any reader of this article with $200 to spare who does not donate it to an overseas aid agency. These readers seem to be acting at least as badly as Bob was acting when he chose to let the runaway train hurtle toward the unsuspecting child. In the light of this conclusion, I trust that many readers will reach for the phone and donate that $200. Perhaps you should do it before reading further.

Now that you have distinguished yourself morally from people who put their vintage cars ahead of a child's life, how about treating yourself and your partner to dinner at your favorite restaurant? But wait. The money you will spend at the restaurant could also help save the lives of children overseas! True, you weren't planning to blow $200 tonight, but if you were to give up dining out just for one month, you would easily save that amount. And what is one month's dining out, compared to a child's life? There's the rub. Since there are a lot of desperately needy children in the world, there will always be another child whose life you could save for another $200. Are you therefore obliged to keep giving until you have nothing left? At what point can you stop?

Hypothetical examples can easily become farcical. Consider Bob. How far past losing the Bugatti should he go? Imagine that Bob had got his foot stuck in the track of the siding, and if he diverted the train, then before it rammed the car it would also amputate his big toe. Should he still throw the switch? What if it would amputate his foot? His entire leg?

As absurd as the Bugatti scenario gets when pushed to extremes, the point it raises is a serious one: only when the sacrifices become very significant indeed would most people be prepared to say that Bob does nothing wrong when he decides not to throw the switch. Of course, most people could be wrong; we can't decide moral issues by taking opinion polls. But consider for yourself the level of sacrifice that you would demand of Bob, and then think about how much money you would have to give away in order to make a sacrifice that is roughly equal to that. It's almost certainly much, much more than $200. For most middle-class Americans, it could easily be more like $200,000.

Isn't it counterproductive to ask people to do so much? Don't we run the risk that many will shrug their shoulders and say that morality, so conceived, is fine for saints but not for them? I accept that we are unlikely to see, in the near or even medium-term future, a world in which it is normal for wealthy Americans to give the bulk of their wealth to strangers. When it comes to praising or blaming people for what they do, we tend to use a standard that is relative to some conception of normal behavior. Comfortably off Americans who give, say, 10 percent of their income to overseas aid organizations are so far ahead of most of their equally comfortable fellow citizens that I wouldn't go out of my way to chastise them for not doing more. Nevertheless, they should be doing much more, and they are in no position to criticize Bob for failing to make the much greater sacrifice of his Bugatti.

At this point various objections may crop up. Someone may say: "If every citizen living in the affluent nations contributed his or her share I wouldn't have to make such a drastic sacrifice, because long before such levels were reached, the resources would have been there to save the lives of all those children dying from lack of food or medical care. So why should I give more than my fair share?" Another, related, objection is that the Government ought to increase its overseas aid allocations, since that would spread the burden more equitably across all taxpayers.

Yet the question of how much we ought to give is a matter to be decided in the real world — and that, sadly, is a world in which we know that most people do not, and in the immediate future will not, give substantial amounts to overseas aid agencies. We know, too, that at least in the next year, the United States Government is not going to meet even the very modest United Nations-recommended target of 0.7 percent of gross national product; at the moment it lags far below that, at 0.09 percent, not even half of Japan's 0.22 percent or a tenth of Denmark's 0.97 percent. Thus, we know that the money we can give beyond that theoretical "fair share" is still going to save lives that would otherwise be lost. While the idea that no one need do more than his or her fair share is a powerful one, should it prevail if we know that others are not doing their fair share and that children will die preventable deaths unless we do more than our fair share? That would be taking fairness too far.

Thus, this ground for limiting how much we ought to give also fails. In the world as it is now, I can see no escape from the conclusion that each one of us with wealth surplus to his or her essential needs should be giving most of it to help people suffering from poverty so dire as to be life-threatening. That's right: I'm saying that you shouldn't buy that new car, take that cruise, redecorate the house or get that pricey new suit. After all, a $1,000 suit could save five children's lives.

So how does my philosophy break down in dollars and cents? An American household with an income of $50,000 spends around $30,000 annually on necessities, according to the Conference Board, a nonprofit economic research organization. Therefore, for a household bringing in $50,000 a year, donations to help the world's poor should be as close as possible to $20,000. The $30,000 required for necessities holds for higher incomes as well. So a household making $100,000 could cut a yearly check for $70,000. Again, the formula is simple: whatever money you're spending on luxuries, not necessities, should be given away.

Now, evolutionary psychologists tell us that human nature just isn't sufficiently altruistic to make it plausible that many people will sacrifice so much for strangers. On the facts of human nature, they might be right, but they would be wrong to draw a moral conclusion from those facts. If it is the case that we ought to do things that, predictably, most of us won't do, then let's face that fact head-on. Then, if we value the life of a child more than going to fancy restaurants, the next time we dine out we will know that we could have done something better with our money. If that makes living a morally decent life extremely arduous, well, then that is the way things are. If we don't do it, then we should at least know that we are failing to live a morally decent life — not because it is good to wallow in guilt but because knowing where we should be going is the first step toward heading in that direction.

When Bob first grasped the dilemma that faced him as he stood by that railway switch, he must have thought how extraordinarily unlucky he was to be placed in a situation in which he must choose between the life of an innocent child and the sacrifice of most of his savings. But he was not unlucky at all. We are all in that situation.

On the Obligation to Keep Informed about Distant Atrocities
Carlo Filice

One must know about faraway moral atrocities if one is to attempt to remedy them. Ignorance of these atrocities is at times a legitimate excuse for failure to make such attempts but not generally. It certainly is not a legitimate excuse when one deliberately keeps oneself uninformed of major atrocities; an example of such a person would be the well-educated, refined hedonist whose world revolves, by conscious choice, around private pleasure. On the other hand, it is a legitimate excuse in many cases when one simply lacks the means for being informed; an example of such would be the seriously underprivileged, culturally deprived, illiterate person.

But what about the cases of those people who fall somewhere between these two extremes? What about the single mother, working fulltime as a nurse, who takes care of her children's needs most of the remainder of her hours? What about the young businessman almost wholly preoccupied with his struggle to make it in the business world? What about the medical student whose workload saps her of all desire to look at additional printed pages? What about the secretary whose after-work life is dedicated to cultivating her interest in French literature? What about the real estate agent in constant pursuit of new listings and loan agreements, who finds barely enough time to spend with her family? What about the small farmer in whose circle of friends and relatives questions about what might be happening in China, Brazil, or Mozambique do not come up? Is their relative ignorance of major moral atrocities excusable? Is their consequent inaction excusable?

This is the issue I would like to explore in this essay. My claim will be that this type of ignorance is not excusable in most cases of "average" Westerners and of "average" U.S. citizens in particular. Consequently this ignorance does not excuse their doing nothing about large-scale abuses.

Consider the events in East Timor during the last twenty-five years. They constitute a typical major moral atrocity. The choice of this example is recommended by a number of factors: (1) the relative magnitude of the evil; (2) the supportive (military, economic, diplomatic) role played by the U.S. government and others in this bloody episode; (3) the fact that most of us have remained unaware of this atrocity; (4) the fact that sources of information concerning it have been available in the public arena (particularly in the last few years), though generally they have had to be sought out.

The following are the basic facts of the East Timor situation as assembled already in 1979, from pretty reliable sources, by Noam Chomsky and Edward S. Herman:

> On December 7, 1975, Indonesian armed forces invaded the former Portuguese colony of East Timor, only a few hours after the

departure of President Gerald Ford and Henry Kissinger from a visit to Jakarta. Although Indonesia has effectively sealed off East Timor from the outside world, reports have filtered through indicating that there have been massive atrocities, with estimates running to 100,000 killed, about one-sixth of the population. An assessment by the Legislative Research Service of the Australian Parliament concluded that there is "mounting evidence that the Indonesians have been carrying out a brutal operation in East Timor," involving "indiscriminate killing on a scale unprecedented in post-World War II history."[1]

The above account reflects the number of dead as of 1979. Current estimates, that include the additional victims since then, put the total to 200,000 dead. The entire population of East Timor was estimated by *The New York Times* in 1974 to be 620,000. One can do the numbers. The main reason for the Indonesian invasion was the 1975 popular victory in East Timor (one year after East Timor was granted independence from Portugal) of a party named FRETILIN and the defeat of more conservative parties. FRETILIN's character is summarized by Chomsky and Herman on the basis of independent reports:

> FRETILIN was a moderate reformist national front, headed by a Catholic seminarian and initially involving largely urban intellectuals, among them young Lisbon-educated radical Timorese who "were most eager to search for their cultural origins" and who were "to lead the FRETILIN drive into the villages initiating consumer and agricultural cooperatives, and a literary campaign conducted in (the native language) along the lines used by Paulo Freire in Brazil . ... It was "more reformist than revolutionary," calling for gradual steps towards complete independence, agrarian reform, transformation of uncultivated land and large farms to people's cooperatives, educational programs, steps towards producer-consumer cooperatives supplementing existing Chinese economic enterprises "for the purposes of supplying basic goods to the poor at low prices, controlled foreign aid and investment, and a foreign policy of non-alignment."[2]

This victorious party's platform did not please the Indonesian leadership which ten years earlier had carried out an internal purge of half a million suspected "communists." Thus, under a pretext to end a civil war in East Timor (there had in fact been some fighting between followers of FRETILIN and of UDT that had, however, quickly come to an end due to the former's preponderance of public support), Indonesia invaded and sealed the area from international observers and organizations, including the International Red Cross, and finding widespread

---

[1] Noam Chomsky and Edward S. Herman, *The Washington Connection and Third World Fascism*, vol. I of *The Political Economy of Human Rights* (Boston: South End Press, 1979), 30.
[2] Ibid., 134. The internal quotation quotes Jill Joliffe, *East Timor: Nationalism and Colonialism* (Australia: University of Queensland Press, 1978), 79.

indigenous resistance, proceeded to carry out the slaughter.

It is important to note that between 1973 and 1977 Indonesia received $254 million of military aid (in arms military aid grants, and military sales credit), and $634 million in economic aid from the U.S.[3] Moreover, during this time 1,272 Indonesian military officers received U.S. military training.[4] Such aid and training has continued more or less unabated till the present. These facts, together with the timing of the invasion, (just after high-level consultations with Ford and Kissinger), the continued close ties between the Indonesian and the U.S. governments, and the lack of serious protests over more than twenty years by United States officials, show complicity on the part of the U.S. government and establishment (not excluding the media and the intellectual community).[5]

Meantime the attempt by Indonesia to "pacify" East Timor has continued till the end of 1999. By this time the Suharto-led military dictatorship in Indonesia was forced by internal popular forces to cede much of its power to a newly established civilian government. On August 30, 1999 the East Timorese were given the chance to vote either for a partial "autonomy" or for independence. 99% of the registered voters went to the polls, ignoring open threats issued by Indonesian-sponsored armed groups. 78% of them voted for independence, and rejected "autonomy" within Indonesia. A near quarter century of massive repression had been for naught. Angered by the election results the Indonesian-inspired armed groups went on a final killing and destruction binge. The UN reports that the resulting property damage alone-including the destruction of hospitals, schools and power plants-"ranges from 60 to 80 per cent in the whole country."[6] It also appears that the plans to destroy most of the country were hatched months in advance, and were known both by the UN and by Western intelligence.[7] Nothing significant was done to stop it (while a similar situation was handled quite differently in Kosovo). Instead, Western arms have continued to flow to Indonesia's military up through the time of this last massacre. With the damage done, a UN-sponsored international force (mainly Australians) has now taken control of East Timor.

One could go on with such depressing details. One could also tell similar stories about other states within the U.S. sphere of influence such as Guatemala, Congo, El Salvador, Brazil, Turkey, or Colombia. The point is that the case of East Timor is not an anomaly. The factors which make it an example of a slaughter relevant for the present essay apply to many other cases. One need only look at

---

[3] Ibid., 45. The original sources of these data are the following: United States Department of Defense, *Foreign Military Sales and Military Assistance Facts* (Washington, 1976); U.S. Department of Defense, *Security Assistance Program, Presentation to Congress*, F.Y, 1978 (Washington, 1977); U.S. Agency for International Development, *U.S. Overseas Loans and Grants*, 1 July 1945-30 June 1975 (Washington, 1976).

[4] Chomsky and Herman, 45.

[5] Repeatedly mainstream publications such as *The New York Times* and *Newsweek* have distorted what actually occurred, by relying upon official Indonesian accounts, by ignoring reports offered by refugees in Portugal, and at least on one occasion, by deliberately altering the published version of events given by an Australian reporter who was in East Timor during the early weeks of the 1975 invasion, Chomsky and Herman, 136-38.

[6] United Nations Office of the High Commissioner for Human Rights. Report of the International Commission of Inquiry on East Timor to the Secretary General, January 2000, paragraph #130.

[7] This according to the report in the *London Observer*, "Revealed: Army's Plot to Destroy a Nation," September 12, 1999.

nearby Guatemala, where U.S. supported military dictatorships have slaughtered hundreds of thousands of poor people over the past half century. That our current U.S. president took the step (possibly unparalleled in American history) of issuing a near-apology to Guatemalans for the US. role in this long reign of terror speaks volumes.[8] Yet how many of us can find Guatemala on a world map?

Because the "average" U.S. citizen does not know these massacres occur, nor of the government's relatively close ties to the regimes perpetrating them, the average citizen does nothing to help end the slaughters. Is this ignorance and resulting inaction morally excusable? The following is one line of argument in favor of a "no" answer. It tries to establish that most of us are under a *prima facie* obligation to keep informed about cases such as East Timor. What it maintains about U.S. citizens would also apply to citizens of other major powers whose governments play supportive roles in the atrocities of other governments.

1. One has a *prima facie* obligation[9] to help prevent harm, especially major, avoidable suffering and death, whenever helping to do so requires only trivial sacrifices such as buying fewer or no luxury items, spending less time watching television, etc., and whenever there is some chance that one's efforts will produce at least some success.
2. One will not be in a position to help prevent harm if one is unaware of the occurrence of this harm.
3. One who has a *prima facie* obligation to help prevent X also has a *prima facie* obligation to attempt to position oneself so as to be able to help prevent X, particularly if these positional attempts are likely to be successful (e.g., if A has a *prima facie* duty to prevent his own violent behavior, A also has a *prima facie* duty to attempt to remain sober if drunkenness tends to make A violent, and if A's attempts to remain sober are not absolutely hopeless).
4. Therefore, each of us has a *prima facie* obligation to make serious attempts to become and remain informed about the occurrence of major, avoidable harm whenever these attempts at gaining the necessary information are likely to succeed and require small sacrifices, and whenever there is some chance for the prevention of at least some harm.
5. Major moral atrocities, such as the systematic and large-scale torture and killing by a government for political reasons, constitute one class of major avoidable harm.
6. Therefore, each of us has a *prima facie* obligation to make serious attempts to be informed about the occurrence of major moral atrocities (whenever the conditions in 4 above obtain).

---

[8] President Clinton, while in Guatemala, issued a statement claiming that the U.S. had made a "mistake" in supporting "a repressive, right-wing government during its 36-year civil war, which claimed 200,000 victims." *Boston Globe*, 15 March 1999.

[9] The notion of "*prima facie* obligation" employed in this argument is most naturally derivative from consequentialist moral theories. However, I believe that it can also be grounded on deontological theories of rights and obligations. I would think that victims of torture and killing are entitled, by virtue of having basic "negative" rights, to receiving our help in avoiding being tortured and killed. However, this topic is too vast for it to be properly addressed here. I choose not to rely on the notion of rights generally, because I find rights to be metaphysically suspect unless they are taken as derived from more basic values such as harm and benefit.

7. Most people in developed countries who attempt to gain the necessary information are likely to succeed.
8. Most people in developed countries can make serious attempts to gain the necessary information about current moral atrocities without such attempts resulting in major sacrifices.
9. The preventive actions based on such information have some likelihood of leading to the prevention of at least some harm resulting from major moral atrocities.
10. Therefore, most people in developed countries have a *prima facie* obligation to make serious attempts to become informed about the current major moral atrocities, especially those occurring within their country's sphere of influence.

I will enlarge on this argument by considering a number of likely objections.

Objection I: Citizens Are Politically Too Naïve

Attempting to seek information about ongoing atrocities taking place outside the sphere of most mainstream news coverage requires a prior decision to do so. This decision, in turn, cannot come about unless one has a considerable awareness of history and global politics. For example, one must know that mainstream national news services, even in "open" societies, tend to have blind spots concerning stories that would embarrass the fatherland and harm its perceived interests. One must know that there is a vast and complex world outside of one's own borders and that the majority of humans, even in the year 2000, live in very poor circumstances. One must know about the historical tendencies of empires. One must have some inklings about the tentacles of the global economy. The average U.S. citizen, however, lacks this necessary historical and political astuteness, arguably through no fault of his or her own. Thus, since "ought" implies "can," and the average U.S. citizen lacks the cultural-motivational prerequisites to decide to seek information, he or she cannot really make such decisions, and thus cannot be morally obligated to seek such information. Similarly, naive creatures like young children cannot be under a moral obligation to decide to learn how to read so as to become responsible citizens.

This seems plausible, but consider a parallel argument. Johnny has grown up amidst people who perceive women as subservient to men (this is far from fiction in many parts of the world). This assessment is reinforced by his sincere religious beliefs, which are also shared by his family and friends. It does not occur to Johnny to examine the validity of his view of women. Upon marrying, he bullies his wife into a subservient role, often through physical threats. He construes her complaints as symptoms of her rebellious and spoiled character. Shall we say that because Johnny seems motivationally incapable of questioning his own assumptions about gender roles, he has no obligation to do so and consequently no obligation to change?[10]

---

[10] Michael Slote correctly observes that the principle of "ought implies can" is vague because "(s)omeone might, for example, argue that since (a rich person), because of his given nature, is so selfish that he cannot bring himself to give away his money, he has no obligation to do so." The principle "claims the right to be as one oneself is because of one's nature...." Presumably these

Surely such an assertion would be problematic. There may be some extreme cases where a person, for example, a child, is absolutely incapable of examining his own morally dubious beliefs. In most cases, however, people have moments of doubt, even if briefly and rarely-by the time one is an adult one has had at least glimpses of alternative value systems. At such times there is at least the possibility of serious probing. If most individuals who have such momentary doubts choose not to probe and instead slide back into blind self-righteousness, this does not show an absolute incapacity for change. It does show how difficult change is in these circumstances. Needless to say, however, fulfilling moral obligations is often quite difficult. While failure to do what one should may be understood and perhaps even forgiven, this does not lessen one's duty.

Similar things can be said about the alleged incapacity to decide to seek information about massive atrocities generally ignored or downplayed by mainstream media. Most people on at least some occasion do get hints that not all that is important is reported on television or in the local paper. These hints may come from some unusual public broadcasting program; or from one's own or an acquaintance's overseas trip which exposes one to slightly different and more skeptical points of view; or from one too many public confessions by government spokespersons about official lies; or from talk-radio; or from rebel Internet sites. These occasional doubts concerning one's ordinary sources of information constitute tiny motivational openings which can lead to decisions to seek further and to see what additional matters are regularly being kept from one. The fact that on these occasions of doubt most individuals choose not to probe further does not show an absolute incapacity to do so. The additional fact that one's failing to do so can be understood and perhaps even forgiven does not lessen one's obligation to make such decisions.

Objection II: Citizens Are Too Powerless To Find Out

Should the average U.S. citizen decide to seek the relevant information, are there not a number of factors which show that he or she most likely will not succeed in fording out about affairs such as the East Timor or the Guatemala bloodshed? Consider the following: large numbers of people are only semi-literate and would not even read a newspaper. Others more literate lack knowledge of geography, history, international affairs, economics, and political and religious ideologies. They lack the general intellectual sophistication to know where to start looking and how to interpret what they ford. Should this large majority of people not be exempt from the obligation to seek knowledge of matters beyond their intellectual reach?

This second objection can be understood in two ways. It can be asking if it is too much to expect that the average person find data about distant human rights conditions, once one has decided to seek these data. The answer to this question is "No," particularly in light of the Internet revolution. One only has to search on the Internet for, say, Guatemala, and all kinds of informative and action-seeking sites will appear. Newspapers, magazines, and radio stations, from all over the world and from multiple socio-political perspectives, are available to us by literally moving our fingertips. Given that the Internet accessibility is becoming the norm in advanced

---

implications are quite objectionable. M. Slote, "The Morality of Wealth," in *World Hunger and Moral Obligations*, W. Aiken and H. LaFollette, eds. (Upper Saddle River, NJ: Prentice Hall, 1977), 138.

countries, the technical barriers to information are diminishing all the time. One only needs to notice the ingenuity and power shown by ordinary people in searching for data about matters close to their heart-say, about their genealogical roots, or about a certain disease. The essential step, therefore, consists in bringing important moral matters close to one's heart. Failure to do so is not a failure due to research impotence. It is more like the unwillingness to take the moral point of view and thereby recognize "that objectively no one matters more than anyone else."[11]

This brings us to a second way of understanding this "powerless" objection. It could be asking about motivational barriers. That is, would a person not have to be broadly aware and ethically sensitive in the first place before he or she opts to type the word "Guatemala" in one's computer search engine? If this is the understanding of this question, then we axe back to the previous objection. Yes, one needs to have already some open-mindedness, curiosity, and sense that there is more to be known, before one takes any active steps to find out more about anything, not just about moral matters. However, at least regarding the sense that there is more to be known (about moral matters particularly), I maintain that most of us Westerners receive plenty of hints that our ordinary knowledge in this area is less than adequate. As to lacking the general open-mindedness and curiosity prerequisites for seeking knowledge, surely this cannot fully exempt US.[12]

Naturally, mainstream news organizations and the intellectual corps bear preeminent moral responsibility for not taking sufficient measures to inform themselves and the public of moral atrocities-in an impartial and non-selective way. It is one of their professional tasks to keep us abreast of the events of greatest significance for the race and the planet. They have clearly failed us in cases such as Guatemala and East Timor. But given that there are sources of information on these matters, albeit off the main media routes, is this responsibility not shared also by average middle-class literate citizens? Perhaps their responsibility is diminished due to their greater difficulty in attaining access to this information. But clearly one would not want to accept the principle that major wrongdoing can be ignored whenever information about it is not provided for one during one's normal course of daily activities, since such ignorance would have justified ignoring Nazi atrocities during the 1930s and 1940s.

Objection III: Help Only Those You Can, i.e., Your Neighbors

The average individual's attempt to influence matters like the Indonesian policy vis-à-vis East Timor, runs this objection, is not likely to lead to the prevention of any harm. Perhaps if most individuals acted collectively, the likelihood of harm-prevention would be quite significant. But the effort of a lone individual is completely negligible, especially if one sets aside drastic options such as a public hunger strike. Would one not be more effectively beneficent by helping instead local

---

[11] Recognizing this value parity constitutes the "basic moral insight," according to Thomas Nagel. T. Nagel, *The View From Nowhere* (New York, Oxford University Press, 1986), 205.

[12] Whether one has the right not to change and improve oneself is a complex issue. At the very least, however, such a right may conflict with the rights of others (to be given help in preventing their being tortured and killed) which may generate a duty that one keep informed on the condition of these others. I discuss this issue more fully in non-rights terms below. See note 13.

charities, an alcoholic relative, or the neighborhood stray cats? And if so, why waste time and effort in trying to become informed about distant atrocities?

Naturally, there is some validity to this line of thinking. One's replies might include the following observations. First, one must concede that an individual alone will not generally accomplish visible results when speaking out on distant occurrences about which officialdom – government educational institutions, the press – is silent. But surely there are exceptions to this. If nothing else, the average individual may be

heard by a few other individuals, each of whom, in turn, might reach a few others, generating a significant ripple effect. Perhaps, someone will be reached who has considerable power or access to the public ear.

Second, if likelihood of impact were an absolute moral prerequisite for action, then one could argue that a person should also not invest any effort in speaking out on those matters on which many others are already speaking out. Why? Because to add one more voice to a chorus of thousands would make no noticeable difference. Hence, the principle here presumed – i.e., that one should speak out only when one's voice is likely to have some non-negligible effect – will justify a policy of almost never speaking out on large-scale affairs. Surely this consequence is objectionable, since such affairs are not what they could and should be. At the very least the magnitude of the preventable evil is an additional factor one should consider in deciding what to do.

Third, the ideal conditions for "local morality" cannot be obtained in the actual world. Perhaps in an ideal world where power and resources are somewhat equitably distributed, if each tends only to her own locality where a noticeable difference can be affected, the global result would probably be morally acceptable (though protection of common resources, such as the ozone layer, would require global and collective attention). But in a world like ours, where resources and power are disproportionately distributed, often through past and present injustice, the policy of each tending to her own property and community will not lead to morally acceptable global results. In this askew world, pursuing one's personal interests and community interests may mean keeping those in Timor or Brazil dispossessed; and one's power to do so is likely to more than offset another's power to improve his or her position. Any view that justifies the pursuit of ends benefiting only oneself and one's own, and that neglects to consider seriously the implications of such pursuits for "others," does not deserve the appellation "moral:" Impartiality must be one of the essential features of the moral viewpoint. One aim of this viewpoint is the transcendence of the "one's own/others" dichotomy, hard as this may be.[13]

---

[13] This claim has been contested by a number of contemporary philosophers: Philippa Foot, *Virtues and Vices and Other Essays in Moral Philosophy* (Berkeley: University of California Press, 1978); Bernard Williams, *Moral Luck* (Cambridge: Cambridge University Press, 1981); Susan Wolf, "Moral Saints," *Journal of Philosophy* 79 (1982): 419-31; Michael Slote, *Goods and Virtues* (Oxford: Clarendon Press, 1983); and Thomas Nagel, *The View From Nowhere*. In different ways each argues that it is not necessarily immoral to pursue personal, familial, or local goals at the expense of "common good" goals. The personal vs. impersonal dilemma is at the center of Nagel's moral and general philosophy. His opinion is that "the impartial standpoint of morality ... will give to everyone a dispensation for a certain degree of partiality-in recognition of the fact that it is one aspect of the human perspective." In other words, an objective moral theory, in acknowledging all the facts in our universe, must take into account the fact that humans encounter the world from the subjective perspective of self, family,

Impartiality in an interconnected world implies a cosmopolitan outlook.

Thus, the principle at issue – only speak out on those issues where one's voice is *likely* to have a noticeable effect – must be rejected on moral grounds. It may be necessary, of course, to choose those ways of speaking out that are most likely to be productive, since the goal is not to attain some empty psychological and moral purity. Thus, one should, perhaps, write to those legislators, newspapers, and organizations which are most likely to listen and which can help publicize one's cause. There is no point in sending letters or articles to *The National Review* about East Timor or Guatemala and then expressing outrage when this material is not printed. As I have argued, however, the need for intelligence in one's efforts must not collapse into the need to limit one's focus to parochial matters.

Needless to say, having an obligation to find out about, and speak out on, distant matters does not exempt one from obligations to help the local indigent, alcoholic, or cat. Many of us can do both. In fact, since parochial and distant matters often causally interact, one may need to do both. But, one might ask, where does one draw the line? And where does one find the time? One does have to earn a living so as to be in a position to help both the local and the distant needy. One does have to fulfill one's family obligations. And one needs to take care of oneself, to do things for sheer pleasure, or to develop artistic and other skills, and not out of moral considerations.

Obviously these questions lead to immense complexities. One suggestion may be that in the interest of time and effectiveness what each individual should devote herself to, in addition to providing for self, family, and friends, depends on the individual's circumstances and expertise. For instance, the lawyer might most effectively use some of her time to defend the interests of the local disenfranchised and speak out about the uses and self-serving misuses of international law by powerful countries such as the U.S.; the local radio announcer might best use her position to insert unusual and personally researched news items into ordinary broadcasts; the corporate employee might best explore the policies of the firm's international division, and if necessary blow the whistle on ethically dubious practices. Despite countless idiosyncrasies and complications, it remains a fact that most (or at least many) individuals can afford to sacrifice some of the time and resources ordinarily allotted for personal pleasure for the sake of those less fortunate.

These sacrifices need not result in significant "losses." One might, in fact, find that these "moral" pursuits will turn into creative and satisfying projects. These projects may even become replacements for some of one's more mindless leisure

---

race, and nationality. The theory's moral demands cannot ignore this human fact. Consequently, an objective moral theory, such as utilitarianism, cannot be strictly impartial. I admit that the issue is profound and fascinating. But I would lean toward the hard line considered, but finally rejected, by Nagel: "One might take the severe line that moral requirements result from a correct assessment of the weight of good and evil, impersonally revealed, that it is our job to bring our motives into line with this, and that if we cannot do it because of personal weakness, this shows not that the requirements are excessive but that we are bad-though one might refrain from being too censorious about it:" This view strikes me as rationally unavoidable once one grants the equal moral value of virtually every human. The partiality toward self that the abovementioned philosophers defend goes directly against this moral axiom, particularly in a world of limited resources where my having x often deprives another or others. Were each of us insulated from others, the case might be different. Thomas Nagel, *The View From Nowhere*, 202-05.

activities. Perhaps this is hoping for too much. At any rate, being embattled by myriad *prima facie* moral obligations, as well as by various practical exigencies, psychological addictions, and other demands, need not paralyze a person. To be sure, juggling all of these interests is quite a challenge; yet, given our present global interdependency and our wide informational access, it must be part of the condition of the average Westerner. As Sartre might say, choose one must. Such choices can be made intelligently and consciously, or nonreflectively and haphazardly. Morally speaking, there is no dilemma here...

Objection IV: It Would Be Great to Help, But Is It Wrong Not to Help?

Philosophers of ethics distinguish between acts that are morally required and acts that, while commendable if done, are not obligatory, called "supererogatory" acts. Sharing one's salary with some group of destitute strangers constitutes a commendable but not an obligatory act. What about taking steps to broaden oneself culturally and intellectually in order to be able to keep abreast of foreign developments so as to help fight against major moral abuses? Wouldn't this also be a commendable but not required course of action? If so, the average citizen is not under any compelling obligation to engage in this course of action.

Let us assume that the commendable/obligatory distinction is valid. Even so, by appealing to certain considerations of compensatory justice it can be shown that the information-seeking course of action is obligatory. Consider the salary sharing example. While generally your sharing your salary with some poor strangers is not morally required (though some historical figures, like Jesus have thought otherwise), what if you have contributed – even if only to a tiny degree – to their systematic impoverishment and have done so in some unfair way? One would think then that by way of compensation you owe them at least some help or some fraction of your possessions.

Has the average citizen contributed to a tiny degree, and in an unfair way, to the moral atrocities committed by some foreign governments? Those who would answer "yes" can advance the following argument:

1. In a democratic country, the government speaks for citizens and invests some of their tax money in foreign affairs. It performs this general function with their knowledge and approval. It is, thus, their agent or broker.
2. The U.S. government has helped, and continues to help, many brutal foreign regimes, often with some of its citizens' tax money.
3. Therefore, U.S. citizens' agent has clearly supported brutal foreign regimes.
4. A person shares responsibility with the agent for what latter does while carrying out the duties with which it is charged; and the responsibility is shared even when the agent's actions are taken without the person's knowledge, so long as the agent is granted broad powers of action.
5. The U.S. government is given broad powers of action, especially in foreign affairs, and often does not fully inform the citizens about its foreign policies.
6. Therefore, the average U.S. citizen shares responsibility with the government for its foreign affairs policies which often support brutal foreign regimes.

Having thus contributed to moral atrocities, U.S. citizens are morally obligated to help the victims of such atrocities by way of compensation, if nothing else.[14]

But what about the case of those citizens who oppose the government's policies and vote for or otherwise support candidates and parties who call for an end to support to brutal regimes? Are these citizens not exempt from any complicity in these atrocities? Must they take further and more drastic actions, such as not paying a proportional share of their income taxes, in order to satisfy their moral obligations? Considered in its own right, this is a very difficult issue. For our purposes it suffices to say that this group constitutes a very small minority (most people, again, do not cast their votes and support on the basis of a candidate's position on foreign policy issues). Moreover, the type of person who is aware of and, by voting, has opposed these immoral foreign policies has thereby shown currency with the relevant world events. This person is already likely to take steps to help alleviate the atrocities. For most of the rest of us, the argument still stands.

But what if the government, as our agent, conceals from us or at least fails to explicitly inform us about its activities in other parts of the world? Would this not relieve us of the responsibility for the related atrocities despite our contribution to these atrocities through, for example, unwitting financial support? To answer this, we would have to know how actively we tend to seek the relevant information from our agent; how willing we are to close our eyes to its practices; and whether there are sources which can, if necessary, provide us with the relevant information. What has already been said on these issues shows that we can uncover our government's role in foreign atrocities.[15] In that case we, the citizens, remain partially responsible for its foreign deeds and our compensatory obligation stands. In fact, once the moral obligation is seen as deriving from the principle of compensatory justice, our duty to help alleviate systematic human rights abuses becomes much stronger than would be the case if it derived merely from a general obligation to prevent harm to people we have in no way affected. Our actions and omissions have affected and do affect distant people, however, unwitting we may be in this.

Because of this contribution to the harm, we have a particularly compelling duty to inform ourselves about these distant atrocities. Indeed, there are many other major sources of harm in our world, such as famines, diseases, environmental destruction, and the nuclear arms threat. My earlier argument, based on a general obligation to prevent harm, can also be used to spur us into keeping informed about these other evils. But if the demands upon our personal time and energy become too burdensome, and we must choose among subjects about which to keep informed, then we ought to inform ourselves first about those major evils to which we contribute-directly, through our actions, and indirectly, through the actions of our representative government. And while such major evils will not be confined to distant atrocities, some of these atrocities will surely fall under this most stringent category.

---

[14] A similar point is made by Slote in discussing whether wealthy individuals and nations who omit to share some of their wealth with the poor are justified in this omission. He observes that "(o)missions may not be permissible ... if they in some sense preserve or perpetuate commissive wrongdoings."
And since he thinks that in fact most wealthy individuals and nations become and remain wealthy by immoral means, they are obligated to share their wealth with those at whose expense this wealth becomes accumulated. M. Slote, "The Morality of Wealth," 141-45.

[15] Note that here I am not relying on the conclusion of my earlier argument based on the general obligation to prevent harm. I am merely borrowing one premise from that argument.

One must add that this argument has made no mention of the economic benefits that accrue to us through big business' exploitation of favorable foreign conditions (e.g., cheap labor, cheap resources, lenient safety regulations, low taxes, etc.). These favorable investment conditions are often systematically maintained by repressive regimes at steep human rights costs. Most of us benefit considerably from the success of these multinational firms. We benefit as consumers through cheaper products. We benefit as investors in stocks, banks, pension funds, and through greater dividends. And we benefit many other ways, given the support by multinationals for media organizations, hospitals, universities, and the arts. Accordingly, are we not obligated to compensate those who are violently repressed so that such benefits will continue to flow our way?...

The victims in Guatemala, East Timor, and elsewhere are not simply children and perhaps they are not our "neighbors," but in our current global village, their cries can be heard by most of us, if we are willing to listen. And many of us unwittingly benefit from and contribute to their suffering. In such circumstances, one would think that the distance of the victims would not lessen our obligation to pay attention and take action.

GLOBALIZATION AND SEPTEMBER 11
MICHAEL MANN

The term "globalization" refers to the extension of social relations over the globe. There is no doubt that this is occurring. The more difficult questions are, how fast? How far? How evenly? Are some regions or groups of people being left out? Will it go further in the future? Many imply that globalization is a singular process, moving toward one encompassing global society. Given the dominance of materialism in modern Western thought, their analysis tends to centre on economic matters – transnational capitalism is breaking through the boundaries of states to create a unitary network of interaction across the globe. Others would stress technological and cultural versions – a revolution in the technology of communications, or in new mass markets of consumer capitalism. There are also less economistic conceptions: the emergence of a single global culture, or world order – more usually seen as a convergence of the many existing states into a single political model, rather than the emergence of a single world state. These visions are essentially pacific: the world will be integrated into a more or less harmonious whole.[1]

These views are false. Though globalization is occurring, it is not singular but multiple, and it disintegrates as well as integrating. Globalization diffuses onto a world scale the unevenness and contradictions of the 'West' and the 'North', and then adds to them those of the 'South' and of North-South relations. Such plural globalizations involve much conflict – often amenable to negotiation and settlement, but at other times sparking armed combat. I will attempt to delineate these varied outcomes, focusing especially on tracing the links between globalizations and the terrible sequence of events begun on September 11. I am not the first to make such arguments. Some emphasize that a capitalist 'world system' generates its own contradictions and conflicts as each of its successive hegemonic Powers begins to falter.[2] This is quite a forceful argument, attempting to analyse both economics and politics, but it is still too narrow and systemic a view.

Some historians of international relations have stressed that globalization has been Janus-faced, providing both order and fragmentation. Thus the Cold War is seen both as having divided the world and as having given it an essential order, either side of its main fault-line—including the partial incorporation of the 'Third' into the 'First World'.[3] There are also many analyses of the 'new world disorder'. But I will place such perspectives within a broader theory of society. In the two volumes of *The Sources of Social Power*, I argued that, in pursuit of their goals, human beings set up

---

[1] Originally given as a lecture at the Russian State University for the Humanities, 24 September 2001. Revised November 9.
[2] See Giovanni Arrighi and Beverly Silver, *Chaos and Governance in the Modern World System*, Minneapolis 1999.
[3] See Ian Clark, *Globalization and Fragmentation*, Oxford 1997.

four main types of power organizations: ideological (or cultural, if you prefer); economic; military; and political.[4] This model sees globalization as consisting of expansions of all four of these networks of interaction, each of which may have differing boundaries, rhythms and results, diffusing distinctive forms of integration and disintegration across the globe. Discussion of globalization should not neglect any of these. Recent events should bring this home, since they clearly involve a mixture of ideological, economic, military and political processes.

The multiple nature of globalization had already been evident in its earlier phases. These lasted many centuries, going into higher gear when, at the end of the fifteenth century, European explorers became the first humans to conceive of conquering and settling the whole globe—and then largely proceeded to do so. But their expansion was multiple. It included the global expansion of European capitalism; of imperialism; and of ideologies—Christianity, individualism and racism, with liberalism, socialism and democracy added later. This bundle of European ideologies was internally contradictory; it also provoked much resistance. To give two examples: firstly, European racism undermined European imperialism's ability to integrate its conquered peoples into enduring empires. Two millennia previously, North Africans had *become* Romans, contributing to the longevity of the Empire. But in the eighteenth and nineteenth centuries Africans did not become British. Excluded as racial inferiors, they kicked out their British overlords as soon as they had the chance. The Russian Empire similarly failed to integrate Caucasian peoples; they never succeeded in subduing the Chechens, while the Circassians were completely wiped out.

Secondly, the expansion globalized militarism between rival European states, bringing wars that initially disrupted globalization but then redirected and even enhanced it—the Napoleonic Wars, enhancing the global power of Britain, and the Asian power of Russia; World War II, followed by the Cold War, generating the first global hegemon: the United States. In the past, therefore, globalization was multiple and contradictory, with all four sources of social power entwining to determine its trajectory. This remains true today. States, imperialism and militarism still exist; and though racism may have declined, ethnic and religious nationalism have surged. To put such phenomena in a broader context, I examine the four power sources in turn.

I. Economic Power

The transnational growth of capitalism has now risen back up to the high levels achieved before World War I—and greatly exceeds these in communications and direct foreign investment. Capitalism is formally transnational: oriented to profit on markets wherever these are found, regardless of national, regional, religious or other boundaries. It could be seamlessly global—but it still contains three main divides, which also cut across a peculiar facet of this recent phase of globalization. For this has not been a period of general economic growth but of overall relative stagnation amid great unevenness between regions.

---

[4] Cambridge 1986 and 1993.

An Exclusive Imperialism

The most important divide is created by the contradictory relations of what I shall call 'ostracizing imperialism'. The term indicates that one part of the world both avoids and dominates the economy of the other, the precise mixture of these relationships varying by region and through time. On the one hand, most of the world's poorest countries are not being significantly integrated into transnational capitalism, but are 'ostracized' by a capitalism which regards them as too risky for investment and trade. It is conventional to describe this economic fault-line as being between 'North' and 'South', though this is too crude a division and is not strictly geographical. Much of Russia, China and the ex-Soviet Central Asian republics are classified as 'South', while Australia and New Zealand are 'North'.

International trade and investment are becoming increasingly concentrated within the North. Between 1850 and 1950, North-South trade comprised about 30 per cent of the global total, and North-South investment about 50 per cent. Both proportions then began to decline, reaching below 20 per cent by the early 1980s. But in these figures, Japan and the 'little Tiger' countries of East Asia – the post-World War II economic success stories – are included in the South. Reallocating them to the North would increase the proportion of global investment and trade within this region to an astonishing 90 per cent. Indeed, if present trends continue, the share of Africa, the Middle East, Latin America, Central Eastern Europe and the countries of the former Soviet Union, all combined, would be down to only 5 per cent of world trade by the year 2020 – in regions that contain over 40 per cent of the world's population.[5] So economic 'globalization' is mostly Northernization, integrating the advanced countries but excluding much of the world's poor; and thus widening inequalities in growth and wealth between North and South.[6]

But such ostracism is only partial. The North does trade with and invest in the South, which it still dominates economically. This has increasingly involved two mechanisms of unequal exchange. Firstly, a secular downward trend in the price of raw materials as compared to finished goods: the South unfortunately depends on raw materials, which also involve lower-end technologies; the gap in wealth and technology widens. Secondly, fluctuations in interest rates, initially generated within Northern (and oil) economies. In the 1970s, low interest rates encouraged Southern countries to borrow heavily, to finance economic development; interest rates shot up, generating a massive Southern debt crisis in the 1980s. This, in turn, generated interventions by the North, to cope with both the debt crisis of depressed Southern economies and the threatened insolvency of Northern banks. In their current, neoliberal form, structural adjustment programmes by the IMF, World Bank and banking consortia involve disruptive cut-backs in Southern state expenditure, welfare, and labour-market regulation. If their net economic effect has sometimes been positive, they have almost always widened inequalities. Thus such interventions are often plausibly perceived in the South as constituting economic imperialism.

---

[5] Ricardo Petrella, 'Globalization and Internationalization: the Dynamics of the Emerging World Order', in Robert Boyer and Daniel Drache, *States Against Markets: The Limits of Globalization*, New York 1996, p. 80.
[6] As argued by Ankie Hoogvelt, in *Globalization and the Postcolonial World*, Basingstoke 1997.

Of course, the world is not neatly divided into two blocs—although the appearance of such a duality is reinforced by the fact that there are far fewer 'middle-class' countries, where per capita GDP hovers around the global average, than there are rich or poor ones. But North and South contain much internal variation, and some countries do straddle the fault-line between them. East Asia and Southern Europe only became part of the North after 1945, and the picture could look very different soon if even a few of the large, poorer countries were to follow suit. Forty per cent of the world's population live in China and India, both currently developing quite rapidly. Their liberalizing economies are built on top of cohesive historic cultures and solid states – one led by a Communist, the other a Hindu Nationalist party – so these are not simply neoliberal success stories. But China alone absorbs well over half of current Northern investment in the South and, its enormous population notwithstanding, may 'join the North' in the not-too-distant future. Another large country, Russia, seems to be bifurcated by the faultline, with the Moscow-St. Petersburg axis becoming quite Northern, while much of the rest of the country is in the South. The world has never seen an evenly diffused process of global development. Some areas have shot forward while others crawl, stagnate or even regress. Development has tended to spread to neighbours, and to those with distinctive natural or social resources. The North creeps outward, but a divide remains.

Persistence of Nation-states

Nation-states remain obdurate networks of economic interaction as they provide the vast majority of the political regulation that capitalism requires. About 80 per cent of the world's production is currently traded within national boundaries. Only in Western Europe has there been a serious decline in this figure, due to the regulated common market the EU provides. Finance capital has become considerably more transnational; labour remains more border-bound – though international labour migration has been increasing, it has not yet returned to the levels of pre-World War I. Nonetheless, vigorous national economic planning has fallen, in both North and South. Socialism's decline seems terminal, and the dominant trend remains toward less protectionism and a more open world economy. In the North, while nation-states may remain important actors, their economic conflicts are peacefully regulated by inter-national institutions. Here there is some movement toward greater economic integration, if of a rather mixed transnational and inter-national form.

Within the South things are more complex. Since the economic power of most Southern countries is in decline, relative to the North, their ability to resist a Northern-defined globalization is lessening. In addition, many Southern regimes are now staffed with 'realists' and Chicago School economists, who argue that their government must do whatever it takes to attract foreign capital and trade, and abandon whatever protectionisms were previously in place. Few Southern elites resist their imperial masters. This displaces serious economic conflict away from the North-South division and situates it within each Southern nation-state as realist elites are challenged by a discontented populace – or by corrupt or privileged patron-client networks, whose control of the state is threatened by the more positive side of neoliberal measures. Such three-way internal conflicts are now weakening the cohesion of many Southern societies and states, further reducing their capacity to resist. If economic development fails, collaborating elites become dangerously exposed to attacks that identify them as tools of foreign imperialists.

Macro-regional variations in economic policy also remain, mainly generated by older ideological-power differences. Esping-Andersen and others have usefully identified three types of 'Western' regimes: liberal, or Anglo-Saxon; corporatist---conservative Catholic, or 'Rhenish'; and social-democratic—mostly, the Nordic states.[7] Liberals are currently the most powerful of the three, with the US leading the way in imposing the 'Washington Consensus' (i.e., neoliberalism) on client states, usually through the US-dominated international institutions – the IMF, World Bank, etc. But the American economy, unlike the US military, is not hegemonic over its rivals; only the first among trilateral equals. The continental Western European countries maintain their corporatist or social-democratic versions of capitalism, involving larger welfare states (though these are no longer expanding). Inequalities have widened much more in liberal than in corporatist or social-democratic states.[8] Japan and the East Asian 'Little Tigers' have their own brands of corporatist-statist capitalisms. And if China, India or Russia do 'join the North', this will only widen regional variation, since they also have very distinctive political economies. Differences between the US, Europe and Japan over many global issues have been growing recently. They may result in bigger fissures within the North in the future, especially if American hegemony lessens. Again, however, these are likely to be solved by peaceful inter-national negotiations. They may produce economic crises but these are unlikely to worsen to military ones.

So capitalism is globalizing, but with a Northern face. The overall drift remains mediated by national and macro-regional differences, but their conflicts are generally resolved peacefully, by international institutions. More destabilizing, as we shall see, are the conflicts arising in the South from the effects of 'ostracizing imperialism'. But these alone are insufficient to cause violent conflict at a global level, for most are deflected into intra-state struggles.

II. Military Power

The most dramatic recent changes have been in relations of military power. For the first time in the entire history of humanity war – at least among the greatest powers – has become absolutely irrational as a means of pursuing human goals. This is not yet so among lesser powers, who may still go to war without obliterating each other, or the entire globe. But it will be true for them too, in time, as they acquire nuclear, chemical or biological weapons of immense destructive power.

Since human beings do often act irrationally, war may not be entirely obsolete, even in the North. But in the meantime, the effects have been profound. US military hegemony left the old West almost entirely pacified. War between West European states, or between them and the US, or between Japan and either of these, has become almost unthinkable. The collapse of the Soviet Union deepened US military hegemony. The US now spends as much on defense as the next twelve

---

[7] Gosta Esping-Andersen, *The Three Worlds of Welfare Capitalism*, Princeton 1990; Evelyne Huber and John Stephens, *Development and Crisis of the Welfare State*, Chicago 2001.
[8] See the data in Michael Mann and Dylan Riley, 'Global Inequality', forthcoming.

Powers combined—dwarfing Britain's nineteenth-century imperialism, under which the strength of the Royal Navy (not the army) was kept a little greater than that of the next two largest navies combined. The rest of the North accepts US military dominance as necessary for its own defense, most Northern states being US allies. Such Northern consensus makes this a historically unprecedented degree and form of military hegemony. We should not assume that consensus spreads to the South. If 'ostracizing imperialism' seems to be imposed with the help of American military power, then resistance might be expected—should that power falter. The consequence in the North, however, has been pacification. Along with the technological revolution in communications, this has been the main cause of the surge in globalization with a Northern face that has occurred from the 1970s onwards. The North is becoming integrated as a single military system, as its many states huddle loosely together under the American umbrella. But outside, two military divides remain.

Regional Powers

There remain major regional powers whom the US has neither the stomach nor the capacity to coerce. Though they seek economic benefits from agreements with the US and its client international institutions, they do not accept American leadership. China and Russia remain the obvious cases, though the US has little influence over India and Pakistan – who also now have nuclear weapons. These cases are all very different. There are no serious differences with Russia, and the US has largely ignored Moscow's local difficulties in Chechnya. The US has no major dispute with either India or Pakistan, though their own mutual antagonism is potentially more than a neighbourhood threat. All these states also have a common interest in redefining some of their own enemies as 'Islamic fundamentalists' – thus supposedly legitimizing their repression. (In Chechnya, this is actually turning an essentially secular separatist movement into a more Islamic one.) The US does have a major dispute with China, over Taiwan. Here, the US desperately hopes that China will not pursue reunification aggressively; US governments have some kind of commitment to a military defense of Taiwan for which they have no stomach. Nonetheless, these are fairly rational powers concerned to regulate their relations with each other. They can hope to work out their conflicts by international negotiation, involving tension perhaps, but without war. This type of divide may involve risk of serious disintegration, though perhaps of rather low probability. But who can ultimately say? The 'Great Game' popularized by Kipling was a simple bi-polar struggle, in which Britain and Russia played chessboard geopolitics over central Asia. Today's struggle over Afghanistan concerns one global superpower, the US, plus several regional powers (Russia, China, Iran, Pakistan, India) each with considerable autonomy of action and each possessing, or close to possessing, nuclear weapons. I suspect that Kipling's was the more rule-governed version of the game.

American Weaknesses

Northern military dominance over the South has been weakening in two ways, over the last decades. First, the North's internal pacification has undermined its own militarism, its stomach for a fight, its ability to take losses among its own citizen-soldiers. In the Lebanon and Somalia, US forces fled precipitously when, respectively, 200 and 20 of its soldiers were unexpectedly killed. This was noted by Osama bin Laden, who declared in his 1997 CNN interview that, in both cases, the victors were 'poor, unarmed people whose only weapon is the belief in Allah the almighty'. In recent years the US has been happy to bomb from a safe height, but has avoided infantry combat—except, as in the Gulf War, in an open desert and with oil at stake. US combat troops are about to be used again in Afghanistan, but it remains doubtful whether American public opinion is prepared to accept heavy American losses.

A second weakening was long obscured by the obsession with the twentieth-century hi-tech weaponry revolution, symbolized by nuclear fission and laser-guided missiles. These do indeed give Northern Powers, and especially the US, extraordinary superiority in traditional forms of inter-state warfare. But at the same time, there has been a more subversive revolution in the 'weapons of the weak' – one that has made a Russian inventor, Mikhail Kalashnikov, a household name. The AK-47 – a simplified, mass-produced hand-held automatic rifle – has been followed by shoulder-held surface-to-air and anti-tank missiles which are now, ironically, serving to undermine Russian military might. A single Chechen fighter cradling a $200 anti-tank missile launcher can pop up out of a cellar behind a $1 million tank and destroy it – providing the infantrymen supposedly guarding the vehicle do not wish to expose themselves to the risk of death. But Russia, it seems, has also experienced some demilitarization. Rather sensibly, Russian infantrymen lag behind a little when their tanks advance. Of course, the guerrilla also has access to a particular global industry: arms smuggling – through which globalization fragments and kills while it unites.

September 11 revealed a more spectacular example of the use of the weapons of the weak. A dozen or so terrorists, armed with knives and civilian airliners, killed just over 3,000 people, demolished the twin towers of the World Trade Centre – just off Wall Street – and one of the Pentagon's five sides: key symbols of US economic and military power.[9] This atrocity also continues another trend in twentieth-century warfare: the increasing targeting of civilians as the enemy. The citizens of the North are not fully and safely pacified, after all. It is likely that Southern dissident movements and refugee camps will continue to generate these militants, while the weapons needed to create mayhem – small arms, Semtex, mobile phones, the internet, even pilot training – are now minimal, and freely available on global markets throughout the world. Even bringing supposed 'rogue states' like Libya or Iraq to heel may make little difference: they are barely needed now – provided suicide volunteers are forthcoming.

Thus the military and political capacity of the great powers to overwhelm the South may be declining. Nineteenth-century empires possessed the concentrated firepower to defeat almost all native forces. They would mount punitive expeditions,

---

[9] The roster of missing and dead at the WTC issued by the companies involved--including those lost by Cantor Fitzgerald, the New York Fire Department, the passengers on the planes and over 165 diners and staff at Windows on the World--comes to 2,405. Estimates from the *New York Times*, *Associated Press* and *USA Today* range from 2,600 to 2,950. At the Pentagon, 189 were killed, including 64 plane passengers. Forty-five people died in the Pittsburgh plane crash: *New York Times*, 25 October 2001; *Washington Post*, 4 November 2001.

sending ships equipped with relatively small infantry, cavalry and artillery units to seize native capitals; they then turned to political power, to persuade local, native leaders to rule as their clients. Bombing from a safe height is not an adequate modern substitute, since it cannot easily effect a regime change. The rise of ethnic and religious nationalism means that, in most Southern countries, it is not so easy to find local clients (rather tribalized countries like Afghanistan may remain exceptions to this). True, economic power often substitutes effectively for political power. Structural adjustment programmes constitute an effective, indirect form of imperialism, constraining the actions of economically motivated Southern regimes. But their populations may resist this; and not all Southern elites are so economically motivated, anyway.

Thus a dual military world emerges. It has been described as consisting of 'zones of peace, zones of turmoil': a largely pacified North exists alongside regions of armed turbulence elsewhere.[10] Of course, such turmoil characterizes only parts of the South and, as we will see, it takes two distinct forms. So I use the plural concept: zones of turmoil. Though these are usually found in poorer regions, the military divide is not identical to the economic one—nor to the political and ideological divides; the sources of social power have distinct rhythms of their own.

III. Political Power

Despite the widespread belief that the nation-state is being undermined by globalization, the actual trends are quite varied. European nation-states are ceding some of their powers to quasi-federal Euro[11] institutions, although this model is not spreading significantly elsewhere. Weak states may cede political powers to strong states in their region, but they have always done so. The US can induce Latin American governments to restructure their economies more easily than it can East Asian ones; but this was also true in the past. Keynesian economic planning may be declining, but looming environmental crises will probably bring new forms of intervention. Global warming, polluted air, water shortages, fuel exhaustion require coordinated negotiations and actions between states – the only actors with authoritative regulatory powers over their territories and airspace. Either states collectively negotiate and plan, or our great-grandchildren perish. This means a growing role for 'soft geopolitics' between states. Diplomacy concerning economic development and environmental agreements will hopefully dominate over water wars.

If such soft geopolitics are predominantly peaceful, they may even encourage the diffusion of a single global political culture, less riven by serious conflict, as John Meyer and others have argued.[12] Governments everywhere have the same cabinet ministers; sponsor the same tripartite education systems; develop the same central banks, the same regulatory agencies, the same national parks. There is no fascism, no

---

[10] Max Singer and Aaron Wildavsky, *The Real World Order: Zones of Peace/Zones of Turmoil*, Chatham, NJ 1993.

[11] See my 'Has Globalization Ended the Rise and Rise of the Nation-State?', *Review of International Political Economy*, Vol. 4, 1997, pp. 472-96.

[12] John Meyer, 'The Changing Cultural Content of the Nation-State: a World Society Perspective', in George Steimnetz, ed., *State / Culture*, Ithaca 1999.

socialism. There are very few monarchies with executive power; no confederal empires. All claim to be democracies and all seek capitalist economic growth. States remain, but the degree of convergence between them is developing a high level of integration at the global level. This would be a single, international world order.

Obstacles to Democracy

Yet democracy and development remain elusive. They have not, so far, diffused evenly across the world, but only to neighbours and peculiarly favoured countries. One obstacle in particular began to loom large in the twentieth century: the difficulty of achieving democracy in a multiethnic or multi-religious environment. There 'rule by the people' has increasingly meant domination over others by one ethnic or religious group, followed by resistance, civil war and ethnic cleansing. This was the past of many Northern countries; it is the present of many Southern ones. It is essentially a modern problem, generated by the global diffusion of the ideal of 'rule by the people' in an environment where 'the people' is prone to be defined in ethnic or religious terms. Ethnic cleansing is the dark side of the democratization process, as I have argued elsewhere.[13] Thus wars, most of them ethnic or religious, increased fairly steadily during the second half of the twentieth century (though some detect a little slackening in the late 1990s). The political faultlines of modernity are being globalized.

Similarly, though all states aspire to economic development, 'ostracizing imperialism' ensures that parts of the South lag further behind the North. This is especially galling since global media and consumerism dangle a fantasy life of economic plenty in front of most of the world's population. Developmental failure weakens regime legitimacy and increases political conflict, both within many Southern countries and between them and the North. These two processes – of ethnic/religious conflict and economic failure – combine as fuels, igniting the zones of turmoil to which I referred above. They yield desperate extremists, roving teenage paramilitaries, civil wars and anarchy. They create turbulence within states, and conflict between them. These zones are scattered rather unevenly across the South, and mainly generated by local conditions. Three types of Northern intervention, however, can exacerbate them.

i. Declining terms of trade and debt crises, followed by neoliberal restructurings, may give local economic resentments a broader, more global resonance. But in these cases discontented locals may be unsure as to who to blame: their own political leaders, or the North?
ii. Northerners, especially the US, prop up Southern regimes for their own purposes, arming them against their local enemies and domestic dissidents. If these regimes become more unpopular, discontent may be turned against the Northern power, whose arms are being used for repression.
iii. Northerners – again, especially the US – may take sides in local ethnic/religious conflicts and help repress one group. There, the

---

[13] 'Explaining Modern Ethnic Cleansing: the Macro-Level', in Montserrat Guibernau and John Hutchinson, eds., *Nationalism*, Cambridge 2000.

discontented have an even clearer sense of who is the enemy, and weapons of the weak enable them to attack.

US policy in the Middle East exacerbates local conflicts on all three grounds. The US provides massive military aid to authoritarian states like Egypt and Saudi Arabia. If it provides much less economic aid, its hand is seen in every IMF or World Bank restructuring, and it appears to prop up Israel, seen as the oppressor of the Palestinians. All these helped generate the extreme response of September 11.

But I stress: this is the extreme case. No other zone of turmoil sees all three interventions, and some see virtually none. Sub-Saharan Africa mainly suffers from ostracism, not imperialism. Its regimes and factions receive little help from the US. Its political power relations are not so much polarized as fragmented. Its resistance is turned inward, in civil wars and wars against neighbours; not directed against Northern imperialism. Conflicts in the African Great Lakes Region, for example, may reach desperate levels, involving genocide in Rwanda, large-scale killing in Burundi and the Congo, and serious economic regress in the whole region. But we blame the UN Security Council for not intervening in Rwanda. The region offers little threat to the rest of the world. The North stills gets copper, diamonds and rare metals from the Congo, though local and regional warlords and smugglers now take a bigger cut of the profits. Political globalization may include a number of such 'black holes', but these do not suck in the rest of the globe. Black holes differ from anti-imperialist struggles; and these differences are exacerbated by ideology.

IV. Ideological Power

Ideological power is wielded by those who can offer meaning systems and mobilizing rituals that make plausible sense of the world in which we live. It generates powerful social movements and normative communities. If globalization was proceeding toward a single, seamless world society, it would generate a single cultural community, converging in norms, meaning systems and ritual practices. Indeed, some degree of convergence into a single Northern global culture is occurring in the realms of consumerism, liberal humanism and the English language all emphasized by advocates of seamless globalization.

The most successful globalization is of cheap, cultural-consumption goods – fashion, drinks, fast food, popular music, TV and movies, The cheapest products are available to almost all the world's population, including low-income teenagers, generating a global youth culture. Though adapted to local conditions, this is also subverting many local norms and rituals that govern such important social spheres as marriage practices, parent-child relations and the submission of women. This is probably the most important integrating effect of globalization, since it carries capitalist consumption globally through very cheap products into people's intimate lives. But it tends to produce more homogenization in the micro-sphere of everyday life and style than in macro-areas like politics. Serbian paramilitaries in the Yugoslav wars, sporting leather jackets and sunglasses, declared that they modelled themselves on Rambo or Mad Max. They then engaged in blood-letting against similar Croat and Albanian groups. Consumer capitalist culture does not necessarily produce either war or peace; it can make profits out of either.

The second cultural diffusion is of liberal humanism – through liberal and social-democratic political movements, the United Nations, countless NGOs, and the concept of 'basic human rights'. This often has a decidedly secular and rather American tone, and so is somewhat contested. Many Southern regimes, especially Asian ones, counter that economic subsistence and social security should take priority over liberal conceptions of rights. The 'arrogance' of Western feminism in proposing individualist and labour-market-centred views of women's liberation is also denounced in many places. But this liberal humanism is of broader appeal than either a Northern restructuring capitalism or American military power; and its attraction is likely to grow since it can offer a critique of the exploitation, repression and corruption imposed by Northern and Southern regimes alike. But it is, at present, undercut by Northern imperialism and Southern religious revivals. The US policy of bombing starving Afghans in the name of democracy is hardly likely to increase trust in Northern democracy.

The third cultural diffusion, that of the English language, is even thinner. English is advancing as the medium of public communication in the most modern sectors; but while many use the language to do business, they do not tell jokes or make love in it. Nor do their social movements mobilize in English, either peacefully or in battle.

Against these globalizing ideological currents, we must also set more divisive ones. These increasingly concern ethnicity and religion. Ethno-nationalism and religious resistance movements are surfacing ubiquitously across the South. Ethno-nationalism destabilizes countries, making them less attractive to Northern investors and traders, reinforcing ostracizing imperialism. I argued above that ethno-nationalism intensifies through the global diffusion of democratic aspirations: it is a part of global modernization, not a peripheral reaction against it. Yet it mostly results in ideological fragmentation, as hundreds of ethno-nationalist movements claim their own uniqueness, their own rights against some purely local 'imperialism'. There are six such movements within Indonesia alone. This is the story across most zones of turmoil, offering no threat to the North.

Broader ideologies can offer more global resistance. This was the traditional role of socialism in the South, plausibly interpreting colonial and post-colonial oppression in terms of capitalist imperialism. But socialist influences have been waning. Movements like the Colombian FARC, the Sendero Luminoso of Peru, the Mexican Zapatistas and the Naxalites of India remain quite strong, but they are largely localized. 'Third World Socialism' has become more an ideology of black holes than of global change. It has probably declined most in the Middle East.

Religion and Resistance

Over the course of the post-war period, religious revivals have come to replace many socialist movements as self-proclaimed resistors of imperialism. We have become obsessed in the last few years with Islam, but across South Asia, Hindu, Sikh and Buddhist – and, in Israel, Jewish – 'fundamentalisms' have arisen, as forms of resistance against local, secularized regimes that are identified with domination by the West or North. The revival began in the last days of colonialism, and was aimed mostly at the British, French or Dutch imperialists. Once these powers had gone, the main enemy was the local political elites, who had abandoned the essentially religious nature of the community and embraced 'Western' versions of socialism, liberalism and nationalism. The local struggle remains primary in Sri Lanka and India. But elsewhere, the assertion of American military hegemony, leading Northern ostracizing imperialism, brought in the US as the third element in the 'fundamentalist' perception of struggle: the religious people fighting against local secular elites in the service of American imperialism.

The main thrust of such movements has therefore been within Islam. Samuel Huntington has rightly emphasized the religious 'faultline' emerging between Islam and other religions in a great swath across two continents, Africa and Asia – though he offers little explanation for this.[14] The two main reasons for Islam's preeminence among such movements are not doctrinal but social and historical. First, Muslim movements have long been able to nourish resistance against foreign imperialism. The Ottoman Empire shared with China and Japan the distinction of never having been conquered by the West; while Caucasian Muslim forces have always been the most effective rebels against Russian (and Soviet) imperialism. Even in the inter-war period, after the collapse of the Ottoman Empire, substantial parts of the Islamic world retained some independence from the Western powers.

In the last few decades, however, Muslim and, especially, Arab power has declined, with some states becoming clients of the US and few achieving much for their citizens. In his videotaped statement of October 9, Osama bin Laden declared that, over 80 years – i.e., since the granting of the British mandate – Islam had been 'tasting… humiliation and disgrace, its sons killed and their blood spilled, its sanctities desecrated'. Yet Muslim memories remain of much greater historical strength, independence and resistance. Second, Islam has particularly nourished 'warrior sects', which have conquered Muslim cities and states defined as corrupt and authoritarian to re-establish the 'fundamentals' of Muhammad's teachings. The cycle from warrior tribes to settled city-states, conquered in turn by warrior tribes, was first identified by the Muslim sociologist, Ibn Khaldun, in the fifteenth century. Many point to the Wahhabis as a recent version of such a warrior sect, detecting their hand in September 11. Yet today most Wahhabis have settled down into comfortable domination of the Saudi and other Gulf states – just as Ibn Khaldun would have predicted.

Combat Fundamentalism

Once again, however, a few 'fundamentalists' are now reviving this tradition. The overwhelming majority of them focus their activities locally, attempting to impose the *shari'a*, Islamic law, on their own community. They hate foreign influences in their own region, but remain uninterested in any broader 'imperialism'. Yet some among them additionally emphasize *qital*, 'combat' against the enemies of Islam, within the broader injunction of *jihad*, meaning 'struggle/striving in the name of Allah' (which does not necessarily imply violence). I will call these people 'combat fundamentalists' – those who, materially or ideologically, support armed struggle in the name of Islam. There are also comparable small movements among Hindu nationalists in India – in fact, some are a part of the ruling BJP's broad family of

---

[14] *The Clash of Civilizations and the Remaking of World Orders*, New York 1996.

movements – and Buddhists in Sri Lanka; although Tamil extremists so far remain secular. All manage to find among their holy texts some phrases appearing to endorse such combat; as do Christian 'fundamentalists'. The Islamic movements focus on the Koran's repeated injunctions to resist oppression – 'for oppression is even worse than killing' (2:191) – and to 'fight against them until there is no more oppression and all worship is devoted to Allah alone' (2:193). It is their oppression that allows certain rulers in the Muslim world to be defined as 'no longer Muslims', thus setting aside the normal Koranic injunction against overthrowing a Muslim leader. Clearly, when both Muslim and infidel oppressors seem entwined in a secular and materialist embrace, the resonance of the call to arms is even greater.

Of course, Islam is as varied as Christianity. In the past, there were long periods when Christian aggression far exceeded Muslim; but most Christian states later became secularized – they still fight, but not in the name of God. In contrast, across much (not all) of the Islamic world, the tide has turned against the secularists over the last decades. The main reason for the difference is that, during the period in which Christians have ruled the world, Muslims have felt themselves oppressed – and not without reason. Combat fundamentalism offers an explanation of real social conditions, and a plausible if high-risk strategy for remedying them.

But this also means that combat fundamentalism involves two elements neglected by Huntington. First, it resonates most strongly where Southern poverty meets Northern imperialism. In Islam, this is especially marked in Palestine. Israel is part of the North, backed up by the Northern superpower; while the Palestinians are the quintessential poor and dispossessed Southerners. Chechnya also bears some traces of such a division. Other countries in the Middle East are caught in an economic vise between low growth and population explosion, part of which they attribute to imperialism. In these cases local ethnic-religious solidarities and conflicts are reinforced, and made more globally resonant, by resistance to Northern infidel imperialism. The economic aspects of this conflict lie somewhat concealed: they figure little in fundamentalist discourse, which actually denounces all materialism as foreign. But were Muslim countries to experience economic development and redistribution, who can doubt that combat fundamentalism would be undercut?

Second, conflict also rages within Islam, as it does among Hindus, Sikhs, Buddhists and Christians, ranging fundamentalists against secularists and religious conservatives. But Muslim secularists and conservatives are often backed by the North, especially the US; they can plausibly be attacked both as authoritarian oppressors and as imperialist lackeys. Bin Laden/s short videotaped statement of October 7 referred three times to the oppressed Palestinians and once to the removal of 'the army of infidels' from 'the land of Muhammad' – i.e., of American forces from Saudi Arabia, or perhaps from Arab lands in general. His previous rhetoric had focused much less on the Palestinians, much more on Saudi Arabia. This is partly opportunism, though only in recent years has the combat fundamentalism of Hamas come to rival the secular PLO among the Palestinians, giving him allies in that struggle.

Cosmology of the Weak

Once in power, 'fundamentalist' regimes tend to establish harsh religious dictatorships, whose popular appeal can be difficult to understand. But we should remember that, while operating as opposition movements, they are populists, calling on the people as a whole to rebel, first against colonial rulers and then post-colonial ones. They advocate what the Pakistani Madoudi, the leading Sunni fundamentalist theorist, termed 'theo-democracy' – not a theocratic state but self-rule by the *umma*, the whole religious community, in obedience to the dictates of the Koran. As populists they can mobilize resistance to authoritarian and corrupt Muslim states, whether secular ones like Egypt, or conservative religious ones like Saudi Arabia. Their pressure then forces some regimes toward more authoritarianism (as in Algeria or Turkey). And it has persuaded more Muslims to define their enemies in religious terms (as in Israel, Kashmir or Chechnya), giving the local struggle a more global cosmology. According to bin Laden, the struggle ranges the Muslim against the infidel. To transplant Judeo-Christian symbols of heroism, it is also David against Goliath, and Robin Hood, stealing from the rich to give to the poor – not to mention Good against Evil, God against Satan. This is an appeal of some resonance, especially able to recruit young, educated dissidents in authoritarian states and young refugees, displaced by conflicts right across the Muslim world – neither having much future amid stagnating economies. These two groups are not very large, rarely generating the resources to seize power. But their capacity to disrupt and re-group is considerable, since they enjoy the sympathy of much of the poor and the middle class of the Muslim world.

It seems safe to predict that military power alone will not eliminate the threat of combat fundamentalism in any of these religions. Indeed, it will probably only fuel the fires, since it seems to confirm the cosmology offered by the combat fundamentalists. Discontented educated leaders and refugee 'foot-soldiers' are the core constituencies that will provide generations of young men, and perhaps young women, willing to risk and even sacrifice their lives for such a powerful vision. As we have seen repeatedly – in car- and body-bombs; in the assassinations of secular leaders, like the three Gandhis or Sadat; and, most terribly, on September 11 – among these will be a very few who will deliberately choose combat suicide. This has become the ultimate weapon of the weak against the powerful of this earth. Whether they will ever be able to repeat a coup as horrific as that of September 11 depends on finding equally unexpected technical means. But Northerners in general now have to fear that possibility.

Sources of Bitterness

This present, terrible confrontation was by no means inevitable. That combat fundamentalism's enemy is the US resulted mainly from the unintended consequences of three American policies – toward Communism, Israel and oil. Through the 1950s the US was mostly a force for decolonization and development in the Islamic world – although the CIA-sponsored coup against Mossadegh in Iran in 1953 already revealed a tendency to label dissidents as Communists that alienated many Muslims. The US then backed the increasingly corrupt and authoritarian secular regime of the Shah of Iran. The enemy was perceived as Communism, not a religious fundamentalism whose revolutionary powers proved a genuine surprise, to the US and everyone else. Second, the legacy of the Holocaust, the political influence of American Jews and earlier Cold War alignments were the main pressures leading the US to back Israel and its dispossession of Palestinians, even when the state of

Israel moved to become less victim than oppressor. The US continues to provide military and economic aid to Israel, even though nowadays it also deplores further Israeli settlements in Palestine. In the televised foreign-policy debate between the two US Presidential candidates in 2000, both Gore and Bush mentioned only one 'ally' by name – Israel. In seeking a solution to this cancerous dispute, the US also backed – mainly militarily – states who had become moderates vis-à-vis Israel, like Egypt and Jordan. Such military aid helped these regimes repress internal dissent, while the smaller amounts of economic aid could not outweigh the effects of ostracizing imperialism to achieve either economic development or domestic legitimacy. Third, oil interests have led the US to install a large number of armed forces in Saudi Arabia and the Gulf sheikdoms, and to attack Iraq as a rogue state – as it did not attack Indonesia's annexation of East Timor. Similar geopolitical contingencies have also affected the combat fundamentalists, who now exploit the Palestinian issue, despite their deep antipathy to the secular PLO, but refrain from attacking hated regimes, such as Iraq or Libya, that happen to oppose the US.

Such convoluted geopolitics only reinforce the conclusion that the war between Islamic 'fundamentalism' and Northern imperialism is not a necessary one. It could be undercut by three measures: a more evenhanded approach to Israel/Palestine; less military and more economic aid to Arab regimes; and a more progressive international development strategy, with redistribution and growth its twin goals. This would reduce both major conflicts: that between Muslim and Christian worlds, and that between fundamentalists and others within the Muslim world. Such a geopolitical re-orientation is a tall order, but even partial success might be enough. There would still be Islamic fundamentalists, but they would gain fewer recruits; and their conception of *jihad* would be less combative and less directed against the US.

Ideological globalization is uneven and unpredictable. It includes thin layers of a potentially common transnational culture; ideological fragmentation across parts of the South; and broader confrontations across major religious faultlines, in which a few combat fundamentalists are exploiting new weapons of the weak. Tamils, Buddhists, Hindus and Christians, plus some peasant revolutionaries, can all provide a few suicide bombers, the ultimate form of ideological military morale, able to counterbalance great disparities in conventional weapons. But only Islamic combat fundamentalists hurl themselves, not only against their local secular enemies, but also against the North and its 'Great Satan', the United States. This particular struggle is now generating a tidal wave of threat and combat across large slices of the world, which could be stemmed by changed polices from the North. But amid such complexity, who knows whence the next tidal wave will come?

Globalization is a real process; but it is multiple and contradictory. The globe is divided into more and more nation-states; it is driven by a paradoxical 'ostracizing imperialist' fault-line between North and South; and there are also potentially dangerous great-power rivalries. Most of these divisions generate not armed combat but tensions that can usually be resolved by peaceful negotiation between converging nation-states. Nonetheless, where ideological power stiffens resistance and 'weapons of the weak' level the battlefield, some divisions do result in intense conflict. These new ideologies and weapons are as much a part of globalization as the dollar, the internet or Coca-Cola. Some of these trends destabilize only at a local or regional level, generating 'zones of turmoil' in the world; some of these degenerate into 'black holes' of desperate violence and instability, ostracized by the rest of the world. But one faultline cuts a more systematically disintegrating swathe across continents: the resistance to secular imperialism launched by 'combat fundamentalism' will remain until its appeal is diminished by cutting away the sense of exploitation on which it thrives.

These mixed patterns mean that we are not, at present, moving toward a singular global society. Northern capitalism unevenly but simultaneously integrates, dominates and ostracizes across the world. The power of the military hegemon, the United States, is somewhat undercut by its own increasing pacification; by its reliance on supposedly safe but decidedly blunt long – range weaponry; and by new weapons of the weak. Political power remains primarily wielded by nation – states, though some of these are more stable than others. Ideological power expresses all these diverse relations. Such complexity is not new to human societies. Globalization merely changes its scale. Like its predecessors, globalization blends different sources of social power, peace and war, order and chaos; it will do so for a good while longer yet.

INSTANTIATION$_2$

THE DEVELOPMENT QUESTION

INTRODUCTION

Deciding whether intervention is obligatory, as we investigated in Instantiation$_1$, does little toward establishing exactly how that intervention should take place. Even if obligations or simple desires to aid are taken as a given, much work is left to be done. Specifically, answering the question "what form should that aid take (and who decides)?" is both complex and contested.

In the age of globalization, aid is often packaged in the form of economic development – helping people help themselves. Programs meant to spur economic growth and diminish poverty and suffering have been proposed and implemented at a global scale. International institutions like the World Bank and the International Monetary Fund have been established in the years following World War II to facilitate forms of economic develop\ment. Thus, perhaps one answer to the preponderance of suffering in the world is to model that world on particular ideals like free trade, liberalization, and privatization. Perhaps a truly one-world phenomenon can emerge through the unification of economic interdependence.

Of course, as the protests in Seattle, New York City, and Genoa have demonstrated, not everyone believes that the path of globalization is smooth and desirable. For those that seek to problematize globalization as a simple solution to global misery and inequality, there are many possible points of emphasis. Some claims emphasize the effects of globalization, which are viewed as multiple and contradictory, often creating as much ill as good (see Instantiation$_1$, esp. Mann). Various groups acknowledge the good intentions of development advocates, but point out the potential and real negative impacts such unsolicited assistance can have on those being developed, including the natural environment (see also Instantiation$_3$). Another complaint lodged against development in the model of current globalization involves the reduction of human interaction to the level of economic exchange. A number of people argue that the current deleterious effects result from particular mistakes in application of this form of development; others contend that the flaws are systematic and unfixable. Development, it appears, is far from an easy answer.

Part of the issue at hand regards how development is defined, and who defines it. Development is a loaded word, often associated with progress. Whether qualities like efficiency and economic growth are necessarily progressive, however, is not self-evident. Many different definitions of development can be reached, and as such many people would like to see these different forms being promoted or at least offered. In the current context, many peoples who may genuinely benefit from some sort of aid are told, rather than asked, what they need. The underlying question is whether there is one best way, or many good ways, to develop.

The essays in this section provide differing critiques of the current mode of development, focusing on either particular impacts on groups being aided or on more systematic problems with the manner in which development takes place.

Vandana Shiva is director of the Research Foundation for Science Technology and Natural Resource Policy in India. Her essay, "Development, Ecology and Women," explores the impact of development on women and nature in India (and by extension, many other parts of the world). Dealing with the issue of visibility, Shiva argues that the current development discourse, which seeks to enlarge the Gross National Product as a sign of progress, renders the value of women and the environment invisible. That is, people who seek to develop regions of the world under the western model fail to take into account the value that women and nature provide because such value is unpaid. Because of this failure, the impact on women and ecological resources is especially negative and severe – turning relative poverty into real poverty. Thus, Shiva claims, such measures should be labeled "maldevelopment." She concludes that alternative visions of development should be entertained that give voice to the desires and needs of those typically excluded from decision making. Development is necessary, but what counts as development is the real issue.

The second essay in this section, by Theresa Ebert, professor of English at the University at Albany, looks at a more particular impact of development. Retaining the focus on women, this excerpt from *Excess-ive Bodies* examines the effects of baby formula on the social and familial bonds in developing countries. Ebert argues that the marketing of baby formula to mothers in these countries mostly benefits corporations interested in selling these products, and even runs counter to received wisdom in developed countries about the benefits of breast milk. The question of development for whom surfaces again.

Herman Daly is Senior Research Scholar, School of Public Affairs, University of Maryland. In "Globalization and its Discontents," Daly argues for a stronger form of internationalization rather than globalization. Seeing the former as filtered through strong nation states and the latter as an expression of commonality through economy, he contends that development through globalization will serve to concentrate and legitimate corporate power at the expense of the natural environment and humankind in general. Identifying four trends in globalization which are touted as necessary for development – including competition, mergers, increased interdependence, and the establishment of strong intellectual property rights – Daly asserts that all tend to guarantee advantage to only a few at the cost of the many.

David Harvey, a professor of geography at Johns Hopkins University, wants to make a case for the importance of the Communist Manifesto in understanding the current economic situation. In "An Anniversary of Consequence and Relevance," he argues that a Marxist analysis of globalization can lend insights into the path that current modes of development are taking. Read along with the original Manifesto (see website), Harvey's piece places a more systematic spin on the processes shaping the globe. Whether one finds Marx's conclusions credible or not, Harvey contends that Marx provides valuable tools for understanding the goals and impacts of globalization.

Luis Camacho is professor of philosophy at the University of Costa Rica. In his essay, "Consumption as a Theme in the North-South Dialogue," he analyzes how modes of consumption impact relations, and understanding, between industrialized and developing countries. Camacho explains that dreams of the North, in the form of malls and commercial products, are present in the South but remain pure dreams for the majority of the populace. On the other hand, the nightmares of the South, found in slums and homelessness, make their way North. This dual presence serves to validate the consumptive drives of all involved, by holding out the promise of development to some and showing the effects of its lack to others. In the end, Camacho argues, too much emphasis on overpopulation in the South and overconsumption in the North mask important interconnections in both regions, where the problem of survival is both real and shared.

In the last essay in this section, Claude Ake, professor of political science in Nigeria (deceased, 1996), argues that emphasis on the idea of human rights is detrimental to a truly African notion of progress. In "The African Context of Human Rights," he asserts that too often, Western concepts of cultural development center around abstract rights while ignoring socioeconomic realities. Securing a stable ability to fulfill certain basic physical needs (food and shelter) may be more pressing than securing freedom of the press. Emphasis on the latter, however, validates certain forms of development over others, despite the needs of the people that are purportedly being helped. This emphasis serves a conservative function in reinforcing the privilege of those who can legitimately enjoy those kinds of rights, while implying no obligation to ensure all can reach that level of self-sufficiency. There is also the cross-cultural difference of attending to individual rights versus more communal responsibilities. In the end, Ake contends that what really should be emphasized is the economic and social empowerment of all people, so that human rights as currently constituted take on more universal meaning.

Development for whom? Defined how? By whom? These are vital questions to consider when pondering the ethical form development might take.

Development, Ecology and Women
Vandana Shiva

Development as a New Project of Western Patriarchy

'Development' was to have been a post-colonial project, a choice for accepting a model of progress in which the entire world remade itself on the model of the colonising modern west, without having to undergo the subjugation and exploitation that colonialism entailed. The assumption was that western style progress was possible for all. Development, as the improved well-being of all, was thus equated with the westernisation of economic categories-of needs, of productivity, of growth. Concepts and categories about economic development and natural resource utilisation that had emerged in the specific context of industrialisation and capitalist growth in a centre of colonial power, were raised to the level of universal assumptions and applicability in the entirely different context of basic needs satisfaction for the people of the newly independent Third World countries. Yet, as Rosa Luxemberg has pointed out, early industrial development in western Europe necessitated the permanent occupation of the colonies by the colonial powers and the destruction of the local 'natural economy'.[1] According to her, colonialism is a constant necessary condition for capitalist growth: without colonies, capital accumulation would grind to a halt. 'Development' as capital accumulation and the commercialisation of the economy for the generation of 'surplus' and profits thus involved the reproduction not merely of a particular form of creation of wealth, but also of the associated creation of poverty and dispossession. A replication of economic development based on commercialisation of resource use for commodity production in the newly independent countries created the internal colonies.[2] Development was thus reduced to a continuation of the process of colonisation; it became an extension of the project of wealth creation in modern western patriarchy's economic vision, which was based on the exploitation or exclusion of women (of the west and non-west), on the exploitation and degradation of nature, and on the exploitation and erosion of other cultures. 'Development' could not but entail destruction for women, nature and subjugated cultures, which is why, throughout the Third World, women, peasants and tribals are struggling for liberation from 'development' just as they earlier struggled for liberation from colonialism.

The UN Decade for Women was based on the assumption that the improvement of women's economic position would automatically flow from an

---

[1] Rosa Luxemberg, *The Accumulation of Capital*, London: Routledge and Kegan Paul, 1951.
[2] An elaboration of how 'development' transfers resources from the poor to the well-endowed is contained in J. Bandyopadhyay and V. Shiva, 'Political Economy of Technological Polarisations,' in *Economic and Political Weekly*, Vol. XVIII. 1982, pp. 1827-32; and J. Bandyopadhyay and V. Shiva, 'Political Economy of Ecology Movements', in *Economic and Political Week*, forthcoming.

expansion and diffusion of the development process. Yet, by the end of the Decade, it was becoming clear that development itself was the problem. Insufficient and inadequate 'participation' in 'development' was not the cause for women's increasing underdevelopment; it was rather, their enforced but asymmetric participation in it, by which they bore the costs but were excluded from the benefits, that was responsible. Development exclusivity and dispossession aggravated and deepened the colonial processes of ecological degradation and the loss of political control over nature's sustenance base. Economic growth was a new colonialism, draining resources away from those who needed them most. The discontinuity lay in the fact that it was now new national elites, not colonial powers, that masterminded the exploitation on grounds of 'national interest' and growing GNPs, and it was accomplished with more powerful technologies of appropriation and destruction.

Ester Boserup[3] has documented how women's impoverishment increased during colonial rule; those rulers who had spent a few centuries in subjugating and crippling their own women into de-skilled, de-intellectualised appendages, disfavoured the women of the colonies on matters of access to land, technology and employment. The economic and political processes of colonial under-development bore the clear mark of modern western patriarchy, and while large numbers of women and men were impoverished by these processes, women tended to lose more. The privatisation of land for revenue generation displaced women more critically, eroding their traditional land use rights. The expansion of cash crops undermined food production, and women were often left with meager resources to feed and care for children, the aged and the infirm, when men migrated or were conscripted into forced labor by the colonisers. As a collective document by women activists, organisers and researchers stated at the end of the UN Decade for Women, 'The almost uniform conclusion of the Decade's research is that with a few exceptions, women's relative access to economic resources, incomes and employment has worsened, their burden of work has increased, and their relative and even absolute health, nutritional and educational status has declined.'[4]

The displacement of women from productive activity by the expansion of development was rooted largely in the manner in which development projects appropriated or destroyed the natural resource base for the production of sustenance and survival. It destroyed women's productivity both by removing land, water and forests from their management and control, as well as through the ecological destruction of soil, water and vegetation systems so that nature's productivity and renewability were impaired. While gender subordination and patriarchy are the oldest of oppressions, they have taken on new and more violent forms through the project of development. Patriarchal categories which understand destruction as 'production' and regeneration of life as 'passivity' have generated a crisis of survival. Passivity, as an assumed category of the 'nature' of nature and of women, denies the ,activity of nature and life. Fragmentation and uniformity as assumed categories of progress and development destroy the living forces which arise from relationships within the 'web of life' and the diversity in the elements and patterns of these relationships.

---

[3] Ester Boserup, *Womens Role in Economic Development*, London: Allen and Unwin, 1970.
[4] Dawn, *Development Crisis and Alternative Visions: Third World Women's Perspectives*, Bergen: Christian Michelsen Institute, 1975, p. 25.

The economic biases and values against nature, women and indigenous peoples are captured in this typical analysis of the 'unproductiveness' of traditional natural societies:

> Production is achieved through human and animal, rather than mechanical, power. Most agriculture is unproductive; human or animal manure may be used but chemical fertilizers and pesticides are unknown. ...For the masses, these conditions mean poverty.[5]

The assumptions are evident: nature is unproductive; organic agriculture based on nature's cycles of renewability spells poverty; women and tribal and peasant societies embedded in nature are similarly unproductive, not because it has been demonstrated that in cooperation they produce *less* goods and services for needs, but because it is assumed that 'production' takes place only when mediated by technologies for commodity production, even when such technologies destroy life. A stable and clean river is not a productive resource in this view: it needs to be 'developed' with dams in order to become so. Women, sharing the river as a commons to satisfy the water needs of their families and society are not involved in productive labor: when substituted by the engineering man, water management and water use become productive activities. Natural forests remain unproductive till they are developed into monoculture plantations of commercial species. Development thus, is equivalent to maldevelopment, a development bereft of the feminine, the conservation, the ecological principle. The neglect of nature's work in renewing herself, and women's work in producing sustenance in the form of basic, vital needs is an essential part of the paradigm of maldevelopment, which sees all work that does not produce profits and capital as non or unproductive work. As Maria Mies[6] has pointed out, this concept of surplus has a patriarchal bias because, from the point of view of nature and women, it is not based on material surplus produced *over and above* the requirements of the community: it is stolen and appropriated through violent modes from nature (who needs a share of her produce to reproduce herself) and from women (who need a share of nature's produce to produce sustenance and ensure survival).

From the perspective of Third World women, productivity is a measure of producing life and sustenance; that this kind of productivity has been rendered invisible does not reduce its centrality to survival - it merely reflects the domination of modern patriarchal economic categories which see only profits, not life.

Maldevelopment as the Death of the Feminine Principle

In this analysis, maldevelopment becomes a new source of male-female inequality. 'Modernisation' has been associated with the introduction of new forms of dominance. Alice Schlegel[7] has shown that under conditions of subsistence, the interdependence and complementarity of the separate male and female domains of

---

[5] M. George Foster, *Traditional Societies and Technological Change*, Delhi: Allied Publishers, 1973.
[6] Maria Mies, *Patriarchy and Accumulation on a World Scale*, London: Zed Books, 1986.
[7] Alice Schlegel (ed.), *Sexual Stratification: A Cross-Cultural Study*, New York: Columbia University Press, 1977.

work is the characteristic mode, based on diversity, not inequality. Maldevelopment militates against this equality in diversity, and superimposes the ideologically constructed category of western technological man as a uniform measure of the worth of classes, cultures, and genders. Dominant modes of perception based on reductionism, duality and linearity are unable to cope with equality in diversity, with forms and activities that are significant and valid, even though different. The reductionist mind superimposes the roles and forms of power of western male-oriented concepts on women, all non-western peoples and even on nature, rendering all three 'deficient', and in need of 'development'. Diversity, and unity and harmony in diversity, become epistemologically unattainable in the context of maldevelopment, which then becomes synonymous with women's underdevelopment (increasing sexist domination), and nature's depletion (deepening ecological crises). Commodities have grown, but nature has shrunk. The poverty crisis of the South arises from the growing scarcity of water, food, fodder and fuel, associated with increasing maldevelopment and eco- logical destruction. This poverty crisis touches women most severely, first because they are the poorest among the poor, and then because, with nature, they are the primary sustainers of society.

Maldevelopment is the violation of the integrity of organic, interconnected and interdependent systems, that sets in motion a process of exploitation, inequality, injustice and violence. It is blind to the fact that a recognition of nature's harmony and action to maintain it are preconditions for distributive justice. This is why Mahatma Gandhi said, 'There is enough in the world for everyone's need, but not for some people's greed.'

Maldevelopment is maldevelopment in thought and action. In practice, this fragmented, reductionist, dualist perspective violates the integrity and harmony of man in nature, and the harmony between men and women. It ruptures the co-operative unity of masculine and feminine, and places man, shorn of the feminine principle, above nature and women, and separated from both. The violence to nature as symptomatised by the ecological crisis, and the violence to women, as symptomatised by their subjugation and exploitation arise from this subjugation of the feminine principle. I want to argue that what is currently called development is essentially maldevelopment, based on the introduction or accentuation of the domination of man over nature and women. In it, both are viewed as the 'other', the passive non-self. Activity, productivity, creativity which were associated with the feminine principle are expropriated as qualities of nature and women, and transformed into the exclusive qualities of man. Nature and women are turned into passive objects, to be used and exploited for the uncontrolled and uncontrollable desires of alienated man. From being the creators and sustainers of life, nature and women are reduced to being 'resources' in the fragmented, anti- life model of maldevelopment.

Two Kinds of Growth, Two Kinds of Productivity

Maldevelopment is usually called 'economic growth', measured by the Gross National Product. Porritt, a leading ecologist has this to say of GNP:

> *Gross* National Product -for once a word is being used correctly. Even conventional economists admit that the hey-day of GNP is over, for the

simple reason that as a measure of progress, it's more or less useless. GNP measures the lot, all the goods and services produced in the money economy. Many of these goods and services are not beneficial to people, but rather a measure of just how much is going wrong; increased spending on crime, on pollution, on the many human casualties of our society, increased spending because of waste or planned obsolescence, increased spending because of growing bureaucracies: it's all counted.[8]

The problem with GNP is that it measures some costs as benefits (e.g. pollution control) and fails to measure other costs completely. Among these hidden costs are the new burdens created by ecological devastation, costs that are invariably heavier for women, both in the North and South. It is hardly surprising, therefore, that as GNP rises, it does not necessarily mean that either wealth or welfare increase proportionately. I would argue that GNP is becoming, increasingly, a measure of how real wealth - the wealth of nature and that produced by women for sustaining life - is rapidly decreasing. When commodity production as the prime economic activity is introduced as development, it destroys the potential of nature and women to produce life and goods and services for basic needs. More commodities and more cash mean less life - in nature (through ecological destruction) and in society (through denial of basic needs). Women are devalued first, because their work cooperates with nature's processes, and second, because work which satisfies needs and ensures sustenance is devalued in general. Precisely because more growth in maldevelopment has meant less sustenance of life and life-support systems, it is now imperative to recover the feminine principle as the basis for development which conserves and is ecological. Feminism as ecology, and ecology as the revival of Prakriti, the source of all life, become the decentred powers of political and economic transformation and restructuring.

This involves, first, a recognition that categories of 'productivity' and growth which have been taken to be positive, progressive and universal are, in reality, restricted patriarchal categories. When viewed from the point of view of nature's productivity and growth, and women's production of sustenance, they are found to be ecologically destructive and a source of gender inequality. It is no accident that the modern, efficient and productive technologies created within the context of growth in market economic terms are associated with heavy ecological costs, borne largely by women. The resource and energy intensive production processes they give rise to demand ever increasing resource withdrawals from the ecosystem. These withdrawals disrupt essential ecological processes and convert renewable resources into non-renewable ones. A forest for example, provides inexhaustible supplies of diverse biomass over time if its capital stock is maintained and it is harvested on a sustained yield basis. The heavy and uncontrolled demand for industrial and commercial wood, however, requires the continuous overfelling of trees which exceeds the regenerative capacity of the forest ecosystem, and eventually converts the forests into non-renewable resources. Women's work in the collection of water, fodder and fuel is thus rendered more energy and time-consuming. (In Garhwal, for example, I have seen women who originally collected fodder and fuel in a few hours,

---

[8] Jonathan Porritt, *Seeing Green*, Oxford: Blackwell, 1984.

now travelling long distances by truck to collect grass and leaves in a task that might take up to two days.) Sometimes the damage to nature's intrinsic regenerative capacity is impaired not by over-exploitation of a particular resource but, indirectly, by damage caused to other related natural resources through ecological processes. Thus the excessive overfelling of trees in the catchment areas of streams and rivers destroys not only forest resources, but also renewable supplies of water, through hydrological destabilisation. Resource intensive industries disrupt essential ecological processes not only by their excessive demands for raw material, but by their pollution of air and water and soil. Often such destruction is caused by the resource demands of non-vital industrial products. In spite of severe ecological crises, this paradigm continues to operate because for the North and for the elites of the South, resources continue to be available, even now. The lack of recognition of nature's processes for survival *as factors in the process of economic development* shrouds the political issues arising from resource transfer and resource destruction, and creates an ideological weapon for increased control over natural resources in the conventionally employed notion of productivity. All other costs of the economic process consequently become invisible. The forces which contribute to the increased 'productivity' of a modern farmer or factory worker for instance, come from the increased use of natural resources. Lovins has described this as the amount of 'slave' labor presently at work in the world.[9] According to him each person on earth, on an average, possesses the equivalent of about 50 slaves, each working a 40 hour week. Man's global energy conversion from all sources (wood, fossil fuel, hydroelectric power, nuclear) is currently approximately 8×10^{12} watts. This is more than 20 times the energy content of the food necessary to feed the present world population at the FAO standard diet of 3,600 cal/day. The 'productivity' of the western male compared to women or Third World peasants is not intrinsically superior; it is based on inequalities in the distribution of this 'slave' labor. The average-inhabitant of the USA for example has 250 times more 'slaves' than the average Nigerian. 'If Americans were short of 249 of those 250 'slaves', one wonders how efficient they would prove themselves to be?'

It is these resource and energy intensive processes of production which divert resources away from survival, and hence from women. What patriarchy sees as productive work, is, in ecological terms highly destructive production. The second law of thermodynamics predicts that resource intensive and resource wasteful economic development must become a threat to the survival of the human species in the long run. Political struggles based on ecology in industrially advanced countries are rooted in this conflict between *long term survival options and short term over-production and over-consumption*. Political struggles of women, peasants and tribals based on ecology in countries like India are far more acute and urgent since they are rooted in the *immediate threat to the options for survival* for the vast majority of the people, *posed by resource intensive and resource wasteful economic growth* for the benefit of a minority.

In the market economy, the organising principle for natural resource use is the maximisation of profits and capital accumulation. Nature and human needs are managed through market mechanisms. Demands for natural resources are restricted to those demands registering on the market; the ideology of development is in large

---

[9] A. Lovins, cited in S.R. Eyre, *The Real Wealth of Nations*, London: Edward Arnold, 1978.

part based on a vision of bringing all natural resources into the market economy for commodity production. When these resources are already being used by nature to maintain her production of renewable resources and by women for sustenance and livelihood, their diversion to the market economy generates a scarcity condition for ecological stability and creates new forms of poverty for women.

Two Kinds of Poverty

In a book entitled *Poverty: the Wealth of the People*[10] an African writer draws a distinction between poverty as subsistence, and misery as deprivation. It is useful to separate a cultural conception of subsistence living as poverty from the material experience of poverty that is a result of dispossession and deprivation. Culturally perceived poverty need not be real material poverty: subsistence economies which satisfy basic needs through self-provisioning are not poor in the sense of being deprived. Yet the ideology of development declares them so because they do not participate overwhelmingly in the market economy, and do not consume commodities produced for and distributed through the market *even though they might be satisfying those needs through self-provisioning mechanisms.* People are perceived as poor if they eat millets (grown by women) rather than commercially produced and distributed processed foods sold by global agri-business. They are seen as poor if they live in self-built housing made from natural material like bamboo and mud rather than in cement houses. They are seen as poor if they wear handmade garments of natural fibre rather than synthetics. Subsistence, as culturally perceived poverty, does not necessarily imply a low physical quality of life. On the contrary, millets are nutritionally far superior to processed foods, houses built with local materials are far superior, being better adapted to the local climate and ecology, natural fibres are preferable to man-made fibres in most cases, and certainly more affordable. This cultural perception of prudent subsistence living as poverty has provided the legitimisation for the development process as a poverty removal project. As a culturally biased project it destroys wholesome and sustainable lifestyles and creates real material poverty, or misery, by the denial of survival needs themselves, through the diversion of resources to resource intensive commodity production. Cash crop production and food processing take land and water resources away from sustenance needs, and exclude increasingly large numbers of people from their entitlements to food. 'The inexorable processes of agriculture-industrialisation and internationalisation are probably responsible for more hungry people than either cruel or unusual whims of nature. There are several reasons why the high-technology-export-crop model increases hunger. Scarce land, credit, water and technology are pre-empted for the export market. Most hungry people are not affected by the market at all. ...The profits flow to corporations that have no interest in feeding hungry people without money.'[11]

The Ethiopian famine is in part an example of the creation of real poverty by development aimed at removing culturally perceived poverty. The displacement of nomadic Mars from their traditional pastureland in Awash Valley by commercial agriculture (financed by foreign companies) led to their struggle for survival in the

---

[10] R. Bahro, *From Red to Green*, London: Verso, 1984, p. 211.
[11] R.J. Barnet, *The Lean Years*, London: Abacus, 1981, p. 171.

fragile uplands which degraded the ecosystem and led to the starvation of cattle and the nomads.[12] The market economy conflicted with the survival economy in the Valley, thus creating a conflict between the survival economy and nature's economy in the uplands. At no point has the global marketing of agricultural commodities been assessed against the background of the new conditions of scarcity and poverty that it has induced. This new poverty moreover, is no longer cultural and relative: it is absolute, threatening the very survival of millions on this planet. The economic system based on the patriarchal concept of productivity was created for the very specific historical and political phenomenon of colonialism. In it, the input for which efficiency of use had to be maximised in the production centres of Europe, was industrial labor. For colonial interest therefore, it was rational to improve the labour resource *even at the cost of wasteful use of nature's wealth*. This rationalisation has, however, been illegitimately universalised to all contexts and interest groups and, on the plea of increasing productivity, labour reducing technologies have been introduced in situations where labor is abundant and cheap, and resource demanding technologies have been introduced where resources are scarce and already fully utilised for the production of sustenance. Traditional economies with a stable ecology have shared with industrially advanced affluent economies the ability to use natural resources to satisfy basic vital needs. The former differ from the latter in two essential ways: first, the same needs are satisfied in industrial societies through longer technological chains requiring higher energy and resource inputs and excluding large numbers without purchasing power; and second, affluence generates new and artificial needs requiring the increased production of industrial goods and services. Traditional economies are not advanced in the matter of non-vital needs satisfaction, but as far as the satisfaction of basic and vital needs is concerned, they are often what Marshall Sahlins has called 'the original affluent society'; The needs of the Amazonian tribes are more than satisfied' by the rich rainforest; their poverty begins with its destruction. The story is the same for the Gonds of Bastar in India or the Penans of Sarawak in Malaysia.

Thus are economies based on indigenous technologies viewed as 'backward' and 'unproductive'. Poverty, as the denial of basic needs, is not necessarily associated with the existence of traditional technologies, and its removal is not necessarily an outcome of the growth of modern ones. On the contrary, the destruction of ecologically sound traditional technologies, often created and used by women, along with the destruction of their material base is generally believed to be responsible for the 'feminisation' of poverty in societies which have had to bear the costs of resource destruction.

The contemporary poverty of the Afar nomad is not rooted in the inadequacies of traditional nomadic life, but in the *diversion of the productive pastureland of the Awash Valley*. The erosion of the resource base for survival is increasingly being caused by the demand for resources by the market economy, dominated by global forces. The creation of inequality through economic activity which is ecologically disruptive arises in two ways: first, inequalities in the distribution of privileges make for unequal access to natural resources- these include privileges of both a political

---

[12] U.P. Koehn, 'African Approaches to Environmental Stress: A Focus on Ethiopia and Nigeria' in R.N. Barrett (ed.), *International Dimensions of the Environmental Crisis*, Boulder, CO: Westview, 1982, pp. 253-89.

and economic nature. Second, resource intensive production processes have access to subsidised raw material on which a substantial number of people, especially from the less privileged economic groups, depend for their survival. The consumption of such industrial raw material is determined purely by market forces, and not by considerations of the social or ecological requirements placed on them. The costs of resource destruction are externalised and unequally divided among various economic groups in society, but are borne largely by women and those who satisfy their basic material needs directly from nature, simply because they have no purchasing power to register their demands on the goods and services provided by the modern production system. Gustavo Esteva has called development a permanent war waged by its promoters and suffered by its victims.[13]

The paradox and crisis of development arises from the mistaken identification of culturally perceived poverty with real material poverty, and the mistaken identification of the growth of commodity production as better satisfaction of basic needs. In actual fact, there is less water, less fertile soil, less genetic wealth as a result of the development process. Since these natural resources are the basis of nature's economy and women's survival economy, their scarcity is impoverishing women and marginalised peoples in an unprecedented manner. Their new impoverishment lies in the fact that resources which supported their survival were absorbed into the market economy while they themselves were excluded and displaced by it.

The old assumption that with the development process the availability of goods and services will automatically be increased and poverty will be removed, is now under serious challenge from women's ecology movements in the Third World, even while it continues to guide development thinking in centres of patriarchal power. Survival is based on the assumption of the sanctity of life; maldevelopment is based on the assumption of the sacredness of 'development'. Gustavo Esteva asserts that the sacredness of development has to be refuted because it threatens survival itself. 'My people are tired of development', he says, 'they just want to live.'[14]

The recovery of the feminine principle allows a transcendance and transformation of these patriarchal foundations of maldevelopment. It allows a redefinition of growth and productivity as categories linked to the production, not the destruction, of life. It is thus simultaneously an ecological and a feminist political project which legitimises the way of knowing and being that create wealth by enhancing life and diversity, and which deligitimises the knowledge and practise of a culture of death as the basis for capital accumulation.

---

[13] Gustavo Esteva, 'Regenerating People's Space,' in S.N. Medlowitz and R.B.J. Walker, *Towards a Just World Peace: Perspectives From Social Movements*, London: Butterworths and Committee for a Just World Peace, 1987.
[14] G. Esteva, Remarks made at a Conference of the Society for International Development, Rome, 1985.

EXCERPT FROM EXCESS-IVE BODIES
THERESA EBERT

Currently, lactation and breast feeding are being revalorized in advanced capitalist countries, especially among the middle and upper middle classes. A recent spate of scientific studies and media stories in the West, for example, are proclaiming the nutritive and health benefits of mother's milk and breast feeding. One report declares in its headline "Mother's Milk Found to Be Potent Cocktail of Hormones" and goes on to claim that "The latest studies of peptides and other hormones in milk offer yet another reason why, whenever possible, mothers should breast-feed their babies" (Natalie Angier, *New York Times*, 24 May 1994, C1, C10). The power of breast milk "is so evident that in Sweden, at least, 'it's considered unethical to feed infants anything but human milk,' said Dr. Neuringer. After the birth of a child, a woman is given plenty of time off from work to nurse an infant. For those who cannot nurse, there are banks of human milk, just as there are rivers of life" (C10).

Significantly, these studies validating breast feeding – and the corporeality of the subjectivity of mother – are appearing at a tithe of considerable unemployment and corporate attempts to downsize the labor force – including managerial and professional positions – in the United States. It is also a time of a corporate and small-business backlash against providing social and medical benefits to workers, as reflected in the increasing employment of temporary workers without benefits, and in business opposition to universal health coverage. The renewed valorization of breast feeding and maternal care, the celebration of the "intensities of flows" of the body in such texts as Grosz's *Volatile Bodies*, are complicit with the political status quo in that they contribute to current efforts to recall women from the labor force and are linked to other regressive efforts to reinstate domesticity, the traditional family and the regime of the social as composed of specific bodies.

In the neocolonies of global late capitalism, however, the ideological construction of such corporeal practices as lactation is often quite otherwise. The political economy of breast feeding is very different, for example, in the Alto do Cruzerio of northeastern Brazil, a poverty-stricken region of "cloying sugarcane fields amid hunger and disease" (Scheper-Hughes, *Death* 31). Nancy Scheper-Hughes examines the "'political economy' of emotions" in this region, focusing particularly on "culture and scarcity, both material and psychological, and their effects . . . on 'maternal thinking'" (*Death* 341, 15; see also "Death"). Northeastern Brazil, according to Scheper-Hughes, accounts for a quarter of "all childhood deaths in Latin America," deaths in large part attributable to the "precipitous" decline in breast feeding, from 96 percent in 1940 to less than 40 percent in 1975; it has since decreased further (*Death* 316-17). Scheper-Hughes argues that "a fairly direct and positive correlation exists between infant survival and breast feeding," yet "each generation of mothers in the Third World is less likely than the previous one to breast-feed offspring. This is especially true of rural migrants to urban areas, where wage labor and the work available to women are incompatible with breast-feeding"

(*Death* 316-17). As one Alto woman described her work situation, "Her patrons would never allow her to enter their homes if they even suspected that she were lactating. '*Da nojo* (It's disgusting)!' Irene exclaimed... One could not run the risk of suddenly having a wet blouse, she explained, in the middle of serving the family meal: 'It would make everyone lose their appetites'" (323). The choice to bottle-feed, for most women engaged in wage labor, is not a matter of desire but of economic necessity; it is really no choice at all.

Moreover, the transition from semisubsistence peasants to wage laborers has also involved the extensive commodification of food, including infant food (323). The United States played a leading role in the commodification of baby's milk, dumping its excess dairy production in the Third World in the 1960s in the form of free powdered milk under the auspices of Food for Peace. It thereby fostered, as Scheper-Hughes notes, "a powdered-milk dependency in the populace, which Nestle and other companies took advantage of when the free distribution ended in the 1970s" (322) in order to mass-distribute their infant formulas, which have become one of the primary food commodities – and by far the most expensive – among the Alto families, "consuming about a fifth of their weekly income" (318).

The changing relations of production in northeastern Brazil, which have brought not only wage labor and the commodification of food but also extreme hunger and scarcity, have produced radical changes in the ideological representation and meaning of lactation and baby's milk. Many women of the Alto, nearly all of whom suffer from acute hunger and overwork, perceive their breast milk as bad, according to Scheper-Hughes, and "described it as salty, watery, bitter, sour, infected, dirty, and diseased... as 'unfit' for the infant" (326). For these women, "human milk appeared blue, thin, watery" in contrast, to the rich, strong infant formulas they offer to their "often small, puny infants" in the form of a "heavy, thickened 'pap'" (325). Moreover, the provision of infant formula plays a crucial role in demonstrating paternity and establishing the child's legitimacy. With the transition to wage labor, marriages have become "less formal, more consensual, and more transitory in the shantytown . . . [T]he definition of a 'husband' . . . is a functional one. A husband is the man who provides food for his woman and her children," especially the expensive infant formula (323). It is, in short, the father, rather than the mother, who has now become the source, the provider of baby's milk. As the father arrives "bearing the prestigious purple-labeled can of Nestle... a woman will say to her newborn... 'Clap your hands, little one; your milk has arrived!'" (323-24). In northeastern Brazil, then, women are called to stop breast feeding, and this is validated by "commonsense" knowledge and economic practices. In the United States, however, women are recalled from the labor force to breast-feed, and science provides the evidence for the naturalness of such practices. Both Brazilian and U.S. women are provided with knowledges that affirm the practices that capitalism needs.

Contrary to the scientific as well as the romanticized claims for breast feeding among the middle and upper middle classes, especially in overdeveloped countries, breast milk is neither self-evidently perceived as healthy nor universally recognized as a "river of life." Nor are women's bodies universally experienced as the source of creative, sensuous unity and redemption from alienating relations of production as claimed by feminist-standpoint epistemologists and ludic writers like Irigaray and, in her more recent ludic work, Iris Young. For instance, Young, following Irigaray, writes that in a

> woman-centered experience of breasts... the breasted body becomes blurry, mushy, indefinite, multiple... A metaphysics generated from feminine desire, Luce Irigaray suggests, might conceptualize being as fluid rather than as solid substances, or things... Fluids surge and move, and a metaphysic that thinks being as fluid would tend to privilege the living, moving, pulsing over the inert dead matter of the Cartesian World view. (*Throwing* 192-93)

Such valorized meanings are, to a large degree, the privilege of prosperity: they are class specific. For the superexploited women living at the "foot of the cane" – at the foot of global capitalism – the body is where "the contradictions of the social order are reproduced in the disquieting image of needy, hungry, dependent women who must withhold their milk from their babies to keep from being devoured by them first" (Scheper-Hughes, *Death* 326). It is not women's bodies that redeem alienating production but rather the exploitative relations of production in capitalism that produce women's alienation from their own bodies.

References

Scheper-Hughes, N. 1992. *Death Without Weeping: Everyday Violence in Northeastern Brazil*. Berkeley: University of California Press.

Young, I. M. 1990. *Throwing Like a Girl and Other Essays in Feminist Philosophy and Social Theory*. Bloomington: Indiana University Press.

GLOBALIZATION AND ITS DISCONTENTS[1]
HERMAN E. DALY

The newspapers and TV say that if you oppose globalization you must be an "isolationist" or even worse a "xenophobe". Nonsense. The relevant alternative to globalization is internationalization, which is neither isolationist nor xenophobic. The media don't know the difference, so let us define the terms clearly:

Internationalization refers to the increasing importance of relations between nations: international trade, international treaties, alliances, protocols, etc. The basic unit of community and policy remains the nation, even as relations among nations, and among individuals in different nations, become increasingly necessary and important.

Globalization refers to global economic integration of many formerly national economies into one global economy, by free trade, especially by free capital mobility, and also, as a distant but increasingly important third, by easy or uncontrolled migration. Globalization is the effective erasure of national boundaries for economic purposes. National boundaries become totally porous with respect to goods and capital, and increasingly porous with respect to people, viewed in this context as cheap labor, or in some cases cheap human capital.

In sum, globalization is the economic integration of the globe. But exactly what is "integration"? The word derives from "integer", meaning one, complete, or whole. Integration means much more than "interdependence"--it is the act of combining separate albeit related units into a single whole. Since there can be only one whole, only one unity with reference to which parts are integrated, it follows that global economic integration logically implies national economic disintegration -- parts are torn out of their national context (dis-integrated), in order to be re-integrated into the new whole, the globalized economy. As the saying goes, to make an omelette you have to break some eggs. The disintegration of the national egg is necessary to integrate the global omelette. This obvious logic, as well as the cost of disintegration, is frequently met with denial.

Denial aside, all that I have just said was expressed with admirable clarity, honesty, and brevity by Renato Ruggiero, former director-general of WTO: *"We are no longer writing the rules of interaction among separate national economies. We are writing the constitution of a single global economy."* This is a clear affirmation of globalization and rejection of internationalization as just defined. It is also a radical subversion of the Bretton Woods Charter. Internationalization is what the Bretton Woods Institutions were designed for, not globalization.

After the April disruption of its meetings in Washington DC, the World Bank sponsored an internet discussion on globalization. The closest they came to offering a definition of the subject under discussion was the following: *"the most*

---

[1] Based in part on a discussion given at The Aspen Institute's 50th Anniversary Conference, "Globalization and the Human Condition", 8/20/00, Aspen, CO.

common core sense of economic globalization.....surely refers to the observation that in recent years a quickly rising share of economic activity in the world seems to be taking place between people who live in different countries (rather than in the same country)". Mr. Wolfensohn, president of the World Bank, told the audience at the Aspen Institute's Conference, that *"Globalization is a practical methodology for empowering the poor to improve their lives."* That is a wish, not a definition. It also flies in the face of the real consequences of global economic integration. One could only sympathize with the demonstrators from the Mountain Folks for Peace and Justice who were protesting Mr. Wolfensohn's speech some fifty yards from the Aspen music tent. The reaction of the Aspen elite was to repeat the title of Mr. Wolfensohn's speech, "Making Globalization Work for the Poor", and then ask in grieved tones, "How could anyone demonstrate against that?" Well, maybe they were fed up with the vacuity and doublespeak of official World Bank pronouncements, as well as with an elitist celebration of globalization in their valley-- one that excluded labor and NGOs, and thought it appropriate to serve bottled water imported all the way from Fiji to the participants.

The World Bank's definition conflates globalization and internationalization as defined above. Consequently, much of the long internet discussion was beside the point--assuming the point was not simply to encourage the venting of anger into cyberspace rather than into the streets of Seattle, Washington D.C., or Prague. The missed point, in the form of a question, is, should these increasing transactions between people living in different countries take place across national boundaries that are economically significant, or within an integrated world in which national boundaries are economically meaningless? Do we really want to give up national monetary and fiscal policy, as well as the minimum wage?

Does economic integration imply or entail political and cultural integration? I suspect it does over the long run, but I honestly do not know which would be worse--an economically integrated world with, or without, political integration. Everyone recognizes the desirability of community for the world as a whole-- but we have two very different models of world community: (1) a federated community of real national communities (internationalization), versus (2) a cosmopolitan direct membership in a single abstract global community (globalization).

If the IMF-WB-WTO are no longer serving the interests of their member nations as per their charter, then whose interests are they serving? The interests of the integrated "global economy" we are told. But what concrete reality lies behind that grand abstraction? Not real individual workers, peasants, or small businessmen, but rather giant fictitious individuals, the transnational corporations.

Consider a few consequences of globalization, of the erasure of national boundaries for economic purposes. Briefly, they include: (1) standards-lowering competition to externalize social and environmental costs to achieve a competitive advantage--the race to the bottom in terms of both efficiency in cost accounting and equity in income distribution; (2) increased tolerance of mergers and monopoly power in domestic markets in order to be big enough to compete internationally; (3) more intense national specialization according to the dictates of competitive advantage with the consequence of reducing the range of choice of ways to earn a livelihood, and increasing dependence on other countries. Free trade negates the freedom not to trade; (4) world-wide enforcement of a muddled and self-serving doctrine of "trade-related intellectual property rights" in direct contradiction to Thomas Jefferson's dictum that "knowledge is the common property of mankind".

Let us look at each of these in a bit more detail.

1. Globalization undercuts the ability of nations to internalize environmental and social costs into prices. Economic integration under free market conditions promotes standards-lowering competition (a race to the bottom). The country that does the poorest job of internalizing all social and environmental costs of production into its prices gets a competitive advantage in international trade. More of world production shifts to countries that do the poorest job of counting costs-- a sure recipe for reducing the efficiency of global production. As uncounted, externalized costs increase, the positive correlation between GDP growth and welfare disappears, or even becomes negative.

Another dimension of the race to the bottom is the increasing inequality in the distribution of income in high-wage countries, such as the US, fostered by globalization. In the US there has been an implicit social contract established to ameliorate industrial strife between labor and capital. Specifically, a just distribution of income between labor and capital has been taken to be one that is more equal within the US than it is for the world as a whole. Global integration of markets necessarily abrogates that social contract. US wages will fall drastically because labor is relatively much more abundant globally than nationally. It also means that returns to capital in the US will increase because capital is relatively more scarce globally than nationally. Theoretically, one might argue that wages would be bid up in the rest of the world. But the relative numbers make this a bit like saying that, theoretically, when I jump off a ladder gravity not only pulls me to the earth, but also moves the earth towards me.

Free trade, and by extension globalization, is often defended by appeal to comparative advantage. The logic of comparative advantage assumes that factors of production, especially capital, are immobile between nations. Only products are traded. With capital mobility now the major defining feature of globalization we have left the world of <u>comparative</u> advantage and entered a regime of <u>absolute</u> advantage which guarantees gains from trade <u>to the world as a whole</u>, but does not guarantee that each nation will share in those gains, as was the case under comparative advantage. Global gains under absolute advantage are theoretically greater than under comparative advantage, but there is no reason to expect these gains to be shared by all trading partners. Mutual gain could be restored under absolute advantage by redistributing some of the global gains from trade. But I have never heard that idea discussed by globalization advocates. Often they appeal, quite illogically, to the doctrine of comparative advantage as a guarantee of mutual benefit, conveniently forgetting that the logic of comparative advantage requires immobile capital, and that capital is not immobile. Indeed, some even argue for free capital mobility by extension of the comparative advantage argument-- if free trade in goods is mutually beneficial then why not also have free trade in capital? However, one cannot use the conclusion of an argument to abolish one of the premises upon which the argument is based!

2. Fostering global competitive advantage is used as an excuse for tolerance of corporate mergers and monopoly in national markets (we now depend on international trade as a substitute for domestic trust busting to maintain competition). It is ironic that this is done in name of deregulation and the free market. Chicago School economist and Nobel laureate Ronald Coase in his classic article on the Theory of the Firm, said "—*Firms are islands of central planning in a sea of*

market relationships". The islands of central planning become larger and larger relative to the remaining sea of market relationships as a result of merger. More and more resources are allocated by within-firm central planning, and less by between-firm market relationships. And this is hailed as a victory for markets! It is no such thing. It is a victory for corporations relative to national governments which are no longer strong enough to regulate corporate capital and maintain competitive markets in the public interest. Of the 100 largest economic organizations 52 are corporations and 48 are nations. One-third of the commerce that crosses national boundaries does not cross a corporate boundary, i.e. is an intra-firm non market transfer. The distribution of income within these centrally planned corporations has become much more concentrated. The ratio of salary of the Chief Executive Officer to the average employee has passed 400 on its way to infinity--what else can we expect when the chief central planners set their own salaries!

3. Free trade and free capital mobility increase pressures for specialization according to competitive (absolute) advantage. Therefore the range of choice of ways to earn a livelihood become greatly narrowed. In Uruguay, for example, everyone would have to be either a shepherd or a cowboy in conformity with the dictates of competitive advantage in the global market. Everything else should be imported in exchange for beef, mutton, wool, and leather. Any Uruguayan who wants to play in a symphony orchestra or be an airline pilot should emigrate.

Most people derive as much satisfaction from how they earn their income as from how they spend it. Narrowing that range of choice is a welfare loss uncounted by trade theorists. Globalization assumes either that emigration and immigration are costless, or that narrowing the range of occupational choice within a nation is costless. Both assumptions are false.

While the range of choice in earning one's income is ignored by trade theorists, the range of choice in spending one's income receives exaggerated emphasis. For example, the US imports Danish butter cookies and Denmark imports US butter cookies. (And, as I learned at the Aspen conference, Colorado imports drinking water from Fiji, and perhaps Fiji imports rocky mountain water from Colorado.) The cookies cross each other somewhere over the North Atlantic. Although the gains from trading such similar commodities cannot be great, trade theorists insist that the welfare of cookie connoisseurs is increased by expanding the range of consumer choice to the limit.

Perhaps, but could not those gains be had more cheaply by simply trading recipes? One might think so, but recipes (trade related intellectual property rights) are the one thing that free traders really want to protect.

4. Of all things knowledge is that which should be most freely shared, because in sharing it is multiplied rather than divided. Yet, our trade theorists have rejected Thomas Jefferson's dictum that *"Knowledge is the common property of mankind"* in exchange for a muddled doctrine of "trade related intellectual property rights" by which they are willing to grant private corporations monopoly ownership of the very basis of life itself--patents to seeds (including the patent-protecting, life-denying terminator gene) and to knowledge of basic genetic structures.

The argument offered to support this grab is that, unless we provide the economic incentive of monopoly ownership for a significant period of time, little new knowledge and innovation will be forthcoming. Yet, as far as I know, James Watson and Francis Crick, who discovered the structure of DNA, do not share in the patent royalties reaped by the second rate gene-jockeys who are profiting from their monumental discovery. Nor of course did Gregor Mendel get any royalties--but then he was a monk motivated by mere curiosity about how Creation works!

Once knowledge exists, its proper allocative price is the marginal opportunity cost of sharing it, which is close to zero, since nothing is lost by sharing it. Yes, of course you do lose the monopoly on the knowledge, but then economists have traditionally argued that monopoly is inefficient as well as unjust because it creates an artificial scarcity of the monopolized item.

Of course the cost of production of new knowledge is not zero, even though the cost of sharing it is. This allows biotech corporations claim that they deserve a fifteen or twenty year monopoly for the expenses they incur in research and development. Of course they deserve a profit on their efforts, but not on Watson and Crick's contribution without which they could do nothing, nor on the contributions of Gregor Mendel, and all the great scientists of the past who made the fundamental discoveries. As economist Joseph Schumpeter emphasized, being the first with an innovation already gives one a temporary monopoly. In his view these recurring temporary monopolies were the source of profit in a competitive economy whose theoretical tendency is to compete profits down to zero.

Believe it or not, most important discoveries were made without the benefit of granting monopoly ownership of the knowledge to the discoverer. Can you imagine such a thing--scientists motivated by the pure love and excitement of discovery, and content with a university salary that puts them only in the top ten percent, but not the top one percent, of income recipients!!

As the great Swiss economist, Sismondi, argued long ago, not all new knowledge is a benefit to mankind. We need a social and ethical filter to select out the beneficial knowledge. Motivating the search for knowledge by the purpose of benefiting mankind rather than by securing monopoly profit, provides a better filter.

This is not to say that we should abolish all intellectual property rights--that would create more problems than it would solve. But we should certainly begin restricting the domain and length of patent monopolies rather than increasing them so rapidly and recklessly. And we should become much more willing to share knowledge. Shared knowledge increases the productivity of all labor, capital, and resources. Further, international development aid should consist far more of freely-shared knowledge, and far less of foreign investment and interest-bearing loans.

Let me close with my favorite quote from John Maynard Keynes, one of the founders of the recently subverted Bretton Woods Institutions:

"I sympathize therefore, with those who would minimize, rather than those who would maximize, economic entanglement between nations. Ideas, knowledge, art, hospitality, travel – these are the things which should of their nature be international. But let goods be homespun whenever it is reasonably and conveniently possible; and, above all, let finance be primarily national."

AN ANNIVERSARY OF CONSEQUENCE AND RELEVANCE[1]
DAVID HARVEY

The *Communist Manifesto* is one hundred and fifty years old. Those words that Marx and Engels penned back in 1847-48 are worth rereading. The *Manifesto* is an extraordinary document, full of insights, rich in meanings, and bursting with political passions and possibilities. In it Marx and Engels sought to give tangible shape and form to the 'spectre' of communism that then haunted Europe.

Much has changed since those revolutionary days. Fortunately, the *Manifesto* freely acknowledges the contingency of its own making. "The practical application of the principles", wrote Marx and Engels (1952 edition, page 8) in the 1872 preface to the German edition, "will depend, as the *Manifesto* itself states everywhere and at all times, on the historical conditions for the time being existing".

But although there are passages where the *Manifesto* appears quaint, outdated or downright objectionable to those who cling to socialist sentiments in these equally troubling but by no means revolutionary times, there is so much that comes through with such force and clarity that it is quite literally stunning to contemplate the contemporary relevance of this text.

Consider, for example, some of those familiar passages that will strike at the core of contemporary alienations and sensibilities. The bourgeoisie, say Marx and Engels:

> "has left remaining no other nexus between man and man than naked self-interest, than callous 'cash payment'.... It has resolved personal worth into exchange value, and in place of the numberless indefeasible chartered Freedoms, has set up that single unconscionable freedom – Free Trade.... The bourgeoisie has stripped of its halo every occupation hitherto honoured and looked up to with reverent awe. It has converted the physician, the lawyer, the priest, the poet, the man of science, into its paid wage laborers..." (page 44).

> "The bourgeoisie cannot exist without constantly revolutionising the instruments of production, and thereby the relations of production, and with them the whole relations of society... Constant revolutionising of production uninterrupted disturbance of all social

---

[1] *An* extended analysis of some of the themes in this essay can be found in L Panitch and C Leys (Eds.) 1998 *The Communist Manifesto Now* a special issue of *Socialist Register* (Merlin Press, Rendlesham, Suffolk). This issue of the *Socialist Register* has several important articles relating to the *Manifesto* and concludes with a republication of the original text.
"Guest Editorial: An Anniversary of Consequence and Relevance" from *Environment and Planning D: Society and Space*, Vol 16, pages 379-385 by D. Harvey. Copyright © 1998. Reprinted by permission of Pion Ltd, London.

> conditions, everlasting uncertainty and agitation distinguish the bourgeois epoch from all earlier ones. All fixed, fast-frozen relations, with their train of ancient and venerable prejudices and opinions, are swept away, all new formed ones become antiquated before they can ossify. All that is solid melts into air, all that is holy is profaned ..." (pages 45-46).

The rhetorical power of such passages, the certitude of enunciation, the acute combination of admiration and horror for the immense powers unleashed under capitalism [later compared, in one of those most striking of Faustian metaphors, to a "sorcerer, who is no longer able to control the powers of the nether world whom he has called up by his spells" (page 49)] is impressive indeed.

We also read of the inevitability of the crises that periodically shake society to its very foundations, crises of creative destruction that are characterized by the 'absurdity' of overproduction and of famine in the midst of abundance, of spiralling inequalities and of massing technological changes that completely transform the surface of the earth and our relation to nature at the same time as they produce unemployment, disinvestments, and destruction of ways of life that even the bourgeoisie holds dear:

> "And how does the bourgeoisie get over these crises? On the one hand by enforced destruction of a mass of productive forces; on the other by the conquest of new markets and by the more thorough exploitation of the old ones. That is to say, by paving the way for more extensive and more destructive crises, and by diminishing the means whereby crises are prevented" (page 50).

The perceptive geographer will immediately detect the specifically spatial and geographical dimension to this argument And indeed a closer inspection of the *Manifesto* reveals it to contain a very distinctive polemic as to the role of geographical transformations, of 'spatial fixes' and of uneven geographical development in the long history of capitalist accumulation. This geographical dimension to the *Manifesto* deserves excavation.

To begin with, the rise of the bourgeoisie in Europe connects to its global activities and strategies. The bourgeoisie effectively circumnavigated land-based feudal powers and converted the state (with it military, organizational. and fiscal powers) into the executive of its own ambitions (page 44). Once in power, it pursued its revolutionary mission in part via geographical transformations. Internally, rapid urbanization brought the towns to rule over the country, reducing the peasantry to a subaltern class. Urbanization concentrated productive forces as well as labor powers in space, transforming scattered populations and decentralized systems of properly rights into massive concentrations of political and economic power And then:

> "The need for a constantly expanding market chases the bourgeoisie over the whole surface of the globe. It must settle everywhere, establish connexions everywhere.... The bourgeoisie has through its exploitation of the world market given a cosmopolitan character to production and consumption in every country.... All old established

national industries have been destroyed or are daily being destroyed. They are dislodged by new industries, whose introduction becomes a life and death question for all civilized nations, by industries that no longer work up indigenous raw material, but raw material drawn from the remotest zones; industries whose produces are consumed, not only at home, but in every quarter of the globe. In place of the old wants, satisfied by the production of the country, we find new wants, requiring for their satisfaction the products of distant lands and climes. In place of the old local and national seclusion and self-sufficiency, we have intercourse in every direction, universal interdependence of nations. And as in material, so also in intellectual production. The intellectual creations of individual nations became common property. National one-sidedness and narrow-mindedness become more and more impossible, and from the numerous national and local literatures, there arises a world literature..." (pages 46-47).

Through thus process of what we now call 'globalization', the bourgeoisie:

"compels all nations on pain of extinction, to adopt the bourgeois mode of production: it compels them to introduce what n calls civilization into their midst, i.e. to become bourgeois themselves. In one word, it creates a world after its own image" (page 47).

The theme of the globalizing and 'civilizing' mission' of the bourgeoisie is here enunciated (albeit with a touch of irony). The effect is to construct an ever-widening and deepening geographical base for the contradictions of capitalism and socialist revolution. Class struggle becomes global and workers of all countries have no option except to unite.

But there are problems with this account. They, too, deserve an airing.

1. The division of the world into 'civilized' and 'barbarian' nations is anachronistic if not downright objectionable even if it can be excused as typical of the times. The center-periphery model of capital accumulation which accompanies it is at best a gross oversimplification and at worst misleading (see Blaut, 1977; 1993). It makes it appear as if capital originated in one place (England or Europe) and then diffused outwards to encompass the rest of the world. Although this did occur, such an account is inconsistent with what happened in Japan after the Meiji restoration or what is happening today as countries such as South Korea and China engage in primitive accumulation and insert their labor powers and products into global markets.

The geography of capital accumulation deserves a far more elaborate treatment than the diffusionist sketch provided in the *Manifesto*. Geographical contingency has had a lot of play within capitalist world history. Furthermore, the geographical dispersal of bourgeois power has geopolitical implications for class struggle. In 1858 Marx (cited in Meszaros, 1995, page xii) worried that:

"For us the difficult question is this: the revolution on the Continent is imminent and its character will be at once socialist: will it not be

> *necessarily crushed* in this *little corner of the world*, since on a much larger terrain the development of bourgeois society is still in the *ascendant*."

It is chastening to reflect upon the number of socialist revolutions around the world that have been geographically encircled and crushed by an ascendant bourgeois power.

2. The *Manifesto* quite correctly highlights the importance of reducing spatial barriers through innovations and investments in transport and communications. "The annihilation of space through time", as Marx later dubbed it, emphasizes the relativity of space relations and locational advantages, thus making comparative advantage in trade a highly dynamic rather than stable affair. Spatial tracks of commodity flows have to be mapped in relation to flows of capital, labor power, military advantage, technology transfers, information news, and the like. In this regard, the *Manifesto* was not wrong as much as under-elaborated upon and under-appreciated for its prescient insights.

3. One of the biggest absences in the *Manifesto* is its lack of attention to territorial organization. If, for example, the state is an "executive arm of the bourgeoisie" then the state must he territorially defined, organized, and administered. The 19th century was the great period of territorial definitions (with most of the world's boundaries being established between 1870 and 1925 by colonial powers). But state formation and consolidation entail more than territorial definition and it has proven a long drawn out and often unstable affair (particularly, for example, in Africa). Only after 1945 did decolonization push state formation worldwide a bit closer to the highly simplified model that the *Manifesto* envisages. Yet in a curious way the *Manifesto* is far more prescient in this regard too than many might care to admit. For is it not now the case that the state almost everywhere and at all levels is far more the 'executive committee' of capital than ever before in human history?

4. The *Manifesto* also remains silent on the question of money and finance. There are two ways to approach this question. World money can be viewed as a universal representation of value to which territories relate (through then own currencies) and to which capitalists conform. This is a very functionalist view (it is the dominant conception in the contemporary neoclassical ideology of globalization). Or money can be seen as a representation of value that arises out of a dialectical relation between concrete labors undertaken in particular places and times and the universality of values (abstract labor) achieved as commodity exchange becomes a normal social act on the world market. Central banks and other financial institutions mediate this relation. Such institutions are often unstable (and territorially based) suggesting a problematic relation between local conditions and universal values. But these institutions also affect concrete labors and class relations and shape patterns of uneven geographical development through their command over capital assembly and capital flows. This second interpretation is more deeply consistent with the underlying thrust of the *Manifesto* even though it is not explicitly developed.

5. The argument that the bourgeois revolution laid the seedbed for a more united working-class politics through urbanization and industrial concentration is

important. It says that the production of spatial organization is not neutral with respect to class struggle. This is a vital principle no matter how critical we might be with respect to the three-stage model sketched out in the *Manifesto*. These stages are (a) individual struggle begins to collectivize around particular factories, trades, and localities; (b) such struggles come together through geographical concentration of activities and the formation of trades unions that begin to communicate with each other, and (c) class struggle emerges at the national level where the working class confronts and deals with its own national bourgeoisie (pages 53-57).

For much of the 19th century this account captures a common enough path to the development of class struggle. And similar trajectories can be discerned in the 20th century (for example, South Korea). But it is one thing to portray this as a useful descriptive sketch and quite another to argue that these are necessary stages through which class struggle must evolve en route to the construction of socialism. Furthermore, the bourgeoisie may also evolve its own spatial strategies of dispersal, of divide and rule, of geographical disruptions to the rise of concentrated class opposition. The current attack on union power by dispersal and fragmentation of production processes across space (often to countries where working-class organization is weakest) has proven a powerful weapon for the bourgeoisie. The active stimulation of inter-worker competition across space has likewise worked to capitalist advantage to say nothing of the problem of localism and nationalism within working-class movements. In general, the capitalist class has used its superior powers of spatial maneuver to defeat place-bound proletarian/socialist resolutions (compare Marx's 1858 worry cited above). Although none of this is inconsistent with the basic underpinning of the argument in the *Manifesto* it does depart from the actual sketch provided of class-struggle dynamics.

6. Although global working-class unity still stands as the only appropriate response to the globalizing strategies of capital accumulation, the manner of conceptualizing that response deserves critical scrutiny. The *Manifesto* argues that modern industry and wage labor have stripped the workers "of every trace of national character" so that "the working men have no country":

> "National differences and antagonisms between peoples are daily more and more vanishing owing to the development of the bourgeoisie, to freedom of commerce, to the world market. to uniformity in the mode of production and in the conditions of life corresponding thereto.
>
> In proportion as the exploitation of one individual by another is put an end to, the exploitation of one nation by another will also be put an end to. In proportion as the antagonism between classes within the nation vanishes, the hostility of one nation to another will come to an end" (pages 71-72).

This guiding vision is noble enough but there is a lot of wishful thinking here. At best, the *Manifesto* mildly concedes that socialist strategy must "be different in different countries". The task of communists, however, is to bring unity to these different causes, to define the commonalities within the differences, and to make a movement in which workers of the world can unite.

Critical reflection suggests how difficult that task might be. Although there is a sense in which the market and commodifications homogenize, capitalism simultaneously differentiates, sometimes feeding off ancient cultural distinctions, gender relations, ethnic predilections, and religious beliefs. Capital also converts market choice into a mechanism for group differentiation. The result is the implantation of all manner of class, gender, and other social divisions into the geographical landscape of capitalism. Divisions such as those between cities and suburbs, between regions as well as between nations cannot be understood as residuals from some ancient order. They are actively produced through the differentiating powers of capital accumulation and market structures. Place-bound loyalties proliferate and in some respects strengthen rather than disintegrate through the mechanisms of class struggle as well as through the agency of both capital and labor working for themselves (Herod, 1997). But class struggle can then all too easily dissolve into geographically fragmented communitarian interests, easily co-opted by bourgeois powers or exploited by the mechanisms of neoliberal market penetration

The dialectic of commonality and difference, particularly that expressed between space and place, has not worked out in the way that the sketch supplied in the *Manifesto* implied, even if the injunction to unite is indubitably correct. Yet the conditions that demand workers to unite on the world stage through class struggle have in no way disappeared. The World Bank (1995, page 9) estimates that the global labor force doubled in size between 1966 and 1995. It now stands at an estimated 7.5 billion men and women, more than a billion of whom live on a dollar or less a day. In many countries "workers lack representation and work in unhealthy, dangerous, or demeaning conditions. Meanwhile 120 millions or so are unemployed worldwide, and millions more have given up hope of finding work". This condition exists at a time of rapid growth in average levels of productivity (reported also to have doubled since 1965 worldwide) and a rapid growth in world trade fuelled by reductions in costs of movement and a wave of trade liberalization As a result, says the International Labour Office (1996, page 2):

> "The number of workers employed in export- and import-competing industries has grown significantly... . It could be said that labour markets across the world are becoming more interlinked ... Some observers see in these developments the emergence of a global labour market wherein 'the world has become a huge bazaar with nations peddling their workforces in competition against one another, offering the lowest prices for doing business'... . The core apprehension is that intensifying global competition will generate pressures to lower wages and labour standards across the world".

Massive movements into the global labor force have also occurred (for example, in China, Indonesia, and Bangladesh). Cities such as Jakarta. Bangkok, and Bombay have become meccas for formation of a transnational working class – heavily dependent upon women – under conditions of poverty, violence pollution, and fierce repression (see Moody, 1997; Seabrook, 1996).

Inequalities have likewise spiralled out of control. The UN Development Program (1996, page 94) reports that 'between 1960 and 1991 the share of the richest 20% rose from 70% of global income to 85%-while that of the poorest declined from 2.3% to 1.4%. By 1991, "more than 85% of the world's population received only 15% of its income" and "the net worth of the 358 richest people, the dollar billionaires, is equal to the combined income of the poorest 45% of the world population - 2.3 billion people". This polarization of wealth and power is as obscene as it is astounding. Seabrook (1996, pages 103-105) reports:

> "Indonesia, in the name of the free market system, promotes the grossest violations of human rights and undermines the right to subsist of those on whose labour its competitive advantage rests. Many transnationals are subcontracting here: Levi-Strauss, Nike, Reebok. A lot of the subcontractors are Korean-owned. They all tend to low wages and brutal management".

Conditions of labor, the impacts upon laboring bodies, are nothing short of appalling. In the Nike plants in Vietnam, Herbert (1997, page A29) reports:

> "[Mr. Nguyen] found that the treatment of workers by the factory managers in Vietnam (usually Korean or Taiwanese nationals) is a 'constant source of humiliation', that verbal abuse and sexual harassment occur frequently, and that 'corporal punishment' is often used. He found that extreme amounts of forced overtime are imposed on Vietnamese workers. 'It is a common occurrence', Mr. Nguyen wrote in his report, 'to have several workers faint from exhaustion, heat and poor nutrition during their shifts.' We were told that several workers even coughed up blood before fainting."

In *Capital*, Marx (1976, pages 364-365) recounts the story of the milliner, Mary Anne Walkely, twenty years of age, who often worked 30 hours without a break (though revived by occasional supplies of sherry, port, and coffee), until after a particularly hard spell necessitated by preparing "magnificent dresses for the noble ladies invited to the ball in honour of the newly imported Princess of Wales", died, according to the doctor's testimony, "from long hours of work in an overcrowded work-room, and a too small and badly ventilated bedroom".

The comparisons between then and now are terrifying The material conditions that sparked the moral outrage in the *Manifesto* have not gone awry. They are embodied to everything from Nike shoes, Disney products, GAP clothing to Liz Claiborne products (for example, see Ross, 1997).

The setting for the *Manifesto* has not, then, radically changed at its basis. The global proletariat is larger than ever. The imperative for workers of the world to unite is greater than ever. But the barriers to that unity are far more formidable than they were in the Europe of 1848. The work force is now far more geographically dispersed, culturally heterogeneous, ethnically and religiously diverse, racially stratified, and linguistically fragmented. Modes of resistance to capitalism and the definitions of alternatives get radically differentiated. And whereas means of communication and opportunities for translation have greatly improved, this has little meaning for the billion or so workers living on a dollar a day possessed of quite different cultural histories, literatures, and understandings. Differentials (both geographical and social) in wages and social provision within the global working class are increasing. This means that a certain segment of the working class (mostly but not exclusively in the advanced capitalist countries and often possessing by far the most powerful political voice) has a great deal to lose besides it chains. Add to all of this the problematics of changing gender relations in the work force, massive urbanization, severe ecological disruptions, transnational migratory movement, and the terrain for constructing a socialist alternative appears as differentiated and uneven as it is complicated (see Moody, 1997)

The socialist movement has to come to terms with these extraordinary geographical transformations and develop tactics to deal with them. It has to recognize, for example, that it may be a feminized proletariat that stands to be the real agent of socialist transformation in the 21st century. This in no way dilutes the importance of the final rallying cry of the *Manifesto* to unite. But we cannot make either our history or our geography under historical-geographical conditions of our own choosing. A geographical reading of the *Manifesto* emphasizes the nonneutrality of spatial structures and powers in the intricate spatial dynamics of class struggle. It reveals how the bourgeoisie acquired its powers vis-à-vis all preceding modes of production by mobilizing command over space as a productive force peculiar to itself. It shows how the bourgeoisie has continuously enhanced and protected its power by that same mechanism. It therefore follows that, until the working-class movement learns how to confront that bourgeois power to command and produce space, it will always play from a position of weakness rather than of strength. Until that movement comes to terms with the geographical conditions and diversities of its own existence, it will be unable to define, articulate, and struggle for a realistic socialist alternative to capitalist domination.

Geographers have contributed much to this work in the past and continue to do so. But there is plenty more to do. The potential for major contributions is there if only the optimism of the will can overcome that pessimism of the intellect so characteristic of our times. The political passion that Marx and Engels evinced needs to be rekindled. That is the sort of spark that a rereading of the *Manifesto* can provide.

References

Blaut J, 1977, "Where was capitalism born?" in *Radical Geography* Ed. R Peet (Maaroufa Press, Chicago, IL) pp 95-107

Blaut J, 1993 *The Colonizer's Model of the World* (Guilford Press, New York)

Herbert B, 1997, "Brutality in Vietnam" *New York Times* 28 March, page A29

Herod A, 1997, "Labor as an agent of globalization and as a global agent", in *Spaces of Globalization Reasserting the Power of the Local* Ed. K Cox (Guilford Press, New York) pp 167-200

International Labour Office, 1996 *World Employment 1996/97: National Policies in a Global Context* (International Labour Office, Geneva)

Marx K, 1976 *Capital. Volume I* (Viking Press, New York)

Marx K, Engels F, 1952 *Manifesto of the Communist Party* (Progress Publishers, Moscow)

Meszaros I, 1995 *Beyond Capital* (Merlin Press, London)

Moody K, 1997 *Workers in a Lean World* (Verso, London)

Ross A (Ed.), 1997 *No Sweat: Fashion Free Trade and the Rights of Garment Workers* (Verso, London)

Seabrook J, 1996 *In the Cities of the South: Scenes from a Developing World* (Verso, London)

UN Development Program, 1996 *Human Development Report, 1996* (United Nations Publications, New York)

World Bank, 1995 *World Development Report: Workers in an Integrating World* (Oxford University Press, New York)

Consumption as a Theme in the North-South Dialogue
Luis N. Camacho

In connection with consumption, three issues seem especially relevant for the North South dialogue: (a) What is the relation between mass consumption in the North and mass destitution in the South? (b) Is there an ongoing discussion in the South on the influence of patterns of Northern consumption and, if there is one, what can we learn from it? (c) Is there something like a perspective on consumption typical of the South?

Two remarks may be useful before any answer to these questions is attempted:

1. "North" and "South," like "West" and "East" before them, are to be taken as very imprecise designations. In addition to the truism that there is no correspondence between geography and economics (New Zealand is in the geographic South but in the economic North; Russia is in the geographic North but in the economic South), there is another, more important fact: intra-regional differences are almost as great as regional ones. Any characterization of "the South," then, must be understood as an approximation. The only justification for the use of such terms is usual practice and lack of a better terminology.
2. Twenty years ago in Latin America, many theorists tried to explain the underdevelopment of the South by pointing to its extreme dependency on developed countries. One answer to this dependency, they argued, was the creation of a non-consumerist society. Such a society would affirm local traditions against the encroachments of modernization, and insist that development in imitation of the North was not necessarily the best course for the non-industrial world.

This "dependence theory" was undoubtedly one-sided. In stressing Southern dependency, it failed to consider the ways in which relations between developed and underdeveloped regions are reciprocal; and in placing so strong an emphasis on external dependency, it tended to miss the internal contradictions that are characteristic of the developing world. Nonetheless, the theory performed a useful function by asking what an alternative model of development, and thus an alternative society, might look like. It is not difficult to locate examples of wasteful consumption, on the one hand, and severe deprivation, on the other. But is there not a third option, one that would be open to the majority?

Real Options and Unfulfilled Desires

Unfortunately, in the South today, a privileged minority engage in ostentatious consumption while large sectors of the population remain in dire poverty. Patterns of wasteful consumption by elites in the South have come to mimic and exaggerate usual consumption in the North.

The promotion of high consumption in the South is, of course, advantageous to Northern industrial and service companies. It has been argued that consumption patterns in the North are likewise beneficial to Southern countries, since exports sold in the North provide developing countries with badly needed hard currencies. Indeed, one rationale for signing North-South trade agreements like NAFTA is that an increase in international commerce is good business for all concerned.

However, the fact that international trade may lead to more consumption in the South does not necessarily mean that poverty will be reduced. For millions of destitute persons in the world, consumption is primarily something that a few inhabitants of their countries can engage in as a privilege; with respect to the majority, it is denied or severely restricted - either because of rampant unemployment or because of great disparities between wages and prices. From a Southern perspective, then, what is of primary interest is not so much the distinction between good and bad consumption, but the distinction between consumption as a real option for some and as an unfulfilled desire for most.

This approach to the issue gives us a start toward an answer to the third of the initial questions. As seen from the North, consumption is largely associated with the pleasures of shopping, and perhaps with the depression resulting from not finding happiness in what can be bought. As seen from the South, consumption is connected to the ostentation of the rich, daydreams of the poor, and food riots by hungry crowds.

In the South, the external signs of the latest onslaught in the battle for a consumer society are very visible. Huge closed malls take the place of open shopping centers, which in turn had taken the place of small grocery stores; flashy cars substitute for inexpensive public transportation; designer clothes are worn by a small minority. Malls are especially interesting because they represent such a massive disruption of local conditions – both climatological and social. Only a profound distortion of the economy and of social values (together with a modification of political conditions) can explain the existence of these huge air-conditioned buildings in countries where the temperature is comfortable all year round. Within the shopping malls, English is the written language, even in countries where people do not speak it; giant parking lots accommodate dozens of cars, while outside most of the roads are filled with potholes.

The visual impact of these monstrous buildings is likewise remarkable: both their size and style – or lack thereof – amount to a violent imposition on the landscape. To attract customers, they are often built in populated neighborhoods, which instantly become noisy, exhaust-filled places and lose any human intimacy they may have had in the past. Everything inside the malls is geared toward selling and buying; all human transactions are reduced to a single function, and the scale of the whole enterprise seems to foster no behavior other than buying as much as possible. However, the prices tend to be astronomical for a substantial majority of the population, who are reduced thereby to gawking without buying.

The few remaining traditional grocery stores and even the more modern supermarkets which began to sprout in the 1950s, were and continue to be visited by people with specific needs and wants, as well as the money to pay for what they buy. The malls, on the contrary, give rise to a new phenomenon: the reduction of most people to passive onlookers, who dream of the day when twill be able to buy many gadgets whose purpose they do not fully understand. If Homo sapiens becomes homo economicus inside the malls, there by necessity appears what Ivan Illich calls homo miserabilis - persons who are reduced to a marginal condition, not because they cannot perform as an economic agent in another type of society, but because the social conditions are such that they are forced to remain on the periphery of the new economy. It is hard to imagine hordes of visitors getting into supermarkets and grocery stores just to look and to long for the time when they will be able to buy. Yet this has become the everyday occurrence in Third World malls. Physically similar to those in the North, socially they are very different.

The combination of closed spaces, a neat variety of imported goods, and English labels is probably intended to give visitors the impression that they are somewhere in the North and not in a country where shantytowns and beggars are all too common. For many years now, movies, magazines, and television shows have depicted a blissful part of the world where most people live in happiness amid plenty of goods and services; now the malls are just those places. The North has moved South.

The South in the North

But now let us take a look at the other side of the coin. If the presence of Northern consumption patterns in the South is so blatant and disruptive, is there something like a Southern presence in the North? Here I can only offer a highly speculative suggestion. It is likely that for many people in the North, the picture of the destitution in the South operates as a deterrent to change, as a powerful image of what they might become if they do not keep doing what they do every day - working endless hours in jobs they find meaningless or oppressive, jobs whose only justification seems to be the income they provide. So, in the same way that consumption in the North has become a utopian dream for the South, perhaps Southern destitution has become a dreaded possibility for the North. This symmetry is worth exploring. In both cases, an image of life as it is lived elsewhere in the world provides the motive for misguided sentiment or action: a pursuit of the worst features of industrial society for some, a reluctance to change toward more meaningful lives for some others. There is a more tangible symmetry as well: just as showy shops full of consumer goods are the visible part of the North in the South, homeless people and inner-city slums may be taken as the South in the North.

Mechanisms of Survival

The questions I have addressed about the relation between North and South have largely been bypassed, unfortunately, in recent discussions and debates. What we often find in their stead is the complaint that the South has too many people and the North too much consumption. This slogan has become a powerful political weapon because of its simplicity and its facile use of imagery. It has been voiced in important international gatherings and in policy documents. As usually happens with oversimplified visions, it hides a complex web of related problems, while at the same time it becomes either an excuse for avoiding action or a device for the justification of hasty policies. The North is said to consume more than it needs and the South to need more than it consumes. But since there is a North in the South, external problems of unequal relations become internal contradictions.

Expensive consumption has been looked upon with suspicion by many Latin American thinkers as one of the causes of recurrent economic crisis. It is seen as a grave danger for the well-being of society, which is thought to be more secure in a simple life of frugality. One finds such a concern in the 1973 book *The Poverty of Nations*, by the late Costa Rican politician Jose ("Pepe") Figueres (1906-1990), twice President of his country. Figueres saw the consumption of expensive imported goods as an obstacle to the all-important task of creating decent jobs for the population, especially for landless peasants. The cover of his book - a reproduction of a 1936 drawing by a local artist - summarizes this idea. In the drawing, a barefooted peasant, bearing a heavy sack of coffee beans on his back, tries to cross a city street while a luxury car passes by. Coffee exports make it possible to buy the imported car, but this luxury item contributes nothing either to the productive capacity of the country or to the improvement of the conditions of the peasant.

There is one final aspect of the Southern perspective which merits some attention. In spite of all the adverse conditions in which they live, millions of poor people survive with very low levels of consumption. How do they manage to survive? How is it possible to find laughter and joy in poverty? If their mechanisms of survival were well understood in the North, perhaps the fear associated with personal and social change, sometimes perceived as threatening, would abate. Consumption, then, provides a point of entry to a complex set of realities - especially in a world where survival may well be a shared problem.

The African Context of Human Rights
Claude Ake

Nobody can accuse Africa of taking human rights seriously. In a world which sees concern for human rights as a mark of civilized sensitivity, this indifference has given Africa a bad name. It is not unlikely that many consider it symptomatic of the rawness of life which has always been associated with Africa. I am in no position to say with any confidence why Africa has not taken much interest in human rights but I see good reasons why she should not have done so.

Before going into these reasons let us be clear what we are talking about. The idea of human rights is quite simple. It is that human beings have certain rights simply by virtue of being human. These rights are a necessary condition for the good life. Because of their singular importance, individuals are entitled to, indeed, required to claim them and society is enjoined to allow them. Otherwise, the quality of life is seriously compromised.

The idea of human rights, or legal rights in general, presupposes a society which is atomized and individualistic, a society of endemic conflict. It presupposes a society of people conscious of their separateness and their particular interests and anxious to realize them. The legal right is a claim which the individual may make against other members of society, and simultaneously an obligation on the part of society to uphold this claim.

The values implicit in all this are clearly alien to those of our traditional societies. We put less emphasis on the individual and more on the collectivity, we do not allow that the individual has any claims which may override that of the society. We assume harmony, not divergence of interests, competition and conflict; we are more inclined to think of our obligations to other members of our society rather than our claims against them.

The Western notion of human rights stresses rights which are not very interesting in the context of African realities. There is much concern with the right to peaceful assembly, free speech and thought, fair trial, etc. The appeal of these rights is sociologically specific. They appeal to people with a full stomach who can now afford to pursue the more esoteric aspects of self-fulfillment. The vast majority of our people are not in this position. They are facing the struggle for existence in its brutal immediacy. Theirs is a totally consuming struggle. They have little or no time for reflection and hardly any use for free speech. They have little interest in choice for there is no choice in ignorance. There is no freedom for hungry people, or those eternally oppressed by disease. It is no wonder that the idea of human rights has tended to sound hollow in the African context.

The Western notion of human rights lacks concreteness. It ascribes abstract rights to abstract beings. There is not enough concern for the historical conditions in which human rights can actually be realized. As it turns out, only a few people are in a position to exercise the rights which society allows. The few who have the resources to exercise these rights do not need a bill of rights. Their power secures them. The many who do not have the resources to exercise their rights are not helped any by the existence of these rights. Their powerlessness dooms them.

The idea of human rights really came into its own as a tool for opposing democracy. The French Revolution had brought home forcefully to everyone the paradox of democracy, namely that its two central values, liberty and equality, come into conflict at critical points. There is no democracy where there is no liberty for self-expression or choice. At the same time there is no democracy where there is no equality, for inequality reduces human relations to subordination and domination. The French Revolution and Jean Jacques Rousseau revealed rather dramatically the paradoxical relation between these two central values of democracy by leaning heavily towards equality. They gave Europe a taste of what it would be like to take the idea of equality and the correlative idea of popular sovereignty seriously.

Bourgeois Europe was horrified. The idea of a popular sovereign insisting on equality and having unlimited power over every aspect of social life was unacceptable. For such power was a threat to the institution of private property as well as the conditions of accumulation. So they began to emphasize liberty rather than the collectivity. This emphasis was also a way of rejecting democracy in its pure form as popular sovereignty. That was the point of stressing the individual and his rights and holding that certain rights are inalienable. That was the point of holding that the individual could successfully sustain certain claims and certain immunities against the wishes of the sovereign or even the rest of society. It is ironical that all this is conveniently forgotten today and liberal democrats can pass as the veritable defenders of democracy.

Changing Status of Human Rights in Africa

Africa is at last beginning to take interest in human rights. For one thing, the Western conception of human rights has evolved in ways which have made it more relevant to the African experience, although its relevance still remains ambiguous. Because human rights is such an important part of the political ideology of the West, it was bound to register in Africa eventually. Human rights record is beginning to feature in Western decisions of how to relate to the countries and leaders of Africa. Western decisions on this score have been made with such cynical inconsistency that one wonders whether human rights record really matters to them at all. However, our leaders ever so eager to please are obliged to assume that it matters and to adjust their behavior accordingly. Also the authoritarian capitalism of Africa is under some pressure to be more liberal and thereby create political conditions more conducive to capitalist efficiency.

If these are the reasons why Africa is beginning to take more interest in human rights, they are by no means the reason why she ought to do so. The way I see it is that we ought to be interested in human rights because it will help us to combat social forces which threaten to send us back to barbarism. Because it will aid our struggle for the social transformation which we need to survive and to flourish. To appreciate this let us look at the historical conditions of contemporary Africa.

I hope we can all agree that for now, the most salient aspect of these conditions is the crisis. It has been with us for so long we might well talk of the permanent crisis. No one seems to know for sure what its character is but we know its devastating effects only too well. We Africans have never had it so bad. The tragic consequences of our development strategies have finally come home to us. Always oppressed by poverty and deprivation, our lives become harsher still with each passing day as real incomes continue to decline. We watch helplessly while millions of our people are threatened by famine and look pitifully to the rest of the world to feed us. Our social and political institutions are disintegrating under pressure from our flagging morale, our dwindling resources and the intense struggle to control them. What is the problem? I am not sure. But I am convinced that we are not dealing simply or even primarily with an economic phenomenon. There is a political dimension to it which is so critical, it may well be the most decisive factor.

This is the problem of democracy or the problem of political repression. A long time ago our leaders opted for political repression. Having abandoned democracy for repression, our leaders are delinked from our people. Operating in a vacuum, they proclaim their incarnation of the popular will, hear echoes of their own voices, and reassured, pursue with zeal, policies which have nothing to do with the aspirations of our people and which cannot, therefore, mobilize them. As their alienation from the people increases, they rely more and more on force and become even more alienated.

Consequences of the Problem of Democracy

The consequences of this are disastrous. In the first place it means that there is no development. Political repression ensures that the ordinary people of Africa who are the object of development remain silent, so that in the end nobody really speaks for development and it never comes alive practice. Development cannot be achieved by proxy. A people develops itself or not all. And it can develop itself only through its commitment and its energy. That is where democracy comes in. Self-reliance is impossible unless the society is thoroughly democratic, unless the people are the end and not just the means of development. Development occurs, in so far as it amounts to the pursuit of objectives set by people themselves in their own interest and pursued by means of their own resources.

Another consequence of repression is brutalization of our people. Look around you. The willful brutalization of people occurring among us is appalling. Human life is taken lightly, especially if it is that of the underprivileged. All manner of inhuman treatment is meted out for minor offenses and sometimes for no offences at all. Ordinary people are terrorized daily by wanton display of state power and its instruments of violence. Our prison conditions are guaranteed to traumatize. The only consensus we can mobilize is passive conformity arising from fear and resignation. As we continue to stagnate this gets worse.

Yet another disaster threatens us. I am referring to fascism. In all probability this is something which nobody wants. But we might get it anyway because circumstances are moving steadily in that direction. All ingredients of fascism are present now in most parts of Africa: a political class which has failed even by its own standards, which is now acutely conscious of its humiliation and baffled by a world it cannot control; a people who have little if any hope or sense of self-worth yearning for redeemers; a milieu of anomie; a conservative leadership pitted against a rising popular socialism and poised to take cover in defensive radicalism. That is what it takes and it is there in plenty. If Africa succumbs it will be terrible—fascism has always been in all its historical manifestations.

It seems to me that for many African countries the specter of fascism is the most urgent and the most serious danger today. Unless we contain it effectively and within a very short time, then we are in a great deal of trouble.

If this analysis is correct, then our present agenda must be the task of preventing the rise of fascism. To have a chance of succeeding this task requires a broad coalition of radicals, populists, liberals and even humane conservatives. That is, a coalition of all those who value democracy not in the procedural liberal sense but in the concrete socialist sense. This is where the idea of human rights comes in. It is easily the best ideological framework for such a coalition.

An African Conception of Human Rights

We have now seen the relevance of human rights in the African context. But on a level of generality which does not tell us very much and so does not really settle the question of the applicability of the Western concept of human rights. I do not see how we can mobilize the African masses or the intelligentsia against fascism or whatever by accepting uncritically the Western notion of human rights. We have to domesticate it, recreate it in the light of African conditions. Let me indicate very briefly how these conditions redefine the idea of human rights.

First, we have to understand that the idea of legal rights presupposes social atomization and individualism, and a conflict model of society for which legal rights are the necessary mediation. However, in most of Africa, the extent of social atomization is very limited mainly because of the limited penetration of capitalism and commodity relations. Many people are still locked into natural economies and have a sense of belonging to an organic whole, be it a family, a clan, a lineage or an ethnic group. The phenomenon of the legal subject, the largely autonomous individual conceived as a bundle of rights which are asserted against all comers has not really developed much especially outside the urban areas.

These are the conditions which explain the forms of consciousness which we insist on misunderstanding. For instance, ethnic consciousness and ethnic identity. It is the necessary consciousness associated with non-atomized social structures and mechanical solidarity. Ethnic consciousness will be with us as long as these structural features remain, no matter how we condemn it or try to engineer it out of existence.

All this means that abstract legal rights attributed to individuals will not make much sense for most of our people; neither will they be relevant to their consciousness and living conditions. It is necessary to extend the idea of human rights to include collective human rights for corporate social groups such as the family, the lineage, the ethnic group. Our people still think largely in terms of collective rights and express their commitment to it constantly in their behavior. This disposition underlies the zeal for community development and the enormous sacrifices which poor people readily make for it. It underlies the so-called tribalist voting pattern of our people, the willingness of the poor villager to believe that the minister from his village somehow represents his share of the national cake, our traditional land tenure systems, the high incidence of cooperative labor and relations of production in the rural areas. These forms of consciousness remain very important features of our lives. If the idea of human rights is to make any sense at all in the African context, it has to incorporate them in a concept of communal human rights.

For reasons which need not detain us here some of the rights important in the West are of no interest and no value to most Africans. For instance, freedom of speech and freedom of the press do not mean much for a largely illiterate rural community completely absorbed in the daily rigors of the struggle for survival.

African conditions shift the emphasis to a different kind of rights. Rights which can mean something for poor people fighting to survive and burdened by ignorance, poverty and disease, rights which can mean something for women who are cruelly used. Rights which can mean something for the youth whose future we render more improbable every day. If a bill of rights is to make any sense, it must include among others, a right to work and to a living wage, a right to shelter, to health, to education. That is the least we can strive for if we are ever going to have a society which realizes basic human needs.

Finally, in the African context, human rights have to be much more than the political correlate of commodity fetishism which is what they are in the Western tradition. In that tradition the rights are not only abstract, they are also ascribed to abstract persons. The rights are ascribed to the human being from whom all specific determinations have been abstracted: the rights have no content just as individuals who enjoy them have no determination and so do not really exist.

All these problems which usually lurk beneath the surface appear in clear relief when we confront them with empirical reality. Granted, I have the freedom of speech. But where is this freedom, this right? I cannot read, I cannot write. I am too busy trying to survive I have no time to reflect. I am so poor I am constantly at the mercy of others. So where is this right and what is it really? Granted, I have the right to seek public office. That is all very well. But how do I realize this right? I am a full-time public servant who cannot find the time or the necessary resources to put up the organization required to win office. If I take leave from my work, I cannot hold out for more than one month without a salary. I have no money to travel about and meet the voters, even to pay the registration fees for my candidature. If I am not in a position to realize this right, then what is the point of saying that I have it? Do I really have it?

In Africa liberal rights make less sense even as ideological representations. If rights are to be meaningful in the context of a people struggling to stay afloat under adverse economic and political conditions, they have to be concrete. Concrete in the sense that their practical import is visible and relevant to the conditions of existence of the people to whom they apply. And most importantly, concrete in the that they can be realized by their beneficiaries.

To be sure, there are rights which are realizable and there are people in Africa who effectively realize their rights. However the people who are in a position to realize their rights are very few. They are able realize their rights by virtue of their wealth and power. The litmus test for rights is those who need protection. Unfortunately these are precisely the people who are in no position to enjoy rights. Clearly, that will not do in African conditions. People are not going to struggle for formalities and esoteric ideas which will not change lives.

Therefore, a real need arises, namely, to put more emphasis on the realization of human rights. How is this to be? Not in the way we usually approach such matters: by giving more unrealizable rights to the powerless and by begging the powerful to make concessions to them in the name of enlightened self-interest, justice and humanity. That approach will fail us always. Rights, especially those that have any real significance for our lives are usually taken, not given with the cooperation of those in power if possible, but without it if necessary. That is the way it was for other peoples and that is the way it is going to be in Africa.

The realization of rights is best guaranteed by the power of those who enjoy the rights. Following this, what is needed is the empowerment by whatever means, of the common people. This is not a matter of legislation, although legislation could help a little. It is rather a matter of redistributing economic and political power across the board. That means that it is in the final analysis a matter of political mobilization and struggle. And it will be a protracted and bitter struggle because those who are favored by the existing distribution of power will resist heartily.

Conclusion: Human Rights and Social Transformation

It is at this point that the ideal of human rights is fully articulated for it is now that we see its critical dialectical moment. Initially part of the ideological prop of liberal capitalism, the idea of human rights was a conservative force. It was meant to safeguard the interests of the men of property especially against the threatening egalitarianism of popular sovereignty. It was not of course presented as a tool of special interests but a universal value good for humanity. That went down well and it has been able to serve those who propagated it behind this mystification.

But ideas have their own dynamics which cannot easily be controlled by the people who brought them into being. In case of human rights, its dynamics soon trapped it in a contradiction somewhat to the dismay of its protagonists. Fashioned as a tool against democracy, the idea became an important source of legitimation for those seeking the expansion of democracy. But in Europe, this contradiction never fully matured. An agile and accommodating political class and unprecedented affluence saw to that.

In Africa, prevailing objective conditions will press matters much further, particularly the question of empowerment. In all probability, the empowerment of people will become the primary issue. Once this happens, the social contradictions will be immensely sharpened and the idea of human rights will become an asset of great value to radical social transformation. I cannot help thinking that Africa is where the critical issues in human rights will be fought out and where the idea will finally be consummated or betrayed.

INSTANTIATION₃

ENVIRONMENT

INTRODUCTION

Our environment is what surrounds us, where we live. Most of us spend most of our time in environments that are largely artificial, that is to say, unnatural. Nature is the world unaltered by humans. But since humanity is a natural species, perhaps that notion makes no sense. Still, we contrast nature and the natural with the civilized, the altered, and the mechanical. And generally, if incorrectly, the natural is supposed somehow to be the better.

The reading just below, by Sagoff, explores the nature of 'nature' and of 'environment' in American cultural and economic history. Particularly important is the conflict between preservation and conservation that underlies conflict that became highly visible in the last half of the Nineteenth Century and continues through the Twentieth and into the Twenty-first Centuries. We want to preserve things that are valuable in themselves: great art, literature, historical places and records. On the other hand, what we want to conserve are resources, and a resource is something to be used. Oil and coal and timber and credit are resources. They have only use-value. The newly popular term 'human resources' chillingly suggests that people, too, are just things to be used as needed. But humans, many of us believe, are valuable in themselves, not just as tools. And many believe this about forests (not timber) as well.

That there are many global environmental problems is apparent to anyone who has not spent the last decade in total isolation. World-wide, fisheries are collapsing. In some places pollution has rendered large areas of the seas lifeless. The climate is clearly changing. Icecaps are melting and the sea is rising. Frog populations are crashing around the world. Species are disappearing at a very high rate. Other species are prospering as alien invaders, displacing and often destroying the natives. Deserts are spreading and ancient forests are being leveled.

The first question, as always, is 'what matters?'. Just me? Just my people? Just people? Everything that can suffer? All life? Natural systems? Mother Gaia?

To take an *anthropocentric* approach to environmental problems is to concern oneself exclusively with human welfare. This is the most narrow approach, and the one most widely accepted. Even those who believe a much broader approach is the right one will appeal to anthropocentric concerns whenever possible. We should preserve species because they might yield cures for our diseases, or because the system might collapse and ruin our lives. Climate change is a threat to our food supplies and our comfort. We should protect fish and animals and forests so that we can 'harvest' them.

The reading below by Foster is clearly anthropocentric in outlook. Foster is concerned here with injustice to humans, not harm to animals or to the environment.

A *sentientocentric* approach holds that the welfare of anything that can have a welfare is significant. Humans matter, but so do chimpanzees and chipmunks, but not cherry trees. If a being is capable of welfare and misery, its welfare and misery matter. A sentientocentricist does not have to hold that the welfare of every creature matters as much as that of any other, and most do not hold this. Utilitarians, at least in principle, are sentientocentricists, and so are many other moral theorists.

The variety of sentientocentric positions (and of anthropocentric ones) is very large. In the reading below Engel argues that all of us accept principles which commit us to sentientocentric positions of at least enough strength to require that we become vegetarians.

A *biocentric* approach claims that sentientocentricism (and therefore anthropocentricism) draw the boundaries of moral concern far too narrowly. All life, as life, is valuable, and we must choose those actions that benefit as much (or harm as little) life as possible.

A *system-centric* or *geocentric* approach holds that anthropocentric, sentientocentric, and (some forms of) biocentric positions all ask the wrong question. They all presume that separable individuals must be the locus of value. But value resides not in individuals but in species, or natural systems, or the super-individual that is the whole earth. Individuals are valuable only derivatively, and if it is necessary to sacrifice an individual of any sort to preserve a whole, we should not hesitate to do so.

In the final reading in this section, Leo Marx suggests that we may be unable even to understand, much less to attack, some of the environmental problems facing us if we do not get beyond the fixation on 'hard' science and realize that many of these problems have their roots in social and political choices.

That these readings are a tiny selection of the literature available on these topics is especially obvious in this section. We provide no biocentric or system-centric readings. Constraints of space and cost are less important on the web. Please go to www.phil.vt.edu/Global/ for more material on this topic.

NATURE VERSUS THE ENVIRONMENT
MARK SAGOFF

Literature, history, and the arts take up the idea of nature as often as the ideas of humanity or love; indeed, a culture or an intellectual period can be identified by the symbolism it attaches to natural objects. No society has developed a culture that does not discover symbols in nature and attach special significance to them. But are these expressions of reverence for nature merely curious cultural artifacts, or do they have relevance for the contemporary debate on the environment?

Nature as Beauty and Power

"The two most obvious characteristics of Nature," the philosopher Alfred North Whitehead once said, "are loveliness and power." These were the principal characteristics artists and writers of the American Romantic tradition, including the transcendentalists, found in Nature--which they always spelled with a capital "N." Emerson, for example, discovered in the beautiful and the sublime aspects of Nature moral and religious lessons. "Man is fallen; nature is erect, and serves as a differential thermometer, detecting the presence or absence of the divine sentiment in man."

The transcendentalists inherited from the Puritan tradition the vision of Nature as a collection of images and shadows of divine things ("faint clues and indirections," Walt Whitman wrote)--although the buoyant Emerson thought these symbols were a lot easier to read than did the Puritan theologian Jonathan Edwards a century earlier. Similarly, the landscape of the American West impressed preservationists like John Muir as a heritage direct from God's hand--a temple in which we should set foot only to worship.

What is striking today about the Romantic imagination of the nineteenth century is the insistence with which it portrayed Nature in moral, religious, and aesthetic terms - in terms of its beauty and power and avoided mentioning its utility. The literature and art of the period - the paintings of Thomas Cole are an example - suggest that to use Nature is to transgress it, to put something foreign and artificial (i.e., Civilization, in its place). In one passage in which Emerson acknowledges the utility of Nature, he does so apologetically: we "draw our living as parasites from her roots and grains" he wrote, while we receive "the sublime moral of autumn and of noon."

The more Americans exploited the environment--the more they thrust civilization upon it--the more their literature and art celebrated the beauty and power of the Nature they destroyed. The historian Perry Miller observes:

> The astonishing fact about this gigantic material thrust of the early nineteenth century is how few Americans would any longer venture, aside from their boasts, to explain, let alone to justify, the expansion of civilization in any language that could remotely be called that of

utility. The more rapidly, the more voraciously the primordial forests were felled, the more desperately poets and painters - and also preachers - strove to identify the personality of this republic with the virtues of pristine and untarnished, or "romantic" Nature.

When the Western frontier closed after the Civil War, many Americans recognized the contradiction between the cultural attitude and the practical policy of their nation toward the natural environment. How could we continue to celebrate the loveliness and power of Nature while everywhere we mined it, plowed it, dredged it, and turned it to the purposes of our industrial economy?

Preservation or Conservation?

Preservationists at the end of the last century sought to minimize the encroachment of humanity on nature; like Whitehead, they believed the important characteristics of Nature are aesthetic and moral, not economic. They opposed conservationists, like Gifford Pinchot, who valued nature primarily for its useful resources and who believed that "the first duty of the human race is to control the earth it lives upon." Many of the concepts, metaphors, and associated norms and attitudes familiar in environmental controversies derive from a century-long debate between those who would protect nature for its symbolic qualities and those who would manage resources efficiently for human use.

The preservationist ethic drew strong support from American literature and art, which has approached nature as Olmsted perceived Yosemite, as the object of moral and aesthetic attention "aroused in the mind occupied without purpose, without a continuation of the common process of relating the present action, thought, or perception to some future end." F. Scott Fitzgerald said of one of his characters in *The Great Gatsby* that the beauty of nature compelled him "into an aesthetic contemplation he neither understood nor desired, face to face for the last time in history with something commensurate with his capacity to wonder."

The romantic and transcendentalist writers of the early nineteenth century, and Muir, Olmsted, and the preservationists who followed them, form a tradition with the nature writers of our own day--authors like John McPhee, Annie Dillard, Edward Abbey, Bill McKibben, and many others--who recite a litany for a vanishing natural heritage. These writers tend to regard nature and humanity as utterly separate.

The idea that nature is what we cannot control -an independent force working on its own - is precisely the reverse of what conservationists like Pinchot believed. Conservationists held that nature or, more precisely, natural resources belong to humanity, which has a duty to maximize its own welfare, and it can do this best by controlling the earth. "The object of our forest policy," Pinchot announced in 1903 to the Society of American Foresters, "is not to preserve the forests because they are beautiful . . . or because they are refuges for the wild creatures of the wilderness . . . but . . . the making of prosperous homes."

Many economists, policy analysts, and others who, in the tradition of the conservation movement, urge us to use natural resources efficiently describe the object of our concern not as "Nature" but as "the environment," by which they mean the physical and biotic resource base for human sustenance and survival.

Writers concerned with ethical, cultural, and aesthetic issues, by contrast, tend to refer to "nature" rather than to the "environment." The titles of major texts in the field of environmental ethics, like John Passmore's *Man's Responsibility for Nature* and Paul Taylor's *Respect for Nature*, avoid the term "environment." Thus, it seems that concepts that arise in the humanities—"responsibility," "stewardship," and "respect"--concern nature, while concepts in the social, natural, and policy sciences--"efficiency," "energy flows," "costs," and "benefits"--apply to the environment. The environment is what nature becomes when we see it as the object of planning, technology, and management.

While the arts and humanities have taught us to love and appreciate Nature for its beauty and power, the economic, policy, and natural sciences have instructed us to manage the environment to satisfy our wants and needs. We may ask, then, how we are to choose between the idea of Nature found in literature, religion, and art, on the one hand, and the concept of the environment we find in the sciences on the other. How can we deal intelligently with a nature that contains both--that is the locus both of beauty and power and, at the same time, of useful materials and resources?

Putting Nature Back Into the Environment

A century ago, Americans celebrated the beauty and power of pristine Nature while they rapidly developed natural resources. They protected a few magnificent landscapes and converted everything else to economic purposes. To experience Nature, Americans escaped to the Maine woods and to the Sierras; they returned to industrial cities like Chicago to develop the environment.

Today, all this has changed. The idea of an inviolate, self-sustaining pristine Nature has proven a will-of the-wisp, as has the idea of a closed economic system. In place of the separate concepts of Nature and environment, we now look for a single concept of nature (with a lower case "n") to describe a sustainable habitat--one in which to live harmoniously with our surroundings over the long run.

It has become apparent that neither the preservationist ethic nor the conservationist "gospel of efficiency" is adequate as we approach the twenty-first century. First, consider preservationism. While preservationists have fought for a century to keep the Adirondacks "forever wild," they have been pursuing a chimera. The flora and fauna of that region are hardly aboriginal; they got there in large part because of human activity, which had utterly revised virtually every ecological community in northeastern America. The area surrounding Walden Pond had been transformed by human beings even before the time of Thoreau. Wherever we look, we have played an immensely important role, intentional or not, in the course of natural history. Few if any pristine landscapes exist to be preserved.

It is in general too late, then, to preserve nature as we preserve art; too many changes have already taken place. Besides; to preserve nature as we do art--for example, to make forests into living museums--turns nature into art. To "restore" ecological communities to one of many possible earlier states may be a wonderful thing to do, but it involves human intervention, for we must use science and technology both to identify those states and to achieve them.

It is we who decide, moreover, what is "natural," for example, with respect to forest-fire policy in national parks and in managing populations of wild animals in the absence of extinct predators. Preservationists today, therefore, no longer think in terms of maintaining a hermetic separation between nature and humanity. Rather, they look for ways human beings may play a stabilizing, harmonizing role in or as part of the natural world.

Accordingly, many who stand in the tradition of Muir are concerned to guide and inform the human role we play in nature--not to keep apart from it. New sciences like conservation biology try to understand this appropriate human role--to understand how we may manage our economy to sustain the complexity and stability of nature and how we may manage the complexity and stability of nature to sustain our economy.

Even if we must modify the preservationism of Muir and Olmsted to make it relevant to our present circumstances, however, we need not embrace the "gospel of efficiency" associated with instrumentalists like Pinchot. Too many of us have lost faith in the ability of science and technology continually to subdue, control, and manipulate nature to facilitate economic expansion. As many of our writers, artists, and religious leaders suggest, we may succeed better by accommodating our interests and desires to the limits nature sets than by trying to push at those limits to accommodate our insatiable desires.

Many economists, like Herman Daly [eds: see this volume], have argued, therefore, that modern economic theory has failed to address environmental problems realistically because it conceives of the economy as a closed system, in which abstract exchange value circulates in a loop between production and consumption, in splendid isolation from the larger ecological systems of which it is a part. In such an abstract circle of trading, in which goods and services are substitutable in terms of price, environmental problems are perceived as "tradeoffs" to be captured by markets or, when markets fail, by experts; who can get the prices of things right.

This approach--which regards all environmental problems as problems of efficient resource allocation--neglects the general problems of aggregate resource depletion and the limited capacity of natural systems to carry the macroeconomy as a whole. Daly suggests the image of a boat that sinks when it is overloaded even though everyone in it has allocated his weight in an "optimal" or "efficient" way. The representation of nature as the boat that carries us - rather than a star that guides us or the materials we have on board - offers an important metaphor to supplement familiar images of "Nature" and "environment."

The Challenge to the Humanities

In a remarkable passage toward the beginning of A *Week on the Concord and Merrimack Rivers (1849)*, Henry David Thoreau writes:

> Late in the afternoon we passed a man on the shore fishing with a long birch pole, its silvery bark left on, and a dog at his side, rowing so near as to agitate his cork with our oars, . . .; and when we had rowed a mile as straight as an arrow, with our faces turned towards him, and the bubbles in our wake still visible on the tranquil surface, there stood the fisher still with his dog, like statues under the other side of the heavens, the only objects to relieve the extended meadow;

and there would he stand abiding his luck, till he took his way home through the fields at evening with his fish. Thus, by one bait or another, Nature allures inhabitants to all her recesses.

Among the writers of pre-Civil War America, Thoreau dealt most subtly with the relation between nature and our economic needs. The last sentence of this passage, for example, points out that we discover nature's secrets not only when we contemplate its beauty and power but also when we try to wrest a living from it. Today, science and technology take us to recesses in nature undreamed of in Thoreau's time. Yet the "bait" with which nature lures us to split the atom or break the genetic code is much the same as that which brought the fisherman to the river.

Thoreau's description of the scene on the riverbank reflects a sense of proper proportion between humanity, technology, and nature. Now that humanity has increased vastly in number and our technology has increased greatly in power, our problem from an economic as well as ethical and aesthetic perspective is to maintain proper proportion between economic activity and the natural world. Our task is not simply to control nature but to control ourselves so that the human economy can fit appropriately within the natural one.

It is easy to read a preservationist message in the famous remark in chapter two of *Walden* that "a man is rich in proportion to the number of things he can afford to let alone." In its context, however, this statement also suggests that from an economic point of view we must maintain intact the resources on which we depend. The fisherman, in satisfying his needs, does not destroy the river; he leaves it as he found it for another day. Similarly, we increase our wealth when we bring economic activity into a sustainable relationship with nature, for example, by renewing the resources we deplete and by maintaining the functioning of the ecological systems on which we depend.

An important challenge to the humanities in our time is to show us how we may regard nature not simply as a system of resources or raw materials for our use or, at the other extreme, as a preserve apart from economic life, but as the habitat in which we and all other species live. The task of developing nature as habitat has been the traditional work of human culture.

The word "culture" derives from *colere*--to cultivate, to dwell, to care for, and to preserve. The attitude of loving care is the lesson the humanities can teach. The writers, artists, and theologians of the nineteenth century taught us to appreciate and revere the loveliness and power of nature (i.e., the beautiful and the sublime). We must now learn how to respect the complex and sometimes fragile ecological systems that support the diversity of life, including our own. If we must abandon the preservationist ideal of a pristine nature from which humanity is excluded, we must at the same time resist the conservationist view of nature as a mere resource for humanity's exclusive benefit.

"LET THEM EAT POLLUTION":
CAPITALISM AND THE WORLD ENVIRONMENT
JOHN BELLAMY FOSTER

On December 12, 1991, Lawrence Summers, chief economist of the World Bank, sent a memorandum to some of his colleagues presenting views on the environment that are doubtless widespread among orthodox economists, reflecting as they do the logic of capital accumulation, but which are seldom offered up for public scrutiny, and then almost never by an economist of Summers' rank. This memo was later leaked to the British publication, *The Economist*, which published part of it on February 8, 1992, under the title "Let Them Eat Pollution." The published part of the memo is quoted in full below:

Just between you and me, shouldn't the World Bank be encouraging more migration of the dirty industries to the LDCs, [Less Developed Countries]? I can think of three reasons:
(1) The measurement of the costs of health-impairing pollution depends on the foregone earnings from increased morbidity and mortality. From this point of view a given amount of health-impairing pollution should be done in the country with the lowest cost, which will be the country with the lowest wages. I think the economic logic behind dumping a load of toxic waste in the lowest-wage country is impeccable and we should face up to that.
The costs of pollution are likely to be non-linear as the initial increments of pollution will probably have very low cost. I've always thought that under-populated countries in Africa are vastly *under*-polluted; their air quality is probably vastly inefficiently low [sic] compared to Los Angeles or Mexico City. Only the lamentable facts that so much pollution is generated by non-tradeable industries (transport, electrical generation) and that the unit transport costs of solid waste are so high prevent world-welfare-enhancing trade in air pollution and waste.
(3) The demand for a clean environment for aesthetic and health reasons is likely to have very high income-elasticity The concern over an agent that causes a one-in-a million change in the odds of prostate cancer is obviously going to be much higher in a country where people survive to get prostate cancer than in a country where under-five mortality is 200 per thousand. Also, much of the concern over industrial atmospheric discharge is about visibility-impairing particulates. These discharges may have very little direct health impact. Clearly trade in goods that embody aesthetic pollution concerns could be welfare-enhancing. While production is mobile the consumption of pretty air is a non-tradeable.
The problem with the arguments against all of these proposals for more pollution in LDCs (intrinsic rights to certain goods, moral rights, social concerns, lack of adequate markets, etc.) [is that they] could be turned

around and used more or less effectively against every Bank proposal for liberalization.

The World Bank later told *The Economist* that in writing his memo Summers had intended to "provoke debate" among his Bank colleagues, while Summers himself said that he had not meant to advocate "the dumping of untreated toxic wastes near the homes of poor people." Few acquainted with orthodox economics, however, can doubt that the central arguments utilized in the memo were serious. In the view of *The Economist* itself (February 15, 1992), Summers' language was objectionable but "his economics was hard to answer."

Although its general meaning could not be clearer, this entire memo deserves to be summarized and restated in a way that will bring out some of the more subtle implications. First, the lives of individuals in the Third World, judged by "foregone earnings" from illness and death, are worth less–the same logic says frequently hundreds of times less – than that of individuals in the advanced capitalist countries where wages are often hundreds of times higher. The low wage periphery is therefore the proper place in which to dispose of globally produced toxic wastes if the overall economic value of human life is to be maximized worldwide. Second, Third World countries are "vastly *under*polluted" in the sense that their air pollution levels are "inefficiently low" when compared with highly polluted cities like Los Angeles and Mexico City (where schoolchildren had to be kept home for an entire month in 1989 because of the abysmal air quality). Third, a clean environment can be viewed as a luxury good pursued by rich countries with high life expectancies where higher aesthetic and health standards apply; worldwide costs of production would therefore fall if polluting industries were shifted from the center to the periphery of the world system. Hence, for all of these reasons the World Bank should encourage the migration of polluting industries and toxic wastes to the Third World. Social and humanitarian arguments against such world trade in waste, Summers concludes, can be disregarded since they are the same arguments that are used against all proposals for capitalist development.

It is important to understand that this policy perspective, with the utter contempt that it displays both for the world's poor and the world environment, is by no means an intellectual aberration. As the World Bank's chief economist Summers' role is to help create conditions conducive to world capital accumulation, particularly where the core of the capitalist world system is concerned. Neither the welfare of the majority of the population of the globe nor the ecological fate of the earth – nor even the fate of individual capitalists themselves – can be allowed to stand in the way of this single-minded goal.

Perhaps the most shocking part of the Summers memo is the openly exploitative attitude that it demonstrates toward the world's poor. And yet nothing is more characteristic of bourgeois economics. *The Economist,* which went on to defend Summers' general conclusions about the desirability of the migration of polluting industries to the Third World in subsequent commentaries, nonetheless dismissed Summers' specific references to the valuation of life, as "crass," denying that such exploitative attitudes toward human life are likely to play an explicit role in government policy in free societies. "Few governments," *The Economist* stated in its February 15, 1992 issue, "would care to defend a policy based on differences in valuations among groups – arguing, for instance, that society values an extra year of life for a white collar worker more highly than for a blue-collar worker. Yet this is the counterpart, within a rich country, of what Summers appeared to be suggesting for the Third World." The truth, however, as *The Economist* itself admitted at another point in the same article, is that governments constantly do make decisions – whether in regard to health, education, working conditions, housing, environment, etc. – that are "based on differences in valuations" among classes, whether or not they "care to defend" their policies in this way. Indeed, such differences in valuation, as anyone with the slightest knowledge of history and economics must realize, are at the very core of the capitalist economy and state.

To illustrate this we only need to turn to the United States. The OMB (Office of Management and Budget) under the Reagan administration endeavored to promote calculations of the dollar value of a human life based on "the wage premiums that workers require for accepting jobs with increased risk." On this basis a number of academic studies concluded that the value of a worker's life in the United States is between $500 thousand and $2 million (far less than the annual salary of many corporate CEOs). The OMB then used these results to argue that some forms of pollution abatement were cost-effective, while others were not, in accordance with President Reagan's executive order No. 12291 that regulatory measures should "be chosen to maximize the net benefit to society."

"Some economists," Barry Commoner informs us:

> . . . have proposed that the value of a human life should be based on a person's earning power. It then turns out that a woman's life is worth much less than a man's, and that a black's life is worth much less than a white's. Translated into environmental terms, harm is regarded as small if the people at hazard are poor – an approach that could be used to justify locating heavily polluting operations in poor neighborhoods. This is, in fact, only too common a practice. A recent study shows, for example, that most toxic dumps are located near poor black and Hispanic communities.

In 1983 a study by the U-S. General Accounting Office determined that three out of the four off-site commercial hazardous waste landfills in the southern states were located in primarily black communities even though blacks represented only 20 percent of the population in the region.[1]

Summers' argument for dumping toxic wastes in the Third World is therefore nothing more than a call for the globalization of policies and practices which are already evidenced in the United States, and which have recently been unearthed in locations throughout the capitalist world. The developed countries ship an estimated 20 trillion tons of waste to the Third World each year. In 1987 dioxin-laden industrial ash from Philadelphia was dumped in Guinea and Haiti. In 1988 4,000 tons of PCB-contaminated chemical waste from Italy was found in Nigeria, leaking from thousands of rusting and corroding drums, poisoning both soil and

---

[1] Barry Commoner, *Making Peace with the Planet* (New York, The New Press, 1992), pp. 64-66; Robert Bullard, "The Politics of Race and Pollution: An Interview with Robert Bullard," *Multinational Monitor* (vol. 13, no. 6, June 1992), pp. 21-22.

groundwater.[2] There can be few more blatant examples of the continuing dominance of imperialism over Third World affairs.

This same frame of mind which sees toxic pollution less as a problem to be overcome than one to be managed in accordance with the logic of the free market, is evident in the approach adopted by orthodox economists to issues as fateful as global warming. Writing in the May 30, 1992 issue of *The Economist*, Summers illustrates this perspective and the general attitude of the World Bank by stating that,

> The argument that a moral obligation to future generations demands special treatment of environmental investments is fatuous. We can help our descendants as much by improving infrastructure as by preserving rain forests . . . as much by enlarging our scientific knowledge as by reducing carbon dioxide in the air. ... The reason why some investments favored by environmentalists fail...a [rigorous cost-benefit] test is that their likely effect on living standards is not so great. ...In the worst-case scenario of the most pessimistic estimates yet prepared (those of William Cline of the Institute for International Economics), global warming reduces growth over the next two centuries by less than 0.1 percent a year. More should be done: dealing with global warming would not halt economic growth either. But raising the specter of our impoverished grandchildren if we fail to address global environmental problems is demagoguery.

The problem with such arguments is that they are based on forms of economic calculation that consistently undervalue natural wealth and underestimate the dependence of the economy on ecological conditions. The rebuilding of infrastructure cannot be equated with preserving the world's tropical rainforests since the loss of the latter would be irrevocable and would mean the extinction of both a majority of the world's species and the world's greatest genetic library. The absurdity of William Cline's attempt to quantify the potential economic damages of "very long-term global warming" up through the year 2,300 – to which Summers refers – should be apparent to anyone who considers the obvious impossibility of applying economic values to the scale of climatic change anticipated. Thus the Cline estimates are based on a projected rise in global mean temperatures of 10° to 18° C (18° to 32° F) by the year 2300. The cost of this to the U.S. economy, Cline expects us to believe, will be long-term damages equal to 6 to 12 percent of GNP under the best assumptions, 20 percent under the worst.[3] All of this is nonsense, however, from an ecological standpoint, since a temperature rise of 4° C would create an earth that was warmer than at any time in the last 40 million years. In the midst of the last ice age the earth was only 5° C colder than it is today. Viewed from this standpoint the question of whether or not long-term damages would equal 6, 12 or 20 percent

---

[2] Bill Weinberg, *War on the Land* (London: Zed Books, 1991), pp. 37-39; Edward Goldsmith, et. al., *The Imperilled Planet* (Cambridge, Mass.: MIT Press, 1990), p. 147; Center for Investigative Reporting and Bill Moyers, *Global Dumping Ground* (Cambridge: The Lutterworth Press, 1991), pp. 1-2, 12; Third World Network, *Toxic Terror* (Penang, Malaysia: Third World Network, 1989), pp. 8-25.
[3] William R. Cline, *The Economics of Global Warming* (Washington, D C : Institute for International Economics, 1993) pp. 4-6, 55-58, 130-33, 300.

of GNP must give way to the more rational question of whether human civilization and life itself could persist in the face of such a drastic change in global temperatures.

An even more alarming example of the same general argument was provided, again in the May 30, 1992 issue of *The Economist*, in a special report published in advance of the June 1992 Earth Summit in Rio. After examining estimates on the economic costs and benefits of averting global warming and the political obstacles to change under existing capitalist regimes, *The Economist* declares:

> The chances that the climate treaty will significantly change the world's output of fossil fuels over the next century is extremely slender. Does this matter? If the figures ... for the costs of damage likely to be done by climate change are accurate, then the honest answer is "no." It would be, of course, wise for countries to take the free lunches available to them ... and to price their energy sensibly. It might be wise to go some way beyond that point, in the interests of buying insurance against nasty surprises. ... Beyond that, adapting to climate change, when it happens, is undoubtedly the most rational course, for a number of reasons. Most countries will be richer then, and so better able to afford to build sea walls or develop drought resistant plants. Money that might now be spent on curbing carbon-dioxide output can be invested instead, either in preventing more damaging environmental change (like rapid population growth, the most environmentally harmful trend of all) or in productive assets that will generate future income to pay for adaptation. Once climate change occurs, it will be clearer – as it now is not – how much needs to be done, and what, and where. Most of the decisions involved in adapting will be taken and paid for by the private sector rather than (as with curbing greenhouse-gas output) by government. Above all, adapting requires no international agreements.[4]

The answer then is "let them build sea walls or develop drought resistant plants." And this in response to "very probable" rises in global mean temperature of 1.5° to 5.0 ° C (2.7° to 9° F) over the next century if "business as usual" continues, a prospect that scientists all over the world regard as potentially catastrophic for the entire planet![5] The threat of heat waves, droughts, floods, and famines suggests the likelihood of incalculable losses in lives, species, ecosystems, and cultures. Nevertheless, for *The Economist* the adaptation of the capital accumulation process and thus world civilization to irreversible global warming once it has taken place and many of its worst effects are evident is easy to contemplate, while any attempt to head off disaster – however defensible in social, moral, and ecological terms –

---

[4] See also Frances Cairncross, *Costing the Earth* (London: Economist Books, 1991), pp. 30-31, 130-33.
[5] National Academy of Sciences, *One Earth, One Future* (Washington D.C.: National Academy Press, 1990), pp. 67-71; Helen Caldicott, *If You Love This Planet* (New York: W. W. Norton, 1992), p. 24; Mostafa K. Tolba, *Saving Our Planet* (New York: Chapman and Hall, 1992), pp. 27-28; Intergovernmental Panel on Climate Change, *Climate Change* (New York: Cambridge University Press, 1990), p. xxii.

besides being difficult to institute under present-day capitalist regimes, would interfere with the dominance of capital and must therefore be unthinkable.

The wait and see attitude promoted by *The Economist* was of course the general stance adopted by the United States (and to a lesser extent Britain) at the Earth Summit. Through its actions in watering down the climate treaty, refusing to sign the biological diversity treaty, and hindering initiatives on weapons of mass destruction and nuclear waste, the United States signaled in no uncertain terms that it was prepared to take on the task of opposing radical forces within the global environmental movement, adding this to its larger role as the leading defender of the capitalist world. According to the U.S. government's position, the concept of "sustainable development" means first and foremost that any environmental goals that can be interpreted as interfering with development must be blocked. Thus in his defense of U.S. intransigence on global environmental issues at the Earth Summit in June George Bush explained, "I think it is important that we take both those words-- environment and development--equally seriously. And we do." No environmental action could therefore be taken, Bush declared, that would jeopardize U.S. economic interests. "I am determined to protect the environment. I am also determined to protect the American taxpayer. The day of the open checkbook is over ... environmental protection and a growing economy are inseparable." In what was intended not only as a re-election ploy but also a declaration of U.S. priorities where questions of environmental costs and controls were concerned, Bush declared, "For the past half century, the United States has been the great engine of global economic growth, and it's going to stay that way." (Guardian [London], June 13, 1992)

The consequences of such shortsighted attention to economic growth and profit before all else are of course enormous since they call into question the survivability of the entire world. It is an inescapable fact that human history is at a turning point, the result of a fundamental change in the relationship between human beings and the environment. The scale at which people transform energy and materials has now reached a level that rivals elemental natural processes. Human society is adding carbon to the atmosphere at a level that is equal to about 7 percent of the natural carbon exchange of atmosphere and oceans. The carbon dioxide content of the atmosphere as a result has grown by a quarter in the last 200 years, with more than half of this increase since 1950. Human beings now use (take or transform) 25 percent of the plant mass fixed by photosynthesis over the entire earth, land and sea, and 40 percent of the photosynthetic product on land. Largely as a result of synthetic fertilizers, humanity fixes about as much nitrogen in the environment as does nature. With human activities now rivaling nature in scale, actions that in the past merely produced local environmental crises now have global implications. Moreover, environmental effects that once seemed simple and trivial, such as increases in carbon dioxide emissions, have now suddenly become threats to the stability of the fundamental ecological cycles of the planet. Destruction of the ozone layer, the greenhouse effect, annihilation of ancient and tropical forests, species extinction, reductions in genetic diversity, production of toxic and radioactive wastes, contamination of water resources, soil depletion, depletion of essential raw materials, desertification, the growth of world population spurred by rising poverty - all represent ominous trends the full impact of which, singly or in combination, is scarcely to be imagined at present. "With the appearance of a continent-sized hole in the Earth's protective ozone layer and the threat of global warming," Barry

Commoner has written, "even droughts, floods, and heat waves may become unwitting acts of man."[6]

The sustainability of both human civilization and global life processes depends not on the mere slowing down of these dire trends, but on their reversal.[7] Nothing in the history of capitalism, however, suggests that the system will be up to such a task. On the contrary there is every indication that the system, left to its own devices, will gravitate toward the "let them eat pollution" stance so clearly enunciated by the chief economist of the World Bank.

Fortunately for the world, however, capitalism has never been allowed to develop for long entirely in accordance with its own logic. Opposition forces always emerge – whether in the form of working class struggles for social betterment or conservation movements dedicated to overcoming environmental depredations – that force the system to moderate its worst tendencies. And to some extent the ensuing reforms can result in lasting, beneficial constraints on the market. What the capitalist class cannot accept, however, are changes that will likely result in the destruction of the system itself. Long before reform movements threaten the accumulation process as a whole, therefore, counterforces are set in motion by the ruling interests, and the necessary elemental changes are headed off.

And there's the rub. Where radical change is called for little is accomplished within the system and the underlying crisis intensifies over time. Today this is particularly evident in the ecological realm. For the nature of the global environmental crisis is such that the fate of the entire planet and social and ecological issues of enormous complexity are involved, all traceable to the forms of production now prevalent. It is impossible to prevent the world's environmental crisis from getting progressively worse unless root problems of production, distribution, technology, and growth are dealt with on a global scale. And the more that such questions are raised, the more it becomes evident that capitalism is unsustainable – ecologically, economically, politically, and morally – and must be superseded.

---

[6] IPCC, *Climate Change*, p. xvi; Donella Meadows, et. al., *Beyond the Limits* (London: Earthscan, 1992), pp. 65-66; Jim MacNeill, et. al., *Beyond Interdependence* (New York: Oxford University Press, 1991), pp. 8-9; Paul R. Ehrlich and Anne H. Ehrlich, *Healing the Planet* (New York: Addison-Wesley, 1991), pp. 26-27; Peter M. Vitousek, et. al., "Human Appropriation of the Products of Photosynthesis," *Bioscience* (vol. 36, no. 6, June 1986), pp. 368-73; Commoner, p.3.

[7] Paul M. Sweezy, "Capitalism and the Environment," *Monthly Review* (vol. 41, no. 2, June 1989), p. 6; Meadows, *Beyond the Limits*, p. xv.

THE CONSISTENCY ARGUMENT FOR ETHICAL VEGETARIANISM:
WHY YOU ARE COMMITTED TO THE IMMORALITY OF EATING MEAT AND OTHER ANIMAL PRODUCTS
MYLAN ENGEL, JR.

Most arguments for the moral obligatoriness of vegetarianism take one of two forms. Either they follow Singer's lead and demand equal consideration for animals on utilitarian grounds,[1] or they follow Regan's deontological rights-based approach and insist that most of the animals we routinely consume possess the very same rights-conferring properties which confer rights on humans.[2,3] While many people have been persuaded to alter their dietary habits on the basis of one of these arguments, most philosophers have not. My experience has been that when confronted with these arguments meat-loving philosophers often casually dismiss them as follows:

> Singer's preference utilitarianism is irremediably flawed, as is Regan's theory of moral rights. Since Singer's and Regan's arguments for vegetarianism are predicated on flawed ethical theories, their arguments are also flawed. Until someone can provide me with clear moral reasons for not eating meat, I will continue to eat what I please.

A moment's reflection reveals the self-serving sophistry of such a reply. Since no ethical theory to date is immune to objection, one could fashion a similar reply to "justify" or rationalize virtually any behavior. One could "justify" rape as

---

[1] See Peter Singer's *Animal Liberation*, 2d ed. (New York: Avon Books, 1990) or his "All Animals are Equal" in *Animal Rights and Human Obligations*, 2d ed., eds. Regan and Singer (Englewood Cliffs, NJ: Prentice Hall, 1989), 73-86.

[2] See Tom Regan's *The Case for Animal Rights* (Berkeley: University of California Press, 1983), or his "The Case for Animals Rights" in *In Defense of Animals*, ed. Peter Singer (New York: Harper and Row Perennial Library, 1985), 13-26.

[3] Utilitarian and rights-based arguments for ethical vegetarianism have dominated the philosophical discussion for the last twenty-five years. For defenses of ethical vegetarianism that do not presuppose utilitarianism or animal rights, see Jordan Curnutt's "A New Argument for Vegetarianism," *Journal of Social Philosophy* 28 (1997): 54-73. Here, using a Feinbergian analysis of harm, Curnutt defends ethical vegetarianism by appealing to the *prima facie* wrongness of causing harm. Also see Andrew Tardiff's "Simplifying the Case for Vegetarianism," *Social Theory and Practice* 22 (fall 1996): 299-314, wherein Tardiff defends ethical vegetarianism with a series of intuitive examples and analogical arguments. In S. F. Sapontzis' *Morals, Reason, and Animals*, Chapters 6 and 11 (Philadelphia: Temple University Press, 1987), Sapontzis offers three independent reasons (only one of which presupposes utilitarianism) in support of ethical vegetarianism and liberating animals. In addition to his utilitarian argument, Sapontzis appeals to considerations of fairness and our concern with character development to defend ethical vegetarianism.

follows: An opponent of rape might appeal to utilitarian, Kantian, or contractarian grounds to establish the immorality of rape. Our fictitious rape-loving philosopher could then point out that all of these ethical theories are flawed and *ipso facto* so too are all the arguments against rape. Our rape proponent might then assert: "Until someone can provide me with clear moral reasons for not committing rape, I will continue to rape whomever I please."

The speciousness of such a "justification" of rape should be obvious. No one who seriously considered the brutality of rape could think that it is somehow justified/permissible *simply because* all current ethical theories are flawed. But such specious reasoning is used to "justify" the equally brutal breeding, confining, mutilating, transporting, killing and eating of animals all the time. My aim is to block this spurious reply by providing an argument for the immorality of eating meat which does not rest on any particular ethical theory. Rather, it rests on beliefs which you already hold.[4]

Before turning to your beliefs, two prefatory observations are in order. First, unlike other ethical arguments for vegetarianism, my argument is not predicated on the wrongness of speciesism,[5] nor does it depend on your believing that all animals are equal or that all animals have a right to life. The significance of this can be explained as follows: Some philosophers remain unmoved by Singer's and Regan's arguments for a different reason than the one cited above. These philosophers find that the nonspeciesistic implications of Singer's and Regan's arguments just *feel* wrong to them. They sincerely *feel* that humans are more important than nonhumans.[6] Perhaps, these feelings are irrational in light of evolutionary theory and our biological kinship with other species, but these feelings are nonetheless real. My argument is neutral with respect to such sentiments. It is compatible with both an anthropocentric and a biocentric worldview. In short, my argument is designed to show that even those of you who are steadfastly committed to valuing humans over nonhumans are nevertheless committed to the immorality of eating meat, given your other beliefs.

---

[4] Obviously, if you do not hold these beliefs (or enough of them), my argument will have no force for you, nor is it intended to. It is only aimed at those of you who do hold these widespread commonsense beliefs.

[5] *Speciesism* is the widespread view that one's own species is superior to and more valuable than the other species and that, therefore, members of one's own species have the right to dominate members of these other species. While 'speciesism' and its cognates are often used pejoratively in the animal rights literature, I use them only descriptively and imply no negative or condescending appraisal of the individual so described.

[6] Bonnie Steinbock's criticism of Singer's view seems to be rooted in such a sincerely held feeling. See her "Speciesism and the Idea of Equality," *Philosophy* 53 (April 1978): 247-256. Therein Steinbock writes:

> I doubt that anyone will be able to come up with a concrete and morally relevant difference that would justify, say, using a chimpanzee in an experiment rather than a human being with less capacity for reasoning, moral responsibility, etc. Should we then experiment on the severely retarded? Utilitarian considerations aside . . . ,we feel a special obligation to care for the handicapped members of our own species, who cannot survive in this world without such care. . . . although one can imagine oneself in the monkey's place, one feels a closer identification with the severely retarded human being. Here we are getting away from such things as 'morally relevant differences' and are talking about something much more difficult to articulate, namely, the role of feeling and sentiment in moral thinking (p. 255f, my emphasis).

Second, ethical arguments are often context-dependent in that they presuppose a specific audience in a certain set of circumstances. Recognizing what that intended audience and context is, and what it is not, can prevent confusions about the scope of the ethical claim being made. My argument is context-dependent in precisely this way. It is not aimed at those relatively few indigenous peoples who, because of the paucity of edible vegetable matter available, must eat meat to survive. Rather, it is directed at people, like you, who live in agriculturally bountiful societies in which a wealth of nutritionally adequate alternatives to meat are readily available. Thus, I intend to show that your beliefs commit you to the view that eating meat is morally wrong for anyone who is in the circumstances in which you typically find yourself and *a fortiori* that it is morally wrong for you to eat meat in these circumstances.[7] Enough by way of preamble, on to your beliefs.

1. The Things You Believe

The beliefs attributed to you herein would normally be considered noncontentious. In most contexts, we would take someone who didn't hold these beliefs to be either morally defective or irrational. Of course, in most contexts, these beliefs are not a threat to enjoying hamburgers, hotdogs, steaks, and ribs; but even with burgers in the balance, you will, I think, readily admit believing the following propositions: (p_1) Other things being equal, a world with less pain and suffering is better than a world with more pain and suffering; and (p_2) A world with less unnecessary suffering is better than a world with more unnecessary suffering.[8] Anyone who has felt the force of the atheistic argument from evil based on gratuitous suffering is committed to (p_1) and (p_2). After all, the reason we think a *wholly good* God would prevent unnecessary suffering is because we think that such suffering is intrinsically bad and that the world would be better without it.[9] Since you think that unnecessary suffering is an intrinsically bad state of affairs, you no doubt also believe: (p_3) Unnecessary cruelty is wrong and *prima facie* should not be supported or encouraged. You probably believe: (p_4) We ought to take steps to make the world a better place. But even if you reject (p_4) on the grounds that we have no positive duties to benefit, you still think there are negative duties to do no harm, and so you believe: ($p_{4'}$) We ought to do what we reasonably can to avoid making the world a worse place. You also believe: (p_5) A morally good person will take steps to make the world a better place and even stronger steps to avoid making

---

[7] Accordingly, throughout the text my claim that "your beliefs commit you to the immorality of eating meat" should be understood as shorthand for the following more cumbersome claim: Your beliefs commit you to the immorality of eating meat for anyone who is in the circumstances in which you typically find yourself.

[8] By "*unnecessary* suffering" I mean suffering which serves no greater, outweighing justifying good. If some instance of suffering is required to bring about a greater good (e.g. a painful root canal may be the only way to save a person's tooth), then that suffering is not unnecessary. Thus, in the case of (p_2), no *ceteris paribus* clause is needed, since if other things are not equal such that the suffering in question is justified by an overriding justifying good which can only be achieved by allowing that suffering, then that suffering is not unnecessary.

[9] Interestingly enough, one of the most powerful versions of the atheistic argument from unnecessary suffering is predicated on gratuitous animal suffering, namely, the suffering of a fawn severely burned in a naturally occurring forest fire. See William Rowe's "The Problem of Evil," in *Philosophy of Religion: An Introduction*, 2d ed. (Belmont, CA: Wadsworth, 1993), 79-82.

the world a worse place; and (p_6) Even a "minimally decent person"[10] would take steps to help reduce the amount of unnecessary pain and suffering in the world, *if s/he could do so with little effort on her/his part*.

You also have beliefs about yourself. You believe one of the following propositions when the reflexive pronoun is indexed to yourself: (p_7) I am a morally good person; or (p_8) I am at least a minimally decent person. You also believe of yourself: (p_9) I am the sort of person who certainly would take steps to help reduce the amount of pain and suffering in the world, *if I could do so with little effort on my part*. Enough about you. On to your beliefs about nonhuman animals and our obligations toward them.

You believe: (p_{10}) Many nonhuman animals (certainly all vertebrates) are capable of feeling pain. I do not have to prove (p_{10}). You already believe it, as is evidenced by your other beliefs: (p_{11}) Other things being equal, it is morally wrong to cause an animal pain or suffering; and (p_{12}) It is morally wrong and despicable to treat animals inhumanely *for no good reason* [Remember Harman's cat.[11]]. In addition to your beliefs about the wrongness of causing animals unnecessary pain, you also have beliefs about the appropriateness of killing animals, e.g. you believe: (p_{13}) We ought to euthanatize untreatably injured, suffering animals to put them out of their misery whenever feasible; and (p_{14}) Other things being equal, it is worse to kill a conscious sentient animal than it is to kill a plant. Finally, you believe: (p_{15}) We have a duty to help preserve the environment for future generations (at least for future *human* generations); and consequently, you believe: (p_{16}) One ought to minimize one's contribution toward environmental degradation, *especially in those ways requiring minimal effort on one's part*.

2. Factory Farming and Modern Slaughter: The Cruelty Behind the Cellophane

Before they become someone's dinner, most farm animals raised in the U.S. are forced to endure intense pain and suffering in "factory farms." Factory farms are intensive confinement facilities where animals are made to live in inhospitable unnatural conditions for the duration of their lives. The first step in intensive farming is early separation of mother and offspring. Chickens are separated from their mothers *before* birth, as they are hatched in incubators and never get to see their mothers, veal calves are removed from their mothers within a few days, and piglets

---

[10] By a "minimally decent person" I mean a person who does the very minimum required by morality and no more. I borrow this terminology from Judith Jarvis Thomson who distinguishes a *good* Samaritan from a *minimally decent* Samaritan. See her "A Defense of Abortion," *Philosophy and Public Affairs* 1 (1971): 62-65.

[11] See Gilbert Harman's *The Nature of Morality: An Introduction to Ethics* (New York: Oxford University Press, 1977), 4, where he presents the following much discussed example: "If you round the corner and see a group of young hoodlums pour gasoline on a cat and ignite it, you do not need to *conclude* that what they are doing is wrong; you do not need to figure anything out; you can *see* that it is wrong." What is relevant about this example for our purposes is that no one considering the example seriously doubts whether a cat so treated would feel pain [Hence, no one seriously doubts (p_{10}).] nor does anyone seriously doubt that cruelly burning a cat for no good reason is wrong [Hence, no one seriously doubts (p_{11}) or (p_{12}) either.].

are separated from their mothers two to three weeks after birth.[12] The offspring are then housed in overcrowded confinement facilities. Broiler chickens and turkeys are warehoused in sheds containing anywhere from 10,000-100,000 birds[13] [The poultry industry recommends--but does not require--that each chicken be allotted seven-tenths of a square foot of floor space.[14]]; veal calves are kept in crates 22" x 54" and are chained at the neck, rendering them unable to move or turn around;[15] pigs are confined in metal crates (which provide 6 square feet of living space) situated on concrete slatted floors with no straw or bedding;[16] and beef cattle are housed in feedlots containing up to 100,000 animals.[17] The inappropriate, unforgiving surfaces on which the animals must stand produce chronic foot and leg injuries.[18] Since they cannot move about, they must stand in their own waste. In these cramped, unsanitary conditions, virtually all of the animals' basic instinctual urges (e.g. to nurse, stretch, move around, root, groom, build nests, rut, establish social orders, select mates, copulate, procreate, and rear offspring) are frustrated, causing boredom and stress in the animals. The stress and unsanitary conditions together compromise their immune systems. To prevent large-scale losses due to disease, the animals are fed a steady diet of antibiotics and growth hormones.[19] When it comes to feed, disease prevention isn't the only consideration. Another is cost. The USDA has approved all sorts of cost-cutting dietary "innovations" with little regard for the animals' well-being including: (i) adding the ground up remains of dead diseased animals (unfit for human consumption) to these herbivorous animals' feed,[20] (ii)

---

[12] Jim Mason and Peter Singer, *Animal Factories*, 2d ed. (New York: Harmony Books, 1990), 5, 10, 11f.
[13] These overcrowded conditions make it impossible for the birds to develop a pecking order, the lack of which generates aggression, feather pecking, and cannibalism in the birds. See Karen Davis, *Prisoned Chickens, Poisoned Eggs: An Inside Look at the Modern Poultry Industry* (Summertown, TN: Book Publishing Co., 1996), 65-71; Singer, *Animal Liberation*, 99f; and Mason and Singer, *Animal Factories*, 7.
[14] Suzanne Hamlin, "Free Range? Natural? Sorting Out Labels," *New York Times*, 13 Nov. 1996, sec. C, p. 2.
[15] John Robbins, *Diet for a New America* (Walpole, NH: Stillpoint, 1987), 114; Humane Farming Association, "Modern Farming Is Inhumane," in *Animal Rights: Opposing Viewpoints* (San Diego, CA: Greenhaven Press, 1989), 118; and Mason and Singer, *Animal Factories*, 12.
[16] Humane Farming Association, "Modern Farming Is Inhumane," 117. For further details, see Robbins' discussion of the "Bacon Bin" in *Diet for a New America*, 83.
[17] Robbins, *Diet for a New America*, 110.
[18] Mason and Singer, *Animal Factories*, 30f; and Davis, *Prisoned Chickens, Poisoned Eggs*, 21, 56f.
[19] Oestrogens, gestagens, and androgens are routinely administered to cattle, veal calves, hogs and sheep. Recommended dosages are described in *Hormones in Animal Production*, Food and Agricultural Organization of the United Nations (Rome 1982), 3. Mason and Singer report, "Nearly all poultry, 90 percent of veal calves and pigs, and a debatable number of cattle get antibacterial additives in their feed" (*Animal Factories*, 66). Residues often remain in their flesh, despite the fact that many of these drugs are known carcinogens not approved for human use. According to *Problems in Preventing the Marketing of Raw Meat and Poultry Containing Potentially Harmful Residues* (Washington, D.C.: General Accounting Office [GAO], April 17, 1979), i: "Of the 143 drugs and pesticides GAO has identified as likely to leave residues in raw meat and poultry, 42 are known to cause cancer or are suspected of causing cancer; 20 of causing birth defects; and 6 of causing mutations" (cited in Mason and Singer, *Animal Factories*, 72).
[20] "Ten billion pounds of processed animal remains were sold for animal feed in the U.S. in 1995." See Eric Haapapuro, "Piling It High and Deep," *Good Medicine* 5, no. 4 (autumn 1996): 15. It should be noted that feeding cattle the rendered remains of sheep infected with scrapie is the suspected cause of bovine spongiform encephalopathy (BSE or as it is commonly called "mad cow disease"). Consuming BSE-infected cattle is believed to be the cause of one variant of Creutzfeldt-Jacob disease,

adding cement dust to cattle feed to promote rapid weight gain,[21] and (iii) adding the animals' own feces to their feed.[22]

The animals react to these inhumane, stressful conditions by developing "stereotypies" (i.e. stress and boredom-induced, neurotic repetitive behaviors) and other unnatural behaviors including cannibalism.[23] For example, chickens unable to develop a pecking order often try to peck each other to death, and pigs, bored due to forced immobility, routinely bite the tail of the pig caged in front of them. To prevent losses due to cannibalism and aggression, the animals receive preemptive mutilations. To prevent chickens and turkeys from pecking each other to death, the birds are "debeaked" using a scalding hot blade which slices through the highly sensitive horn of the beak leaving blisters in the mouth;[24] and to prevent these birds from scratching each other to death (which the industry refers to as "back ripping"), their toes are amputated using the same hot knife machine.[25] Other routine mutilations include: dubbing (surgical removal of the combs and wattles of male chickens and turkeys), tail docking, branding, dehorning, ear tagging, ear clipping, teeth pulling, castration, and ovariectomy. In the interest of cost efficiency, <u>all</u> of these excruciating procedures are performed *without* anaesthesia. *Unanaesthetized* branding, dehorning, ear tagging, ear clipping, and castration are standard procedures on nonintensive family farms, as well.[26]

Lives of frustration and torment finally culminate as the animals are inhumanely loaded onto trucks and shipped long distances to slaughterhouses without food or water and without adequate protection from the elements. Each year millions of animals die or are severely injured as a result of such handling and transportation. For example, in 1998, USDA inspectors condemned 28,500 ducks, 768,300 turkeys and 37.6 million chickens before they entered the slaughter plant, because they were either dead or severely injured upon arrival.[27] Once inside the

---

a fatal brain disease in humans. See "Mad Cow Disease: The Risk in the U.S.", *Good Medicine* 5, no. 3 (summer 1996): 9.

[21] Mason and Singer, *Animal Factories*, 51.

[22] Haapapuro, "Piling It High and Deep," 15. Also see Eric Haapapuro, N. Barnard, and M. Simon, "Animal Waste Used as Livestock Feed: Dangers to Human Health," *Preventive Medicine* 26 (1997): 599-602; as well as Mason and Singer, *Animal Factories*, 53. Detailed feed recipes, some containing as much as 40% chicken manure, are outlined in *Feed from Animal Wastes: Feeding Manual*, Food and Agricultural Organization of the United Nations (Rome 1982). Forced coprophagia has been an industry practice since the mid-1970s. See "Animal Wastes Can Be Fed in Silage," *The American Farmer* (January 1974): 14f, an article describing the "suitability" of adding cattle and poultry manure to feed.

[23] Mason and Singer, *Animal Factories*, 21-24; and Davis, *Prisoned Chickens, Poisoned Eggs*, 65-71.

[24] Debeaking is the surgical removal of the birds' beaks. When beaks are cut too short or heal improperly, the birds cannot eat and eventually starve to death in their cages/shed (Davis, *Prisoned Chickens, Poisoned Eggs*, 48, 65-71; Mason and Singer, *Animal Factories*, 39f; and Robbins, *Diet for a New America*, 57).

[25] Davis, *Prisoned Chickens, Poisoned Eggs*, 47; and Mason and Singer, *Animal Factories*, 40.

[26] Singer, *Animal Liberation*, 145.

[27] *Poultry Slaughter*, National Agricultural Statistics Service [NASS], United States Department of Agriculture [USDA] (Washington, D.C.: February 2, 1999): 2, 4f. The ante-mortem condemnation statistics just cited are estimates, since NASS tracks ante-mortem condemnations in pounds, not birds, and were deduced as follows: The total weight of ante-mortem condemnations for a given bird-type was divided by the average live weight of birds of that type. For example, in 1998 ante-mortem chicken condemnations totaled 182,705,000 lb. and the average live weight of the chickens

slaughterhouse, the animals are hung upside down [Pigs, cattle, and sheep are suspended by one hind leg which often breaks.] and are brought via conveyor to the slaughterer who slits their throats and severs their carotid arteries and jugular veins.[28] In *theory*, animals covered by the Federal Humane Slaughter Act are to be rendered unconscious by electric current or by captive bolt pistol (a pneumatic gun which, when aimed properly, renders the animal unconscious by firing an eight-inch pin into the animal's skull). Chickens, turkeys, ducks, and geese are not considered animals under the Act and receive no protection at all.[29] In *practice*, the Act is not enforced, and as a result, many slaughterhouses elect not to use the captive bolt pistol in the interest of cost efficiency.[30] As for electric shock, it is unlikely that being shocked into unconsciousness is a painless process, based on reports of people who have experienced electroconvulsive therapy.[31] A consequence of the lax enforcement of the Federal Humane Slaughter Act is that in many cases (and all kosher cases), the animals are fully conscious throughout the entire throat-slitting ordeal.[32] For some, the agony does not even end here. According to Gail Eisnitz, chief investigator for the Humane Farming Association, the killing line speeds are so fast in modern slaughterhouses that animals frequently do not have time to bleed out before reaching the skinners and leggers. As a result, those animals which were unstunned or improperly stunned often have their legs cut off and their skin removed while they are still alive.[33,34]

These animal rearing and slaughtering techniques are by no means rare: 97% of all poultry are produced in 100,000+ bird operations,[35] 98% of pigs are raised in confinement systems,[36] 59% of the nation's dairy cows are raised in confinement

---

slaughtered was 4.86 lb. Dividing pounds condemned by average pounds per bird yields 37,593,621 chickens condemned.

[28] Gail Eisnitz, *Slaughterhouse: The Shocking Story of Greed, Neglect, and Inhumane Treatment Inside the U.S. Meat Industry* (Amherst, NY: Prometheus Books, 1997), 20, 145, 198.

[29] Robbins, *Diet for a New America*, 139.

[30] Singer, *Animal Liberation*, 153.

[31] Ibid., 152.

[32] While only 5% of U.S. meat is sold as kosher, as many as 50% of the animals are slaughtered while fully conscious in conformity with antiquated ritual slaughter laws (Robbins, *Diet for a New America*, 142).

[33] Eisnitz, *Slaughterhouse*, 28f, 126-128. Unstunned or improperly stunned hogs which do not bleed out properly are lowered into the 140°F scalding tank while still conscious (p. 71).

[34] The farming, transporting, and slaughtering practices just described have been documented in the following films and videos: Frederick Wiseman's *Meat* (Kine Films, Inc., 1976); Victor Schonfeld's *The Animals Film* (Slick Pics International, 1981); Humane Farming Association's *The Pig Picture* (1995); PETA's *The Diner Video* (1996); and PETA's *Pig Farm Investigation* (1999).

[35] *Animal Agriculture: Information on Waste Management and Water Quality Issues*, a U.S. GAO Report to the U.S. Senate Committee on Agriculture, Nutrition, and Forestry (June 1995), 2, 47.

[36] Confinement is the norm in hog operations with 100+ head. In 1997, 98% of the total U. S. hog inventory was housed in operations with more than 100 head. In fact, 87% of hogs were raised in facilities with 500+ head and 40% were raised in operations with 5000+ head (*Hogs and Pigs: Final Estimates 1993-97*, NASS, USDA [Washington, D.C.: December 22, 1998]: 40ff. All NASS publications can be accessed on the web at: www.usda.gov/nass/). The trend toward consolidation of the hog industry with ever larger operations is continuing. According to the U.S. GAO, "From 1978 to 1994, the total number of [hog] operations (of all sizes) decreased by about 67 percent--from 635,000 to 209,000--while inventory remained the same at about 60 million head" (*Animal Agriculture*, 41). In 1997, the number of hog farms plummeted to 122,160, down 14% from 1996 and 27% below 1995, while inventory increased slightly to 61.2 million head (*Hogs and Pigs: Final Estimates 1993-97*,

systems,[37] all veal calves are crate-raised by definition, and 74% of beef cattle experience feedlot confinement before slaughter.[38] To see just how many animals suffer the institutionalized cruelties of factory farming, consider the number slaughtered in the U.S. each year. According to the National Agricultural Statistics Service [NASS], 35.6 million cattle, 1.5 million veal calves, 101.2 million pigs, 3.9 million sheep and lamb, 23.5 million ducks, 273.0 million turkeys, and 7,995.4 million chickens were slaughtered in the U.S. in 1998.[39] In sum, 8.43 *billion* animals are raised and slaughtered in the U.S. annually (not counting horses, goats, rabbits, emu, other poultry, or fish);[40] and even this number underestimates the number of farm animals killed by animal agriculture by over 10%, since it does not include the 921.4 million animals who suffer lingering deaths from disease, malnutrition, injury or suffocation before reaching the slaughterhouse either as a result of the abysmal unsanitary conditions in factory farms or as a result of brutal handling in transit.[41] Extrapolation reveals that over 25 million animals per day (i.e. roughly 297 animals per second) are killed as a result of the food animal industry. Suffice it to say that no other human activity results in more pain, suffering, frustration and death than factory farming and animal agribusiness.[42]

3. The Implications of <u>Your</u> Beliefs: Why <u>You</u> Are Committed to the Immorality of Eating Meat

I will now offer an argument for the immorality of eating meat predicated on <u>your</u> beliefs (p_1)-(p_{16}). Actually I will offer a family of related arguments, all predicated on different subsets of the set $\{(p_1),(p_2),...,(p_{16})\}$. While you do not have to believe all of (p_1)-(p_{16}) for my argument to succeed, the more of these propositions you believe, the greater <u>your</u> commitment to the immorality of eating meat.[43] For convenience, (p_1)-(p_{16}) have been compiled in an appendix at the end of the article.

NASS, USDA, 1, 36).

[37] Again confinement is the norm in operations with 100+ dairy cows. According to NASS, in 1997, 59% of the nation's dairy cows were housed in operations with 100+ head (*Milk Cows and Production: Final Estimates 1993-97*, NASS, USDA, [Washington, D.C.: January 19, 1999], 35-40).

[38] In 1997, feedlots of all sizes marketed 26.8 million (or 74%) of the 36.3 million cattle sold for commercial slaughter, with 63% (22.8 million) of the total commercial slaughter coming from feedlots with 1000+ head (*Livestock Slaughter 1997 Slaughter*, NASS, USDA [Washington, D.C.: March 1998], 1; and *Cattle: Final Estimates 1994-1998*, NASS, USDA [Washington, D.C.: January 19, 1999], 81).

[39] *Livestock Slaughter 1998 Summary*, NASS, USDA (Washington, D.C.: March 1999), 2; and *Poultry Slaughter*, NASS, USDA (Washington, D.C.: February 2, 1999), 1f.

[40] These numbers are for the United States alone. Worldwide, cattle, poultry, goats, and sheep total 15 billion (U.N. Food and Agricultural Organization, *Production Yearbook 1989* [Rome, 1989], vol. 43, table 89).

[41] According to *The Farm Report* (spring 1997), 530.8 million broilers, 252.6 million layers, 115.7 million turkeys, 1.4 million ducks, 1.8 million cattle, 2.8 million veal calves, 15.1 million pigs and 1.2 million sheep died in 1997 *before* reaching the slaughterhouse. These numbers are only for the United States.

[42] With the possible exception of the seafood industry which, strictly speaking, should be viewed as an extension of animal agribusiness since it is in the business of harvesting animals for human food consumption.

[43] If you believe (p_1), (p_2), (p_6), and (p_{10}), my argument will succeed. In fact, an argument for the immorality of eating meat can be constructed from (p_{15}) and (p_{16}) alone.

Your beliefs (p_{10})-(p_{13}) show that you already believe that animals are capable of experiencing intense pain and suffering. I don't have to prove to you that *unanaesthetized* branding, castration, debeaking, tail docking, tooth extraction, etc. cause animals severe pain. You already believe these procedures to be excruciatingly painful. Consequently, given the husbandry techniques and slaughtering practices documented above, you must admit the fact that: (f_1) Virtually all commercial animal agriculture, *especially* factory farming, causes animals intense pain and suffering and, thus, *greatly increases* the amount of pain and suffering in the world. (f_1) and your belief (p_1) together entail that, other things being equal, the world would be better without animal agriculture and factory farms. It is also a fact that: (f_2) In modern societies the consumption of meat is *in no way necessary* for human survival,[44] and so, the pain and suffering which results from meat production is entirely *unnecessary*, as are all the cruel practices inherent in animal agriculture. Since no one *needs* to eat flesh, all of the inhumane treatment to which farm animals are routinely subjected is done *for no good reason*, and so, your belief that it is morally wrong and despicable to treat animals inhumanely *for no good reason* [(p_{12})] forces you to admit that factory farming and animal agribusiness are morally wrong and despicable. Furthermore, your belief that a world with less unnecessary suffering is better than a world with more unnecessary suffering [(p_2)], together with (f_2), entails that the world would be better if there were less animal agriculture and fewer factory farms, and better still if there were no animal agriculture and no factory farms. Moreover, your belief in (p_3) commits you to the view that factory farming is wrong and *prima facie* ought not be supported or encouraged. When one buys factory farm-raised meat, one <u>is</u> supporting factory farms monetarily and thereby encouraging their *unnecessary* cruel practices. The only way to avoid actively supporting factory farms is to stop purchasing their products, for as Singer rightly notes:

> The people who profit by exploiting large numbers of animals do not need our approval. They need our money. The purchase of the corpses of the animals they rear is the main support the factory farmers ask from the public.... They will use intensive methods as long as they can sell what they produce by these methods.[45]

Since, per (p_3), you have a *prima facie* obligation to stop supporting factory farming and animal agriculture, you have a *prima facie* obligation to become a vegetarian.[46] Of course, *prima facie* obligations are overridable. Perhaps they can

---

[44] According to the USDA, "Vegetarian diets are consistent with the Dietary Guidelines for Americans and can meet Recommended Dietary Allowances for nutrients." *Nutrition and Your Health: Dietary Guidelines for Americans*, 4th Ed., USDA, U.S. Department of Health and Human Services (1995), 6.
[45] Singer, *Animal Liberation*, 161f.
[46] Here I am bracketing hunting. I realize that not all meat comes from factory farming and animal agriculture. Some comes from hunting. Hunting itself results in all sorts of unnecessary pain and suffering for the animals killed, maimed and wounded by bullets, shot, and arrows. Every year in the U.S. alone, hunters kill 175 million animals, and for every animal killed two are seriously wounded and left to die a slow agonizing death (Anna Sequoia, *67 Ways to Save the Animals* [New York: Harper Perennial, 1990], 38); and for every deer killed by crossbow, 21 arrows are shot since crossbow hunters rarely hit a vital organ (Ingrid Newkirk, *Save the Animals! 101 Easy Things You Can Do* [New York:

even be overridden simply by the fact that fulfilling them would be excessively burdensome or require enormous effort and sacrifice on one's part. Perhaps, but this much is clear: When one can fulfill *prima facie* obligation O *with little effort on one's part* and *without thereby failing to perform any other obligation*, then obligation O becomes very stringent indeed.

As for your *prima facie* obligation to stop supporting factory farming, you can easily satisfy it without thereby failing to perform any of your other obligations simply by refraining from eating meat and eating something else instead. For example, you can eat: Boca burgers rather than hamburgers, pasta with marinara sauce rather than meat sauce, bean burritos or bean tostadas rather than beef tacos, red beans and rice rather than Cajun fried chicken, barbecued tofu rather than barbecued ribs, moo shoo vegetables rather than moo shoo pork, minestrone rather than chicken soup, hummus-filled whole wheat pitas rather than BLTs, five bean vegetarian chili rather than chili with ground beef, chick pea salad rather than chicken salad, fruit and whole wheat toast rather than bacon and eggs, scrambled tofu vegetable frittatas rather than ham and cheese omelets, etc.[47] These examples underscore the <u>ease</u> with which one can avoid consuming flesh, a fact which often seems to elude meat eaters.

From your beliefs (p_1), (p_2), and (p_4), it follows that we ought to do what we reasonably can to avoid contributing to the amount of unnecessary suffering in the world. Since one thing we reasonably can do to avoid contributing to unnecessary suffering is stop contributing to factory farming with our purchases, it follows that we ought to stop purchasing and consuming meat.

Your other beliefs support the same conclusion. You believe: (p_5) A morally good person will take steps to make the world a better place and even stronger steps to avoid making the world a worse place; and (p_6) Even a "minimally decent person" would take steps to help reduce the amount of unnecessary pain and suffering in the world, *if s/he could do so with little effort on her/his part.* You also believe that you are a morally good person [(p_7)] or at least a minimally decent one [(p_8)]. Moreover, you believe that you are the kind of person who would take steps to help reduce the amount of pain and suffering in the world, *if you could do so with little effort on your part* [(p_9)]. As shown above, *with minimal effort* you could take steps to help reduce the amount of unnecessary suffering in the world just by eating something other than meat. Accordingly, given (p_6), you ought to refrain from eating flesh. Given (p_9), if you really are the kind of person you think you are, you will quit eating meat, opting for cruelty-free vegetarian fare instead.

Finally, animal agriculture is an extremely wasteful, inefficient, environmentally devastating means of food production. A full discussion of the inefficiencies and environmental degradations associated with animal agriculture is beyond the scope of the present paper, but consider five examples: (1) Animal

---

Warner Books, 1990], 95). Many of these animals are killed for barbaric wall "trophies," but even in those cases where the animals are killed (maimed or wounded) for the sake of obtaining meat, all of the pain and suffering inflicted on them is *unnecessary* since no one in a modern agriculturally-advanced society *needs* to eat any kind of meat, wild or domesticated.

[47] It is worth noting that in every case just mentioned the vegetarian option is significantly more nutritious, more healthful, and much lower in fat, saturated fat, and cholesterol than its meat-based counterpart. In fact, none of the vegetarian options listed contain any cholesterol whatsoever.

agriculture is an extremely energy intensive method of food production. It takes an average of 28 kcal of fossil energy to produce 1 kcal of animal protein, compared with an average of 3.3 kcal of fossil energy per kcal of grain protein, making animal production on average more than 8 times less energy efficient than grain production.[48] (2) Animal production is extremely inefficient in its water usage, compared to vegetable and grain production. Producing 1 kg of animal protein requires around 100 times more water than producing 1 kg of plant protein, e.g. it takes 500 liters of water to grow 1 kg of potatoes and 900 liters of water to grow 1 kg of wheat, but it requires 100,000 liters of water to produce 1 kg of beef.[49] Hence, agricultural water usage, which currently accounts for 87% of the world's freshwater consumption,[50] could be drastically reduced by a shift toward an entirely plant-based agriculture. (3) Animal agriculture is also extremely nutrient inefficient. By cycling grain through livestock to produce animal protein, we lose 90% of that grain's protein, 96% of its calories, 100% of its carbohydrates, and 100% of its fiber.[51] (4) Another negative by-product of the livestock industry is soil erosion. Much of arable land in the U.S. is devoted to feed crop production. Eighty percent of the corn and 95% of the oats grown in the U.S. are fed to livestock, and the excessive cultivation of our farmlands needed to produce these crops is responsible for the loss of 7 billion tons of topsoil each year.[52] David Pimentel, Professor of Agriculture and Life Sciences, Cornell University, describes the magnitude of the problem as follows: "During the last 40 years, nearly one-third of the world's arable land has been lost by erosion and continues to be lost at a rate of more than 10 million hectares per year."[53] The United States is losing soil at a rate 13 times faster than the rate of soil formation.[54] And (5) Animal agriculture creates enormous amounts of hazardous waste in the form of excrement. U.S. livestock produce 250,000 pounds of excrement *per second*, resulting in *1 billion tons* of unrecycled waste per year.[55] According to the U.S. General Accounting Office's Report to the U.S. Senate Committee on Agriculture, Nutrition, and Forestry, animal waste run-off from feedlots and rangeland is a significant factor in water quality, affecting about 72% of impaired rivers and streams, 56% of impaired lake acres, and 43% of impaired estuary miles.[56] This GAO report found that agriculture is one of the main sources of groundwater pollution and also found: "Among five general categories of pollution sources (Municipal Point Sources; Urban Runoff/Storm Sewers;

---

[48] David Pimentel, "Livestock Production: Energy Inputs and the Environment," in *Proceedings of the Canadian Society of Animal Science*, 47th Annual Meeting (Montréal, Québec: July 24-26, 1997), 16, 20. Fish production is equally inefficient requiring, on average, 27 kcal of fossil energy per kcal of fish protein produced (David Pimentel and Marcia Pimentel, *Food, Energy, and Society*, Rev Ed. [Niwot, CO: University Press of Colorado, 1996], 93).

[49] David Pimentel et al., "Water Resources: Agriculture, the Environment, and Society," *Bioscience* 47 (February 1997): 100.

[50] Ibid., 97, 104.

[51] Robbins, *Diet for a New America*, 352.

[52] Ibid., 351, 358.

[53] David Pimentel et al., "Environmental and Economic Cost of Soil Erosion and Conservation Benefits," *Science* 267 (February 24, 1995): 1117.

[54] Pimentel and Pimentel, *Food, Energy, and Society*, 153.

[55] Robbins, *Diet for a New America*, 372. In contrast, humans produce 12,000 pounds of excrement per second, 1/20th that of livestock (p. 372).

[56] *Animal Agriculture: Information on Waste Management and Water Quality Issues*, 2, 8f.

Agriculture; Industrial Point Sources; and Natural Sources), agriculture ranked as the number one cause of impaired rivers and streams and lakes."[57] The upshot is this: Animal agriculture is, by far and away, the most resource intensive, inefficient, environmentally harmful and ecologically unsound means of human food production, and consequently, one of the easiest direct actions one can take to help protect the environment and preserve resources for future generations, *one requiring minimal effort*, is to stop eating meat. And so, since you believe that we have a duty to preserve the environment for future generations [(p_{15})] and you believe that one ought to minimize one's contribution toward environmental degradation [(p_{16})], your beliefs commit you to the obligatoriness of becoming vegetarian, since doing so is a simple way to help to preserve the environment.

The moral of the present section is clear: Consistency forces you to admit that meat consumption is immoral and, thus, necessitates your becoming vegetarian immediately.

4a. Perhaps Meat Consumption Is Necessary for Optimal Nutrition

A crucial premise in my argument is: (CP1) The pain and suffering which inevitably results from meat production is entirely *unnecessary*. I defended (CP1) on the grounds that in modern societies meat consumption is *in no way necessary* for human survival [(f_2)]. But (CP1) does not follow from (f_2), since eating meat might be necessary for some reason other than human survival. Hence, one might object: "While eating meat is not necessary for survival, it *might* still be necessary for humans to thrive and flourish, in which case (CP1) would be false since the pain and suffering experienced by farm animals would be *necessary* for a significant human benefit."

If meat consumption were *necessary* for humans to flourish, my argument would be seriously compromised, so let us examine the evidence. First, consider the counterexamples. Since world class athletic competition is one of the most grueling and physically strenuous activities in which humans can engage, one would not expect there to be any highly successful vegetarian athletes or vegetarian world record holders, **if** meat consumption were necessary for humans to thrive and flourish. However, the list of world class vegetarian athletes is quite long and includes: Dave Scott (six-time winner of Hawaii's Ironman Triathlon), Sixto Linares (world record holder for the 24-hour triathlon), Edwin Moses (400 meter hurdler undefeated in international competition for 8 straight years), Paavo Nurmi (20 world records, 9 Olympic medals), Andreas Cahling (1980 Mr. International title in body building), and Ridgely Abele (U.S. Karate Association World Champion), to name a few,[58] which strongly suggests that eating meat is not necessary for humans to flourish.

Second, consider the diseases associated with the consumption of meat and animal products--heart disease, cancer, stroke, osteoporosis, diabetes, hypertension, arthritis, and obesity--as documented in numerous highly regarded studies.[59] Four

---

[57] Ibid., 9.

[58] The impressive feats of these world class vegetarian athletes and numerous other vegetarian athletes are discussed in much greater detail in Robbins, *Diet for a New America*, 158-163.

[59] For an excellent well-documented discussion of the positive correlation between meat consumption

examples must suffice: (1) The Loma Linda study, involving over 24,000 people, found that lacto-ovo-vegetarian men (who consume eggs and dairy products, but no meat) had a 61% lower coronary heart disease [CHD] mortality rate than California's general population. Pure vegetarian men (who consume no animal products) fared even better. The CHD mortality rate for these males was 86% lower than that of the California general population.[60] (2) The ongoing Framingham heart study has been tracking the daily living and eating habits of thousands of residents of Framingham, Massachusetts since 1948. Dr. William Castelli, director of the study for the last 15 years, maintains that based on his research the most heart healthy diet is a *pure vegetarian diet*.[61] Perhaps vegetarians suffer from other illnesses or die of other diseases earlier than their meat-eating counterparts. Not according to Dr. Castelli: "The vegetarian societies of the world have the best diet. Within our own country, they outlive the rest of us by at least seven years, and they have only 10 or 15 percent of our heart attack rate."[62] Elsewhere Castelli adds: "Vegetarians not only outlive the rest of us, they also aren't prey to other degenerative diseases, such as diabetes, strokes, etc., that slow us down and make us chronically ill."[63] (3) The Cornell-Oxford-China Health Project systematically monitored the diet, lifestyle and disease patterns of 6,500 families from 65 different counties in Mainland China and Taiwan.[64] The data collected in this study has led its director Dr. T. Colin Campbell to conclude that 80-90% of all cancers can be controlled or prevented by a lowfat (10-15% fat) pure vegetarian diet.[65] Campbell summarizes the results of his study as follows:

> In summary, two general strategies of analysis were used to examine the more holistic relationships between diet and chronic degenerative disease in this massive data set. The first strategy combined diseases into naturally associated groups, then sought the principal risk factors for these groups. The second strategy examined multiple individual diet-disease associations, then compared their individual relationships to the consumption of plant and animal-based foods. In both cases, the same conclusion emerges. A diet comprised of a variety of good quality plant-based foods is the healthiest.[66]

---

and these diseases, see Robbins' *Diet for a New America*, 203-305.
[60] Roland L. Phillips et al., "Coronary Heart Disease Mortality among Seventh-Day Adventists with Differing Dietary Habits: A Preliminary Report," *The American Journal of Clinical Nutrition* 31 (October 1978): S191-S198. CHD mortality rates based on Standardized Mortality Ratios of 39 and 14 for lacto-ovo and pure vegetarian men, respectively (FIG. 5, p. S195).
[61] "An Interview with William Castelli," *Good Medicine* 5, no. 3 (summer 1996): 15.
[62] Ibid.
[63] William Castelli, "Lessons from the Framingham Heart Study: How to Reduce the Risk of Heart Disease," *Bottom Line: Personal* (July 1, 1994): 10.
[64] J. Chen, T. C. Campbell et al., *Diet, Lifestyle, and Mortality in China: A Study of the Characteristics of 65 Counties* (Oxford: Oxford University Press, 1990).
[65] T. Colin Campbell [Professor of Nutritional Biochemistry at Cornell University], *New Century Nutrition* 2, no. 9 (September 1996): 1. Also reported in *Healthcare Foodservice* (March/April 1992): 15.
[66] T. Colin Campbell, "Associations of Diet and Disease: A Comprehensive Study of Health Characteristics in China" (presented at Harvard University, Cambridge, MA, May 23-24, 1997), 24.

Campbell adds:

> ... there are several more specific corollary conclusions to the main finding:
> - There is no threshold of plant food richness beyond which further health benefits are not achieved.
> - The closer the foods of plant origin are to their native state (minimal cooking, salting and processing), the greater will be their benefit:risk ratio.
> - The greater the variety of plant foods within a diet, the greater will be the long-term health benefit.[67]

And (4), the Dean Ornish study in which it was demonstrated that *advanced* coronary artery disease could be *reversed* through a combination of stress reduction and an extremely lowfat vegetarian diet (10% fat). All patients in the study had greater than 50 percent stenosis in one or more of the major coronary arteries. Members of the experimental group participated in stress management training and were fed a 1400 calorie diet consisting of fresh fruits and vegetables, whole grains, legumes, tubers, and soy beans; while the control group continued their routine activities at work and at home. After only six weeks, the experimental group's mean left ventricular ejection fraction had increased 6.4% (compared to pre-intervention ejection rates), whereas the control group's mean left ventricular ejection fraction showed a 1.7% decrease. In addition, the experimental group showed a 20.5% reduction in plasma cholesterol, a 91% mean reduction in the frequency of anginal episodes, and a mean weight reduction of 10 pounds; compared to the control group which showed no significant improvement in any of these areas.[68] These and countless other studies have led the American Dietetic Association, the leading nutritional organization in the country, to assert:

> Scientific data suggest positive relationships between a vegetarian diet and reduced risk for several chronic degenerative diseases and conditions, including obesity, coronary artery disease, hypertension, diabetes mellitus, and some types of cancer. . . . *It is the position of The American Dietetic Association (ADA) that appropriately planned vegetarian*

---

[67] Ibid., 24f. Also see T. C. Campbell et al., "Diet and Chronic Degenerative Diseases: Perspectives from China," *American Journal of Clinical Nutrition* 59, suppl. 5 (May 1994): 1153S-1161S, where Campbell and his co-authors conclude that "even small intakes of foods of animal origin are associated with significant increases in plasma cholesterol concentrations, which are associated, in turn, with significant increases in chronic degenerative disease mortality rates" (p. 1153S).

[68] Dean Ornish et al., "Effects of Stress Management Training and Dietary Changes in Treating Ischemic Heart Disease," *Journal of the American Medical Association* 249 (1983): 54-59. These findings were confirmed in the Lifestyle Heart Trial. See Dean Ornish et al., "Can Lifestyle Changes Reverse Coronary Heart Disease?" *Lancet* 336 (July 21, 1990): 129-133. [NOTE: Left ventricular ejection fraction (LVEF) is indicative of the amount of blood expelled from the left ventricle in a single contraction of the heart muscle. As such, LVEF is an important indicator of heart function and efficiency.]

diets are healthful, are nutritionally adequate, and provide health benefits in the prevention and treatment of certain diseases.[69]

An article in *The Journal of the American Medical Association* concurs, claiming: "A vegetarian diet can prevent 90% of our thrombo-embolic disease and 97% of our coronary occlusions."[70] In light of these findings, the Physicians Committee for Responsible Medicine [PCRM] recommends centering our diets around the following **new** four food groups: I. Whole Grains (5+ servings/day), II. Vegetables (3+ servings/day), III. Fruits (3+ servings/day), and IV. Legumes (2+ servings/day).[71] Gone are meat and dairy, the two principal sources of fat and cholesterol in the American diet. The evidence is unequivocal: A vegetarian diet is nutritionally superior to a meat-based diet. One cannot reject (CP1) on the grounds that eating meat is necessary for human flourishing, because it isn't. On the contrary, it is *detrimental* to human health and well-being.[72]

[Editors' Note: two substantial sections of the paper, dealing with other objections to vegetarianism, are omitted here. The full text of the paper is available on the web site at www.phil.vt.edu]

6. Conclusion

Let me conclude by noting an additional implication of your beliefs. Not only do your beliefs commit you to the obligatoriness of vegetarianism, they also commit you to the obligatoriness of a vegan diet, i.e. a diet devoid of all animal products. Here's why: In section 4a, we found a vegan diet to be the most nutritious and healthful diet a human can consume.[73] Plus, contrary to what many

---

[69] "Position of the American Dietetic Association: Vegetarian Diets," *Journal of the American Dietetic Association* 97 (November 1997): 1317. For those wishing to learn more about sound vegetarian nutrition, the ADA has published this article in its entirety at: www.eatright.org/adap1197.html .
[70] "Diet and Stress in Vascular Disease," *Journal of the American Medical Association* 176 (June 3, 1961): 806. Thus, the coronary health benefits of a vegetarian diet have been known for over 35 years.
[71] Neal Barnard, *Food for Life: How the New Four Food Groups Can Save Your Life* (New York: Harmony Books, 1993), 144-147.
[72] These findings are hardly surprising when one considers that both the American Heart Association [AHA] and the American Cancer Society [ACS] recommend a diet that is high in complex carbohydrates and fiber, and low in protein, dietary cholesterol, fat (especially saturated fat), sodium, alcohol, carcinogens and procarcinogens. Specifically, complex carbohydrates should comprise 55-70% of our calories, fat should provide less than 30% (preferably 10-15%) of our calories, protein should make up 10-12% of our calories, dietary cholesterol should not exceed 300 mg/day (0 mg is optimal, since there is no minimum amount of dietary cholesterol required), and fiber consumption should be 25-30 grams per day. In stark contrast, the typical American meat-based diet is 40% fat (most of which is saturated), 30% carbohydrate, 25% protein and contains 400+ mg of cholesterol per day. These statistics are to be expected since meat is high in fat, high in protein, and high in cholesterol (only animal products contain cholesterol), but contains no complex carbohydrates and no fiber. In fact, it is almost impossible to adhere to the AHA's and ACS's dietary guidelines while consuming a meat-based diet, whereas satisfying these guidelines is virtually inevitable when one eats only from the PCRM's new four food groups.
[73] The PCRM recommends a vegan diet centered around the new four food groups. Anyone who eats only from these four food groups will be consuming a vegan diet. Any article advocating a vegan diet would be remiss not to discuss the *only* legitimate nutritional concern facing vegans, namely, vitamin B_{12} deficiency. The conventional wisdom is that vitamin B_{12} is virtually nonexistent in plant

people think, it is relatively easy to adopt a vegan diet. To see how easy, recall that in section 3, I provided a long list of readily available, tasty vegetarian dishes which one could easily eat in place of standard meat fare. Each of the vegetarian dishes listed there is actually vegan. While being vegan may seem like a daunting task to the uninitiated, all one needs to do to eat vegan is to make a conscious choice to consume only those foods listed in the PCRM's new four food groups.[74] Since eggs and dairy products are both nutritionally unnecessary and relatively easy to avoid, we are now in a position to see why your beliefs entail that eating these products is morally wrong.

Let us start by examining the modern egg industry. Two distinct strains of chickens have been developed: "layers" for egg production and "broilers" for meat production. Since layer strains are thought to produce insufficient and inferior meat and since males do not produce eggs, male chicks of the layer strain are identified by chicken sexers, who throw them into plastic bags where they are allowed to suffocate.[75] In 1995, 247 million unwanted male chicks met this fate.[76] Like their broiler counterparts, female layers are debeaked at one week of age. However, since layers are kept alive longer, most egg producers debeak their birds a second time around twelve weeks of age.[77] Worse still, layers are permanently confined in 16" x 18" battery cages, 5-6 birds to a cage.[78] Thus, the average layer has only 48-58 square inches of cage-floor space, not much larger than a 5x8 index card. The cages have slanted wire mesh flooring which is totally inappropriate for the birds' feet, which sometimes grow fast to the cage floor making it impossible to reach food and water.[79] Ninety-eight percent of the eggs produced in the U.S. come from layers permanently confined in such battery cages.[80] After a year and a half of this existence (assuming they don't die in their cages, as do 12-18% of them per year[81]), about the time when their egg production begins to wane, the birds are either crammed even more tightly

---

foods. New evidence suggests: (i) that B_{12} can be found in plants, (ii) that organically grown plants contain higher levels of B_{12} than those grown with chemical fertilizers, (iii) that plant roots are able to absorb vitamins produced by soil microorganisms [B_{12} is only produced by microorganisms.], and (iv) that vegans should be able to obtain B_{12} by consuming organically grown produce (T. Colin Campbell, "B_{12} Breakthrough: Missing Nutrient Found in Plants," *New Century Nutrition* 2, no. 11 [November 1996]: 1). Because this evidence is preliminary, those following a vegan diet should make sure they have a reliable source of vitamin B_{12} in their diets [Reliable sources include: fortified soy, rice, and nut milks; fortified cereals; fortified textured soy protein; and Red Star T-6635+ nutritional yeast.] or they should take a B_{12} supplement.

[74] This is not to deny that being vegan requires some effort, at least until one becomes habituated to eating this way. For example, one must read labels to check the ingredients in different foods so as to avoid foods containing meat, eggs, and dairy products. But now that most supermarket chains stock a wide variety of soy, rice, and nut milks, countless vegan meat analogues, and a plethora of vegan canned and frozen goods, it requires much less effort than one would initially think.

[75] Robbins, *Diet for a New America*, 54.

[76] Davis, *Prisoned Chickens, Poisoned Eggs*, 105.

[77] Mason and Singer, *Animal Factories*, 39.

[78] Karen Davis, "The Plight of Poultry," *The Animals' Agenda* (July/August 1996): 38. Also see Robbins, *Diet for a New America*, 63.

[79] Singer, *Animal Liberation*, 110. The industry justification for such inappropriate flooring is that it allows urine and feces to drop through the cage and the slant facilitates automatic egg collection.

[80] William Dudley-Cash, "Study Shows Adoption Rate of Technology by Laying Hen Industry," *Feedstuffs* (November 4, 1991): 11; and Robbins, *Diet for a New America*, 53.

[81] Mason and Singer, *Animal Factories*, 25.

into portable crates, transported to the slaughterhouse, and turned into soup and other processed foods,[82] or they are kept for another laying cycle, whichever is cheaper. Those unfortunate enough to be kept and "recycled" are force-molted to prepare them for the next laying cycle. The primary method of forced molting involves the withholding of all food from the hens for a period of 5-14 days.[83] In a typical month, 70 million hens are force-molted.[84] After one or two forced-molt laying cycles, the spent birds will suffer one of two fates: Either they will be sent to slaughter as described above or, as is increasingly favored, they will meet with on farm disposal whereby they are ground up alive and fed to the next generation of hens.[85] During the first six months of 1999, 98.7 million laying hens were sent to slaughter and another 21.9 million met with on farm disposal.[86] These millions of birds are forced to endure all of this inhumane treatment, just so we can indulge in an inherently unhealthful product loaded with cholesterol (300 mg. per egg) and fat (50% of eggs' calories come from fat, most of which is saturated), which has somehow come to be associated with breakfast. Since eggs are nutritionally unnecessary, are reasonably easy to avoid, and come from an unnecessarily cruel industry, your beliefs entail that it is immoral to eat them.

As for dairy products, 57% of dairy cows are raised in factory farms, where their calves are taken away within 1-2 days and where they are constantly reimpregnated, pumped full of antibiotics and bovine growth hormone, milked 2-3 times a day, suffer from mastitis, fed unnatural diets and prevented from moving about freely. After a few years when their milk production wanes, they, like their meat-producing counterparts, will be inhumanely loaded onto trucks and shipped to the slaughterhouse without food or water and without protection from the elements, where they will be transformed into ground beef. Lest one think this a rare occurrence, in 1998, over 2.6 million dairy cows were slaughtered in federally inspected plants.[87] As for their calves, if the calf is female, it will either be kept or sold to another dairy farmer. However, if the calf is male, it will typically be sold to veal farmers who will chain it at the neck and feed it an iron deficient diet for 14-16 weeks before sending it off to slaughter.[88] Consequently, when one purchases dairy products, one is not only supporting the unnecessary and inhumane confinement of dairy cows, one is also indirectly supporting the even more inhumane veal industry. Since, according to both the ADA and the PCRM, dairy products are in no way necessary for optimum human health, since dairy products are relatively easy to

---

[82] Ibid., 6.
[83] Davis, *Prisoned Chickens, Poisoned Eggs*, 74-76. Davis explains molting and the industry rationale behind forced molting as follows: "Molting refers to the replacement of old feathers by new ones. In nature, all birds replace all of their feathers in the course of a year.... Egg laying tapers off as the female bird concentrates her energies on growing new feathers and staying warm" (p. 74). This process naturally takes four months, whereas during a forced molt, the process only takes a month or two (p. 74).
[84] According to NASS, on July 1, 1999, over 17.5 million hens were being forced molted and over 70.3 million hens had just completed a forced molt; the figures for June 1, 1999 were 16.6 million and 70 million, respectively (*Chicken and Eggs*, NASS, USDA [Washington, D.C.: July 23, 1999]: 2-4).
[85] Davis, *Prisoned Chickens, Poisoned Eggs*, 77.
[86] *Chicken and Eggs*, NASS, USDA, Monthly Reports: 3-99, 4-99, 5-99, 6-99, and 7-99, pp. 4f, 3, 3, 2f, and 2-4, respectively.
[87] *Livestock Slaughter 1997 Summary*, NASS, USDA, 82.
[88] Ibid., 12f.

avoid, and since the dairy industry inflicts untold suffering and death on dairy cows and their calves, your beliefs commit you to the immorality of consuming dairy products.

One might object to my argument for the immorality of consuming dairy products by challenging one of its major premises, namely, that milk and other dairy products are in no way essential for optimum human health. Aren't there certain groups, e.g. children and pregnant women, who absolutely must consume milk and other dairy products to meet their nutritional needs? Don't children *need* milk in a way that no one in our culture needs meat? Not according to the American Dietetic Association: "Well-planned vegan . . . diets are appropriate for all stages of the life cycle, including during pregnancy and lactation. Appropriately planned vegan . . . diets satisfy nutrient needs of infants, children, and adolescents and promote normal growth."[89]

One might also object to my argument for the immorality of consuming dairy products as follows: "While it is true that much of the milk produced today is produced inhumanely in factory farms, not all milk is. Some milk is gotten humanely from truly free range dairy cows whose owners allow their cows to die of old age. What's wrong with consuming the milk of humanely raised cows?"[90] Often in ethics (and in philosophy generally), there are gray areas. This may be such an area, but before deeming it such, let us look at the issue more closely. Obviously, if the cows in question are raised completely humanely and are allowed to live out their natural life span, then one cannot object to drinking their milk on the basis of (p_1), (p_2), (p_3), (p_6), (p_{11}), (p_{12}) or (p_{14}). So, if it is morally objectionable to drink the milk of such contented cows, it must be for reasons having nothing to do with unnecessary cruelty and unnecessary killing. The first thing to realize is that even if it is permissible to drink the milk of contented cows, that does not make it permissible to drink the inhumanely produced commercial milk available at your local grocery store. Second, producing milk in an entirely humane way is only economically feasible on very small dairy farms. In 1997, only 3.5% of dairy cows were housed on farms with fewer than 30 head of cattle.[91] So, for most people living in nonrural areas, the opportunity to drink milk from truly contented cows will never avail itself. Thus, since your beliefs commit you to the immorality of consuming inhumanely produced commercial milk, your beliefs entail that it is wrong to drink the only milk available to most of us. But suppose, unlike most of us, you know Mike Milky, a small-scale humane free-range nonkill dairy farmer. Is it permissible to drink Mike's milk? That depends on what Mike does with the offspring of his contented cows [Dairy cows must be continually reimpregnated in order for them to continually produce milk.]. If Mike sells the non-milk-producing male calves to the veal farmer down the road, then by purchasing Mike's milk you would be indirectly supporting the veal industry. Finally, suppose that Mike keeps and humanely raises all of the offspring of his cows until they die of old age. Because of the cost associated with feeding and housing cows, very few farmers can afford to be like Mike. The major moral concerns with Mike's farm are environmental ones. In 1995, dairy cows consumed 12,387 pounds of grain per cow and they converted every 75 pounds of grain consumed into 100

---

[89] "Position of the American Dietetic Association: Vegetarian Diets," 1318.
[90] I wish to thank Louis Pojman for calling to my attention this and the previous objection.
[91] *Milk Cows and Production: Final Estimates 1993-97*, NASS, USDA, 35.

pounds of milk,[92] but since Mike never kills any of his cows' male offspring, he must provide these males with 12,387 pounds of grain per year for their entire lives. If a dairy cow has two males in a row, that will in effect increase the grain-to-milk conversion ratio from .75:1 to 2.25:1, since Mike must now provide grain for three animals rather than one. Another concern is that a typical cow produces more than a ton of manure per year.[93] Since Mike never kills his cows, he quickly finds himself with over 30 cows, half of which are male. [Starting with 6 females, Mike will have 34 cows after just three breeding seasons if all females are impregnated annually.] Now Mike's cattle produce over 30 tons of manure a year, but because his animals are not confined, the manure drops on the ground, where it leaches into the soil and water table. Having 30+ tons of nitrate--and heavy metal-rich manure absorbed by the soil annually will, over time, significantly reduce soil quality. [Mike could, of course, prevent this geometric expansion of his herd by only impregnating one cow each year, but since cows have a natural life span of 20-25 years, in 15 years he will be feeding 15 cows to get milk from one and will be facing an 11.25:1 grain-to-milk conversion ratio, hardly an efficient use of our precious grain resources.] Since dairy production in its most humane form is a very inefficient, resource intensive, environmentally degrading means of protein production, since dairy products are not nutritionally necessary for any subgroup of the population, and since it is relatively easy to avoid consuming dairy products, your beliefs (p_{15}) and (p_{16}) commit you to the immorality of consuming milk, even contented cow's milk.[94]

The implications of your beliefs are clear. Given your beliefs, it follows that: (1) eating meat is morally wrong and (2) eating animal products is also morally wrong. These conclusions were not derived from some highly contentious ethical theory which you can easily reject, but from your own firmly held beliefs.

---

[92] NASS, USDA, *Agricultural Statistics 1997*, Table 1-72, p. I-47.

[93] *Protecting the Nation's Groundwater from Contamination*, vol. 2 (Washington, D.C.: U. S. Congress, Office of Technology Assessment, OTA-O-276, October 1984), 284.

[94] It is worth noting that your beliefs also commit you to the immorality of purchasing personal care and household products that have been tested on animals. These tests include the Draize eye irritancy test, the lethal dose 50% [LD50] test, dermal toxicity tests, and injection tests. Eighty percent of the animals in these tests receive no anaesthesia. Moreover, these tests are unnecessary and unreliable. Consider two examples: (1) the crude LD50 test, in which a test group of animals is force-fed a substance until fifty percent of the animals die (which is often due to stomach rupture rather than the effects of the substance *per se*), provides no useful data which can be reliably extrapolated to humans (Robert Sharpe, "Animal Experiments--A Failed Technology," in *Animal Experimentation: The Consensus Changes*, ed. Gill Langley [New York: Chapman and Hall, 1989], 101-104); and (2) The Draize test involves dripping caustic substances such as bleach or shampoo into restrained rabbits' eyes, frequently resulting in hemorrhage, ulceration, and blindness. Rabbits are used for convenience, because they have no tear ducts to flush out the offending substance. Of course, this makes them poor models for humans who do have tear ducts (Sidney Gendin, "The Use of Animals in Science" in *Animal Rights and Human Obligations, op. cit.*, 199f). In most cases, avoiding products which have been tested on animals is relatively easy, since (1) in many cases, we do not need the products and can live perfectly happy lives without them, and (2) in those cases where we do need a particular product, equally priced, equally safe, alternative products which have not been tested on animals and which contain no animal ingredients are almost always readily available. Moreover, determining which products are cruelty-free will not require a great deal of time or effort on your part, for cruelty-free products typically advertise their cruelty-free status on the label. Since one can easily reduce one's contribution to laboratory-generated animal suffering by buying cruelty-free personal care and household products instead of those tested on animals (usually they are right next to each other on the supermarket shelves), your beliefs entail that you are morally obligated to do so.

Furthermore, these conclusions follow, regardless of your views on speciesism, animal equality, and animal rights. Even those of you who are staunch speciesists are committed to the immorality of these practices, given your other beliefs. Consequently, consistency demands that you embrace the immorality of these practices and modify your behavior accordingly.[95]

Appendix

(p_1) Other things being equal, a world with less pain and suffering is better than a world with more pain and suffering.

(p_2) A world with less unnecessary suffering is better than a world with more unnecessary suffering.

(p_3) Unnecessary cruelty is wrong and *prima facie* should not be supported or encouraged.

(p_4) We ought to take steps to make the world a better place.

($p_{4'}$) We ought to do what we reasonably can to avoid making the world a worse place.

(p_5) A morally good person will take steps to make the world a better place and even stronger steps to avoid making the world a worse place.

(p_6) Even a minimally decent person would take steps to help reduce the amount of unnecessary pain and suffering in the world, *if s/he could do so with little effort on her/his part*.

(p_7) I am a morally good person.

(p_8) I am at least a minimally decent person.

(p_9) I am the sort of person who certainly would take steps to help reduce the amount of pain and suffering in the world, *if I could do so with little effort on my part*.

(p_{10}) Many nonhuman animals (certainly all vertebrates) are capable of feeling pain.

(p_{11}) Other things being equal, it is morally wrong to cause an animal pain or suffering.

(p_{12}) It is morally wrong and despicable to treat animals inhumanely for *no good reason*.

(p_{13}) We ought to euthanatize untreatably injured, suffering animals to put them out of their misery whenever feasible.

(p_{14}) Other things being equal, it is worse to kill a conscious sentient animal than it is to kill a plant.

---

[95]Research on this project was supported by a generous grant from the Culture and Animals Foundation, for which I am extremely grateful. Versions of this paper have been presented at the MidSouth Philosophy Conference, the Illinois Philosophical Association Meetings, the Conference on Value Inquiry, the Society for the Study of Ethics and Animals Meetings, and at the University of Maribor-Slovenia. I would like to thank those in attendance for their comments and criticisms. I would also like to thank John Carroll, Mark Heller, Alastair Norcross, Louis Pojman, Trudy Pojman, Wolfgang Gombocz, Eric Richards, Jim Sauer, Keith Burgess-Jackson, Jim Hudson, Sharon Sytsma, E. W. Van Steenburgh, Ray Dybzinski, Nathan Nobis, Bob Hicks and the philosophy faculty at Southern Methodist University for their helpful suggestions. Special thanks to Lisa Joniak whose detailed comments on numerous prior versions have improved every section of the paper.

(p₁₅) We have a duty to help preserve the environment for future generations (at least for future human generations).

(p₁₆) One ought to minimize one's contribution toward environmental degradation, *especially in those ways requiring minimal effort on one's part.*

Post-Modernism and the Environmental Crisis
Leo Marx

The globalization of the environmental crisis coincides with the crossing of what many consider to be a historic watershed in philosophy. On one side we find the dominant tradition of Western thought, with all its efforts to place human knowledge on a solid, unchanging foundation. On the other side we find certain skeptical, or anti-foundationalist, modes of thinking variously labeled "post-modern," "poststructuralist," or "deconstructionist." Whether or not the emergence of these viewpoints truly constitutes a watershed, and whether or not they actually represent a common tendency of thought, the fact is that many intellectuals have recently adopted an attitude of radical skepticism toward the basic premises of scientific rationalism. Perhaps the most important of these premises has been that human beings can gain access to a stable, context-free foundation for knowledge, and so arrive at a univocal, objective truth.

This widespread skepticism about the foundations of knowledge leads naturally to a rejection of "essentialism"--that is, the belief that our language provides access to immutable essences, or meanings, located in a reality beyond, and hence independent of, the language itself. Defenders of essences are now rare indeed. We find instead a pervasive historicism, acutely sensitive to the unstable, contingent nature of language, and convinced of the historical and societal genesis of all our ideas and practices, including the language or discourses by which they are defined.

Terms such as "nature," "technology," "science," and "environment"--which might be thought to represent constituent properties of an independently existing reality--are seen from a post-modernist perspective as contingent products of historical processes. Like all our words and concepts, they are taken to be "socially constructed." So, far from having a univocal meaning, the import of each term is thought to vary according to historical, social, and cultural circumstances and, more particularly, according to the speaker's assumptions about race, ethnicity, gender, and class.

Whatever its weaknesses, post-modernism is a feature of our intellectual world too important to be ignored; and it may even provide valuable critical analyses of certain cloudy regions of environmentalist thinking. Because its adherents do not offer their own "positive" alternative to the conventional theories of knowledge they dismiss, most versions of post-modernism, like most versions of philosophic skepticism, are valuable chiefly for the critical, anti-metaphysical insights they afford. Indeed, it is difficult to imagine what form such a positive alternative, compatible with the spirit of post-modernist skepticism, might take. We nonetheless believe that the post-modernist critique of traditional assumptions could be useful in rethinking certain theoretical and cognitive presuppositions of environmentalism.

The Hegemony of "Hard" Science

This current tendency, with its bias towards contextualism, may help to break down some long-standing conceptual and practical barriers to collaboration between the "hard" biophysical sciences and the "soft" social or human sciences. To begin with, it calls into question the hegemony of "hard" scientific knowledge and its tacit corollary, a virtually exclusive commitment to reductionist methods of inquiry. That hegemony has created many difficulties for the management of environmental research. It has often meant, for example, that complex problems involving the reciprocal relations between human and natural systems are defined in narrowly technocentric terms.

Because of the perceived "weakness," or "softness," of the social sciences and humanities, the hegemony of the biophysical sciences has also impeded the effective integration of scientific findings about environmental degradation with findings about its behavioral, societal origins. According to *Humankind in the Biosphere*, Martin F. Price's recent survey of international interdisciplinary research on environmental problems, the "research objectives" of many purportedly interdisciplinary projects "tend to be set primarily by natural scientists." Of course, this is hardly a recent development. Price notes that the 1981 international conference aimed at assessing ten years' work by UNESCO's "Man and the Biosphere" program, whose goals were "to develop the basis within the natural and social sciences" for improving the global relationship between man and the environment, found that "less than five percent of projects through mid-1979 integrated the work of natural and social scientists."

These findings compel us to reaffirm our primary assumption, namely, that although the work of scientists and engineers is indispensable for coping with the most urgent environmental problem, the problems themselves are invariably the result of social practices. They are quintessentially *social* problems whose roots lie deep in a long-standing matrix of cultural proclivities. Hence, they are bound to remain intractable until we find ways to integrate (1) scientific analyses of their nature; (2) an adequate understanding of their social, cultural or behavioral genesis; and (3) a plan to change the behavior, or institutional structures, necessary to resolve them. One of the main impediments to coping with urgent environmental problems, in our view, is the deeply ingrained habit of defining them chiefly in terms derived from their biophysical manifestations. Indeed, a fact that scientists and engineers seem reluctant to acknowledge is that many, perhaps even most, environmental problems will have to be resolved in the arena of national and international politics.

All of this suggests that there may be more than coincidence involved in the simultaneous discovery of the global and social nature of environmental degradation and the skeptical, anti-foundationalist drift of contemporary philosophy and critical theory. These current philosophic tendencies direct attention away from the centrality of "hard" scientific knowledge as the key to coping with the problems of the environment. They emphasize the decisive role not of some context-free body of truth, but of the common understandings, or "background" knowledge, shared by a people. On this view, the ultimate determinant of many of the practices causing the deterioration of the environment, as well as of the practices required to cope with it, is the cultural context. Unlike traditional scientific rationalism; this contextualist concept of knowledge might help to foster a collaborative, multidisciplinary approach to environmental problems.

INSTANTIATION₄

FORCE AND RESISTANCE

INTRODUCTION

Is killing other human beings to solve international disputes ever morally defensible? Extreme pacifists would argue that it never is. Extreme militarists would argue it always is. Most of us fall somewhere in between. There seem to be clear cases of the justified use of violence for example, the Jewish uprising in the Warsaw ghetto. There also seem to be clear cases where the use of violence is not justified-- turning again to WW II, Nazi concentration camps provide an obvious example of unjustified and immoral violence. But how do we decide cases that are not so clear-cut, the ambiguous middle cases? Just War theories and traditions (i.e., ethical theories and history of agreed upon conventions for engaging in "civilized warfare") attempt to provide an ethical basis and set of rules for the organized use of violence to resolve disputes between groups. They do not nor were they intended to apply to or regulate individual behavior or unorganized violence (e.g., mob violence, spontaneous protests, etc.). Here, we briefly outline the basic just war framework, then discuss and raise questions and criticisms about its applicability to today's global situation and possibilities for extension. As we assume the majority of students using this book will be predominately American College students, our discussion and selections focus on the American experience.

1. Just War Theories and Tradition[1]

Assumptions:

There are two general assumptions underlying both Just War theories and the Just War tradition

1. War is a great evil and a last resort, which is to be avoided at *almost* any cost.
2. After the war, one hopes to live peacefully with and re-integrate the opposing side into normal international relations.

In order to meet assumption 1, one must be able to demonstrate clearly that one goes to war (uses violence) only after all other options have been exhausted and that one has a compelling and just cause for fighting. Without a just cause, there can be no ethically relevant justification for war. In order to meet assumption 2, one must wage war in such a way that greater enmity will not ensue after the close of the war-- implacable hatred does not make for good neighbors. These two assumptions give rise to the two main components of Just War theory: *jus ad bellum* and *jus in bello*. The first addresses acceptable reasons and requirements for starting and engaging in a just war. The main elements considered under *jus ad bellum* are those of proper

---

[1] (see Moseley for a fuller outline of the history of just war theories and traditions).

authority, just cause, right intention, chance of success and proposed means proportional to desired ends. Given that one can justify engaging in war the second component, *jus in bello*, then provides guidelines for justly conducting a just war. Here, the rules of engagement are laid out and a wide spectrum of concerns about just and unjust actions during war are addressed, including legitimate targets for violence, treatment of prisoners, acceptable weapons and tactics, etc.

Jus ad Bellum: Just Cause & Legitimate Authority, etc.

Jus ad bellum is the requirement that in order to fight a just war--engage in justifiable violence against others--one must first be able to argue that one has just cause. Intuitively, self-defense (including the defense of one's allies as a part of self) seems a self-evident principle for justifying the use of violence against another group. It is standard reason appealed to for justifying killing at the level of individuals and is now merely being translated to the larger political group. Most arguments for what constitute a just cause, though they come in a variety of guises, tend to reduce to some type of "self-defense" reasoning.

Just War theories and traditions also define "who" may engage in a just war. As these theories were being developed alongside the development of the modern nation state, it should not be too surprising that it was decided that only legitimate sovereigns or rulers of nation states could declare and wage just wars. Under *Jus ad Bellum*, one must also be able to show one has a chance of success. Resorting to violence that ultimately will be futile is considered unjust. One must also ensure prior to engagement that the means one will employ are proportional to the end sought.

Jus in Bello: Principles of Discrimination & Proportionality

Jus in Bello is the second component of just war theories and conventions. The two main principles for conducting a just war are discrimination and proportionality. The principle of discrimination covers what are legitimate targets of violence. Traditionally, a distinction is made between civilians and professional soldiers. Targets have been limited to military personnel in uniform and military property (e.g., military bases, ships, supply depots, etc.) The principle of proportionality requires that the amount of force one uses does not extend beyond that necessary for victory and to ensure the original source of injustice is removed and will not soon resurface once hostilities cease.

2. Jus ad Bellum: Revisions, Criticisms and Extensions

Just war tradition is just that--a tradition--historically contingent conventions between particular sovereign states and which obviously benefited those power structures that codified and agreed to them. This does not mean they are bad traditions, but clearly they need to be questioned to see if they fit our historical situation. Is the traditional "*status quo*" itself morally desirable and/or relevant for us today? Answering this question requires asking whom such theories would benefit and disenfranchise. The reminder of this introduction will provide some criticisms of traditional just war theory and try to indicate where a just war theory analysis could be extended in order to evaluate a spectrum of force and resistance actions between groups other than nation states. First, we need to distinguish between three general categories of violence that are applicable to analyzing force and resistance--lethal violence (taking of human life), non-lethal violence (the destruction of property) and non-violence (protest or force without damage to either persons or property).

Legitimate Authority: On Just War Tradition, only sovereigns of nation states or some other geo-political unit were considered legitimate authorities and were the only ones allowed to declare war or sanction acts of violence against other groups. Any other type of group was merely engaging in unjust violence including those enemies (internal and external) who would "overthrow" the sovereign. The American Revolution was unjust given the conventions of the period--by *fiat* given the definition of who could declare war--as was any other revolution.[2] Questions arose, of course, about whether citizens could use violence to resist and replace a government that was grossly unjust and ineffective after all other means of change had failed.[3] But just as history is written by the victors, so too are the conventions of Just Warfare--traditions change. Today, in general, we assume the overthrow of an unpopular government by its own citizens is just.[4]

Revisions: Accepting the view above that rejects only sovereigns of nation states as having the right to declare and engage in just war does not mean any group can use violence to change society. Just war conventions and theorists today have broadened the scope of authority. Groups that can demonstrate they have a military chain of command or hierarchical authority structure, the support of the local populace, and marginally control specific territory—perhaps only at night as is often the case during civil wars and guerrilla conflicts, etc. may be considered for status as legitimate authorities. Most of the criteria offered to extend the notion of legitimate authority modify or relax the characteristics of a nation state to extend this status to internal dissenting groups (See Lackey for a more in-depth discussion of these characteristics and problems resulting from these revisions).

Criticisms: The vagueness and often inconsistent application of these criteria for determining the difference between a "freedom fighter" and a "terrorist" seems in practice to depend less on each group's actions, which are in many respects similar, and more on the interests of the party doing the labeling. Our guys are freedom fighters, their guys are terrorists. If a distinction is going to be made between these two groups, then it does not appear it will come from looking at definitions of who has the authority to make war. However, putting aside these problems, is this extension sufficiently broad?

Extensions: We encounter force and resist (and vice versa) at many levels both from and from within the many international, multinational and transnational groups

---

[2] This does not mean there was no sympathy for the uprising. Indeed, there was support in England for the colonies especially among the Tories. The question of whether or not colonists' rights had been violated; however, does not change the fact that under the just war conventions of that time, rebellion against a sovereign was unjust.

[3] Even with the qualification of overthrowing "brutal" and "ineffective" governments, "taxation without representation" is hardly grounds for engaging in such a great evil as war.

[4] This is part of the legacy we have acquired from the success of both the American and French revolutions.

and communities we belong to or with whom we share our political, economic and social spaces. There are an enormous number of "non-traditional" global powers in the world today. These powers are for all intents and purposes geo-political entities with rights, privileges and powers granted explicitly or implicitly by other more traditional governments though they make no claim to resembling traditional geopolitical entities. These new forces of global power include but are not limited to big business corporations, non-profit organizations, religious groups, non-governmental organizations, ecological and animal rights groups--the list runs the gamut from earthfirsters to the World Trade Organization (WTO). These collectives are major actors in both force and resistance on a global scale. Of deep concern for many is the increasing power and number of multinational and transnational companies and groups that do not fall under the aegis of any one government.

Regardless of how one views such groups "rights" to authority, their power and global impact can not be denied (see Instantiation$_2$, Instantiation$_5$ and our supporting website at http://www.phil.vt.edu/Global/). Should these groups be bound by just war theories and conventions when they use (directly or indirectly through a third party—often a weak government) force or engage in resistance and how could this be implemented? Note the question is not whether to grant them the power to use force and resistance, they already have it and are actively engaged in using it. The question is how to bring the use of such power under international ethical scrutiny and control. Replacing definitions of authority with the demand of showing just cause does suggest that a group, which can show just cause with right intentions, may have legitimate grounds for claiming the authority to use violence to resist or force change given all other methods of resolution have failed. Alternatively, using just war theory, we can say that any group fighting on behalf of themselves or some other "entity" that violates *jus ad bellum* or *jus in bello* conventions forfeits any claim to being a legitimate authority capable of engaging in just war. Though traditional theories de-couple authority and cause, for today's world it may be more fruitful to link them together along with right intentions.

Just Cause: When agriculture was the primary source of both the basic necessities as well as the luxuries of a people's life, then invasion onto one's territorial claims could be seen as a clear case of aggression that required self-defense.

Revisions & Criticisms: In an increasingly global world where industry, information and trade provide, especially for the west, their economic structure (e.g., indirectly a source of food, etc), arguments are forwarded to the effect that protecting businesses, trade and trade routes is essential to self-defense. Are these arguments ethically justifiable? For example, when Castro nationalized all businesses was the US justified in treating this as a military incursion threatening national self-defense that justified a military blockade and assassination attempts on a sovereign rather than an international business dispute[5]? The entangling of economics and national interests with self-defense is deeply problematic. How far claims of self-defense can be extended beyond national boundaries is an area of deep controversy especially given the interconnected and international character of trade today.

---

[5]This particular situation is considerably more complicated given both the US government and the businesses concerned previous involvement in Cuba's internal governmental affairs. The US initially supported Castro. See Chomsky (1999) for a detailed analysis of this situation.

Further, if we view the environment as one tightly interwoven system, do threats to it pose threats to individual countries security and require and justify action to be taken in self-defense?

Another problem with self-defense justifications comes into play with the idea of "preemptive" self-defense. What are, if any are, acceptable reasons for anticipatory self-defense? What evidence would be required to justify such a claim? Clearly, the concept of self-defense as justifying violence is at present vague and open to interpretation. Richard Falk analyses American military actions over the last few decades based on just versus unjust self-defense. Can we figure out workable necessary and sufficient conditions for pining down justified from unjustified claims of "self-defense" in an increasingly interconnected global world?

Extensions: Besides self-defense, war is also justified to aid suffering innocent persons or if it will prevent a greater evil than is had by the use of violence itself. We have in fact if not in theory enlarged just cause to include "Humanitarian Military Intervention" (Lobel and Ratner this volume). Should the international community step in and use violence to stop "atrocities" in other countries even if such atrocities impose no direct threat to them? While on the surface, we are inclined to consent with such interventions, problems arise as to making judgments about which atrocities (unfortunately there are many) ought to receive intervention and in what, if any order, they should be ranked. Here, another tenet of just war theory can prove enlightening, which is that one also needs the right "intentions" in fighting a war. Looking at the patterns of American interventions is our intention to stop horrific atrocities from occurring or do they reflect economic concerns and/or mere self-interest as Jules Lobel and Michael Ratner suggest? Perhaps one way to grapple with intervention is for countries to focus their interventions on those tragedies for which they themselves are either directly or indirectly causally responsible. Thus East Timor (see Filice this volume) would seem to be one place that the US has an obligation to "intervene" as our governmental policies and obstruction of UN action made the continuing genocide possible. Of course, in order to make such decisions, the public must inform themselves and there are many obstacles for doing this though it is not impossible for most Americans (see Wresch, Filice this volume).

If violence is justified on behalf of defenseless innocents suffering greatly at the hands of others, does this open the door for either non-lethal or lethal violence on behalf of animals and/or the environment (see Engle this volume)? We were unable to find a sufficiently rigorous philosophical argument for such resistance but that does not mean there is not one. Attempts to justify such actions based on arguments similar to those given for justifying humanitarian intervention in human communities can be found on the web sites of many animal and earth liberation groups (see our supporting website at http://www.phil.vt.edu/Global/).

Principle of probable success: Traditionally, under *Jus ad Bellum*, one must also consider whether one has a chance of success. Resorting to violence that ultimately will be futile is unjust. One must also ensure that the end is proportional to the means used. The problem with these strictures is they seem to stack the deck in favor of the powerful that can afford the weapons and means to wage war successfully. Poor and weak countries and groups appear to have three options. (1) They can seek protection from a more powerful state or group through an alliance. (2) They could form an alliance with several other weak states or groups to pool their resources and hence increase their power. Finally, (3) they could resort to unconventional tactics. If we keep the requirement of 'reasonable chance of success', then many groups will need to choose one or more of these options if they are to engage in just war against more powerful bodies. We will need to examine *Jus in Bello* to pursue these problems arising from the inequality of various groups.

3. Jus in Bello: Revisions, Criticisms and Extensions

Principle of Discrimination: The principle of discrimination covers what are legitimate targets of violence. Traditionally, targets have been limited to military property and uniformed personnel.

Revisions: Advanced technological weapons to kill from afar take control of who is killed out of the fighters' hands. I can discriminate my killing a soldier from a civilian using a gun in a way that I can not using a bomb. This also holds for other weapons such as land mines and biological or chemical agents. Using euphemisms like "collateral damage" may hide but do remove the fact that the use of such weapons inevitably kills civilians. Modern theories often try to make distinctions between intentional and unintentional killing of civilians to distinguish the just from unjust use of these weapons. Others try to discriminate, using the principle of proportionality, by estimating whether using these weapons will result, in the end, in saving more lives than if the weapons had not been deployed. Some weapons due to their inherent design as weapons of mass destruction are considered unethical such as nuclear and biological weapons. Do those who already possess such weapons have the right to deny other countries acquiring them unless they rid themselves of them? (See Instantiation$_5$ for more on the relationship of ethics and technology.)

However modern weaponry by itself is not the biggest challenge for applying the principle of discrimination in the modern world. The above distinction between civilian and soldier is quite problematic given the modern military industrial complex. The efficient industrial production of weapons is clearly necessary for conducting violence and links workers in industry and technological development as causally efficacious agents in war. Can we still maintain that workers in war production factories are entitled to civilian status? What about scientists engaged in inventing new weapons? Finally, the United States has been fortunate in so far as we have not really had a modern war fought on home shores. If we were invaded, would we, as civilians, sit idly by waiting for the professionals to fight? But if civilians (e.g., men, women and children) forcefully resist the enemy at night while 'acquiescing' at day, is it possible to distinguish between soldier and civilian and if so, how? Many authors and accepted conventions today blur the old line of distinction between soldier and civilian and base target-ability on the level of causal agency a person/group has for either conducting the war or for producing the causes of injustice against which the war is being fought.[6] If I or the institution where I work are directly responsible for your oppression or for sustaining a war against to you, then my institution or I are a legitimate target on a causal analysis. My target-ability is directly proportional to my causal efficacy (e.g.. my status as a direct versus indirect causal agent, major versus

---

[6] Mosely, Wilkins, and others also address the issue of responsibility here, (e.g., causal connection between civilians and successful waging of war.)

minor causal agent, etc.) Ascribing target-ability based on causal arguments would also seem to make members of democratic nations (i.e., those who have a voice in government policies) more responsible for the actions of their governments than those who live under tyrannies and have no voice in government policies. Using causal arguments requires one to face up to questions about collective versus individual responsibility (See Wilkins for a more detailed discussion on this point).

Criticisms: Problems arise from blurring the distinction between "innocent" civilians and "professional" soldiers using a causal analysis as it can quickly lead one down a slippery slope to the point that either everyone is responsible and hence a target or no one is (Wilkins). Today, many terrorist groups target "capitalism" as disguised imperialism, oppressing them and hence *any* American business and worker are claimed to be legitimate targets. This seems absurd to many Americans, especially the idea of declaring a war against an economic system—an abstract concept. While denying the legitimacy of such reasons, we must look to the weight of our own cold war history of targeting the abstract idea of "communism" as a threat to democracy and our way of life. Both superpowers used, trained and financially supported unpopular regimes or put other groups into power in third world countries (all the little "hot" wars of the cold war). Adding the component of causal agency and making distinctions based on direct versus indirect agency may help contain, if not fully stop the abuses that arise from wars about abstractions be it capitalism, communism, religious fundamentalism, democracy etc. by shifting focus to specific concrete actions by specific concrete persons. However, a critical point of just war is even if one is able to make such a discrimination that does not mean one has an unrestricted field of possible actions open. The second principle of *jus in bello*, proportion, determines how much and what type of force can be justly used to resolve disputes.

In sum, there are deep problems making a distinction between soldier and civilian in today's modern technological society. Causal analysis based on direct versus indirect involvement in producing injustice and sustaining war efforts, may provide guidance for discrimination but must be based on the specifics of the case at hand.

Extensions: How is one to determine legitimate targets if a group's being and livelihood are not being threatened by a nation state but by another civilian group particularly one in which you have no voice? One example of using targeted non-lethal violence based on causal arguments by one non-governmental group against another is illustrated by the Animal Liberation Movement's targeting laboratories and businesses that conduct and support animal experimentation, the fur industry, etc. with non-lethal force (property destruction). Some "right to life" anti-abortion groups also attempt to make similar arguments for using both non-lethal and lethal force. One way, perhaps, to distinguish relevant differences, if there are any, between these two groups--in order to argue if either, neither or both are engaged in justified violence--is to examine their actions under the next requirement, proportionality. A further ethical question arises here. At what point, if any, is violence justified in democracies where the majority determines the legality of actions such as abortion and animal experimentation? Many anti-globalization protesters engage in non-violent protests and some attempt to justify non-lethal violence against groups such as the WTO using causal analysis and self-defense criteria along with the claim that these organizations bypass democratic processes. (See our webpage for relevant articles about these groups.)

Principle of Proportion: If we consider proportionality, then it seems that unless lethal violence is directed at us, we ought not to use lethal violence to resolve the dispute and so on. However, the above statement is qualified on just war theory. We are allowed and indeed required to use as much violence as is necessary to ensure that the cause of war will not continue nor resurface a short time later and this consideration must also be calculated into considerations of proportionality.

Revisions: If violence will stop a greater injustice than the violence itself, then it is just. Arguments have been given by Victor Hanson that the destruction of southern plantations during Sherman's march through Georgia was justified, as its aim was to destroy the institutions and economic lifestyle that both required and defended the immoral institution of slavery. In short, plantation property was the embodiment of this great evil. As slavery was a greater evil than property destruction, the destruction was justified. Similarly, Jewish groups during WW II requested the allies to bomb the trains and train tracks used to deport Jews to concentration camps. This would be targeting civilian populations and rails. The argument to support this request was that those on the trains were already 'dead' and only by stopping the terrible speed and efficiency of train transportation could the death camps grisly task be slowed down. The request was denied. Many argue this denial was unjust based on the principle of proportion that more lives would have been saved compared to those lost had the rails been bombed and that a greater evil was left unmolested rather than committing a smaller injustice. Hanson also argues that Sherman's march was justified by the principle of proportion because by attacking property in the heart of the South's territory, the psychological terror that inspired brought a close to the war without direct battle and thus with a great saving of lives on both sides. One justification for dropping a nuclear bomb on Hiroshima has been that ultimately it, too, brought the war to a speedy end and ultimately saved more lives (at least American lives) that would have been lost by a direct invasion. At the time, this argument was also used to support dropping another nuclear bomb on Nagasaki.

Criticisms: Determining proportion is an empirical matter and one alternative (the road not taken) will always remain hypothetical. Thus, this is perhaps the most contentious area for determining just from unjust actions and our only guides seem to be forecasting methods, experience and, ultimately, hindsight.

Extensions: Very little has been said about non-violence and only a bit said about non-lethal (i.e., property) violence. Clearly, both those engaged in force and resistance ought to first try non-violent means to secure a solution to a dispute (legal actions, public protest marches, letters to those in power, etc.). Given the rule of proportionality, this is especially true for fighting injustices that are not life threatening. Non-lethal violence normally entails either the destruction of property or non-life threatening harassment. Examples of these tactics include 'Black Fax' days, where animal rights groups send hundreds of dark black faxes to companies that support animal testing or labs that engage in it thus costing them money and tying up their fax lines. The Earth Liberation Front's destruction of the Vale resort lodge is another example of property destruction. These groups and actions are often labeled "eco-terrorism." Implicitly accepting the principle of proportionality, animal rights groups require that members do not engage in acts that endanger the life of other sentient beings. (This extension of lethal force to non-humans is both consistent and coherent within their larger philosophy.) They also require in 'rescuing' animals that alternative arrangements for their welfare are in place. This requirement has evolved from a history of past mistakes. Even though we may contest whether or not such groups have 'just cause', we can at least, right now, scrutinize their actions based on the principles of discrimination and proportionality. At issue here, is whether or not the use of non-lethal violence is proportional to both the ends desired as well as to other existing options for forcing change.

4. Just War Theory and Tradition & Non-violence

Many of you may be wondering if just war theory has anything to say to those who believe and follow the tenets of non-violence? Just War theory and tradition are useful for analyzing and guiding actions all along the violent/non-violent spectrum. Non-Lethal violence (i.e., property destruction) is a continuing and growing concern among non-violent activists. Is it ever justified and if so how and where? Some argue that as property is a social construct of capitalism, that to speak of treating it with violence is incongruous-property is not living and only living things are the types of things that can be done violence to. You can not destroy or harm life where it never existed (e.g., Stephens). However, if the destruction has a severe and negative impact on a living being then such an argument seems quite shallow. True, if you burn my house while I am gone, you have not technically physically harmed a living being, but if such arson results in my freezing to death, surely you have caused me, a living being, great harm. (Indeed, this is the rationale for scorch and burn policies. The Russians used this tactic quite successfully when they were invaded. By burning everything behind them as they fled, invaders could not live off the land and would starve.)

However, most non-violence protesters tend to analyze and justify non-lethal violence using (implicitly) the principles of just war theory. For example, many non-violence activists argue that property destruction is ethical provided one has "right intentions." They argue breaking a window if it is planned as part of a well thought out and organized protest may be justified. If one breaks a window due to rage, mob psychology, etc. then it is not justified. Non-violent movements also share the requirement that the means are to be proportional to ends and the second assumption of just war theory and traditions--the expectation of negotiating after the "war" or violent act. Several groups in the non-violence movement, following Ghandi, argue that premeditated, announced or unannounced property damage is acceptable if and only if the instigators remain behind and accept the consequences of their actions. This is because the ultimate aim of nonviolence is to resolve disputes through negotiation. If you are not there, (e.g., the action is taken at night, no one is caught, or one takes action while masked and then flees the scene) there is no chance to peacefully discuss why one has done what one has done. Thus the opportunity is lost to talk with the opposing side to give reasoned moral convictions for your actions and persuade them to change their ideology. Again, several groups who hold this Ghandian view argue that the arrest and subsequent court trial in democratic nations itself is really the most important part of the action--this is a chance to publicly defend and persuade others of your position. For the majority of non-violent activists for property damage to be effective nonviolent protest, one must stand up and accept responsibility and use the damage as a platform for discussion (e.g., Carter).

5. A final note on Just War Theories and Conventions: The Third Assumption

Just war theories and conventions are based on and can only work within a framework of trust. Trust, implicitly or explicitly, is the primary assumption underlying—indeed is the very foundation of--both Just War theories and Just War conventions. Onora O'Neil argues that one of the consequences of terrorist acts is that they fundamentally and irrevocably violate trust--the sort of daily trust we have that others will behave decently and follow the rules for getting along together and resolving disputes in a rational manner. Internationally, just war conventions are a concrete embodiment of how we expect or trust others will behave. Thus, returning to the question of the possibility of and requirements for extending the definition of legitimate authority for engaging in just war/violence beyond sovereigns of nation states, clearly authority can only be legitimately assumed or granted based on trust. This is the trust that in general those who take on and who we grant the mantle of authority accept the underlying assumptions behind just war and that they will, in general, follow the (perhaps suitably extended) conventions for engaging in and conducting violence. Some minimal level of trust ultimately underlies all just war theories and conventions. The question is how to build trust and act on it given the shrinking physical, temporal and communication distances between communities brought about by modern technologies combined with the large cultural differences and gaps that exist in our world today. Optimistically, one hopes that just war theories and traditions can give us guidance provided we localize and re-conceptualize them to our own time and place. Our first selection below by Johnathan Glover explains and explores the concept of nationalism and examines both the positive and negative aspects of this phenomenon. Richard Falk, Jules Lobel & Michael Ratner and Onora O'Neil (see our webpage for this last) provide thoughtful reflections and arguments on the application of just war theories and traditions to the global situations we Americans find ourselves in today.

References

Chomsky, N.(1999). *Profit Over People: Neoliberalism and Global Order*. New York: Seven Stories Press.

Carter, M. "Hearts, Minds & Property destruction" *NonViolent Activists: The Magazine of the War Resisters League* Special Section: The Parameters of Nonviolent Action –What Makes an Action Nonviolent (July-August 2001) an on-line journal at www.warresisters.org/nva0701-2.htm

Hanson, V. (1999). "Sherman's War". *American Heritage* November 1999. (58-67).

Lackey, D.P., (2002). "Just War Theory" in *Applied Ethics: A Multicultural Approach* 3rd edition. (eds.) Larry May, Shari Collins-Chobanian and Kai Wong. Upper Saddle River, new Jersey: Prentice Hall. (275-284) (This is a good discussion with reference to Geneva War Conventions)

Moseley, A., (2002) "Just War Theory" in *Internet Encyclopedia of Philosophy* at: www.utm.edu/research/eip/j/justwar.htm

O'Neil, O. (2002) "A Question of Trust". Reith Lectures on the BBC (July 2002) http://www.bbc.co.uk/radio4/reith2002/

Stephens, K. "Breaking a Store Window Violent? Nonsense!" *NonViolent Activists: The Magazine of the War Resisters League* Special Section: The Parameters of Nonviolent Action –What Makes an Action Nonviolent (July-August 2001) an on-line journal at www.warresisters.org/nva0701-2.htm

Wilkins, B. (2002). "Can Terrorism Be Justified?" in *Applied Ethics: A Multicultural Approach* 3rd edition. (eds.)Larry May, Shari Collins-Chobanian and Kai Wong. Upper Saddle River, New Jersey: Prentice Hall. (301-308).

Nations, Identity, and Conflict[1]
Jonathan Glover

We lived happily together for many years and now it has come to killing each other's babies. What is happening to us?
-Indira Hadziomerovic, mourning in Sarajevo, reported in the London Independent, August 8, 1992

There are two histories of nationalism. One history, repeated many times, is of a people rightly struggling to be free. They eventually break away from their large neighbor, a colonial power, or the Soviet Union to attain the dignity of self-governing nationhood. The other history, repeated many times, is of nationalism as tribal conflict. This is the story of the European nations and their quarrels that culminated in war in 1914. More recently it is the story of seemingly endless reciprocal killing: the story of Armenia and Azerbaijan, of Israel and Palestine, of the factions in the Nigerian civil war, of Iran and Iraq, of Greeks and Turks in Cyprus, of nationalists and unionists in Northern Ireland, of the participants in the ethnic conflict in Sri Lanka. It is the story of what was once Yugoslavia.

Are these two histories or one? Is there a good nationalism, linked to freedom and self-government, that can be distinguished from the kind of nationalism whose results can be seen from Belfast to Bosnia? Or is commitment to the idea of a nation-state a dangerous psychological weakness, something to be contained and, if possible, eradicated?

I will approach these questions by exploring three issues. The first is the nature of nationalism. The second is its psychology. Finally, I will put the psychological comments to use in thinking about nationalist conflict and how to contain it.

Nations and Nation-States

Nationalism is the belief that a nation should have self-determination. This is usually thought of in terms of every nation having its own state. There is a universal version: every nation should have self-determination. And there is the particular version: this nation should have self-determination.

Nationalism can function as a solvent, as when it undid the links between Czechs and Slovaks. And it can function as a glue, bringing together people previously separate, as in the Risorgimento. Both aspects can be seen in Giuseppe Mazzini's slogan: "Every nation a state, only one state for the entire nation."[2]

---

[1] "Nations, Identity and Conflict" by Jonathan Glover, from *The Morality of Nationalism*, edited by Robert McKim and Jeff McMahan, copyright © 1997 by Oxford University Press, Inc. Used by permission of Oxford University Press, Inc.
[2] Quoted in Eric Hobsbawm, *Nations and Nationalism since 1780: Programme, Myth, Reality* (Cambridge, 1990) p. 101.

The belief that a nation should have its own state is not clear. The trouble does not come from the phrase "its own state;" which refers to a constitution and set of laws and the existence of an independent government. (There is vagueness. How independent is the government of a member state of the European Community or the government of a banana republic? But even these fuzzy edges are relatively unimportant here.) The main obscurity is in the concept of a nation.

The Social Construction of the Nation

Nationality is often thought of as something "natural" or presocial. Swedes are different from Italians in the way the fish of the Baltic are different from those of the Mediterranean. This sense of naturalness is reinforced by stories nations often have about their own antiquity. But some historians and social scientists emphasize the relative modernity of the European nation-states, dating them from around the end of the eighteenth century.[3]

Various influences on the rise of those nation-states are cited. It is suggested that the division of labor created by the transition from an agrarian to an industrial capitalist economy required large economic units. These in turn may have needed some centralized control of public order and defense, together with a standardized education system. The dominance of national languages may have come partly from the decline of the idea of Christendom and the resulting fading of Latin. The economic need for communication within large units and for national administration is cited to explain why national languages defeated regional dialects. A national base provided a more profitable market than a regional one for the products of print technology.

If these suggestions are correct, European states arose partly for other reasons in addition to being a vehicle for a preexisting national consciousness. In at least some cases, the state may have come into existence before there was much sense of nationhood. Eric Hobsbawm quotes a speaker in the first meeting of the Parliament of the new Kingdom of Italy as saying that "we have made Italy, now we have to make Italians"[4]

In Africa there are more extreme cases of nation-states arising independently of any sense of nationhood. Many state boundaries were lines drawn on maps by colonial governments and administrators, often cutting through the middle of territories inhabited by Africans who felt part of a single community and often putting together groups who had no sense of shared identity.[5]

These accounts by historians and social scientists tend to describe nations as products of nation-states rather than the other way around. And nation-states in turn are explained by citing their usefulness, whether to industrialists and capitalists or to colonial rulers.

No doubt in many cases such factors are part of the explanation of nationhood. But it is hard to believe they are the whole story. I suggest that once we

---

[3] Benedict Anderson, Imagined Communities; Reflections on the Origin and Spread of Nationalism (London, 1983); Ernest Gellner, Nations and Nationalism (Oxford, 1983); Hobsbawm, Nations and Nationalism.
[4] Hobsbawm, *Nations and Nationalism*, p. 44.
[5] Basil Davidson, *The Black Man's Burden: Africa and the Curse of the Nation-State* (New York, 1992).

go beyond economic interests or the interests of colonizers, we can see the psychological needs that are met by the sense of nationhood and by the nation-state. A deeper explanation of nationalism requires exploration of these other needs. It is important for this exploration to note that people emotionally committed to nations do not think of them in instrumental terms or as social constructions. They are often thought of in more tribal terms.

The "Tribal" Nation as an Ideal Type

Nationalists often think of their nation in ways influenced by a traditional model of a "pure" or "ideal" case. This ideal version is of a people inhabiting a single, unified territory. All territorial boundaries are clear and undisputed, and there are no minorities over the border. The "people" are a tribe. They are a single ethnic group. They have a common language. They have a shared history, which involves their having a common culture. This culture typically includes shared religious beliefs. The unity of the culture is sustained partly by a common pattern of education and partly by access to such things as the same newspapers and the same television programs.

To talk in this way of a tribal nation is to use a metaphor that may not be very securely grounded in reality. The word "tribe" is typically used by Europeans to describe African groupings, and some are skeptical about its usefulness there. Basil Davidson suggests that the word has no clear meaning and that colonial rulers intent on dividing Africans into tribes sometimes had to invent the tribes.[6] Even if some of the tribes were partly European constructions, the great physical and cultural differences that are sometimes found suggest that not all tribes were merely colonial inventions. But even if originally there had been no tribes in Africa (or anywhere else), the word would still be useful, if only to stand for an ideal type.

The pure case of the tribal nation might seem ideal in another way. Without the conflicts generated by blurred or disputed borders, there might be the hope that tribal nations would live together as good neighbors. Each nation would delight in its own ethnicity, religion, culture, and language, without any hostility to the nation next door.

Why does this seem so unlike most of the real world? One obvious answer is that much of the real world has territorial boundaries only of the messy or disputed kind. And there are other complications. According to one view, the Jewish people before the founding of Israel were a nation without a territory. (This would not mean they had to want their own state. The members of a nation do not have to be, in that way, nationalists.) The United States is only one example of a state with great ethnic variety. Belgium, Switzerland, and Canada are among states without a single unifying language. Between 1945 and 1989, the people of Germany had a divided history. And many states have religious diversity. These departures from the ideal type may lead to a good deal of social construction, such as the efforts to create a shared sense of being American.

---

[6] Ibid., p. 206

Groups, Tribalism, and Identity

If it is true that nationalism arose in Europe only about the time of the industrial revolution, some more general term is needed to include whatever made Englishmen and Frenchmen fight each other at Agincourt. Even without the modern nation-state, it was still the English versus the French and not short versus tall or peasants versus lords. I will use the word "tribalism" to cover the psychological attachments that made the English versus the French the natural conflict even before the nation-state. Tribalism may be the deeper phenomenon, of which nationalism is the currently dominant variant.

In most group conflicts, members of different groups are marked off from each other by some distinguishing characteristics that typically carry an emotional charge, such as religion or ethnicity. One question is whether the psychological core of tribalism is a shared possession of such "charged" characteristics or whether the core has to do with group membership as such....

Identity, Self-Creation, and Tribalism

The hypothesis I want to put forward is a partial explanation of tribalism in terms of our need to create something coherent out of ourselves and our own lives. If there is anything in this, tribalism has roots that go very deep in our psychology. Those roots make its elimination impossible or at least dauntingly difficult. Some will welcome this. Others will find it depressing. Those who, like me, find it depressing to accept that tribalism is virtually indestructible will have to think of ways of taming it.

A natural way of thinking of oneself is as a Cartesian ego. My empirical characteristics, both physical and mental, are subject to change. Old age may ravage my body, my memory may go, and my personality may change. But behind all of this, I am still fully there.

This Cartesian view has variants in religious beliefs about the soul and in the Kantian "noumenal self." It has fallen on bad times. Lichtenberg argued that Descartes's cogito proves only the occurrence of a perhaps impersonal thought, not the existence of a thinking self. Nietzsche agreed, suggesting that we get used to "getting along without that little 'it' (which is what the honest old 'I' has evaporated into)." Hume attacked the ego for its empirical unobservability....

This reductionist view seems to leave personal unity across a lifetime a more precarious affair than we have usually supposed. Our unity rests on shifting ground: on physical and mental characteristics that may come and go rather than on the persisting ego that was supposed to own them all. The reductionist view is sometimes supported by an analogy with nations. Hume says: "I cannot compare the soul more properly to anything than to a republic, or commonwealth." [In the present Derek] Parfit agrees: France exists, but it is not an entity distinct from its citizens and its territory...[7]

If personal identity is thought of as a "fact," the strong grounds for skepticism about the Cartesian ego do indeed help to undermine its importance. A

---

[7] Derek Parfit, *Reasons and Persons* (Oxford, 1984), pp. 211-12, 339, 340.

person's life may consist of a series of stages that are related only contingently and perhaps weakly. In principle, at least, there may be little more coherence between the stages of life than there is between the stones in a pile. Any one stone that happens to be part of this pile could well have been part of another. According to this viewpoint, death becomes less important, as all any individual's death means is that there will be no future experiences related in certain ways to these present ones. There will be similar experiences; it is just that they will be members of series other than this one. There will be other stones; they will just be in piles other than this one.

But the unity of life is perhaps not best seen as a "fact" that is discovered to be there to some degree or other. An alternative view is that this unity is something we, at least in part, create. The analogy with nations holds in more complex ways than Hume and Parfit suggest. Nations and people are not just similar in that there exists neither a national soul nor a metaphysical ego. They are also similar in being to some extent artifacts rather than things whose nature is given.

Many of us care about what sort of people we are, and many of the characteristics we want to have are long-term. The psychoanalyst Carl Jung may have wanted to be someone of integrity, wisdom, and spiritual depth. Perhaps his early life fitted this description. But in 1933 he replaced the editor of a psychiatric journal who resigned because he could not accept its subordination to Nazi ideology. The first issue under Jung's editorship published a Nazi statement saying that *Mein Kampf* was essential reading for psychiatrists. Jung himself wrote in the journal that "the Jewish race as a whole" had an unconscious that could be compared with the Aryan "only with reserve." Saying that Freud and his followers had not understood the German psyche, Jung asked: "Has the formidable phenomenon of National Socialism, on which the whole world gazes with astonished eyes, taught them better?"[8] The conception of Jung as a man of integrity and wisdom is destroyed by these remarks.

It is possible to defend the integrity of a "time slice" of Jung. Jung-before-1933 may have had integrity. But some of us want our central characteristics to be more durable. And this may involve a long-term process of self-creation. This is one reason why an early death can be tragic. To return to the stone metaphor, the thought that it does not matter if there are fewer stones on a particular heap is unconvincing if the stones were being used to create a building that will now remain unfinished.

People care about what their lives add up to. It may seem paradoxical to give this as a reason for the importance of self-creation. Must not the person already be a persisting ego in order to have this kind of concern? Or does the concern belong merely to a momentary time slice? Neither of these need be true. The importance of the concern is bound up with its depth and persistence. But a deep and persistent concern need not presuppose an ego to which this concern belongs. Or, to put it the other way around, the nonexistence of an ego does not entail that all concerns are shallow and brief.

The process of self-creation is partly that of a novelist telling a coherent story about a character. The mixture of freedom and constraint is similar. Various possibilities may be open, but what the character can do depends partly on circumstances and partly on other people in the story. There are also limits on how far

---

[8] Jeffrey Masson, *Against Therapy* (London, 1993), pp. 134-64.

acting "out of character" is possible. This story we create about ourselves, partly by what we do and partly by how we edit and narrate the story of our past, is central to our sense of our own identity.

But the story is bound up with the context in which it takes place. This is partly physical context; to be forced into exile is, among other things, to be excluded from the places where the earlier parts of the story took place. It is partly the context of other people. What I did was done with them or done in response to what they did or said. I still carry their hopes and expectations with me. The values that guided what I have done (and that color the tone of the narrative) inevitably were shaped partly by them.

Because both the people and the places we have known are intrinsic to the story, loss of either is a complex deprivation. We lose the pleasures of being with those people in those places. We also lose some of the grip we had on the reality of our earlier story, more of which now has to rely on fugitive memory images. And we lose people who were part of our story's perhaps unconsciously half-intended audience. After someone has died, we may later become aware of this role he or she had when we do something and notice that the deceased is not there to see or be told about it. Not only do particular people shape the content and narrative tone of the story, but also we may see them partly as libraries in which our lives' stories are safely kept. And as we tell the story or act it out, we need these people to listen, and we hope for their recognition of what we are like.

The role of places in our self-creative story makes the emotional pull of territory unsurprising. This makes it more natural to identify with the interests of a geographically based nation than, for instance, with the interests of farmers.

And the role of particular people in our self-creative story makes our identification with them natural, too. (This is of course just one reason why we identify with people we know. Other, less egocentric reasons are usually at least as strong.) But this account of the role of people close to us faces a problem parallel to that faced by the sociobiological account of tribalism. Just as the nations and other groups with which we identify are far larger than the group of those we are genetically related to, so they are far larger than the group of people who have a role to play in our personal story.

The relationships that are so important to us, both for our sense of identity and for other reasons, normally draw heavily on a shared cultural background. A shared frame of reference, a common history (passed on by a common education), and a shared sense of humor all create a context in which relationships and identity can flourish. And in turn this cultural context is tied up in obvious ways with a shared language. (Anyone who knows, as I do, what it is to speak another language badly will know how this coarsens the texture of relationships and forces you to present a drastically simple and crude version of what you want to say and hence of yourself.)

The ways in which we think of our identity and shape it are in these different ways bound up with a shared language and culture. Because of this, we care about the survival of our language and cultural traditions. We want what has mattered to us to survive. The nation is often seen as at least the best defense of these things and sometimes as their embodiment.

It is also within a particular culture and language that our created identity is validated by the recognition bestowed by others.[9] So any lack of respect for our culture and language in turn devalues our personal self-respect.

Nationalism and the Roots of Conflict

Tribes are marked off from one another by some combination of ethnicity, religion, shared territory, language, and shared culture. Needs linked to creating and maintaining personal identity are part of the explanation of why these particular differences between people are the basis of tribal identification. (Other needs and interests, for instance economic ones, may also play a part. The interaction between economic and deeper psychological needs can be very complex.)[10]

Mazzini's nationalist slogan could be rephrased as: "Every tribe a nation-state, only one nation-state for the entire tribe." Tribal loyalties both find expression in nationalism and, are partly created by it. These loyalties and this way of expressing them bring both benefits and risks. The questions are whether the benefits are worth the risks and whether there are ways of reducing the risks.

Benevolent Nationalism: Self-Respect and Moral Identity

There is little doubt that people's sense of their own worth is enhanced by feeling that they run their own affairs. To live in a country ruled by a colonial power or in one leaned on heavily by a big neighbor (whether the neighbor is the United States or the former Soviet Union) may create the feeling of being deprived of what is rightfully yours, perhaps even of being treated like a child. Whether it comes as formal independence after colonial rule or as release from the domination of a large neighbor, national independence may bring a gain in self-respect. This can give support to people's sense of their own moral identity: the sense of being a person of a particular kind, who lives by some values rather than others.

Moral identity is sometimes bound up with national identity in impressive ways. During the Nazi occupation of most of Europe, many Jewish children were hidden in convents. One nun, asked afterward why she had risked hiding some children, replied, "Je suis française a la fin:" Guelfo Zamboni, as the Italian consul general in Salonika in 1943, saved the lives of many Jews by issuing false Italian documents to them. When rebuked by the SS chief in Salonika for his defense of Jews, Zamboni replied, "As long as the Italian flag flies here, under this flag I am the only one who decides what to do or what not to do:" When the Jews in Denmark were about to be rounded up by the Nazis, Danish non-Jews gave massive support to the Jews and saved over 90 percent of them. Jews were stopped on the streets and offered keys to people's flats and houses. Some Jews were hidden in hospitals by doctors and nurses who gave them false medical records. Taxis, ambulances, fire engines, and cars were used to take them to the coast for their escape to Sweden. In the public statement made by the Danish church, the roundup was described as being "in conflict with the sense of justice inherent in the Danish people and inseparable from our Danish Christian culture through centuries."

---

[9] Charles Taylor, *Multiculturalism and "The Politics of Recognition"* (Princeton, 1992).
[10] Michael Hechter, "The Dynamics of Secession," *Acta Sociologica*, 1992.

Some of the benefits of national consciousness are real. But there is also the conflict risked by the more competitive kinds of nationalism.

Some Causes of Nationalist Conflict

What turns benevolent nationalism into the more menacing version of nationalism? Blurred boundaries and disputed territories play an obvious role. But there are other causes. Sometimes politicians have their own motives for whipping up competitive nationalism. Sometimes it results from fear and entrapment. Sometimes views of a Social Darwinist kind make people think conflict between national groups is unavoidable. And closer to the heart of nationalism are some tendencies toward conflict in the very processes by which national identity is socially constructed.

Political Manipulation

Sometimes nationalist rivalries are whipped up by politicians for domestic political reasons. There was at least an element of this in the German naval expansion that made a contribution to the outbreak of World War I. The German government and its supporters were worried by the growing support for the radical policies of the Social Democrats. In the 1890s, Adm. Alfred von Tirpitz had advocated a bigger navy, giving as one reason that "the great patriotic task and the economic benefits to be derived from it will offer a strong palliative against educated and uneducated Social Democrats." Bernhard Bulow, the chancellor when the naval arms race began, took the same view. He urged "a policy which appeals to the highest national emotions;" mentioning the need to "regain the sympathies of the Social Democrat workers for the state and the monarchy."[11]

The events of 1914 are of course a spectacular case of "the highest national emotions" contributing to catastrophe. But this pattern has been repeated many times. Most recently, Slobodan Milosevic chose to base his own power on the appeal of "Greater Serbia" while Franjo Tudjman manipulated Croatian national feeling in a parallel way.

Fear and Entrapment

In many countries, some politicians like to play the patriotic card for their own purposes. Something more needs to be said about when this finds a response. One explanation of the case of Yugoslavia appeals to fear. In the former Yugoslavia, most people cannot have wanted ethnic conflict. Close to half of all families were ethnically mixed. But the communist period had not allowed the development of a political culture in which people learned how to settle differences peacefully. And with the collapse of Tito's federation, ethnic national units seemed the only protection against threats from other groups.

The Hobbesian picture of people subordinating themselves to any government able to provide safety and security may apply here. And the

---

[11] V R. Berghahn, *Germany and the Approach of War in 1914* (London, 1973), pp. 29-31.

manipulation of ethnic and religious tribalism by politicians only added to the fear in other groups and thus made escape from the trap of conflict harder. When the conflict starts, its psychology entraps almost everyone. The Croatian writer Slavenka Drakulic wrote of an airplane flight from London: "I hear a girl next to me, no older than twelve, say to her friend as the aeroplane flies over Croatia: "If we were forced to land in Zagreb, I would have to lie about my Serbian nationality, or those Croats would kill me on the spot. We are all trapped. The two girls are at war, too, and even if hostilities were to cease instantly, how long would it take for these girls not to be afraid of landing at Zagreb?"[12]

Hobbesian fear leads to the creation of a new state for protection. Different kinds of fear and entrapment play a part in conflicts between already-existing nations. Going back again to 1914, the mutual sense of entrapment clearly played a part in bringing about World War I. Russia, France, and Britain feared the growth of German power and formed an alliance to "contain" it, which was in turn seen in Germany as "encirclement...." Sir Edward Grey, the British foreign secretary, later wrote that "armaments were intended to produce a sense of security in each nation .... What they really did was to produce fear in everybody."[13]

A similar story is found still further back. Thucydides said of the Peloponnesian War: "What made war inevitable was the growth of Athenian power and the fear this caused in Sparta."[14]

Social Darwinism

Sometimes the sense of entrapment in unavoidable conflict is reinforced by an unarticulated Social Darwinism. Those who accept the sociobiological hypothesis that a disposition to group loyalty is genetically programmed as a result of its contribution to inclusive fitness may be tempted to go further. The Social Darwinist extrapolation sees nations as the units engaged in a Darwinian struggle for survival. Nations unwilling to fight will go under.

The heyday of explicit Social Darwinism was the period before World War I. In England this Social Darwinism was expressed by Karl Pearson, who said that the nation should be "kept up to a high pitch of external efficiency by contest, chiefly by way of war with inferior races, and with equal races by the struggle for trade routes and for the sources of raw materials and food supply."[15] Lord Salisbury said that "you may roughly divide the nations of all the world as the living and the dying.... The living nations will gradually encroach on the territory of the dying and the seeds and causes of conflict among civilised nations will speedily appear."[16]

In Germany at that time, Social Darwinism was even more influential...

---

[12] Slavenka Drakulic, *Balkan Express: Fragments from the Other Side of War* (London, 1993), p. 20.
[13] Viscount Grey of Falloden, *Twenty-Five Years, 1892-1916*, vol. 2 (London, 1925), p. 52.
[14] Thucydides, *The Peloponnesian War*, trans. Rex Warner (Harmondsworth, 1986), pp. 35-49.
[15] James Joll, *The Origins of the First World War*, 2d ed (London, 1992), p. 172.
[16] Zara Steiner, *Britain and the Origins of the First World War* (London, 177), p. 16.

National Identity and Perceived Characteristics

Political manipulation, together with entrapment in mutual fear, contributes to national conflict. And a residual Social Darwinism may make it seem inevitable. But these explanations do not go deep enough. Other causes are found in the fact that national consciousness is itself a social construct. National consciousness draws on a narrative about national history. It also draws on people's perception of what they take to be their own nation's distinctive characteristics.

One can only respect and admire the Danes who stood up to the Nazis because they believed the sense of justice was inherent in the Danish people. But there is another side to the belief in the good qualities of one's own nation.

National self-images require the selection of some features rather than others. Unsurprisingly, the preferred traits are characteristically favorable. We are intelligent and witty, open-minded and brave. But these are comparative characteristics. It is a daunting conceptual feat to maintain the view that we score so well on them without thinking that by comparison our neighbors are stupid and humorless, bigoted and cowardly.

We are rightly uneasy about the idea of racial pride, seeing at best a murky boundary between that and objectionable racism. But the same considerations should make us ask questions about national pride. It is true, as Benedict Anderson has argued, that racial hostility is often dehumanizing in a way that national hostility is not. Racism tends to define people in terms of biological categories such as skin color, while national insults at least focus on human cultural creations.[17]

But the boundary between national or cultural stereotypes and racial ones is less well defined than this suggests. A student at a university in Northern Ireland... mentioned one of the stereotypes she had been taught as a child, that the primitiveness of the members of the other community was shown by their having one long eyebrow rather than two brows with a gap between them. Her friends in the other community reported exactly the same stereotype in reverse. These mirror images were not racist; the two communities were not of different races. Yet the hostile physical stereotype is the stuff of which racism is made.

Because national self-image is often (even if misleadingly) cast in terms of the tribal nation, the favorable national characteristics are easily thought of as ethnic ones. And from thinking of one's own ethnic characteristics as particularly good, the slide to the evils of "ethnic cleansing" can too easily take place.

National Identity and Narrative

National identity, like personal identity, is constructed partly by means of a story about the past. The narrative used to shape national consciousness can contribute to conflict in a way not completely separate from the contribution of perceived characteristics.

Much of the story of a nation is made up of its relations with other nations, who often turn out to have behaved ingloriously. The narrative of the Croats emphasizes the stifling nature of communism, conceived as a system primarily imposed by

---

[17] Anderson, *Imagined Communities*, chap. 8.

Serbs. The narrative of the Serbs emphasizes the period of Croatian fascism, the evils of the Ustasi, and the Serbian part in defeating the Croats and their Nazi allies. (The Croatian government reinforced this narrative by renaming streets after fascist leaders.) These are only the more recent chapters of the two stories. And new chapters are now being written...The narratives do not have to be entirely "fantasies." A selective reading of the past, a Serb one or a Croat one, can have the same effect on the heart.

There are narratives of victory and narratives of defeat. Narratives of victory can slide into a triumphalism that arouses resentment in those whose ancestors were on the other side. The Orange parades in Northern Ireland, which celebrate the defeat of the Catholics by William of Orange, are an extreme case of this.

Narratives of defeat, kindling a desire to redress a grievance, also play an obvious part in entrapping people in a spiral of hostility Slavenka Drakulic says: "After the war the role will be reversed and the victims will judge not only the executioners, but their silent accomplices. I am afraid that, as we have been forced to take sides in this war, we--all of us, on both sides--will get caught in that cruel, self-perpetuating game for ever"[18]

Isaiah Berlin quotes Schiller's "bent twig" theory of nationalism as a reaction to oppression or humiliation and suggests that the nationalism of Israelis and Palestinians may be so intractably strong because both are reacting against having been victims.[19]

In South Africa, Afrikaner nationalism can also be seen as something springing back like a bent twig. The brother of John Vorster, the former prime minister, described being at school a decade and a half after the Boer defeat: "If you were caught speaking Afrikaans, you had to carry a placard round your neck bearing the words 'I must not speak Dutch.' When the bell went for school to start again the last man with what was called the Dutch mark had to write out one thousand times 'I must speak English at school.'""[20] It is not hard to see how this sort of thing contributed to the stubborn defensiveness whose effects black Africans later were to feel.

One of the strengths of nationalism is the contribution it can make to self-respect. But the strengths and the weaknesses are closely interwoven. Slights to self-respect are often the first step in the spiral of conflict.

Defusing Nationalism

If the account given here is for the most part correct, nationalism is partly the expression of a tribalism that goes very deep in our psychology. It is linked partly to a general disposition to group loyalty and partly to the way distinguishing tribal features play a role in our creation of identity. In principle, this could all be harmless. But, for reasons we have seen, this tribalism is dangerous. Yet because it goes so deep, it is very hard--perhaps impossible--to eliminate. This casts doubt on the

---

[18] Slavenka Drakulic, *Balkan Express*, p. 55.
[19] Isaiah Berlin, "The Bent Twig," in *The Crooked Timber of Humanity: Chapters in the History of Ideas* (New York, 1992), pp. 238-61
[20] David Harrison, *The White Tribe of Africa* (Johannesburg, 1981), p. 54.

expectation among thinkers of the Enlightenment that national loyalties would fade away.

The best strategy is to attempt to contain the tendencies toward hostility and conflict within nationalism. Because nationalist conflict has a variety of sources, there is no single "solution" to the problem. A variety of strategies can be adapted to fit different cases.

One central point, which may appear paradoxical, is that often the best way to contain tribalism is to grant the demands of nationalism. This applies particularly where there is the prospect of a tribal nation or of something close to it. The former Czechoslovakia provides a model. If the Slovaks want to separate from the Czechs, both groups will live more happily together without the tribal conflict generated by the refusal of a divorce. And this applies to many other possible cases. If the majority of Scots or Basques or Quebecois really want their own independent nation, "yes" is the answer that defuses tribal conflict, and "no" is the answer that starts the spiral of resentment.

The Soft-Edged Nation-State

In many cases, the tribal nation is not possible. Shared or disputed territory necessitates some sort of pluralism. We need to be more imaginative about the kinds of pluralism that are possible.

A worthwhile response to the problem of blurred or disputed geographical boundaries may be the blurring of the conceptual boundaries of the nation-state. Northern Ireland might benefit from thinking along these lines. Northern Ireland is nearly always seen either as a duck or as a rabbit. "The six counties belong in the Republic" versus "Ulster is part of the United Kingdom" is a classic duck-rabbit figure, and no solution is likely to work unless it takes account of both ways of viewing Northern Ireland. Ideally, a solution would encourage tolerance of ambiguity, a recognition that Northern Ireland is not quite a duck, nor quite a rabbit.

One approach would be to give up the assumption that nation-states must have hard borders, that any piece of territory is either part of one country or part of another. Avishai Margalit once proposed that Jerusalem should be the capital both of Israel and of a Palestinian state. If the possibility of soft-edged countries is introduced, the territory of Northern Ireland could be part of both the Republic and the United Kingdom. People already have the choice of citizenship of either country (or of dual nationality). There could be autonomous local administration, with internationally backed guarantees of respect for minority rights. Policing this could perhaps be done by the European Community. It should not be done by the British, who are one of the historically involved tribes.

Any approach of this kind is obviously going to raise many questions and problems: Can two independent countries harmonize sufficiently to share a province or a city? What happens when they disagree? What should be left to local administration, and what limits on majority decisions should be set in the interests of the minority? I am not putting forward a detailed policy but suggesting that some scheme of this sort is worth looking into. It will be messy. But duck-rabbit figures are messy. The policies tried so far have been of duck fanciers trying to twist the figure one way and rabbit fanciers trying to twist it the other way. These policies have not been such a success that messy alternatives should be excluded.

Northern Ireland is just an example. Around the world enough places are shared between tribes to make some experiments worth trying. In such places the hard-edged nation-state can be Procrustean. Adapting states to fit people rather than making people fit states is a policy that might make use of nation-states with soft edges.

Limits to National Autonomy

In other ways, too, the concept of the nation-state is sometimes too rigid. As Henry Shue suggests in chapter 20 of this volume[21], we need to think in terms of limited sovereignty. World government has been proposed as a solution to national conflicts, a suggestion often dismissed as either utopian or undesirable. But there are many gradations between world government and the unlimited sovereignty of autonomous nation-states. We are already growing accustomed to a degree of policing of conflicts between nations by the world community. And because of our common interest in the avoidance of nuclear war, many of us accept the idea of some international policing of nuclear proliferation.

After years of accepting that the United Nations cannot interfere in a country's "internal affairs," we are starting to think in terms of international intervention to prevent genocide, "ethnic cleansing," and other horrors. This is an important development of the principle of limited national sovereignty. A strong enough policy of this kind is the Hobbesian solution to the fear that generates nationalist conflict, for instance in Yugoslavia.

International intervention does not have to use military force. Different kinds of breach might call for different degrees of response. Linkage of respect for minority rights with loans from the World Bank or the International Monetary Fund is a weaker form of international pressure. Given the principle that national sovereignty is limited, we need a debate on what the limits are and on what forms of intervention are justified in different cases. Clear answers to these questions could help avoid some of the horrors we now see.

Limited sovereignty, like the soft-edged nation-state, blurs traditional conceptual boundaries. This is occurring through the development of groups such as the European Union. It could be taken further with the aim of reducing nationalist conflict. For instance, a constitution for the European Union might have provisions for minority rights within member nations. This constitution might include the rights of "subnations" to vote to secede from their parent nations, provided that these subnations in turn respect the rights of minorities within their borders....

States in Eastern Europe wanting to join the Union would have to accept the constitution. In some cases this acceptance might substitute the Czechoslovak model for the Yugoslav one. Minorities in the countries of the existing Union might benefit, too.

Again, this is not intended as a blueprint for detailed policy. I am gesturing toward the kind of conceptual and political innovations that may be worth considering if we want to reduce nationalist conflict.

---

[21]Shue, H. (1997). Chapter 20 in *The Morality of Nationalism*, edited by Robert McKiim and Jeff McMahan, Oxford: Oxford University Press, Inc.

The Long, Slow Strategy

These possible strategies for containing the dangers of nationalism start by accepting our tribal psychology as a fact of life. At present, this is the only realistic option. But I am reluctant to abandon the hope of the Enlightenment that in the long run these tribal loyalties may take second place to a more general humanism. Immediate strategies for containing conflict could be supplemented by greater self-consciousness about the tribal loyalties themselves. In the long run, this could lead these simpleminded commitments to evolve into something more complex.

Some of the changes of outlook I hope for may come through the growth of intellectual understanding. One instance is something already under way: the growing appreciation of the limitations of Social Darwinism.

Today considerably more people grasp the fact that we do not have to see nations as fighting each other to the death in a Darwinian struggle for survival than in 1914. Even if there is some truth in the sociobiological hypothesis of a genetic disposition to group loyalty, this by no means entails the Social Darwinist view. It entails nothing about nations being the units loyalty must attach to. And, in particular, it does not entail genetic determinism: the view that our genetic composition makes certain behavior, for instance group conflict, inevitable. Especially with modern weapons, cooperation may do more than conflict for inclusive fitness. And even where some menacing trait has biological origins, the best strategy of containment may be environmental, for instance by making sure that conflict does not pay.

Our understanding could usefully grow in other ways, too. The spread of a more sophisticated understanding of the way national self-images and narratives are constructed could slowly erode uncritical nationalism. And seeing the ways in which modern pluralist nations differ from tribal nations may have the same effect. Belief in "Greater Serbia," and so forth, depends on myths that are unlikely to survive the growth of a more critical outlook.

Greater awareness of the links between tribalism and identity might accompany an awareness of the variety of other resources we can draw on for self-creation. We have more than just our tribal membership. We are mothers and fathers, sons and daughters, brothers and sisters, friends, architects, scientists, fans of the Grateful Dead, supporters of the Liverpool Football Club, mountaineers, vegetarians, amateur photographers, lovers of Mozart, admirers of Tolstoy, and haters of Heidegger. To have a self-conception only in terms of being a Serb or a Croat would be a great impoverishment. Slavenka Drakulic has expressed this result of the Yugoslav conflict:

> I had fought against treating nationality as a main criterion by which to judge human beings; I tried to see the people behind the label; I kept open the possibility of dialogue with my friends and colleagues in Serbia even after all telephone lines and roads had been cut off and one third of Croatia had been occupied and bombed .... In the end none of that helped me. Along with millions of other Croats, I was pinned to the wall of nationhood--not only by outside pressure from Serbia and the Federal army but by national homogenization within Croatia itself. That is what the war is doing to us, reducing us to one dimension: the Nation. The trouble with this nationhood,

> however, is that whereas before, I was defined by my education, my job, my ideas, my character and, yes, my nationality too--now I feel stripped of all that. I am nobody because I am not a person any more. I am one of 4.5 million Croats.[22]

As more people see this for the impoverishment that it is, we may hope that tribal psychology itself may be changed. Perhaps self-creation will become less centered on the narrow range of charged tribal characteristics. Because this hope of tribalism being weakened depends on long-term changes of consciousness, it may seem utopian. Year by year, changes of consciousness are imperceptible, just like the day-by-day growth of children. But children do grow up, and our consciousness really has changed from that of medieval people.

The thinkers of the Enlightenment did not see the importance of tribalism or the contribution national loyalties make to our psychology. Seeing what they missed makes us, in one way, more sympathetic to nationalism. The case for this greater sympathy is based on the contribution of national loyalties to people and their sense of identity. This makes nations only of instrumental value. They are to be judged by the good and bad contributions they make to the lives of people. In this way the Enlightenment thinkers who kicked nations off their pedestal got it right. A good Enlightenment principle might be: Always treat nations merely as means and never as ends in themselves.

For the present we have to accept the strong psychological pull of nationalism as a fact of life. But if we are lucky, we may move toward a rather different world. I hope for a world of many small countries, which are only relatively autonomous. I also hope that many of them may be like W H. Auden's Arcadia, where the only statues allowed are of great dead chefs.

Notes
In the final version of this essay, I have been helped a great deal by perceptive comments from David Little, Michael Hechter, Jeff McMahan, and Robert McKim.

---

[22] Slavenka Drakulic, *Balkan Express*, p. 51.

DEFINING A JUST WAR[1]
RICHARD FALK

I have never since my childhood supported a shooting war in which the United States was involved, although in retrospect I think the NATO war in Kosovo achieved beneficial results. The war in Afghanistan against apocalyptic terrorism qualifies in my understanding as the first truly just war since World War II. But the justice of the cause and of the limited ends is in danger of being negated by the injustice of improper means and excessive ends. Unlike World War II and prior just wars, this one can be won only if tactics adhere to legal and moral constraints on the means used to conduct it, and to limited ends.

The perpetrators of the September 11 attack cannot be reliably neutralized by nonviolent or diplomatic means; a response that includes military action is essential to diminish the threat of repetition, to inflict punishment and to restore a sense of security at home and abroad. The extremist political vision held by Osama bin Laden, which can usefully be labeled "apocalyptic terrorism," places this persisting threat well outside any framework of potential reconciliation or even negotiation for several reasons: Its genocidal intent is directed generically against Americans and Jews; its proclaimed goal is waging an unconditional civilizational war--Islam against the West--without drawing any distinction between civilian and military targets; it has demonstrated a capacity and willingness to inflict massive and traumatizing damage on our country and a tactical ingenuity and ability to carry out its missions of destruction by reliance on the suicidal devotion of its adherents.

There are three types of responses to the attack, each of which contains some merit and enjoys some support. None of them are adequate, however.

I. Antiwar/Pacifist Approach

The pacifist position opposing even limited military action overlooks the nature of the threat and is thus irrelevant to meeting the central challenge of restoring some sense of security among our citizenry and in the world generally.

Also, in the current setting, unlike in the civil rights movement and the interventionist conflicts of the cold war era (especially Vietnam), antiwar and pacifist stands possess little or no cultural resonance with the overwhelming majority of Americans. It may be that at later stages of the war this assessment will prove to have been premature, and even now Quaker, Christian, Gandhian and Buddhist forms of pacifism offer a profound critique of wars. These critiques should be seriously heeded, since they lend weight to the the view that the use of force should be marginal and kept to an absolute minimum. Certainly the spiritually motivated pacifist witness can be both inspirational and instructive, and help to mitigate and interrogate militarist postures.

---

[1] Reprinted with permission from the October 29, 2001 issue of *The Nation*.

Another form of antiwar advocacy rests on a critique of the United States as an imperialist superpower or empire. This view also seems dangerously inappropriate in addressing the challenge posed by the massive crime against humanity committed on September 11. Whatever the global role of the United States--and it is certainly responsible for much global suffering and injustice, giving rise to widespread resentment that at its inner core fuels the terrorist impulse--it cannot be addressed so long as this movement of global terrorism is at large and prepared to carry on with its demonic work. These longer-term concerns--which include finding ways to promote Palestinian self-determination, the internationalization of Jerusalem and a more equitable distribution of the benefits of global economic growth and development--must be addressed. Of course, much of the responsibility for the failure to do so lies with the corruption and repressive policies of governments, especially in the Middle East, outside the orbit of US influence. A distinction needs to be drawn as persuasively as possible between inherently desirable lines of foreign policy reform and retreating in the face of terrorism.

II. Legalist/UN Approach

International treaties that deal with terrorism on civil aircraft call for cooperation in apprehending suspects and allow for their subsequent indictment and prosecution by national courts. Such laws could in theory be invoked to capture Osama bin Laden and his leading associates and charge them with international crimes, including crimes against humanity. A tribunal could be constituted under the authority of the United Nations, and a fair trial could then be held that would avoid war and the ensuing pain, destruction and associated costs. The narrative of apocalyptic terrorism could be laid before the world as the crimes of Nazism were bared at Nuremberg.

But this course is unlikely to deal effectively with the overall threat. A public prosecution would give bin Laden and associates a platform to rally further support among a large constituency of sympathizers, and conviction and punishment would certainly be viewed as a kind of legal martyrdom. It would be impossible to persuade the United States government to empower such a tribunal unless it was authorized to impose capital punishment, and it is doubtful that several of the permanent members of the Security Council could be persuaded to allow death sentences. Beyond this, the evidence linking bin Laden to the September 11 attacks and other instances of global terrorism may well be insufficient to produce an assured conviction in an impartial legal tribunal, particularly if conspiracy was not among the criminal offenses that could be charged. European and other foreign governments are unlikely to be willing to treat conspiracy as a capital crime. And it strains the imagination to suppose that the Bush Administration would relinquish control over bin Laden to an international tribunal. On a more general level, it also seems highly improbable that the US government can be persuaded to rely on the collective security mechanisms of the UN even to the unsatisfactory degree permitted during the Gulf War. To be sure, the UN Security Council has provided a vague antiterrorist mandate as well as an endorsement of a US right of response, but such legitimizing gestures are no more than that. For better and worse, the United States is relying on its claimed right of self-defense, and Washington seems certain to insist on full operational control over the means and ends of the war that is now under way. Such a reliance is worrisome, given past US behavior and the somewhat militaristic character of both the leadership in Washington and the broader societal orientation in America toward the use of overwhelming force against the nation's enemies.

Yet at this stage it is unreasonable to expect the US government to rely on the UN to fulfill its defensive needs. The UN lacks the capability, authority and will to respond to the kind of threat to global security posed by this new form of terrorist world war. The UN was established to deal with wars among states, while a transnational actor that cannot be definitively linked to a state is behind the attacks on the United States. Al Qaeda's relationship to the Taliban regime in Afghanistan is contingent, with Al Qaeda being more the sponsor of the state rather than the other way around.

Undoubtedly, the world would be safer and more secure with a stronger UN that had the support of the leading states in the world. The United States has for years acted more to obstruct than to foster such a transformation. Surely the long-term effects of this crisis should involve a new surge of support for a reformed UN that would have independent means of financing its operations, with its own peacekeeping and enforcement capabilities backed up by an international criminal court. Such a transformed UN would generate confidence that it could and would uphold its charter in an evenhanded manner that treats people equally. But it would be foolish to pretend that the UN today, even if it were to enjoy a far higher level of US support than it does, could mount an effective response to the September 11 attacks.

III. Militarist Approach

Unlike pacifism and legalism, militarism poses a practical danger of immense proportions. Excessive reliance on the military will backfire badly, further imperiling the security of Americans and others, spreading war and destruction far afield, as well as emboldening the government to act at home in ways that weaken US democracy. So far the Bush Administration has shown some understanding of these dangers, going slowly in its reliance on military action and moving relatively cautiously to bolster its powers over those it views as suspicious or dangerous, so as to avoid the perception of waging a cultural war against Islam. The White House has itself repeatedly stressed that this conflict is unlike previous wars, that nonmilitary means are also important, that victory will come in a different way and that major battlefield encounters are unlikely to occur.

Such reassurances, however, are not altogether convincing. The President's current rhetoric seems to reflect Secretary of State Colin Powell's more prudent approach, which emphasizes diplomacy and nonmilitary tactics, and restricts military action to Al Qaeda and the Taliban regime. Even here, there is room for dangerous expansion, depending on how the Al Qaeda network is defined. Some maximalists implicate twenty or more countries as supporters of terrorism. Defense Secretary Donald Rumsfeld, his deputy Paul Wolfowitz and others are definitely beating the drums for a far wider war; they seem to regard the attacks as an occasion to implement their own vision of a new world, one that proposes to rid the world of "evil" and advances its own apocalyptic vision. This vision seeks the destruction of such organizations as Hezbollah and Hamas, which have only minimal links to

Al Qaeda and transnational terror, and which have agendas limited mainly to Palestinian rights of self-determination and the future of Jerusalem. These organizations, while legally responsible for terrorist operations within their sphere of concerns, but also subject to terrorist provocations, have not shown any intention of pursuing bin Laden's apocalyptic undertaking. Including such groups on the US target list will surely undermine the depth and breadth of international support and engender dangerous reactions throughout the Islamic world, and possibly in the West as well.

Beyond this, there is speculation that there will be a second stage of response that will include a series of countries regarded as hostile to the United States, who are in possession of weapons of mass destruction but are not currently related to global terrorism in any significant fashion. These include Iraq, Libya and possibly even Syria, Iran and Sudan. To expand war objectives in this way would be full of risks, require massive military strikes inflicting much destruction and suffering, and would create a new wave of retaliatory violence directed against the United States and Americans throughout the world. If military goals overshoot, either by becoming part of a design to destroy Israel's enemies or to solve the problem of proliferation of weapons of mass destruction, the war against global terrorism will be lost, and badly.

Just as the pacifist fallacy involves unrealistic exclusion of military force from an acceptable response, the militarist fallacy involves an excessive reliance on military force in a manner that magnifies the threat it is trying to diminish or eliminate. It also expands the zone of violence in particularly dangerous ways that are almost certain to intensify and inflame anti-Americanism. It should be kept in mind that war occasions deep suffering, and recourse to international force should be both a last resort and on as limited a scale as possible.

But there is a fourth response, which has gained support among foreign policy analysts and probably a majority of Americans.

IV. Limiting Means and Ends

Unlike in major wars of the past, the response to this challenge of apocalyptic terrorism can be effective only if it is also widely perceived as legitimate. And legitimacy can be attained only if the role of military force is marginal to the overall conduct of the war and the relevant frameworks of moral, legal and religious restraint are scrupulously respected.

Excessive use of force in pursuing the perpetrators of September 11 will fan the flames of Islamic militancy and give credence to calls for holy war. What lent the WTC/Pentagon attack its quality of sinister originality was the ability of a fanatical political movement to take advantage of the complex fragility and vulnerability of advanced technology. Now that this vulnerability has been exposed to the world, it is impossible to insure that other extremists will not commit similar acts--even if Osama bin Laden is eliminated.

The only way to wage this war effectively is to make sure that force is used within relevant frameworks of restraint. Excessive force can take several forms, like the pursuit of political movements remote from the WTC attack, especially if such military action is seen as indirectly doing the dirty work of eliminating threats to Israel's occupation of Palestinian territories and Jerusalem. Excessiveness would also be attributed to efforts to destroy and restructure regimes, other than the Taliban, that are hostile to the United States but not significantly connected with either the attack or Al Qaeda.

The second, closely related problem of successfully framing a response is related to the US manner of waging war: The US temperament has tended to approach war as a matter of confronting evil. In such a view, victory can be achieved only by the total defeat of the other, and with it, the triumph of good.

In the current setting, goals have not been clarified, and US leaders have used grandiose language about ending terrorism and destroying the global terrorist network. The idea of good against evil has been a consistent part of the process of public mobilization, with the implicit message that nothing less than a total victory is acceptable. What are realistic ends? Or put differently, what ends can be reconciled with a commitment to achieve an effective response? What is needed is extremely selective uses of force, especially in relation to the Taliban, combined with criminal law enforcement operations--cutting off sources of finance, destroying terrorist cells, using policing techniques abetted, to the extent necessary, by paramilitary capabilities.

Also troubling is the Bush Administration's ingrained disdain for multilateralism and its determination to achieve security for the United States by military means--particularly missile defense and space weaponization. This unilateralism has so far been masked by a frantic effort to forge a global coalition, but there is every indication that the US government will insist on complete operational control over the war and will not be willing to accept procedures of accountability within the UN framework

The Administration has often said that many of the actions in this war will not be made known to the public. But an excessive emphasis on secrecy in the conduct of military operations is likely to make the uses of force more difficult to justify to those who are skeptical about US motives and goals, thus undercutting the legitimacy of the war.

In building a global coalition for cooperative action, especially with respect to law enforcement in countries where Al Qaeda operates, the US government has struck a number of Faustian bargains. It may be necessary to enter into arrangements with governments that are themselves responsible for terrorist policies and brutal repression, such as Russia in Chechnya and India in Kashmir. But the cost of doing so is to weaken claims that a common antiterrorist front is the foundation of this alliance. For some governments the war against apocalyptic terrorism is an opportunity to proceed with their own repressive policies free from censure and interference. The US government should weigh the cost of writing blank checks against the importance of distinguishing its means and ends from the megaterrorist ethos that animated the September 11 attacks. There are some difficult choices ahead, including the extent to which Afghan opposition forces, particularly the Northern Alliance, should be supported in view of their own dubious human rights record.

How, then, should legitimacy be pursued in the current context? The first set of requirements is essentially political: to disclose goals that seem reasonably connected with the attack and with the threat posed by those who planned, funded and carried it out. In this regard, the destruction of both the Taliban regime and the Al Qaeda network, including the apprehension and prosecution of Osama bin Laden and any associates connected with this and past terrorist crimes, are appropriate goals. In each instance, further specification is necessary. With respect to the Taliban, its relation to Al Qaeda is established and intimate enough to attribute primary responsibility, and the case is strengthened to the degree that its governing policies are so oppressive as to give the international community the strongest possible grounds for humanitarian intervention. We must make a distinction between those individuals and entities that have been actively engaged in the perpetration of the visionary program of international, apocalyptic terrorism uniquely Al Qaeda's and those who have used funds or training to advance more traditional goals relating to grievances associated with the governance of a particular country and have limited their targets largely to the authorities in their countries, like the ETA in Spain and the IRA in Ireland and Britain.

Legitimacy with respect to the use of force in international settings derives from the mutually reinforcing traditions of the "just war" doctrine, international law and the ideas of restraint embedded in the great religions of the world. The essential norms are rather abstract in character, and lend themselves to debate and diverse interpretation. The most important ideas are: the principle of discrimination: force must be directed at a military target, with damage to civilians and civilian society being incidental; the principle of proportionality: force must not be greater than that needed to achieve an acceptable military result and must not be greater than the provoking cause; the principle of humanity: force must not be directed even against enemy personnel if they are subject to capture, wounded or under control (as with prisoners of war); the principle of necessity: force should be used only if nonviolent means to achieve military goals are unavailable.

These abstract guidelines for the use of force do not give much operational direction. In each situation we must ask: Do the claims to use force seem reasonable in terms of the ends being pursued, including the obligation to confine civilian damage as much as possible? Such assessments depend on interpretation, but they allow for debate and justification, and clear instances of violative behavior could be quickly identified. The justice of the cause and of the limited ends will be negated by the injustice of improper means and excessive ends. Only the vigilance of an active citizenry, alert to this delicate balance, has much hope of helping this new war to end in a true victory.

HUMANITARIAN MILITARY INTERVENTION
JULES LOBEL AND MICHAEL RATNER

Key Points:
- The history of "humanitarian" military intervention is replete with invocations of humanitarian intentions by strong powers or coalitions in order to conceal their own geopolitical interests.
- The United Nations charter prohibits nations from attacking other states to remedy claimed violations of human rights.
- The requirement that the Security Council must authorize any use of force to protect human rights is critical to the maintenance of world peace and order.

The 1999 U.S.-led NATO air assault against Yugoslavia undertaken with the avowed aim of stopping human rights abuses in Kosovo has been extolled by some as a new model of humanitarian intervention. President Clinton and others have argued that when a nation is committing gross human rights violations against its citizens, other nations or multilateral coalitions have the right to intervene militarily, without the authority of the UN Security Council, to end those abuses.

However, the United Nations charter clearly prohibits nations from attacking other states for claimed violations of human rights. Article 2(4), the central provision of the charter, prohibits the "threat or use of force against" another state. There are only two exceptions to this prohibition. Article 51 allows a nation to use force in "self-defense if an armed attack occurs against" it or an allied country. The charter also authorizes the Security Council to employ force to counter threats to or breaches of international peace. This has been interpreted to allow individual nations to militarily intervene for humanitarian reasons, but only with the explicit authorization of the Security Council. This has occurred in Somalia, Rwanda, Haiti, and Bosnia. In line with post-World War II international law, most governments and jurists have rejected unilateral humanitarian military intervention because of the potential that powerful states will abuse such a doctrine. The history of humanitarian military intervention is replete with examples of powerful states or coalitions invoking the doctrine to conceal their own geopolitical interests. Professors Thomas Franck and Nigel Rodley examined the historical record of such interventions in the 1973 American Journal of International Law and concluded that "in very few, if any, instances has the right [to humanitarian intervention] been asserted under circumstances that appear more humanitarian than self-seeking and power seeking." The International Court of Justice concluded in 1949 that the doctrine of forcible intervention in the name of international justice "has, in the past, given rise to most serious abuses . . . [F]rom the nature of things, it would be reserved for the most powerful states."

Some scholars argue that recent UN practice allows for an exception to Article 2(4)'s prohibition on humanitarian intervention. They assert that the world's interest in countering serious human rights abuses cannot be blocked by the veto of a permanent Security Council member. They would legitimize unilateral military action in instances where the Security Council is silent, where it has condemned the human rights record of the target country, or where the UN is participating in the settlement of the war.

The purported good that might come from allowing countries to intervene unilaterally based upon such arguments is; however, outweighed by the dangers that arise from weakening the international restraints on the use of force. In addition, the UN charter requires that the use of force be a last resort, taken only after all peaceful alternatives have failed. The UN's primary goal is to "save succeeding generations from the scourge of war." To further this goal, its charter requires that decisions to go to war be made by a deliberative body of states representing a broad range of constituents: i.e., the Security Council.

The Kosovo crisis illustrates the danger of bypassing the Security Council and lends credence to those who argue that intervention was not for humanitarian purposes. Had the United States gone to the Security Council, it is possible that a settlement similar to the one that ended the air war could have been achieved without the use of force. The Security Council might have insisted on more negotiations, a more flexible approach to the Rambouillet proposal, or a less prominent role for NATO and the United States. Moreover, the destructiveness of the war and its aftermath undermine Washington's humanitarian claims and reemphasize the reasons that the charter's framers chose peace as its central tenet.

There may, of course, be certain extreme cases of genocide where one country's veto blocks the Security Council from authorizing the use of force. In dealing with those cases, it is preferable to recognize that in rare instances (and the factual evidence indicates that Kosovo was not one of these) a nation or group of nations may need to intervene without UN authorization in order to save lives. That is a less dangerous alternative than permitting an "escape clause" on the prohibition of the unilateral use of force, an exception that would likely be widely and dangerously abused.

Problems with Current U.S. Policy

Key Problems:
- The Clinton doctrine of forceful military intervention to prevent a nation from committing human rights abuses has been highly selective.
- In practice, the U.S. continues to provide arms to repressive regimes and has refused to intervene to stop human rights abuses committed by key allies or occurring where it has strategic or trade interests. Meanwhile, Washington tends to ignore genocide in countries considered of little importance.
- Human rights is but one of the rationales that, along with stopping the drug trade, terrorism, or communism, the United States has used to justify intervention in the internal affairs of other countries.

In the aftermath of the Kosovo War, U.S. administration officials have articulated a Clinton doctrine that proclaims that the United States will forcefully intervene to prevent human rights abuses when it can do so without suffering substantial casualties. This doctrine rhetorically suggests a new, assertive U. S. approach to promoting and defending human rights abroad.

However, the Clinton doctrine is highly selective, as indicated by Washington's decision to intervene in Kosovo—where, over the preceding year, an estimated two thousand had been killed—though ignoring the 1994 Rwandan genocide of over one million civilians within the span of a few weeks.

Although the U.S. failed to act in Rwanda, a country of little strategic or economic importance, in other instances the Clinton administration has chosen not to intervene to defend human rights precisely because the U.S. has strong strategic or trade interests in a country. For instance, though the State Department recognizes that Turkey, a close ally, has committed flagrant human rights violations against its Kurdish minority, the administration not only fails to intervene to protect the Kurds but actually continues to export arms to Turkey. During his October 1999 visit to Turkey, Clinton went so far as to praise Turkey's progress on establishing democracy and to promote its entry into the European Union. If human rights were of serious concern to the U.S., Washington would at least stop selling guns and helicopters to Turkey.

Another close U.S. ally, Indonesia, which invaded and annexed East Timor, causing the death of over 200,000 Timorese, is one of the world's worst human rights violators. Yet, throughout the incursions into East Timor, the U.S. continued to arm and train the Indonesian military. When, in 1999, East Timor voted peacefully and overwhelmingly for independence, the U.S. opposed the rapid creation of an armed UN peacekeeping force that could have stopped the forced exile of hundreds of thousands and the slaughter of Timorese civilians by Indonesian-controlled paramilitaries. Today, the U.S. is giving only limited support to the Australian/UN force; it refuses to supply combat troops but is giving some logistical help and a few helicopters.

By acting selectively, the U.S. not only undermines the authority of the United Nations and the rule of international law but belies the claim that it is acting to protect human rights when it does intervene. President Clinton has attempted to explain the obvious inconsistencies in U.S. policy by contending that America cannot be the world's policeman. Yet the United States has failed to promote UN-sanctioned international responses. Experts say that the genocide in Rwanda, for instance, could have been stopped with a few thousand soldiers. The killings in East Timor could have been curbed with even fewer—perhaps merely by the withdrawal of World Bank and International Monetary Fund credits to Indonesia. In Turkey, Washington (and other NATO countries) could still exert pressure to stop human rights abuses by halting U.S. arms flows. That Washington has not done so suggests not a lack of capacity but an unwillingness to raise human rights concerns in countries viewed as important strategic allies.

The Clinton doctrine of humanitarian intervention is simply the latest in a series of pretexts employed by the United States to justify unilateral military intervention. In recent decades, the U.S. has launched military actions under the rubric of overthrowing totalitarian governments and bringing democracy to people (Cuba, Vietnam, Nicaragua, Chile, Grenada), preventing terrorism (Sudan and Afghanistan), and stopping drug trafficking (Panama).

For over a year, the U.S., acting virtually alone and supported only by a token British military presence, has bombed the so-called no-fly zone in northern Iraq, which was established ostensibly to protect the Kurdish population. Unlike the war to oust Iraq from Kuwait, which had Security Council approval, Washington is currently bombing without UN backing. U.S. motives in continuing this bombing are related not to protecting the Kurds but to Washington's dispute with Iraq over weapons inspectors. With the end of the cold war and the struggle against communism, humanitarian intervention to prevent human rights abuses is providing a rationale for selective U.S. or U.S.-led military interventions, outside the framework of the United Nations.

Toward a New Foreign Policy

Key Recommendations:
- The United States should not employ military force for alleged humanitarian reasons without the explicit approval of the Security Council.
- The United States should end military support of nations committing serious human rights violations.
- The United States should strengthen its own participation in international human rights agreements.

The challenge for U.S. foreign policy in the twenty-first century is to improve the international regime of human rights without undermining the UN charter's prohibition on the unilateral use of force. The most important step toward this goal would be for the United States to eschew military force for alleged humanitarian reasons without the explicit approval of the UN Security Council. The failure to obtain such approval prior to the war against Yugoslavia and prior to the current and continuous bombing of Iraq seriously weakens the key international restraint against the use of force as embodied in the UN charter.

If the real purpose of U.S. humanitarian military intervention is to protect human rights, then America ought to employ peaceful and more principled methods for protecting those rights before resorting to military action. The U.S., which dominates the UN Security Council, should end its political selectivity and begin to work for a more principled human rights stance within the United Nations itself. Humanitarian intervention to stop grave human rights abuses should only be used after multilateral diplomatic and economic measures have been exhausted. This is not currently the case. The United States played the central role in imposing both the UN sanctions on Libya (finally lifted in 1999) and the prolonged, inhumane embargo on Iraq, while blocking sanctions against Israel, Turkey, and other allies that are serious human rights abusers. If Washington truly cares about furthering human rights, it must do so collectively and in a more evenhanded manner.

Former Amnesty International Secretary-General Ian Martin argues that there is too much "enthusiasm in the human rights movement, and especially in the United States, for military intervention on humanitarian grounds." Although he understands that national sovereignty does not necessarily prevail over the responsibility to prevent mass violations of human rights, he emphasizes that "such international responsibility can be properly exercised only by a multilateral decision of the international community through the UN." Martin states that the legitimacy of such decisions by the United Nations depends "upon a proper distribution of power within that organization, the application of a set of principled criteria for military intervention which is not politically selective, and the development of the ability of the UN itself to maintain the control of a military operation."

Although the Clinton administration has shown scant willingness to seek UN authority prior to using force, there is a step that the United States could more easily take: end its military support for nations committing serious human rights violations. In 1998, Congress enacted the Leahy amendment, a provision in the foreign assistance legislation prohibiting foreign aid funds, including U.S. loan guarantees, from being used to bolster units of foreign security forces that are committing human rights violations. This legislation needs to be extended, strengthened, and fully implemented.

In the past, such provisions have often led to executive branch assertions that governments supported by the United States were, in fact, improving their human rights records. During the 1980s, for instance, the Reagan administration repeatedly certified El Salvador during years when that government was committing terrible atrocities. Currently, both the Clinton administration and Congress have pumped military hardware, training, and advisors into Colombia's armed forces and police, despite evidence of corruption and human rights abuses.

A positive sign in an otherwise bleak environment was the State Department's use of the Leahy amendment in December 1998 to deny, in part, a defense contractor's request for U.S.-government financing to underwrite Turkey's purchase of armored vehicles. A key test of administration arms policy toward Turkey is still pending; whether it will issue an export license for Turkey's planned acquisition of 145 attack helicopters, which would likely be used for the destruction of Kurdish civilian targets.

Finally, the United States ought to strengthen its own participation in international human rights agreements and support the international institutions that enforce such agreements. In the long term, stronger international agreements and institutions will save more lives than questionable ad hoc military interventions. The U.S. should sign and ratify the agreement establishing the International Criminal Court. The Senate should remove the reservations added to treaties (such as the International Covenant on Civil and Political Rights) that render them non-self-executing or nonenforceable under U.S. law. At present, U.S. courts have been following a double standard of imposing liability against foreign officials accused of committing serious international human rights abuses, while refusing to recognize such claims brought against U. S. officials. To encourage other nations to apply international human rights law in their domestic courts, we must apply it in our courts.

Changing U.S. foreign policy along these lines will not be easy and is unlikely to happen quickly. However, at the close of a century in which scores of millions have been killed in military conflicts and with the rise of new and extreme ethnic, national, and religious conflicts, multilateral cooperation through a more democratic United Nations is more important than ever.

Sources for More Information

Organizations:
Center for Constitutional Rights
666 Broadway, 7th Floor
New York, NY 10012
Voice: (212) 614-6464
Fax: (212) 243-2007

Publications:
Noam Chomsky, The New Military Humanism: Lessons from Kosovo (Monroe, ME: Common Courage Press, 1999).

Lori Damrosch and David Scheffer, Law and Force in the New International Order (Boulder, CO: Westview Press, 1991).

Richard Falk, "The Complexities Of Humanitarian Intervention: A New World Order Challenge," Michigan Journal of International Law, vol. 17, Winter 1996.

Thomas Franck and Nigel Rodley, "After Bangladesh: The Law of Humanitarian Intervention by Military Force," American Journal of International Law, vol. 67, 1973.

Michael Mandelbaum, "A Perfect Failure: NATO's War Against Yugoslavia," Foreign Affairs, vol. 78, no. 5, September-October 1999.

Sean D. Murphy, "Humanitarian Intervention: the United Nations in an Evolving World Order,"Procedural Aspects of International Law Series, vol. 21 (Philadelphia, PA: University of Pennsylvania Press, 1996).

W. Michael Reisman, "Coercion and Self-Determination: Construing Charter Article 2(4)," American Journal of International Law, vol. 78, July 1984.

Sarah A. Rumage, "Panama and The Myth Of Humanitarian Intervention in U.S. Foreign Policy: Neither Legal Nor Moral, Neither Just Nor Right," Arizona Journal of International Law and Comparative Law, vol. 10, no. 1, 1993.

Oscar Schachter, "The Right of States to Use Armed Forces," Michigan Law Review, vol. 82, April-May 1984.

Stephen Shalom, "Reflections on NATO and Kosovo," available at: http://www.zmag.org/crisescurevts/shalomnp.htm

Wil Verwey, "Humanitarian Intervention Under International Law," Netherlands International Law Review, vol. 32, 1985.

Websites:
Jurist: The Law Professors' Network
http://jurist.law.pitt.edu/kosovo.htm
Human Rights Now
http://www.humanrightsnow.com

INSTANTIATION$_5$

TECHNOLOGIES

INTRODUCTION

Probably the place to begin is with two somewhat controversial theses. The first is that the history of technologies has been coextensive with the history of human evolution. While it is an open question as to whether our tools define our humanity, technologies have been around since humans emerged as humans. This takes the form of spears, axes, agricultural techniques, and even complex languages.[1] This thesis is significant since it forces those dealing with the ethics of technologies to realize that ethical questions about technologies did not begin with, say, the atom bomb. Instead, there is a long narrative to be told about the emerging visibility of technologies as an ethical problematic, that begins to be explicitly formulated by Francis Bacon, developed into a heavenly vision by assorted Enlightenment types, reaching a pinnacle with the works of Marx and Engels. It is probably only since the time of the Industrial Revolutions that it has become obvious to virtually everyone that technologies both create and solve numerous ethical problems.

The second thesis is that there is no such thing as *Technology*. A number of philosophers of technology, most influentially Martin Heidegger and Jacques Ellul, have argued that Technology has an "essence," something that gives it a particular quality, generally making any technology inherently evil.[2] It is proposed here that the essentialist is wrong. Instead there are particular types of technologies which we must look at and assess. Different technologies function in different ways, which means that any ethical assessment of the "goodness" or "evilness" of technologies must also reflect this diversity. While we might be able to use a very general conception of technology to guide ethical judgments, we must also appreciate the context in which particular technologies are used.

In order to bring a bit of order to this chaos, it is useful to introduce just such a general conception. Michel Foucault developed a set of "ideal types" of technology which are a useful heuristic for mapping different sorts of technology. He proposes four types:

> (1) technologies of production, which permit us to produce, transform, or manipulate things; (2) technologies of sign systems, which permit us to use signs, meanings, symbols, or signification; (3) technologies of power, which determine the conduct of individuals and submit them to certain ends or domination, an objectivizing of the subject; (4) technologies of the self, which permit individuals to effect by their own means, or with the help of others, a certain number of operations on their bodies and souls, thoughts, conduct, and way of being, so as to transform themselves in order to attain a

---

[1] This might lead some to the conclusion that higher primates are technology-using creatures as well. While provocative, such a navel-gazing issue might be best left to philosophers of technology.
[2] Less frequently it is argued that technology is inherently good, but critical types find it much more fun to say its evil.

> certain state of happiness, purity, wisdom, perfection, or immortality. (Foucault, 1997: 225)

Needless to say, these different types of technologies overlap with one another in many cases. As will be shown below, these four types illuminate many dimensions of different types of technologies.

Bearing in mind the two theses introduced above, it should be obvious to anyone who watches the evening news that many contemporary technologies function in new ways. Those discussed by the authors in this section have a direct or indirect global impact. From the Industrial Revolutions, becoming clear with the atomic bomb, to the present, many technologies have been developed whose boundaries are either "large and fuzzy" or outright global. This adds a new dimension to ethical judgements regarding technologies.

Joseph Pitt has noted "...ever since a human first used a tree limb to batter or kill another creature, our technologies have out-paced our moral theories." (Pitt, 2000: 113) Matters with more recent technologies make Pitt's statement all the more poignant. No longer is it "simply" a matter of determining the morality of beating things with sticks (a rather local matter), but potentially shutting out nations from a world community, the possibility of a free(r) press, or the future of various species and even the human race. These are technologies that extend beyond locales, nations, cultures and species. This greatly extends the who and what that must count in any ethical judgment regarding such technologies. Further more, these problems are genuinely ethical and not purely technically. As all the texts here demonstrate, these problems will not be solved with more technological fixes. Instead, these are social problems that require serious rethinking of our society.

This point is made clear throughout this section in a number of ways. In "Information Rich, Information Poor" Richard Wresch develops a vivid portrait of who is left in and left out in the so-called "information revolution." In mapping the notion of information and information technologies, he reminds us of the lingering importance of books and social connections as well as computers and the like. This mapping of information shows how these various sign-systems both encourage and prohibit other sorts of activities including political action and changing one's self.

Noam Chomsky takes a different approach to information systems by focusing on the media. His principle concern is to show how the media forms a technology of domination. This domination is never explicit, but exists through the way editors chose stories and media target audiences. By channeling information in this way, various media can channel how the masses act.

The two articles that follow focus on emerging biotechnologies. Both Jeremy Rifkin and Mark Sagoff show these (bio)technologies of production threaten much of what we take as "common sense." Rifkin gives an overview of the enormous threats that biotechnology poses to both humans and non-humans. The claim is that much of this work is done for the "betterment of mankind," he shows the ways in which this is basically a rhetorical ploy to cover a desire to make money. Sagoff's scope is limited to property rights and biotechnology. Many respond to the notion of patenting living organisms with some amount of horror which Sagoff is sympathetic with. In this penetrating analysis, he attempts to navigate between this revulsion and protecting the intellectual property of biotechnologists.

The section concludes with a set of remarks from Monhandas Karamchand (Mahatma) Gandhi on machinery. In this discussion, Gandhi shows reasons to be skeptical of mechanization and industrialization. The power of his words lies in his ability to show that machinery is not merely about producing things. Instead, machinery becomes a means of controlling human subjects; something which Gandhi is rather critical of.

References

Foucault, Michel. 1997. "Technologies of the Self." Pp. 223- 251 in *Ethics: Subjectivity and Truth, The Essential Works of Michel Foucault (1954-1984)*. Edited by Paul Rabinow, Volume 1. New York: New Press.

Pitt, Joseph. 2000. *Thinking About Technology: Foundations of the Philosophy of Technology*. New York: Seven Bridges Press.

INFORMATION RICH, INFORMATION POOR
WILLIAM WRESCH

Theo Shoeman washes his BMW at 5:00 A.M. He is out early in part to beat the heat. While Windhoek, Namibia, sits at fifty-six hundred feet, its elevation can only partially offset the effects of the tropical sun that will rise by 6:30 and take afternoon temperatures into the nineties. Mostly Schoeman is up early because he faces a very full day. President of the family business, Schoeman Computers, he has an endless stream of business information he must absorb. Besides his e-mail connections to the business centers of Europe, he also receives CD-ROMs with thousands of business and technical articles from periodicals around the world. If he can get to his desk by six, he should be able to read his latest CDs for two hours before his employees arrive and the daily routine of meetings and phone calls start.

But not all of his connections are electronic. Fluent in English, German, and Afrikaans, he travels at least once each year to trade shows in Germany and the United States. He has a regular buyer in California who does direct purchasing for him, shipped out on a regular flight each Friday. They converse daily either via phone or via electronic mail. A lifelong Namibian, he has a wide circle of friends, but he supplements that circle with formal relationships he has cultivated over the years. When people in the technology field started talking about forming a group, he helped found the Namibian Information Technology Association (NITA). When the government civil service formed a Data Services Division, he began having regular meetings with its head and supplied her with free training sessions for her new employees.

In many ways Theo Schoeman could be the ideal "Information Man." When people describe the future, he is much of what they hope for—educated, affluent, well traveled. It would be nice to think that most of the world's people will live like Theo sometime soon. But before we get too excited about that future, there are a few additional things we should know about Theo Schoeman's day. After his twelve or fourteen hours at the office, Schoeman will come home. He may put a movie into his VCR, but it won't be a Namibian movie—there is no such thing. He might curl up with a Namibian book, but he won't do it very often—only about half a dozen are published each year. He could turn on the tube, but all he will see on it is American reruns and government propaganda. He might pick up the phone and direct dial dozens of friends in the United States or Germany, but he couldn't call more than a handful of people outside the capital city in his own country. In other words, Schoeman has amazing access to some kinds of information, no access at all to others—either the information doesn't exist or he can't get to it. There are barriers and blind spots in his world. Even the best and the brightest face limits.

Across town is Negumbo Johannes—everyone's nightmare about the information age. Johannes wakes every morning at six. He sleeps on the floor of a friend's house in Wanaheda. The house is a concrete block rectangle about the size of a one-car garage in the United States. Wanaheda is on the northern outskirts of

Windhoek, north because that is where blacks were allowed to live under South African rule. His street is gravel. Water and electricity are planned, but neither has arrived yet. Johannes drinks a glass of water from the bucket on the table and goes next door to meet Filippus Erastus, a friend from his village along the Angolan border. Together they start the one-hour walk that takes them to downtown Windhoek.

Johannes and Erastus are day laborers. Men in their early twenties, they attended five or six years of school in their village and then spent the rest of their youth herding cattle for their family. At sixteen or seventeen they each had younger brothers who could take over the herd, so they started looking for something better. In the north there is nothing. Two or three times a year they went in to Oshikati, the main city of the north, to sell cattle or visit friends. The city is big, but there is little manufacturing, just small retail outlets and a few slaughterhouses. There are no jobs. Under South African rule members of their tribe were forbidden to travel or move to the southern parts of Namibia, but with independence in 1990 all restrictions were dropped. Some of their friends moved to Windhoek. That is where the money was. That is where the jobs were. Johannes and Erastus followed.

They did not find jobs. Windhoek, at 150,000 people, is far larger than Oshikati, and there is some manufacturing there, but not nearly enough to employ the thousands who stream in from the outer reaches of the country. Johannes tried. In his first weeks he walked to every business in the city. Each has a sign mounted by the employees' entrance—No Work it says in three languages. Several times he has used the entrance anyway, only to be chased away before he could even ask for a job. There is no work.

So he and his friends from the north stand on various corners in the downtown area. They arrive by seven and stand until four. On a good day a construction foreman will pull a pickup truck up to the corner. Johannes and all the other men—maybe twenty or thirty—will run to the truck. Some will jump in the back hoping they will be selected. Usually the foreman will order them back out and query each man individually about previous jobs he has done. Johannes will stand and describe work he has done and try to meet the man's eyes as long as he can. Sometimes he is chosen; sometimes he is not. When he is not, he never knows why. He is just ordered away. If he is chosen, he jumps into the back of the truck with the other lucky men.

On the job site, he does whatever he is told. Sometimes it is concrete work, building the walls of new houses. Sometimes it is loading or unloading trucks. Often it is digging foundations or trenches for water or electricity. On rare occasions his boss will give him a small lunch. Usually he works through the day on an empty stomach. At five the foreman will pay the men. It will be some amount between fifteen and twenty-five Namibian dollars (four to seven U.S. dollars). He takes whatever he is given without complaint, for any comments may mean he is never hired again. The foreman may drive the men up to Wanaheda or may let them walk.

Most days Johannes just stands on his corner waiting for work. He talks to the other men about places they may have recently worked, rumors they have heard about jobs. They get no lunch. They have no bathrooms. They debate whether to stay on the corner or move to another corner. Eventually the day passes and Johannes starts the hour-long walk home. He will fix some sort of dinner, his one meal of the day. He will pass the evening talking to his neighbors. The next day he will be back on the corner. In the past, he and his friends spent six days a week waiting for work and played soccer on Sunday. Recently some of the men have started spending Sunday on the corner too. Johannes hasn't yet, but since he is being hired fewer and fewer days each week (three days of work is an exceptional week), he is debating standing Sundays too. It would be a desperate thing to do, ending any break from the monotony of the corner, any break from the tropical sun, any break from the embarrassment of standing so visibly unemployed in a city where many drive Mercedes.

Negumbo Johannes leads a life of brutal poverty. He has no money, he has no skills, he has very little hope. His life has become almost an obsession with finding a job. He talks about it all day and dreams about it at night. His mental health is almost as precarious as his physical health. What he does not know is that his situation is getting worse. The information age has arrived in Africa and new systems are being established. Those systems totally exclude him.

Consider, if you will, Johannes's job search. Public information vehicles are available in Namibia that might tell him about economic trends and job opportunities. But he is excluded from virtually all of them. Newspapers cost N$ 1.50–10 percent of his daily wage on days when he has a wage. So he doesn't buy them. Television is broadcast by the state, but few of his neighbors have a TV, and broadcasts are in English, a language he doesn't know. Radio has one channel broadcasting in Oshiwambo, his only source of news. Professional information excludes him because he has no profession. Namibia has professional societies to help their members stay current, and to help their members find work, but he will never be a member. Organizational information bypasses him as well. None of his employers take the time to inform him of their future directions, their future prospects. He will only be there a day–why should they waste time talking to him? His personal information is virtually nonexistent. He has no connections to church or sports or social groups that might give him job tips. His school friends are as desperate as he is. He has traveled nowhere but Windhoek and his village in the north, so he knows nothing of the world. The only language he speaks is his tribal language, a language few speak in Windhoek or elsewhere in the world. As for the great wired future he will never in his life see a computer, much less use one to communicate or learn.

Both Theo Schoeman and Negumbo Johannes have much to tell us about our age. One is information rich, the other information poor. The gulf between them seems infinite. They might as well be living on separate planets. Yet even the rich man has problems. The information available to him is not nearly as unlimited as might seem the case. Faxes and modems may carry information, but they do not guarantee that information will exist to carry. Cyberspace is populated with numerous black holes–information vacuums that are largely ignored. As for Negumbo Johannes, he just wants to know who might give him a laboring job the next day, and he can't find anyone who will even talk to him. If this is the information age, what age is *he* in?

There may be miracles happening all around us–masses of optical fiber, four-hundred-channel TV, satellite uplinks, a World Wide Web of resources there at the click of a button. But Schoeman and Johannes remind us that, as is usually the case, there is much more to the story. For information rich and poor alike, there are problems. To understand those problems, and then to solve them, we must begin by looking at unexamined assumptions.

Unexamined Assumptions

One of the most basic models of the communication process begins with a simple triangle: sender, message, receiver. Somebody has to talk, something has to be said, somebody has to listen. If we map that model onto an overview of information handling, we could say information has to be generated, it has to be transmitted, and it has to be understood.

Nothing could be simpler. Except we make assumptions about each step in the process. We assume masses of information are being generated, more information every day, more than the world has ever seen before. That's not exactly wrong, but it's not totally right, either. Too much information is unavailable, even to the information rich like Theo Schoeman. We're missing something.

Similarly, we assume that information transmission problems are now a thing of the past. After all, we have optical fiber and satellite delivery systems. But is that all it really takes? If laying fiber means information now flows everywhere, what is Negumbo Johannes's problem?

And what about us as information receivers? Even if untold quantities of new information were suddenly available and delivered free to our door, would we know what to do with it? Where is the evidence to support that assumption?

The central point of this book is that we haven't asked enough about the basics. If information is doubling every three or five or seven or ten years, where has all that information gone? Is the world really awash in information? And if it is, is that the end, to all the world's problems? We are counting articles and pointing to large numbers, but not looking closely enough at the information being generated. We are talking about bandwidth as a solution to information flow without looking carefully enough at how information really moves from one place to another–and why it often cannot move at all. And we are arrogant about our own abilities to handle information despite endless examples of our frailties.

If we are going to take advantage of developments in information access, we have to begin by being honest about the kind of information that is available, the ability of information to move, and our own ability to process it. We will take a quick overview, of those three areas in this chapter, and then spend the rest of the book examining them in detail.

How Much Information Is There?

Over the past decade or two we have been told there is an information explosion going on. We are told we now live in the information age. John Naisbitt summed up much of this sentiment in his massive best seller, *Megatrends* (1982). His first trend: "Although we continue to think we live in an industrial society, we have in fact changed to an economy based on the creation and distribution of information" (1). He goes on to say that "more than 60 percent of us work with information as programmers, teachers, clerks, secretaries, accountants, stockbrokers, managers, insurance people, bureaucrats, lawyers, bankers, and technicians" (14). As support for his assertions, Naisbitt cites the following figures: (1) Between six and seven thousand scientific articles are written each day; (2) scientific and technical information now increases 13 percent per year, which means it doubles every 5.5 years; and (3) the rate will soon jump to perhaps 40 percent per year because of new, more powerful information systems, and an increasing population of scientists (24).

More recently it is Alvin Toffler who has commanded our attention with his series of books describing the changes being brought to our world by new information systems. His descriptions of the information flowing through an ordinary grocery store shows all of us the practical business implications of information systems. His *Powershift* (1990) is a careful case-by-case description of how the availability of information is changing power relationships among individuals, organizations, and nations. He sums up much of the impact this way:
"We are creating new networks of knowledge...linking concepts in startling ways...building up amazing hierarchies of inference...spawning new theories, hypotheses, and images, based on novel assumptions, new languages, codes, and logics. Businesses, governments, and individuals are collecting and storing more sheer data than any previous generation in history" (85).

It is not too surprising that given this mountain of new data, we are already hearing from counselors telling us how to handle the stress such information is bringing us. In his popular book *Information Anxiety* (1989), Richard Saul Wurman describes sixteen warning signs of this new malady. Among his signs: (1) Feeling guilty about that ever-higher stack of periodicals waiting to be read; (2) feeling depressed because you don't know what all the buttons are on your VCR; (3) thinking the person next to you understands everything you don't; and (4) reacting emotionally to information you don't really understand such as not knowing what the Dow Jones really is but panicking when you hear that it has dropped five hundred points (36).

All these authors seem to answer the question, How much information is there? They tell us simply that there is far more than there was before, that the amount is ever increasing, and that it is already more than many of us can handle. Are they right? Without question there is more information available to us than there has been in the past. At least there is more of certain *kinds* of information. There is clearly more scientific information available: we can see the results in new manufacturing processes, new medical treatments, and even in the genetically altered food we eat. But what about other kinds of information? Does Dan Rather tell us twice as much each night as he did five years ago? Does your local paper have twice as much news? Does it even still exist? Does your employer tell you twice as much about your company's progress? Does the company down the block tell you anything about its activities? The World Wide Web has infinitely more information than five years ago, since it did not exist five years ago, but what kind of information is on the Web? What kind of information is not?

Defining Information

If we want to start discussions of an information explosion, and define this as the information age, it would be helpful if we would begin by defining the term *information*. Toffler defines information as "data that have been fitted into categories and classification schemes or other patterns" (18). That's not a bad beginning. It implies that information is something that has been worked on— "fitted" into patterns or other larger structures. But it is still vague. For instance, it does not tell us where we might go looking for information, or what forms we might find it in.

Michael Buckland (1991) at the School of Library and Information Studies at the University of California-Berkeley takes a look at the forms of information. He focuses on "information-as-thing." This is a very practical approach for a librarian to take. In essence he asks, Where is this stuff and how much room will it occupy? His answer is that information comes as:

1. data-records that can be stored on a computer;
2. text and documents–papers, letters, books–that may be on paper, microfilm, or in electronic form;
3. spoken language in any medium;
4. objects–dinosaur bones, rock collections, and skeletons;
5. records of events-photos, news reports, and memoirs.

Such a definition is both insightful and practical. It reminds us that information can come in many forms. The weakness of Buckland's definition is its neutrality. It does not help us later, when we try to determine why there seems to be limitless information in some areas and no information in others.

This book tries a different approach. My assumption is that information is not a neutral object to be discovered and counted, like atoms or zebras, but an expression shaped from the very beginning by the creators of that information. In short, information comes from somebody, and that somebody determines from the beginning how much information there will be, what form it will take, and even if it will exist at all. If you want to understand information, go to its source.

How many sources are there? In one sense there are billions–each of us who has ever occupied our planet. For the sake of brevity, though, we will look at just five sources: public information, personal information, organizational information, professional information, and commercial information. These five do not exhaust all the information sources we may encounter, but they represent major sources. By examining each, we will see how much information is really out there, what form it takes, and how good it is.

Public Information. In our rush to examine all the new opportunities made available by technology, we often forget that much of the information people have still comes from very traditional sources–television, movies, radio, newspapers, and books. It is true digital information is supplementing and even supplanting these earlier forms, but it hasn't totally replaced them and won't anytime soon.

But while these traditional sources of information are still important, they are not always accessible. For instance, CNN is nice, but to see it you not only need a television, you need an electrical outlet to plug the TV into. That may not be a problem in the United States, where we have 850 TV sets per 1,000 population, but it is a problem in countries such as Bangladesh (5 TVs per 1,000) and Kenya (9 TVs per 1,000). Books are still a critical resource for information, but some countries have virtually no publishing industry. The entire continent of Africa, for example, produces just 2 percent of the world's book titles.

Besides availability, there is the question of origination. There are lots of movies circulating through the world, but they come from very few countries. Developing nations occasionally complain about this cultural dependence, and even formed the New World Information and Communications Order, but there is no sign of real change here. In the meantime, not only do some countries struggle under the weight of foreign cultures, but exporting countries such as ours have almost no opportunity to hear other voices or see other perspectives. The information flow is all one way.

Personal Information. "It's not what you know, it's who you know" is cynical, but it is accurate. It might be even more accurate if rephrased: who you know determines what you know. The value of personal contacts may be more difficult to calculate than the number of scientific articles published or the bandwidth of optical-fiber telecommunications networks, but it can be seen in the success rate in job-seekers' networks and in the conscious effort being placed on creating mentorships, especially for women and minorities. All of us also have an anecdote about an opportunity that came our way or a problem we were able to solve because we know someone. It seems a truism that successful people just have a bigger Rolodex than others.

While personal information access is a central process for many people, it poses several problems. The first is the possibility of conscious abuse. Many women's network were setup specifically as a response to the perception that "old boy" networks were creating an unfair advantage for men–men talked to each other, helped each other, in ways that were closed to women.

A second problem is less visible, but may in fact be a more difficult problem to overcome. The problem is cultural. Some cultures interact, others are more aloof. College calculus may serve as the best, if most unlikely, example here. Uri Triesmann tried to determine why Asian students at the University of California-Berkeley were able to pass calculus while black students almost always failed. Both groups had been stars in high school–getting into Berkeley isn't easy–yet blacks just could not pass the course. Some might respond to those results with racial slurs or attacks on affirmative action. Triesmann moved into the dorms and studied how both groups spent their days. What he discovered is that Asian students began each quarter by setting up study groups. These were not just groups for grinds–they had their pizzas and social evenings, too, but most of their time together was for studying. Blacks had social groups too, but these groups were strictly social. When it came time to study, each black student went back to his dorm room, closed the door, and studied alone. That was their culture, and it was a cultural trait that was destroying them.

Cultures of isolation aren't the only problems of personal information channels. Since these channels are largely invisible, they can be filled with myths, lies, and hatreds. Few outsiders even know what is being said, nor do they have opportunities to correct even the most egregious errors. Yet error-prone or not, these are channels that supply much of the world's information.

Organizational Information. Whether organizations are businesses, universities, or government agencies, they seem to be conflicted over information. Internally, organizations seen more willing to share information with members and employees. Externally, organizations seem unwilling to tell the world what is going on, and seem very willing to lie.

Internal organizational communication is based around an ideal and a reality. The ideal is that organizations function best when employees know what is going on.

Maybe they have been asked an opinion, maybe they have played a role in forming policy, maybe not. But at least they know what the organization is trying to do. The reality is that information flows within a context. We can put in new e-mail systems and create a system that is theoretically capable of letting each and every worker have electronic access to the CEO. But that does not mean the CEO will ever read the e-mail coming in. Nor does it mean that all workers will be thrilled with new opportunities to communicate with an organization to which they may have, at best, a tangential relationship.

An area of information flow that may be even more challenging is the new flows being created between organizations. Electronic data interchange (EDI) systems connect companies and government agencies in ways never attempted before. The computer systems needed for this new interchange may be daunting, but they are nothing compared to the ethical and legal challenges on the horizon.

Then there is the question of how organizations communicate with the rest of the world. Whether the organizations are public or private, large corporations or small proprietorships, information is withheld from outsiders as a routine measure.

Professional Information. A major source of information is professional bodies, of which there are many. In the United States the last decade or so has seen a major growth in the number of these bodies (U.S. CENSUS 1993:787):

Professional Bodies	*1980*	*1992*
Scientific, technical, and engineering associations	1,039	1,365
Trade, business, and commercial associations	3,118	3,851
Health and medical associations 2,290	1,413	2,290

With more than seven thousand professional associations in existence in 1992, it would appear every occupational group or subspecialty had some organization they could contact to push their professional interests or communicate professional information. How much information do these associations generate? One calculation says there have now been a million papers published in the mathematics field, half within just the last ten years.

Without question, professions are producing in volume. The problem is whether the large number masks areas of information that are being left empty. Professions tend to have specific biases—who they will let in, who they will listen to, what they will say to the public, and how they will relate to each other. Each bias curbs the kind of information professions produce and the kind of information available to members of the profession.

Commercial Information. Information can be sold. We are used to credit bureaus selling information about our purchasing and payment histories. Now those bureaus are being joined by thousands of businesses whose entire inventory consists of information in a database. Their competitive edge is based solely on the size and contents of that database. Universities are entering the information business in a big way, selling not just collections of other people's information, but original research.

Join any of their research consortia and you too can get the latest data months, or years, before your competition.

As this information industry matures and grows, we begin to see that it will not only be a major force in the economy–an employer of thousands, maybe tens of thousands–but it will be like any other industry. It will produce products for which there is a market. The names of the fifty most credit-worthy individuals in your zip code may be available from many sources. It may be less easy to access the phone numbers of the federal programs an immigrant may turn to for temporary help. Universities may have new sources of funds for building material science research centers. They may have less money available to pay visiting poets. The commercialization of information has commercial consequences. Profitable information is available from many sources; nonprofit information struggles to survive on handouts. Each of these five information sources shapes information, with some of the "shapes" looking more and more like distortions.

How Accessible Is Information?

If the amount of information available is somewhat less than our hopes, at least now we can easily get to information, right? We have all these satellites and optical-fiber networks. Access to information is no longer supposed to be a problem. Naisbitt even divides American history along the fault line of information access: "The following year–1957–marked the beginning of the globalization of the information revolution: The Russians launched Sputnik, the missing technological catalyst in a growing information society. The real importance of Sputnik is not that it began the space age, but that it introduced the era of global satellite communications" (12).

With satellites in the air, information flow seems sure to follow. And any measure of data traffic makes it clear huge amounts of information are in fact moving through space. Some, Toffler among them, have looked at the data traffic and remarked on the global linkages that seem to be following: "As capital flows electronically across national borders, zipping back and forth from Zurich to Hong Kong, Hong Kong to Norway, Norway to Tokyo, Tokyo to Wall Street in milliseconds, information traces equally complex pathways. A change in U.S. T bill rates or the yen-deutsche mark ratio is instantly known around the world, and the morning after the big event in Los Angeles, youngsters in Ho Chi Minh City discuss the latest Grammy winners. The mental borders of the state become as permeable as its financial frontiers" (364).

Toffler and the others are obviously right. Information does flow more easily to many places. Who can help but be impressed by the ability to send e-mail around the world in minutes, the chance to access libraries and databases in other nations, the transportation system that can cross continents in hours. We can get to far more information far more easily than ever before.

At least some of us can. In our excitement to explore the new opportunities before us, we may overlook a few things. For instance,. we may forget to note that half the Americans living on Indian reservations have no telephones. What information will they be downloading? By concentrating on computer information, we may also forget to notice that millions of people around the globe never saw *Schindler's List*–their governments would not let them. We sometimes even ignore our own problems, information that turns out to be lies, datalines that become doorways for thieves.

Despite all the satellites we put in the sky and the cellular-phone networks we build along our interstates, there is some information we cannot get. If this really is the information age, those barriers need to be examined, and ultimately they need to be removed. We will look at three barriers–transmission problems–not because they are the only barriers information faces, but because they represent the kinds of problems that will preoccupy our efforts to make all information available to all people. These are the problems: information exiles, tyranny, and information criminals.

Information Exiles. Information is like any other commodity in that it is not evenly distributed across the world. Some people live in the midst of gold fields; many others can barely find coal. Parts of the information vacuum we instantly recognize. For example, no one expects the Bushmen of the Kalahari to walk around with cellular phones (as we will see, they have a long list of communication problems). Other isolates are less obvious. The growing army of people living in neighborhoods (or countries) too dangerous to visit certainly qualify. In either case, the number of people totally removed from the information infrastructure is huge.

What happens to these people in the information age? As subsistence farming and handicrafts persisted through the industrial age, will the disconnected carry on, barely feeding themselves, producing the primitive and quaint for middle-class coffee tables? Early indications are that the disconnected will fare far worse than their predecessors in previous revolutions. The gap between the rich and the poor, the knowing and the ignorant, will be larger, the room along the margins far smaller.

Tyranny. While previous revolutions created classes of haves and have-nots, the information age is already showing that it will be complicated by the "wills" and "will-nots." You can bring the optical fiber to Johnny, but you can't make him connect. There are no shortages of examples to prove this assertion, but let's take one contemporary example–satellite dishes. In one week's time in late 1993, three distinct comers of the world showed just how arbitrary our species can be.

The week began in China with an announcement that the sale and manufacture of satellite dishes was now banned. Too many comrades were using the dishes to bring in "decadent" news and entertainment shows. Decadent information might lead to decadent ideas and then to decadent actions. So the government stepped in and satellite access ended.

The news from Algeria was more bizarre. Islamic fundamentalists decided it was no longer enough to cleanse Algeria of Western influences by murdering women tourists caught shopping in street malls. Now they had turned their attention to neighbors who had satellite dishes. Since the dishes were pointed toward Europe rather than Mecca, it was obvious Western ideas were entering the country. The response was attacks on dish owners.

But for pure cussedness, no one beats the South Africans. In 1993, with majority rule in the offing, the South African Broadcasting Corporation (SABC) elected a new board of directors, including blacks. The response of the Christian Right was to refuse to pay their TV license fees and to ask SABC to fix their TVs so they could no longer get public television. To these Christians it was obvious SABC was now a communist agency and would begin giving air time to blacks and other atheistic forces. They would rather have no television at all than risk the possibility of an occasional black face flickering across their living room.

China, Algeria, South Africa–all places where people are deciding whether they will or will not listen, view, read, or discuss. The same decision–to include or exclude, to listen or turn away, to read or ignore–is being made individually the world over. Rejectionists are constantly saying, "You don't look like me–I have nothing to learn from you," "You aren't my sex–I won't listen to you," "You are too old, too young, too light, too dark." If information is the currency of this age, much of our species is proud to wear rags.

Information Criminals. While one group kills to keep information secret, another group uses the very technology of information to perform crimes. To remind us of the kind of people we face, let's begin with three brief horror stories–all well known, but worth repeating. Just days before he was elected president of the United States, Republicans seeking to block his election got into Bill Clinton's passport records looking for information that might be embarrassing. Here is a man only weeks from being president of the United States, yet even he is vulnerable to illegal searches.

This incident was preceded by the discovery that Internal Revenue Service agents in St. Louis were calling up tax records on their computers and looking to see how much their friends and neighbors earned. They had the time, they had the technology, they had the curiosity–they did not have the discipline, integrity, or supervision to protect honest taxpayers.

The third example is described in dramatic detail in Cuckoo's Egg (1990) by Clifford Stoll. Stoll describes how he tracked down communist agents who were using the Internet to break into secret military archives–essentially to spy on American military bases without ever leaving their homes in Europe. One of the scarier moments in the book is when Stoll tells the U.S. Army about the agents and they refuse to believe him. If ever there was an organization that should have some security sense . . .

Every advance in electronics means that more information can be held in more places for less money and accessed more easily. Unless criminals (and governments) can be held at bay, the very technology that transmits our new-found data stream will be so dangerous we will refuse to use it. What good is a strand of optical fiber to every door if we are too scared to plug it in?

Are We Ready for Information?

What if there really is an information explosion at some point? And what if it happened at the same time that some combination of luck and technology meant that the information got to everyone effortlessly? Would we know what to do with it? There are three ways of looking at ourselves as information processors. None of the views is very attractive.

Education. Assuming we can find someway to get the optical fiber to Johnny, and assuming that Johnny won't be shot if he hooks up, what if Johnny can't read? A world of information may be physically and politically available to people, but it may be no more useful to them than a library is to illiterates. Some totalitarian governments figured this out long ago. It was the stated public policy of South Africa to limit the education of nonwhites. Dr. Hendrik Verwoerd began his stint as minister of Bantu Education with a very clear statement of policy: "When I have control of Native education I will reform it so that Natives will be taught from childhood to realize that equality with Europeans is not for them. People who believe in equality are not desirable teachers for the Natives. Education must train and teach people in accordance with their opportunities in life, according to the sphere in which they live."

That such words could be uttered in public says much about the tragedy of South Africa. Unfortunately, South Africa is not the only place where education has been used to control, to limit. Education is a weapon demagogues are ready to wield.

Even for those with some connection to basic human values, education is a problem. In the developing world, where fewer than half the citizens may make it to the sixth grade, information resources are inaccessible resources. Barely able to read, what difference does it make that they can review scientific articles from around the globe?

Psychology. Brilliant, well-educated, well-connected people can also miss most of what is happening in the world. In fact, it is quite likely that they will. All it requires is that they take a part of the world and explore it to the exclusion of everything else. An example often given is the railroad industry. Creating railroads is no small matter. These are complicated systems that were the technological and political extremes of their time. Leaders of the railroad industry can be forgiven for being preoccupied with getting lines built, designing locomotives that were powerful and reliable, and getting trains out on time. These were not foolish people. But they were hypnotized. By focusing exclusively on railroads they missed out on larger opportunities in transportation.

How could they and countless industries since them make such an obvious error? The information was there. Why didn't they use it? If we are to prepare for the free flow of information, one place to start working is on our own perceptions.

Noise. Neil Postman's Amusing *Ourselves to Death* is a lengthy indictment of contemporary American culture. It takes only an hour or two of prime time television to fully agree. The print media follow suit. How could our founding fathers ever believe that the First Amendment would be used to protect the right of newspapers to print Elvis sightings, Princess Di's appointment calendar, and conversations with extraterrestrials? Were we always so silly? Will the information age cause us to finally come of age and end this terminal adolescence that seems to control the United States?

Maybe not. For one thing, the sheer volume of information involved leaves plenty of room for trivial pursuits. The typical CD-ROM drive now being built into many home computers holds 600 million bytes of information. This is in excess of three hundred thousand pages of text. After you put all the great books of antiquity (meaning any book on which the copyright has expired) on one disk, what do you put on the others? Articles about Elvis sightings, and Princess Di's activities, and... Suddenly the much-vaunted information highway has become silly street. Maybe that's what we want. Maybe the noise we hear is the noise we crave.

Fighting for Information

While it would be lovely if the nature of the world suddenly changed and we were all suddenly awash in information, as the examples above illustrate, we still live in a world in which information is restricted. The limits come from institutions that reveal and pursue only information that meets their needs. The limits come from tyrants who have already learned how to clamp down the Internet as effectively as they cut off satellite communication and television. The limits may be our own as we routinely ignore or distort information that does not match our prejudices. The limits are there, overwhelming satellite launches and trenches full of fiber. If we want information, we will have to fight for it

The Stakes

Why fight? An increasingly common question is, Is all this really necessary? For the tired executive who spends all day in meetings, uses audix and e-mail by the hour, stares at endless computer printouts, and then goes home to a pile of mail and thirty channels on her cable TV, the answer might appear to be no. Another eighty or hundred channels, yet another computer network, yet another club or association, yet another conference call is like giving someone already eating three thousand calories a day another three or four thousand calories. They are just *as* likely to be sick as grateful. Yet like the person eating lots of food, all of it sugar and preservatives, it may well be wise for that person to take a look at the quality of her diet. She may discover that Theo Schoeman is not the only executive who has total access to some kinds of information but absolute blind spots elsewhere. Hidden by the overflowing e-mail list may be the fact that some kinds of information are absent.

If she is clever, she will survive despite the holes in her information system. others, however, may not fare as well. For the poor, the starving, the abused, the desperate, information access may be the only hope. For these people, the stakes are life and death.

The Invisible

According to a report circulated by Human Rights Watch-Africa in early 1994, slavery still persists in Mauritania. While the practice is officially banned, Human Rights Watch believes there are over one hundred thousand slaves in the country. The government of Maaoviya Ould Sid'ahmed Taya is apparently making no effort to stop slavery or to stop cruel punishments of slaves. It is reported that the punishment for attempted escape is as follows: "The victim is seated flat with his legs spread out and buried in sand up to his waist. Coals are placed between his legs and lit, slowly burning the legs, thighs, and genitals of the victim." Because the country is so obscure, few seem aware of the atrocities being routinely committed.

The report by Human Rights Watch-Africa was picked up by the wire services and carried widely throughout Africa. There was no immediate response from Mauritania, and certainly no indication that the country had suddenly decided to free its slaves. But the publicity still mattered. To the enslaved of that nation at least the possibility of freedom now exists. As long as their treatment was unknown to the rest of the world, there was no reason why it might ever improve. True, just shining the light of day on vermin does not instantly solve the problem. When St. Louis was being gradually drowned by the Mississippi in the summer of 1993, the publicity drew thousands of spectators who stood and watched while people's homes went under. But the publicity also drew thousands of volunteers who worked in the heat and the mud to fill sandbags to save other people's homes. Both groups were out on the levees. Both groups walk the Earth. A human tragedy reduced to a five-minute segment on late-night TV may be ghastly entertainment to the twisted, but it can also be an alarm bell to the many who will risk everything to help. And there are people who will help when they know about a problem. To believe otherwise is to believe oneself a member of a very sad species.

Information makes the invisible visible. It will bring hope. Ultimately it will bring help.

The Vulnerable

Mary Byron lived just one day after her boyfriend was released from jail. That's how long it took him to track her down and shoot her seven times. She had no idea he was stalking her. Why should she? She thought he was in jail. "Had we known the assailant was out, our daughter would not have been working that day," says her father. "Probably not even within the state." But the police did not tell her Donovan Harris was being released from jail, even though he had hurt her before.

It isn't cheap or easy, but some communities are making more of an effort to warn past victims that their assailants are back on the streets. At a cost of fifty-five thousand dollars to start and fifty-seven thousand dollars a year to operate, Louisville, Kentucky, now has a computerized system that keeps track of prisoners as they move through the judicial system and notifies past victims if criminals are about to be released. The computer keeps calling until somebody answers, and a taped message warns victims that their accused attackers are about to be released. It has already saved the life of one woman, who ran out to get a gun when she found out her abusive husband was about to be released from jail. She returned home to find him waiting with a knife (Davis 1995).

Warning people that they are in danger is only part of the solution. The real solution would be to remove the danger. But until that happens, the vulnerable can be helped by at least warning them of the danger they face–giving them a better chance at life than Mary Byron had.

The Ignorant

In *Broca's Brain*, Carl Sagan makes an interesting point about scientific issues that are left unresolved. He says that rich people gamble their money on projects. Scientists gamble their lives. If a scientist invests years and years in a research project that goes nowhere, he has wasted a significant portion of his professional life. So he looks very carefully at areas of research, determining which has the most likely prospect. There is still a chance he will hit a dead end and have nothing to show for years of work, but he tries to improve the odds by looking before he leaps.

Scientists are not the only ones gambling their lives. Negumbo Johannes gambled when he chose to move to Windhoek. But his gamble was less informed.

He knew nothing about the cities of Namibia. His trip to Windhoek was his first trip away from home. When interviewed, he said he chose Windhoek because when men returned from Windhoek around Christmas time, they were well dressed when they got off the bus. On that basis he decided everyone in Windhoek was rich and he should go there.

In the United States, young people the age of Negumbo Johannes are also making decisions, picking colleges and workplaces. Some have been groomed for the decision for years. They have parents who are knowledgeable, or older siblings, or social connections. They have a pretty clear sense of what they are getting into. Other young men and women are wandering blind. At one urban university in the Midwest there is a special program for minority students. It appears attractive, yet records show the program graduates a mere 17 percent of its students even after seven years of study. That information is publicly available, but only to those who know what to ask, and where. The rest are gambling seven years of their lives on a college degree, unaware they have only one chance in six of succeeding. Would they enter the program if they knew the odds? What other situations do they face, what other burdens do they bear, what other losses do they suffer because they never understood what they were getting into? The cost of ignorance is high. People do in fact gamble their lives on their decisions.

The Misdirected

All is not a struggle for jobs and food and safety and housing. There are still poetry and sunsets and music. There are also people who help. One of the world's blessings is the millions of these kind souls. One of the world's torments is the difficulty often encountered in using this help well. One study by the World Bank found less than one project in three was successful. Many were clearly failures, even in the early years, when they were receiving substantial funding. Others collapsed the minute external funding dried up.

Helping isn't easy. Good intentions lie in ruins worldwide. One cause is that people know too little about the problem they are trying to solve. Whether the problem is homelessness, teen pregnancy, or starvation in the Sahel, problems are always more complicated than people originally think. It is especially difficult where problems are only half-seen. Getting the necessary information may involve leaving the office to actually talk to the dirty, the sick, and the powerless, or it may take sneaking TV cameras past the local junta's soldiers, or getting the international accountants past the doctored books, or reading the books or articles some would rather censor. Learning comes before helping. But learning isn't easy.

There are some who are concerned that nations will be marched from one crisis to another by the power of TV images—governments and aid agencies putting out the fire-of-the-week based on the latest CNN broadcast. A bigger problem may be the quality of the images and the quality of other information sources. For too many of the problems of the world, the necessary information just is not coming through. We have the people and right intentions. What we often do not have is a good sense of how to use them.

So what are the stakes? For many, the stakes are life and death. The technical, personal, and social requisites to the information age are substantial and need to be recognized, but the benefits are real. Large-scale, multilevel access of information by trained citizens does not guarantee that people will suddenly drop their prejudices, stop making stupid decisions, or have the courage to act on the data before them, but it certainly gets us closer to that time than we are now. So whatever the current problems of information creation and transfer are, those problems need to be solved. Let's start by first examining the sources of information.

References

Buckland, M. K. 1991. "Information as Thing." *Journal of the American Society for Information Science* 42:351-60.

Naisbitt, J. 1982. *Megatrends: Ten New Directions Transforming Our Lives*. New York: Warner Books.

Toffler, A. 1990. *Powershift: Knowledge, Wealth and Violence at the Edge of the 21st Century*. New York: Bantam Books.

U. S. Bureau of the Census. 1993. *Statistical Abstracts of the United States*. Washington, D.C.

WHAT MAKES MAINSTREAM MEDIA MAINSTREAM
NOAM CHOMSKY

Part of the reason why I write about the media is because I am interested in the whole intellectual culture, and the part of it that is easiest to study is the media. It comes out every day. You can do a systematic investigation. You can compare yesterday's version to today's version. There is a lot of evidence about what's played up and what isn't and the way things are structured.

My impression is the media aren't very different from scholarship or from, say, journals of intellectual opinion—there are some extra constraints—but it's not radically different. They interact, which is why people go up and back quite easily among them.

You look at the media, or at any institution you want to understand. You ask questions about its internal institutional structure. You want to know something about their setting in the broader society. How do they relate to other systems of power and authority? If you're lucky, there is an internal record from leading people in the information system which tells you what they are up to (it is sort of a doctrinal system). That doesn't mean the public relations handouts but what they say to each other about what they are up to. There is quite a lot of interesting documentation.

There are three major sources of information about the nature of the media. You want to study them the way, say, a scientist would study some complex molecule or something. You take a look at the structure and then make some hypothesis based on the structure as to what the media product is likely to look like. Then you investigate the media product and see how well it conforms to the hypotheses. Virtually all work in media analysis is this last part—trying to study carefully just what the media product is and whether it conforms to obvious assumptions about the nature and structure of the media.

Well, what do you find? First of all, you find that there are different media which do different things, like the entertainment/Hollywood, soap operas, and so on, or even most of the newspapers in the country (the overwhelming majority of them). They are directing the mass audience.

There is another sector of the media, the elite media, sometimes called the agenda-setting media because they are the ones with the big resources, they set the framework in which everyone else operates. The *New York Times* and CBS, that kind of thing. Their audience is mostly privileged people. The people who read the *New York Times*—people who are wealthy or part of what is sometimes called the political class—they are actually involved in the political system in an ongoing fashion. They are basically managers of one sort or another. They can be political managers, business managers (like corporate executives or that sort of thing), doctoral managers (like university professors), or other journalists who are involved in organizing the way people think and look at things.

The elite media set a framework within which others operate. If you are watching the Associated Press, who grind out a constant flow of news, in the midafternoon it breaks and there is something that comes along every day that says "Notice to Editors: Tomorrow's *New York Times* is going to have the following stories on the front page." The point of that is, if you're an editor of a newspaper in Dayton, Ohio and you don't have the resources to figure out what the news is, or you don't want to think about it anyway, this tells you what the news is. These are the stories for the quarter page that you are going to devote to something other than local affairs or diverting your audience. These are the stories that you put there because that's what the *New York Times* tells us is what you're supposed to care about tomorrow. If you are an editor in Dayton, Ohio, you would sort of have to do that, because you don't have much else in the way of resources. If you get off line, if you're producing stories that the big press doesn't like, you'll hear about it pretty soon. In fact, what just happened at *San Jose Mercury News* is a dramatic example of this. So there are a lot of ways in which power plays can drive you right back into line if you move out. If you try to break the mold, you're not going to last long. That framework works pretty well, and it is understandable that it is just a reflection of obvious power structures.

The real mass media are basically trying to divert people. Let them do something else, but don't bother us (us being the people who run the show). Let them get interested in professional sports, for example. Let everybody be crazed about professional sports or sex scandals or the personalities and their problems or something like that. Anything, as long as it isn't serious. Of course, the serious stuff is for the big guys. "We" take care of that.

What are the elite media, the agenda-setting ones? The *New York Times* and CBS, for example. Well, first of all, they are major, very profitable, corporations. Furthermore, most of them are either linked to, or outright owned by, much bigger corporations, like General Electric, Westinghouse, and so on. They are way up at the top of the power structure of the private economy which is a very tyrannical structure. Corporations are basically tyrannies, hierarchic, controlled from above. If you don't like what they are doing you get out. The major media are just part of that system.

What about their institutional setting? Well, that's more or less the same. What they interact with and relate to is other major power centers—the government, other corporations, or the universities. Because the media are a doctrinal system they interact closely with the universities. Say you are a reporter writing a story on Southeast Asia or Africa, or something like that. You're supposed to go over to the big university and find an expert who will tell you what to write, or else go to one of the foundations, like Brookings Institute or American Enterprise Institute and they will give you the words to say. These outside institutions are very similar to the media.

The universities, for example, are not independent institutions. There may be independent people scattered around in them but that is true of the media as well. And it's generally true of corporations. It's true of Fascist states, for that matter. But the institution itself is parasitic. It's dependent on outside sources of support and those sources of support, such as private wealth, big corporations with grants, and the government (which is so closely interlinked with corporate power you can barely distinguish them), they are essentially what the universities are in the middle of. People within them, who don't adjust to that structure, who don't accept it and internalize it (you can't really work with it unless you internalize it, and believe it);

people who don't do that are likely to be weeded out along the way, starting from kindergarten, all the way up. There are all sorts of filtering devices to get rid of people who are a pain in the neck and think independently. Those of you who have been through college know that the educational system is very highly geared to rewarding conformity and obedience; if you don't do that, you are a troublemaker. So, it is kind of a filtering device which ends up with people who really honestly (they aren't lying) internalize the framework of belief and attitudes of the surrounding power system in the society. The elite institutions like, say, Harvard and Princeton and the small upscale colleges, for example, are very much geared to socialization. If you go through a place like Harvard, most of what goes on there is teaching manners; how to behave like a member of the upper classes, how to think the right thoughts, and so on.

If you've read George Orwell's *Animal Farm* which he wrote in the mid-1940s, it was a satire on the Soviet Union, a totalitarian state. It was a big hit. Everybody loved it. Turns out he wrote an introduction to *Animal Farm* which was suppressed. It only appeared 30 years later. Someone had found it in his papers. The introduction to *Animal Farm* was about "Literary Censorship in England" and what it says is that obviously this book is ridiculing the Soviet Union and its totalitarian structure. But he said England is not all that different. We don't have the KGB on our neck, but the end result comes out pretty much the same. People who have independent ideas or who think the wrong kind of thoughts are cut out.

He talks a little, only two sentences, about the institutional structure. He asks, why does this happen? Well, one, because the press is owned by wealthy people who only want certain things to reach the public. The other thing he says is that when you go through the elite education system, when you go through the proper schools in Oxford, you learn that there are certain things it's not proper to say and there are certain thoughts that are not proper to have. That is the socialization role of elite institutions and if you don't adapt to that, you're usually out. Those two sentences more or less tell the story.

When you critique the media and you say, look, here is what Anthony Lewis or somebody else is writing, they get very angry. They say, quite correctly, "nobody ever tells me what to write. I write anything I like. All this business about pressures and constraints is nonsense because I'm never under any pressure." Which is completely true, but the point is that they wouldn't be there unless they had already demonstrated that nobody has to tell them what to write because they are going say the right thing. If they had started off at the Metro desk, or something, and had pursued the wrong kind of stories, they never would have made it to the positions where they can now say anything they like. The same is mostly true of university faculty in the more ideological disciplines. They have been through the socialization system.

Okay, you look at the structure of that whole system. What do you expect the news to be like? Well, it's pretty obvious. Take the *New York Times*. It's a corporation and sells a product. The product is audiences. They don't make money when you buy the newspaper. They are happy to put it on the worldwide web for free. They actually lose money when you buy the newspaper. But the audience is the product. The product is privileged people, just like the people who are writing the newspapers, you know, top-level decision-making people in society. You have to sell a product to a market, and the market is, of course, advertisers (that is, other businesses). Whether it is television or newspapers, or whatever, they are selling audiences. Corporations sell audiences to other corporations. In the case of the elite media, it's big businesses.

Well, what do you expect to happen? What would you predict about the nature of the media product, given that set of circumstances? What would be the null hypothesis, the kind of conjecture that you'd make assuming nothing further. The obvious assumption is that the product of the media, what appears, what doesn't appear, the way it is slanted, will reflect the interest of the buyers and sellers, the institutions, and the power systems that are around them. If that wouldn't happen, it would be kind of a miracle.

Okay, then comes the hard work. You ask, does it work the way you predict? Well, you can judge for yourselves. There's lots of material on this obvious hypothesis, which has been subjected to the hardest tests anybody can think of, and still stands up remarkably well. You virtually never find anything in the social sciences that so strongly supports any conclusion, which is not a big surprise, because it would be miraculous if it didn't hold up given the way the forces are operating.

The next thing you discover is that this whole topic is completely taboo. If you go to the Kennedy School of Government or Stanford, or somewhere, and you study journalism and communications or academic political science, and so on, these questions are not likely to appear. That is, the hypothesis that anyone would come across without even knowing anything that is not allowed to be expressed, and the evidence bearing on it cannot be discussed. Well, you predict that too. If you look at the institutional structure, you would say, yeah, sure, that's got to happen because why should these guys want to be exposed? Why should they allow critical analysis of what they are up to take place? The answer is, there is no reason why they should allow that and, in fact, they don't. Again, it is not purposeful censorship. It is just that you don't make it to those positions. That includes the left (what is called the left), as well as the right. Unless you have been adequately socialized and trained so that there are some thoughts you just don't have, because if you did have them, you wouldn't be there. So you have a second order of prediction which is that the first order of prediction is not allowed into the discussion.

The last thing to look at is the doctrinal framework in which this proceeds. Do people at high levels in the information system, including the media and advertising and academic political science and so on, do these people have a picture of what ought to happen when they are writing for each other (not when they are making graduation speeches)? When you make a commencement speech, it is pretty words and stuff. But when they are writing for one another, what do people say about it?

There are basically three currents to look at. One is the public relations industry, you know, the main business propaganda industry. So what are the leaders of the PR industry saying? Second place to look is at what are called public intellectuals, big thinkers, people who write the "op eds" and that sort of thing. What do they say? The people who write impressive books about the nature of democracy and that sort of business. The third thing you look at is the academic stream, particularly that part of political science which is concerned with communications and information and that stuff which has been a branch of political science for the last 70 or 80 years.

So, look at those three things and see what they say, and look at the leading figures who have written about this. They all say (I'm partly quoting), the general population is "ignorant and meddlesome outsiders." We have to keep them out of the public arena because they are too stupid and if they get involved they will just make trouble. Their job is to be "spectators," not "participants."

They are allowed to vote every once in a while, pick out one of us smart guys. But then they are supposed to go home and do something else like watch football or whatever it may be. But the "ignorant and meddlesome outsiders" have to be observers not participants. The participants are what are called the "responsible men" and, of course, the writer is always one of them. You never ask the question, why am I a "responsible man" and somebody else is in jail? The answer is pretty obvious. It's because you are obedient and subordinate to power and that other person may be independent, and so on. But you don't ask, of course. So there are the smart guys who are supposed to run the show and the rest of them are supposed to be out, and we should not succumb to (I'm quoting from an academic article) "democratic dogmatisms about men being the best judges of their own interest." They are not. They are terrible judges of their own interests so we have do it for them for their own benefit.

Actually, it is very similar to Leninism. We do things for you and we are doing it in the interest of everyone, and so on. I suspect that's part of the reason why it's been so easy historically for people to shift up and back from being, sort of enthusiastic Stalinists to being big supporters of U.S. power. People switch very quickly from one position to the other, and my suspicion is that it's because basically it is the same position. You're not making much of a switch. You're just making a different estimate of where power lies. One point you think it's here, another point you think it's there. You take the same position.

How did all this evolve? It has an interesting history. A lot of it comes out of the first World War, which is a big turning point. It changed the position of the United States in the world considerably. In the 18th century the U.S. was already the richest place in the world. The quality of life, health, and longevity was not achieved by the upper classes in Britain until the early 20th century, let alone anybody else in the world. The U.S. was extraordinarily wealthy, with huge advantages, and, by the end of the 19th century, it had by far the biggest economy in the world. But it was not a big player on the world scene. U.S. power extended to the Caribbean Islands, parts of the Pacific, but not much farther.

During the first World War, the relations changed. And they changed more dramatically during the second World War. After the second World War the U.S. more or less took over the world. But after the first World War there was already a change and the U.S. shifted from being a debtor to a creditor nation. It wasn't huge, like Britain, but it became a substantial actor in the world for the first time. That was one change, but there were other changes.

The first World War was the first time there was highly organized state propaganda. The British had a Ministry of Information, and they really needed it because they had to get the U.S. into the war or else they were in bad trouble. The Ministry of Information was mainly geared to sending propaganda, including huge fabrications about "Hun" atrocities, and so on. They were targeting American intellectuals on the reasonable assumption that these are the people who are most gullible and most likely to believe propaganda. They are also the ones that disseminate it through their own system. So it was mostly geared to American intellectuals and it worked very well. The British Ministry of Information documents (a lot have been released) show their goal was, as they put it, to control the thought of the entire world, a minor goal, but mainly the U.S. They didn't care much what people thought in India. This Ministry of Information was extremely successful in deluding hot shot American intellectuals into accepting British propaganda fabrications. They were very proud of that. Properly so, it saved their lives. They would have lost the first World War otherwise.

In the U.S., there was a counterpart. Woodrow Wilson was elected in 1916 on an anti-war platform. The U.S. was a very pacifist country. It has always been. People don't want to go fight foreign wars. The country was very much opposed to the first World War and Wilson was, in fact, elected on an anti-war position. "Peace without victory" was the slogan. But he was intending to go to war. So the question was, how do you get the pacifist population to become raving anti-German lunatics so they want to go kill all the Germans? That requires propaganda. So they set up the first and really only major state propaganda agency in U.S. history. The Committee on Public Information it was called (nice Orwellian title), called also the Creel Commission. The guy who ran it was named Creel. The task of this commission was to propagandize the population into a jingoist hysteria. It worked incredibly well. Within a few months there was a raving war hysteria and the U.S. was able to go to war.

A lot of people were impressed by these achievements. One person impressed, and this had some implications for the future, was Hitler. If you read *Mein Kampf*, he concludes, with some justification, that Germany lost the first World War because it lost the propaganda battle. They could not begin to compete with British and American propaganda which absolutely overwhelmed them. He pledges that next time around they'll have their own propaganda system, which they did during the second World War. More important for us, the American business community was also very impressed with the propaganda effort. They had a problem at that time. The country was becoming formally more democratic. A lot more people were able to vote and that sort of thing. The country was becoming wealthier and more people could participate and a lot of new immigrants were coming in, and so on.

So what do you do? It's going to be harder to run things as a private club. Therefore, obviously, you have to control what people think. There had been public relation specialists but there was never a public relations industry. There was a guy hired to make Rockefeller's image look prettier and that sort of thing. But this huge public relations industry, which is a U.S. invention and a monstrous industry, came out of the first World War. The leading figures were people in the Creel Commission. In fact, the main one, Edward Bernays, comes right out of the Creel Commission. He has a book that came out right afterwards called *Propaganda*. The term "propaganda," incidentally, did not have negative connotations in those days. It was during the second World War that the term became taboo because it was connected with Germany, and all those bad things. But in this period, the term propaganda just meant information or something like that. So he wrote a book called *Propaganda* around 1925, and it starts off by saying he is applying the lessons of the first World War. The propaganda system of the first World War and this commission that he was part of showed, he says, it is possible to "regiment the public mind every bit as much as an army regiments their bodies." These new techniques of regimentation of minds, he said, had to be used by the intelligent minorities in order to make sure that the slobs stay on the right course. We can do it now because we have these new techniques.

This is the main manual of the public relations industry. Bernays is kind of the guru. He was an authentic Roosevelt/Kennedy liberal. He also engineered the public relations effort behind the U.S.-backed coup which overthrew the democratic government of Guatemala.

His major coup, the one that really propelled him into fame in the late 1920s, was getting women to smoke. Women didn't smoke in those days and he ran huge campaigns for Chesterfield. You know all the techniques—models and movie stars with cigarettes coming out of their mouths and that kind of thing. He got enormous praise for that. So he became a leading figure of the industry, and his book was the real manual.

Another member of the Creel Commission was Walter Lippmann, the most respected figure in American journalism for about half a century (I mean serious American journalism, serious think pieces). He also wrote what are called progressive essays on democracy, regarded as progressive back in the 1920s. He was, again, applying the lessons of the work on propaganda very explicitly. He says there is a new art in democracy called manufacture of consent. That is his phrase. Edward Herman and I borrowed it for our book, but it comes from Lippmann. So, he says, there is this new art in the method of democracy, "manufacture of consent." By manufacturing consent, you can overcome the fact that formally a lot of people have the right to vote. We can make it irrelevant because we can manufacture consent and make sure that their choices and attitudes will be structured in such a way that they will always do what we tell them, even if they have a formal way to participate. So we'll have a real democracy. It will work properly. That's applying the lessons of the propaganda agency.

Academic social science and political science comes out of the same thing. The founder of what's called communications and academic political science is Harold Glasswell. His main achievement was a book, a study of propaganda. He says, very frankly, the things I was quoting before—those things about not succumbing to democratic dogmatism, that comes from academic political science (Lasswell and others). Again, drawing the lessons from the war time experience, political parties drew the same lessons, especially the conservative party in England. Their early documents, just being released, show they also recognized the achievements of the British Ministry of Information. They recognized that the country was getting more democratized and it wouldn't be a private men's club. So the conclusion was, as they put it, politics has to become political warfare, applying the mechanisms of propaganda that worked so brilliantly during the first World War towards controlling people's thoughts.

That's the doctrinal side and it coincides with the institutional structure. It strengthens the predictions about the way the thing should work. And the predictions are well confirmed. But these conclusions, also, are not allowed to be discussed. This is all now part of mainstream literature but it is only for people on the inside. When you go to college, you don't read the classics about how to control peoples minds.

Just like you don't read what James Madison said during the constitutional convention about how the main goal of the new system has to be "to protect the minority of the opulent against the majority," and has to be designed so that it achieves that end. This is the founding of the constitutional system, so nobody studies it. You can't even find it in the academic scholarship unless you really look hard.

That is roughly the picture, as I see it, of the way the system is institutionally, the doctrines that lie behind it, the way it comes out. There is another part directed to the "ignorant meddlesome" outsiders. That is mainly using diversion of one kind or another. From that, I think, you can predict what you would expect to find.

THE BIOTECH CENTURY: PLAYING ECOLOGICAL ROULETTE WITH MOTHER NATURE'S DESIGNS[1]
JEREMY RIFKIN

We are in the midst of a great historic transition into the Biotech Age. The ability to isolate, identify and recombine genes is making the gene pool available, for the first time, as the primary raw resource for future economic activity on Earth. After thousands of years of fusing, melting, soldering, forging and burning inanimate matter to create useful things, we are now splicing, recombining, inserting and stitching living material for our own economic interests. Lord Ritchie-Calder, the British science writer, cast the biological revolution in the proper historical perspective when he observed that "just as we have manipulated plastics and metals, we are now manufacturing living materials."

The Nobel Prize-winning chemist Robert F. Curl of Rice University spoke for many of his colleagues in science when he proclaimed that the 20th century was "the century of physics and chemistry. But it is clear that the next century will be the century of biology."

Global "life-science" companies promise an economic renaissance in the coming Biotech Century--they offer a door to a new era of history where the genetic blueprints of evolution itself become subject to human authorship. Critics worry that the re-seeding of the Earth with a laboratory-conceived second Genesis could lead to a far different future--a biological Tower of Babel and the spread of chaos throughout the biological world, drowning out the ancient language of creation.

A Second Genesis

Human beings have been remaking the Earth for as long as we have had a history. Up to now, however, our ability to create our own second Genesis has been tempered by the restraints imposed by species boundaries. We have been forced to work narrowly, continually crossing close relatives in the plant or animal kingdoms to create new varieties, strains and breeds. Through a long, historical process of tinkering and trial and error, we have redrawn the biological map, creating new agricultural products, new sources of energy, more durable building materials, and life-saving pharmaceuticals. Still, in all this time, nature dictated the terms of engagement.

But the new technologies of the Genetic Age allow scientists, corporations and governments to manipulate the natural world at the most fundamental level--the genetic one. Imagine the wholesale transfer of genes between totally unrelated species and across all biological boundaries--plant, animal and human--creating

---

[1] Reprinted with permission from *E/The Environmental Magazine*. Subscription department: PO Box 2047, Marioin, OH 43306. Telephone: (815)734-1242 (Subscriptions are $20 per year). On the Internet: www.emagazine.com. Email: info@emagazine.com.

thousands of novel life forms in a brief moment of evolutionary time. Then, with clonal propagation, mass-producing countless replicas of these new creations, releasing them into the biosphere to propagate, mutate, proliferate and migrate. This is, in fact, the radical scientific and commercial experiment now underway.

Global Powers at Play

Typical of new biotech trends is the bold decision by the Monsanto Corporation, long a world leader in chemical products, to sell off its entire chemical division in 1997 and anchor its research, development and marketing in biotech-based technologies and products. Global conglomerates are rapidly buying up biotech start-up companies, seed companies, agribusiness and agrochemical concerns, pharmaceutical, medical and health businesses, and food and drink companies, creating giant life-science complexes from which to fashion a bio-industrial world. The concentration of power is impressive. The top 10 agrochemical companies control 81 percent of the $29 billion per year global agrochemical market. Ten life science companies control 37 percent of the $15 billion per year global seed market. Meanwhile, pharmaceutical companies spent more than $3.5 billion in 1995 buying up biotech firms. Novartis, a giant new firm resulting from the $27 billion merger of Sandoz and Ciba-Geigy, is now the world's largest agrochemical company, the second-largest seed company and the second-largest pharmaceutical company.

Global life-science companies are expected to introduce thousands of new genetically engineered organisms into the environment in the coming century. In just the past 18 months, genetically engineered corn, soy and cotton have been planted over millions of acres of U.S. farmland. Genetically engineered insects, fish and domesticated animals have also been introduced.

Virtually every genetically engineered organism released into the environment poses a potential threat to the ecosystem. To appreciate why this is so, we need to understand why the pollution generated by genetically modified organisms is so different from the pollution resulting from the release of petrochemical products into the environment.

Because they are alive, genetically engineered organisms are inherently more unpredictable than petrochemicals in the way they interact with other living things in the environment. Consequently, it is much more difficult to assess all of the potential impacts that a genetically engineered organism might have on the Earth's ecosystems.

Genetically engineered products also reproduce. They grow and they migrate. Unlike petrochemical products, it is difficult to constrain them within a given geographical locale. Finally, once released, it is virtually impossible to recall genetically engineered organisms back to the laboratory, especially those organisms that are microscopic in nature.

The risks in releasing novel, genetically engineered organisms into the biosphere are similar to those we've encountered in introducing exotic organisms into the North American habitat. Over the past several hundred years, thousands of non-native organisms have been brought to America from other regions of the world. While many of these creatures have adapted to the North American ecosystems without severe dislocations, a small percentage of them have run wild, wreaking havoc on the flora and fauna of the continent. Gypsy moth, Kudzu vine,

Dutch elm disease, chestnut blight, starlings and Mediterranean fruit flies come easily to mind.

Whenever a genetically engineered organism is released, there is always a small chance that it, too, will run amok because, like non-indigenous species, it has been artificially introduced into a complex environment that has developed a web of highly integrated relationships over long periods of evolutionary history. Each new synthetic introduction is tantamount to playing ecological roulette. That is, while there is only a small chance of it triggering an environmental explosion, if it does, the consequences could be significant and irreversible.

Spreading Genetic Pollution

Nowhere are the alarm bells going off faster than in agricultural biotechnology. The life-science companies are introducing biotech crops containing novel genetic traits from other plants, viruses, bacteria and animals. The new genetically engineered crops are designed to perform in ways that have eluded scientists working with classical breeding techniques. Many of the new gene-spliced crops emanating from laboratories seem more like creations from the world of science fiction. Scientists have inserted "antifreeze" protein genes from flounder into the genetic code of tomatoes to protect the fruit from frost damage. Chicken genes have been inserted into potatoes to increase disease resistance. Firefly genes have been injected into the biological code of corn plants. Chinese hamster genes have been inserted into the genome of tobacco plants to increase sterol production.

Ecologists are unsure of the impacts of bypassing natural species boundaries by introducing genes into crops from wholly unrelated plant and animal species. The fact is, there is no precedent in history for this kind of "shotgun" experimentation. For more than 10,000 years, classical breeding techniques have been limited to the transference of genes between closely related plants or animals that can sexually interbreed, limiting the number of possible genetic combinations. Natural evolution appears to be similarly circumscribed. By contrast, the new gene-splicing technologies allow us to bypass all previous biological boundaries in nature, creating life forms that have never before existed. For example, consider the ambitious plans to engineer transgenic plants to serve as pharmaceutical factories for the production of chemicals and drugs. Foraging animals, seed-eating birds and soil insects will be exposed to a range of genetically engineered drugs, vaccines, industrial enzymes, plastics and hundreds of other foreign substances for the first time, with untold consequences. The notion of large numbers of species consuming plants and plant debris containing a wide assortment of chemicals that they would normally never be exposed to is an unsettling prospect.

Much of the current effort in agricultural biotechnology is centered on the creation of herbicide-tolerant, pest-resistant and virus-resistant plants. Herbicide-tolerant crops are a favorite of companies like Monsanto and Novartis that are anxious to corner the lucrative worldwide market for their herbicide products. More than 600 million pounds of poisonous herbicides are dumped on U.S. farm land each year, most sprayed on corn, cotton and soybean crops. Chemical companies gross more than $4 billion per year in U.S. herbicide sales alone.

To increase their share of the growing global market for herbicides, life-science companies have created transgenic crops that tolerate their own herbicides (see "Say It Ain't Soy," *In Brief*, March/April, 1997). The idea is to sell farmers patented seeds that are resistant to a particular brand of herbicide in the hope of increasing a company's share of both the seed and herbicide markets. Monsanto's new "Roundup Ready" patented seeds, for example, are resistant to its best-selling chemical herbicide, Roundup.

The chemical companies hope to convince farmers that the new herbicide-tolerant crops will allow for a more efficient eradication of weeds. Farmers will be able to spray at any time during the growing season, killing weeds without killing their crops. Critics warn that with new herbicide-tolerant crops planted in the fields, farmers are likely to use even greater quantities of herbicides to control weeds, as there will be less fear of damaging their crops in the process of spraying. The increased use of herbicides, in turn, raises the possibility of weeds developing resistance, forcing an even greater use of herbicides to control the more resistant strains.

The potential deleterious impacts on soil fertility, water quality and beneficial insects that result from the increased use of poisonous herbicides, like Monsanto's Roundup, are a disquieting reminder of the escalating environmental bill that is likely to accompany the introduction of herbicide-tolerant crops.

The new pest-resistant transgenic crops pose similar environmental problems. Life-science companies are readying transgenic crops that produce insecticide in every cell of each plant. Several crops, including Ciba Geigy's pest-resistant "maximizer corn" and Rohm and Haas's pest-resistant tobacco are already available on the commercial market. A growing body of scientific evidence points to the likelihood of creating "super bugs" resistant to the effects of the new pesticide-producing genetic crops.

The new generation of virus-resistant transgenic crops pose the equally dangerous possibility of creating new viruses that have never before existed in nature. Concerns are surfacing among scientists and in scientific literature over the possibility that the protein genes could recombine with genes in related viruses that find their way naturally into the transgenic plant, creating a recombinant virus with novel features.

A growing number of ecologists warn that the biggest danger might lie in what is called "gene flow" - the transfer of genes from altered crops to weedy relatives by way of cross-pollination. Researchers are concerned that manufactured genes for herbicide tolerance, and pest and viral resistance, might escape and, through cross pollination, insert themselves into the genetic makeup of weedy relatives, creating weeds that are resistant to herbicides, pests and viruses. Fears over the possibility of transgenic genes jumping to wild weedy relatives heightened in 1996 when a Danish research team, working under the auspices of Denmark's Environmental Science and Technology Department, observed the transfer of a gene from a transgenic crop to a wild weedy relative - something critics of deliberate-release experiments have warned of for years and biotech companies have dismissed as a remote or nonexistent possibility.

Transnational life-science companies project that within 10 to 15 years, all of the major crops grown in the world will be genetically engineered to include herbicide-, pest-, virus-, bacterial-, fungus- and stress-resistant genes. Millions of acres of agricultural land and commercial forest will be transformed in the most daring experiment ever undertaken to remake the biological world. Proponents of the new science, armed with powerful gene-splicing tools and precious little data on potential impacts, are charging into this new world of agricultural biotechnology, giddy over the potential benefits and confident that the risks are minimum or non-existent. They may be right. But, what if they are wrong?

Insuring Disaster

The insurance industry quietly let it be known several years ago that it would not insure the release of genetically engineered organisms into the environment against the possibility of catastrophic environmental damage, because the industry lacks a risk-assessment science --a predictive ecology--with which to judge the risk of any given introduction. In short, the insurance industry clearly understands the Kafka-esque implications of a government regime claiming to regulate a technology in the absence of clear scientific knowledge.

Increasingly nervous over the insurance question, one of the biotech trade associations attempted early on to raise an insurance pool among its member organizations, but gave up when it failed to raise sufficient funds to make the pool operable. Some observers worried, at the time, and continue to worry--albeit privately--over what might happen to the biotech industry if a large-scale commercial release of a genetically altered organism were to result in a catastrophic environmental event. For example, the introduction and spread of a new weed or pest comparable to Kudzu vine, Dutch elm disease or gypsy moth, might inflict costly damage to flora and fauna over extended ranges.

Corporate assurances aside, one or more significant environmental mishaps are an inevitability in the years ahead. When that happens, every nation is going to be forced to address the issue of liability. Farmers, landowners, consumers and the public at large are going to demand to know how it could have happened and who is liable for the damages inflicted. When the day arrives--and it's likely to come sooner rather than later--"genetic pollution" will take its place alongside petrochemical and nuclear pollution as a grave threat to the Earth's already beleaguered environment.

Allergic to Technology?

The introduction of new genetically engineered organisms also raises a number of serious human health issues that have yet to be resolved. Health professionals and consumer organizations are most concerned about the potential allergenic effects of genetically engineered foods. The Food and Drug Administration (FDA) announced in 1992 that special labeling for genetically engineered foods would not be required, touching off protest among food professionals, including the nation's leading chefs and many wholesalers and retailers.

With two percent of adults and eight percent of children having allergic responses to commonly eaten foods, consumer advocates argue that all gene-spliced foods need to be properly labeled so that consumers can avoid health risks. Their concerns were heightened in 1996 when The *New England Journal of Medicine* published a study showing genetically engineered soybeans containing a gene from a Brazil nut could create an allergic reaction in people who were allergic to the nuts. The test result was unwelcome news for Pioneer Hi-Bred International, the Iowa-based seed company that hoped to market the new genetically engineered soy.

Though the FDA said it would label any genetically engineered foods containing genes from common allergenic organisms, the agency fell well short of requiring across-the-board labeling, leaving The New England Journal of Medicine editors to ask what protection consumers would have against genes from organisms that have never before been part of the human diet and that might be potential allergens. Concerned over the agency's seeming disregard for human health, the Journal editors concluded that FDA policy "would appear to favor industry over consumer protection."

Depleting the Gene Pool

Ironically, all of the many efforts to reseed the biosphere with a laboratory-conceived second Genesis may eventually come to naught because of a massive catch-22 that lies at the heart of the new technology revolution. On the one hand, the success of the biotech revolution is wholly dependent on access to a rich reservoir of genes to create new characteristics and properties in crops and animals grown for food, fiber and energy, and products used for pharmaceutical and medical purposes. Genes containing beneficial traits that can be manipulated, transformed and inserted into organisms destined for the commercial market come from either the wild or from traditional crops and animal breeds (and from human beings). Notwithstanding its awesome ability to transform nature into commercially marketable commodities, the biotech industry still remains utterly dependent upon nature's seed stock--germplasm--for its raw resources. At present, it is impossible to create a "useful" new gene in the laboratory. In this sense, biotechnology remains an extractive industry. It can rearrange genetic material, but cannot create it. On the other hand, the very practice of biotechnology--including cloning, tissue culturing and gene splicing--is likely to result in increasing genetic uniformity, a narrowing of the gene pool, and loss of the very genetic diversity that is so essential to guaranteeing the success of the biotech industry in the future.

In his book *The Last Harvest*, Paul Raeburn, the science editor for *Business Week*, penetrates to the heart of the problem. He writes, "Scientists can accomplish remarkable feats in manipulating molecules and cells, but they are utterly incapable of re-creating even the simplest forms of life in test tubes. Germplasm provides our lifeline into the future. No breakthrough in fundamental research can compensate for the loss of the genetic material crop breeders depend upon."

Agricultural biotechnology greatly increases the uniformity of agricultural practices as did the Green Revolution when it was introduced more than 30 years ago. Like its predecessor, the goal is to create superior varieties that can be planted as monocultures in agricultural regions all over the world. A handful of life-science companies are staking out the new biotech turf, each aggressively marketing their own patented brands of "super seeds"—and soon "super" farm animals as well. The new transgenic crops and animals are designed to grow faster, produce greater yields, and withstand more varied environmental and weather-related stresses. Their cost effectiveness, in the short run, is likely to guarantee them a robust market. In an industry where profit margins are notoriously low, farmers will likely jump at the opportunity of saving a few dollars per acre and a few cents per pound by shifting quickly to the new transgenic crops and animals.

However, the switch to a handful of patented transgenic seeds and livestock animals will likely further erode the genetic pool as farmers abandon the growing of traditional varieties and breeds in favor of the commercially more competitive patented products. By focusing on short-term market priorities, the biotech industry threatens to destroy the very genetic heirlooms that might one day be worth their weight in gold as a line of defense against new resistant diseases or superbugs.

Most molecular biologists and the biotechnology industry, at large, have all but dismissed the growing criticism of ecologists, whose recent studies suggest that the biotech revolution will likely be accompanied by the proliferation and spread of genetic pollution and the wholesale loss of genetic diversity. Nonetheless, the uncontrollable spread of super weeds, the buildup of resistant strains of bacteria and new super insects, the creation of novel viruses, the destabilization of whole ecosystems, the genetic contamination of food, and the steady depletion of the gene pool are no longer minor considerations, the mere grumbling of a few disgruntled critics. To ignore the warnings is to place the biosphere and civilization in harm's way in the coming years. Pestilence, famine, and the spread of new kinds of diseases throughout the world might yet turn out to be the final act in the script being prepared for the biotech century.

This article is adapted from Jeremy Rifkin's new book *The Biotech Century: Harnessing the Gene and Remaking the World* (Tarcher/Putnam).

Animals as Inventions: Biotechnology and Intellectual Property Rights
Mark Sagoff

Since 1988, the U.S. government has granted nine patents for genetically engineered animals. A coalition of religious leaders called last summer for a moratorium on such patents. They declared, in a joint statement issued in the nation's capital, that "the gift of life from God, in all its forms and species, should not be regarded solely as if it were a chemical product subject to genetic alteration and patentable for economic benefit. Moral, social, and spiritual issues deserve far more consideration before binding decisions are made in this area."

For its part, the biotech industry argues that without patents, companies would be unwilling to invest in, or unable to attract capital for, research that benefits humankind. For example, the development of the "Oncomouse" patented by Harvard University may lead to more rapid progress in the management and prevention of breast cancer.

This essay invokes the distinction between "inventions," which are rightfully patented, and mere "products," which are not, in order to cast doubt on current Patent Office policy. However, I also propose reasonable ways of granting protection to biotechnological innovations--ways that might be acceptable to those who object specifically to the patenting of life and not necessarily, to biotechnology itself. I begin with an account of the meaning of creation and ownership, courtesy of John Locke.

The Occasions of their Being

Locke's *First Treatise of Government* (1698), which languishes in the shadow of his more famous *Second Treatise,* refutes Sir Robert Filmer, who had upheld the divine right of kings. Filmer argued that just as God, having made Adam, owned him absolutely, so Adam owned his children, and so princes, who inherit this right from Adam, hold authority over their subjects.

Locke replied that while ownership is, indeed, a consequence of authorship, God alone is able "to frame and make a living Creature, fashion the parts, and mould and suit them to their uses." Humans, starting with Adam, produce offspring but do not frame and fashion and, therefore, do not own them. Even those who desire and intend to beget children are "but the occasions of their being" says Locke, and "do little more towards their making, than Ducalion and his Wife in the Fable did towards the making of Mankind, by throwing Pebbles over their Heads."

Of course, no one thinks that genetic engineers proceed in quite the accidental way that Ducalion and his wife do in the fable to which Locke alludes. Still, Locke's discussion offers guidance on the question of whether genetic engineers can claim an intellectual property right or patent in the organisms they produce. Whether the organisms should be patentable turns, in part, on how we construe the activity of their producers: do biotechnologists create these organisms, or do they serve merely as "the occasions of their being"? It seems to me that many reservations concerning the patentability of these products stem from an uncertainty about how much their producers, as it were, author or design them, and thus have contributed to the world's store not just of useful things but also of useful knowledge.

Technologists may claim intellectual property rights in organisms, I believe, insofar as they design them, using ideas that are not found in nature but are their own. This is the principle that underlies the patenting of inventions generally. Thomas Edison received a patent to the light bulb because he contributed the novel idea--the use of the glowing carbon filament--that made it work. What made the light bulb Edison's intellectual property is that he not only produced but also designed it. To put this distinction in Aristotelian language, the inventor can claim intellectual property rights if he or she provides not just the efficient but also the formal cause of the mechanisms he or she creates.

Consider another example. Samuel Morse could patent telegraphic instruments he invented but not--as he wanted--the use of electromagnetic waves to send and receive signals. Morse claimed as intellectual property "the use of the motive power of the electric or galvanic current, which I call electro-magnetism, however developed for making or printing intelligible characters . . . at any distance." But the Supreme Court held that Morse had invented only a particular instrument to take advantage of electromagnetism, and that he could not prohibit others from harnessing by other means the same natural forces or materials.

Similarly, in *Funk Brothers Seed Company v. Kalo Inoculant* (1948), the Supreme Court held that a scientist's combination of bacterial strains found separately in nature did not constitute "an invention or discovery within the meaning of the patent statutes." According to the Court, "a product must be more than new and useful to be patented; it must also satisfy the requirements of invention." The Court regarded the repackaging of genetic information taken from nature as a commercial not a scientific advance: "Even though it may have been the product of skill, it certainly was not the product of invention."

These and other cases illustrate a fundamental logical limitation on the scope of intellectual property rights. These rights can extend only to what someone designs--what he or she devises and constructs, as it were, from simpler materials, by reason of a plan or principle which that person invents. Intellectual property does not include objects, such as natural forces and materials, which the individual does not design but simply uses or manipulates by applying a novel instrument or process. The instrument (the telegraph) or the process (for combining bacteria) is patentable, but the product is not.

Patenting Organisms

Thus far I have described the traditional conception governing the awarding of intellectual property rights. However, the practice of the U.S. Patent Office changed dramatically after a 1980 decision, *Diamond v. Chakrabarty,* in which the Supreme Court held by a 5-4 majority that Chakrabarty, a microbiologist, could patent a novel organism because "his discovery is not nature's handiwork, but his own." The "discovery" in question was a bacterium which, Chakrabarty had hybridized by inserting plasmids from other bacteria. The Court determined that the hybridized microorganism could be patented because it was not found in nature but was "the result of human ingenuity and research."

The Supreme Court in *Chakrabarty* emphasized that the bacteria it had to consider differed from those in *Funk Brothers* in that they had been genetically changed and were not naturally occurring strains. Yet one might argue that there is no more creation in the second instance than in the first. In both cases, the inventors manipulate design already found in nature; they do not introduce a new design of their own. The organism--although altered slightly from its naturally occurring state and therefore more useful--may result from the application of a novel process to natural materials, but the element of design resides in nature.

On the strength of the *Chakrabarty* decision; however, the Patent Office began routinely to award patents on hybridized and recombinant organisms--and very broad patents at that. The current high-water mark in this flood of patents came with an application from Agracetus of Middletown, Wisc., which in 1992 received a patent covering "all cotton seeds and plants which contain a recombinant gene construction (i.e., are genetically engineered)." By using a well-known process to introduce foreign genes into a cotton plant, Agracetus gained the right to exclude other companies from introducing any other genes into that plant without its consent. "All transgenic cotton products . . . will have to be commercially licensed through us before they can enter the marketplace," a vice president of Agracetus said.

The Patent Office apparently reasoned that anything that is not a product of nature must therefore result from invention or design. This is perhaps not an unwarranted inference from *Chakrabarty,* but it does confuse *invention* with the *production* of anything novel and useful. The Patent Office went on to establish as intellectual property the genome of any organism--Agracetus also received a patent for soy--that a company manages to alter using novel technical means. In several instances when a company seeking to patent an organism had used fairly well-known, if laborious, methods for manipulating its genome, the Patent Office still allowed a patent on that genome as the material for further genetic manipulation. The Patent Office, in other words, failed to distinguish manipulating or changing a genome from designing or inventing it.

Competitors were slow to challenge the Agracetus patent, perhaps believing that their interest would be better served by acquiring similar intellectual property rights to broccoli, bananas, and a host of other organisms whose genomes they could alter using the same technique Agracetus applied. Eventually challenges mounted up, including a major and successful suit by the U.S. Department of Agriculture. The Patent Office is now reviewing the Agracetus patent, which is unlikely to be sustained.

Breeders' Rights

The manipulation of genetic material in nature to produce novel and useful forms of life is not new. Breeders have worked for centuries--and over the past hundred years, *in* the light of Mendelian genetic theory--to give us the crops we eat, the flowers we enjoy, the livestock we raise, and the pets we keep in our homes. The history of patent law with respect to their work casts further light on issues surrounding the patenting of life.

Under the standard or utility patent act, breeders have not traditionally been able to protect their products. Luther Burbank, the man responsible for the Shasta daisy, the Burbank potato, and scores of other important varieties, decried this situation: "A man can patent a mousetrap or copyright a nasty song, but if he gives the world a new fruit that will add millions to the value of the earth's annual harvests, he will be fortunate if he is rewarded by so much as having his name connected with the result." Though Burbank himself did fairly well, he never received the riches he deserved because he could not patent the varieties he created. Thomas Edison is reputed to have told him, "The things you have created for the American people are worth far more than what I have created for them. The law protects my creations but gives no protection to yours."

We can explain this situation. Edison could claim an intellectual property right in his inventions--and therefore a "utility" patent in them--since they arose from new knowledge he discovered and disclosed, thus enabling others intellectually to reproduce his own inventions and to make many more besides. Burbank, a superb breeder for whose work we cannot be too grateful, did not provide new ideas or knowledge that would enable others to build further varieties. Rather, he depended entirely on his skill in conventional techniques of breeding. Thus, the daisy for which Burbank is justly famous can be reproduced biologically but not intellectually. Burbank gave us many wonderful plants, but he left the science of plant breeding essentially unchanged.

Confronted with the inapplicability of intellectual property law to new varieties of plants and animals, Congress enacted the Plant Patent Act of 1930 and the Plant Variety Protection Act of 1970, which protect new varieties respectively against unauthorized asexual and sexual reproduction. In enacting these statutes, Congress sought to "afford agriculture, so far as practicable, the same opportunities to participate in the benefits of the patent system as have been given industry." Congress recognized that plant breeders could not claim to design the new varieties they created; indeed, they could hardly claim that the methods they used were anything but obvious, nor could they describe the genome of the plants they produced. (Under the "specification" requirement of patent law, inventors are required to describe their invention so that others can understand precisely how it works.) Nevertheless, Congress wished to give an adequate economic incentive to breeders and reward their efforts, even if those efforts did not produce new knowledge and therefore did not result in the creation of intellectual property.

The laws written for plant breeders greatly weakened the traditional standards for the awarding of patents. The 1970 statute, for example, replaces the specification requirement with a mandate that seeds be deposited in a public repository. This may represent good social policy, insofar as it encourages plant breeders to continue their useful endeavors. It may also be fair, since Congress, by giving breeders rights over the use of their plants for reproduction, may have recognized the rights of creators to control their personal property, including the seeds and tubers of the plants they produce. But the genetic information contained in these seeds and tubers is the work not of the breeder (who could hardly specify what it is), but of nature. For this reason, the Plant Protection Act does *not* give a breeder intellectual property rights to this information. Rather, the statute provides that anyone who develops the same variety independently does not infringe the patent.

This legislative framework was shaken, in turn, in April 1987, when the Patent Office announced that it "now considers nonnaturally occurring non-human multicellular living organisms, including animals, to be patentable subject matter." The trade paper *Genetic Engineering News* immediately inferred that the ruling "will lead to protection of animals developed not only through genetic alteration but also through animal husbandry and breeding." The intellectual contribution of breeders, after all, may be as great as or greater than that of genetic engineers with respect to the organisms they create. Breeders have to keep dozens of traits in mind and navigate among them, while engineers make a far more surgical strike on the genome of the organism. Plant breeding and artificial selection generally, moreover, typically change the genome of target animals far more broadly than the more surgical techniques employed by genetic engineers.

It is unsurprising, therefore, that conventional plant breeders immediately saw an opening to claim their products as intellectual property--even though these "inventions" may exhibit no more new knowledge than those of Luther Burbank. At first, the Patent Office was unwilling to draw this inference. But a 1985 decision established a precedent whereby, as one law journal noted, "a plant breeder may obtain a utility patent on a newly developed plant variety." Organisms produced by conventional breeding techniques now routinely receive utility patents, as do products of genetic engineering. It seems no longer to matter to the Patent Office whether new knowledge is involved; all that seems to matter is useful innovation.

A Compromise Solution

The religious critique of biotechnology and the patenting of life focuses on our ability to override or obliterate the distinctions between life and matter, nature and technology, humanity and God on which our spiritual estate seemed to depend--distinctions that helped us think that man belongs to nature, not the other way around. The religious leaders who signed the declaration last summer made this point when they asked for a moratorium on the patenting of life forms. These leaders deny that genetic engineers, any more than conventional plant breeders, design organisms, as it were, from scratch, and accordingly that these organisms should be considered intellectual property of anyone but God. As Dr. Richard D. Land of the Southern Baptist Convention testified: "Humans and animals are pre-owned beings. We belong to the creator God. The... decision to grant patents on animal or human genetic information represents a usurpation of the ownership rights of the Sovereign of the Universe."

Insofar as these religious leaders are concerned to dispel the idea that human beings create life forms just as God created Adam, however, there appears to be a way to reconcile their objection with the needs of the biotech industry. This is true because the industry is also concerned to dispel the idea that it is "playing God." It cares less about its pretensions to having designed life than about its access to a particular set of rights to certain products. Whether or not these rights carry with them a pretension to intellectual property in the moral sense is of no concern to the biotech companies; from their perspective, what matters is only the legal effect, not the ethical meaning or basis, of the law.

There seems to be room for compromise between the concerns of the industry and those of religious leaders. Indeed, each group has sought to accommodate the other. Activist Jeremy Rifkin, characterizing the position of the religious leaders he led to Washington, emphasized that they had "no problem" with process patents nor even with protecting biotech products with the sort of marketing exclusivity conferred on "orphan" drugs. Rabbi David Saperstein, who heads the Religious Action Center of Reform Judaism, decried the idea that scientists would "arrogate to themselves the ownership of the life they are creating" but went on to observe that there are "ways through contract laws and licensing procedures to protect the economic investment that people make." Like Rifkin, Saperstein objected to the hubris of claims that organisms are intellectual property, not to legal regimes *per se* intended to reward and encourage effort and investment in biotechnology.

On the industry side, spokespersons have been eager to assure their clerical critics that what they want is not to upstage the Creator but to enjoy a legal regime that protects and encourages investment. Biotechnology Industry Organization President Carl Feldbaum emphasizes this point:

> A patent on a gene does not confer ownership of that gene to the patent holder. It only provides temporary legal protections against attempts by other parties to commercialize the patent holder's discovery or invention. This is a critical distinction because no one, in our view, can or should own life itself.

It is not hard to see the outlines of a solution that can embrace both the view of religious leaders and the needs of the biotech industry. Novel organisms might be covered by a new patent statute which, like the old Plant Protection Acts, recognizes that those who produce these organisms may alter or recombine but do not design and therefore cannot claim to own them as intellectual property. Such a statute might not differ further from utility patents in the terms, conditions, and rights for the patenting of organisms.

A compromise along these lines would bring patent law into harmony with the important distinction between production and invention which we borrowed from Locke at the beginning of this essay. To claim novel organisms as intellectual property is to confuse, as did Sir Robert Filmer, the way God and humans create life. The difference is that God knew what He was doing in a way that plant breeders and even genetic engineers do not. To cross strains of plants or microinject genes into embryos is not to invent, design, or create living things.

References: Edmund L. Andrews, "Religious Leaders Prepare to Fight Patents on Genes," *New York Times* (May 13, 1995); Claudia Mills, "Patenting Life," *Report from the Institute for Philosophy and Public Policy*, vol. 5, no. 1 (Winter 1995); John Locke, *Two Treatises of Government*, Book I, chap. 5, section 53; Fred Powledge, "Who Owns Rice and Beans? Patents on Plant Germplasm," *BioScience*, vol. 45 no. 7 (July 1995); *Pittsburgh Post-Gazette* (Sept. 3, 1995); H.R. Rep. No. 1129, 71st Cong., 2d Sess. 2 (1930) (Rep. Purcell quoting a telegram received from the widow of Luther Burbank); Dienner, "Patents for Biological Specimens and Products," *Journal of the Patent Office Society*, vol. 35 (1953); U.S.C. Section 112, first paragraph; *Graham v. John Deere Co.*, 383 U.S. 1. 17 (1966); Hearing on H.R. 11372 before the House Committee on Patents, 71st Cong., 2d Sess. 4, 7 (1930) (memorandum of Patent Commissioner Robertson); Hearing before the Subcommittee on Departmental Operations of the Committee on Agriculture, 91st Cong., 2d Sess. (1970); Unsigned note, "Altering Nature's Blueprint for Profit: Patenting Multicellular Animals," *Virginia Law Review*, vol. 74 (1988); *Official Gazette of the U.S. Patent and Trademark Office*, vol. 8 (1987); Reid G. Adler, "Controlling the Applications of Biotechnology: A Critical Analysis of the Proposed Moratorium on Animal Patenting." *Harvard Journal of Law and Technology*, vol. 1 (1988); "New Animals Will Be Patented," *New York Times* (April 17, 1987); Neil D. Hamilton, "Why Own the Farm if You Can Own the Farmer (and the Crop)?" *Nebraska Law Review*, vol. 73 (1994); "Transgenic Crops Head to Market," *Chemical Week* (Sept. 27, 1995); Richard D. Land, quoted in Bruce Rubenstein, "Genetic Patents Pit Clients, Religion, Government," *Corporate Legal Times* (Sept. 1995); Reginald Rhein, "Gene Patent Crusade Moving from Church to Court," *Biotechnology Newswatch* (June 5, 1995)

GANDHI ON MACHINERY, 1919-47
MONHANDAS KARAMCHAND GANDHI

1919

"There is thus room in the country for both the mill industry and the handloom weaving. So let mills increase as also spinning-wheels and handlooms. And I should think that these latter are no doubt machines. The handloom is a miniature weaving mill. The spinning-wheel is a miniature spinning-mill. I would wish to see such beautiful little mills in every home. But the country is fully in need of the hand-spinning and hand-weaving industry. Agriculturists in no country can live without some industry to supplement agriculture.... Even if we have sufficient mills in the country to produce cloth enough for the whole country, we are bound to provide our peasantry, daily being more and more impoverished, with some supplementary industry, and that which can be suitable to chores of people is hand-spinning and hand-weaving. Opposition to mills or machinery is not the point. What suits our country is the point. I am not opposed to the movement of manufacturing machines in the country, nor to making improvements in machinery. I am only concerned with what these machines are meant for. I may ask, in the words of Ruskin, whether these machines will be such as would blow off a million men in a minute or they will be such as would turn waste lands into arable and fertile land. And if legislation were in my hands, I would penalise the manufacture of [labour-saving] machines and protect the industry which manufactures nice ploughs which can be handled by every man." (CW 16: 134-5)

1922

"India does not need to be industrialised in the modern sense of the term. It has 750,000 villages scattered over a vast area..... The people are rooted to the soil, and the vast majority are living a hand-to-mouth life. . . . pauperism is growing. There is no doubt also that the millions are living in enforced idleness for at least four months in the year. Agriculture does not need revolutionary changes. The Indian peasant requires a supplementary industry. The most natural is the introduction of the spinning-wheel, not the handloom. The latter cannot be introduced in every home, whereas the former can, and it used to be so even a century ago. It was driven out not by economic pressure, but by force deliberately used as can be proved from authentic records. The restoration, therefore, of the spinning-wheel solves the economic problem of India at a stroke.... I hope you will not allow yourself to be prejudiced by anything you might have heard about my strange views about machinery. I have nothing to say against the development of any other industry in India by means of machinery, but I do say that to supply India with cloth manufactured either outside or inside through gigantic mills is an economic blunder of the first magnitude, just as it would be to supply cheap bread though huge bakeries in the chief centres in India and to destroy the family stove." (CW 22: 401-2)

1924

"What I object to, is the craze for machinery, not machinery as such. The craze is for what they call labour-saving machinery. Men go on 'saving labour' till thousands are without work and thrown on the open streets to die of starvation. I want to save time and labour, not for a fraction of mankind, but for all. I want the concentration of wealth, not in the hands of the few, but in the hands of all. Today machinery merely helps a few to ride on the backs of millions. The impetus behind it all is not the philanthropy to save labour, but greed. It is against this constitution of things that I am fighting with all my might.

"….scientific truths and discoveries should first of all cease to be the mere instruments of greed. Then labourers will not be over-worked and machinery instead of becoming a hindrance will be a help. I am aiming, not at eradication of all machinery, but limitations…

"The supreme consideration is man. The machine should not tend to make atrophied the limbs of man. For instance, I would make intelligent exceptions. Take the case of the Singer Sewing Machine. It is one of the few useful things ever invented, and there is a romance about the device itself. Singer saw his wife labouring over the tedious process of sewing and seaming with her own hands, and simply out of his love for her he devised the sewing machine, in order to save her from unnecessary labour…

"It is an alteration in the condition of labour that I want. This mad rush for wealth must cease, and the labourer must be assured, not only of a living wage, but a daily task that is not a mere drudgery. The machine will, under these conditions, be as much a help to the man working it as to the State, or the man who owns it. The present mad rush will cease, and the labourer will work…under attractive and ideal conditions…. Therefore, replace greed by love and everything will come right." (CW 25: 251-2)

1931

"I hold that the machinery method is harmful when the same thing can be done easily by millions of hands not otherwise occupied……Western observers hastily argue from Western conditions that what may be true of them must be true of India where conditions are different in so many material respects. Applications of the laws of economics vary with varying conditions.

"The machinery method is no doubt easy. But it is not necessarily a blessing on that account… If the craze for the machinery method continues, it is highly likely that a time will come when we shall be so incapacitated and weak that we shall begin to curse ourselves for having forgotten the use of the living machines given to us by God." (CW 47:89-90)

"Machinery is a grand yet awful invention. It is possible to visualise a stage at which the machines invented by man may finally engulf civilisation. If man controls the machines, then they will not; but should man lose his control over the machines and allow them to control him, then they will certainly engulf civilisation and everything." (CW 48: 353)

1934

"When as a nation we adopt the spinning-wheel, we not only solve the question of unemployment but we declare that we have no intention of exploiting any nation, and we also end exploitation of the poor by the rich....When I say I want independence for the millions, I mean to say not only that the millions may have something to eat and to cover themselves with, but that they will be free from the exploitation of people here and outside. We can never industrialise India, unless, of course, we reduce our population from 350 millions to 35 millions or hit upon markets wider than our own and dependent on us. It is time we realised that, where there is unlimited human power, complicated machinery on a large scale has no place....We cannot industrialise ourselves, unless we make up our mind to enslave humanity." (CW 58: 400)

1935

"Machinery well used has to help and ease human effort. The present use of machinery tends more and more to concentrate wealth in the hands of a few in total disregard of millions of men and women whose bread is snatched by it out of their mouths." (CW 61: 416)

1936

[Responding to a Japanese correspondent who asked whether Gandhi was against this machine age]:
"To say that is to caricature my views. I am not against machinery as such, but I am totally opposed to it when it masters us ...
Q. 'You would not industrialise India?'
A. 'I would indeed, in my sense of the term. The village communities should be revived. Indian villages produced and supplied to the Indian towns and cities all their wants. India became impoverished when our cities became foreign markets and began to drain the villages dry by dumping cheap and shoddy goods from foreign lands.'" (CW 64: 118)

1940

"We should not use machinery for producing things which we can produce without its aid and have got the capacity to do so. As machinery makes you its slave, we want to be independent and self-supporting; so we should not take the help of machinery when we can do without it. We want to make our villages free and self-sufficient and through them achieve our goal—liberty--and also protect it. I have no interest in the machine nor [do] I oppose it. If I can produce my things myself, I become my master and so need no machinery." (CW 71: 383)

1945

"Another danger in making more and more use of machinery is that we have to make great efforts for the protection of it, that is to say, we shall have to keep an army as is being done today elsewhere in the world. The fact is that even if there is no danger of aggression from outside we shall be slaves to those who will be in control of the big machinery. Take the case of the atom bomb. Those nations who have atom bombs are feared even by their friends. If we take a wise view, we shall be saved from the working of machinery." (CW 82:132-3)

1946

Gandhi's definition of a machine, as given in his address to the Indian Industries Ministers' Conference, Poona. The text of the address is not available. The following is taken from a report on it published in CW 85: 95. [Ed.]

"'Ours has been described as the machine age, because the machine dominates our economy. Now, what is a machine?--one may ask. In a sense, man is the most wonderful machine in creation. It can be neither duplicated nor copied.'

"He [Gandhi] had, however, used the word not in its wider sense but in the sense of an appliance that tended to displace human or animal labour instead of supplementing it or merely increasing its efficiency. That was the first differentiating characteristic of the machine. The second characteristic was that there was no limit to its growth or evolution. That could not be said of human labour. There was no limit beyond which its capacity or mechanical efficiency could not go. Out of this circumstance arose the third characteristic of the machine. It seems to be possessed of a will or genius of its own. It was antagonistic to man's labour. Thus it tended more to displace man, one machine doing the work of a hundred, if not a thousand, who went to swell the army of the unemployed and the under-employed, not because it was desirable but because that was its law."

Gandhi was asked if he would oppose adoption of the flush system as one way of eradicating untouchability. He replied as follows. [Ed.]

"Where there is ample supply of water and [where] modern sanitation can be introduced without any hardship on the poor, I have no objection to it [the flush system]. In fact, it should be welcomed as a means of improving the health of the city concerned. At the moment, it can only be introduced in towns. My opposition to machinery is much misunderstood. I am not opposed to machinery as such. I am opposed to machinery which displaces labour and leaves it idle." (CW 85: 239-40)

1947

"Machine-power can make a valuable contribution towards economic progress. But a few capitalists have employed machine-power regardless of the interests of the common man and that is why our condition has deteriorated today." (CW 87: 249)

References

Gandhi, M.K.. Collected Works Of Mahatma Gandhi (in 100 volumes). Published by Publications Division, Ministry of Information and Broadcasting, Government of India. (**CW**)

Universals'

A Coda...

A Note on the Value of Gender-Identification[1]
Christine M. Korsgaard

In the course of this conference Susan Wolf raised the question of what role we should like to see the concept of gender playing in an ideal world, perhaps the future world. Could the fact of gender play a far more restricted role in our lives than it does now? As Cass Sunstein put it, could being male or female matter as little to a person as having blue eyes or brown ones? And if it did, would we have lost something of value? Would it be better or worse to live in a world where gender mattered little to the sense of one's identity?

Martha Chen and Margarita Valdés reminded us that such questions, almost science-fictional in their remoteness from the situation even of 'developed' nations, have little to do with the problems of women in the Third World. For these women, progress often depends on getting those in power to focus on the differences between men and women, and on drawing attention to the special features of women's lives. Ruth Anna Putnam reminded us that this is true even in our own society: medical research, for instance, in taking men's bodies to be the basic human bodies, has neglected women's health. But this of course is not because either developing or developed societies have ignored *gender*. It is because they have ignored *women*. That is another matter altogether.

Despite its remoteness, Susan's question is an important one for anyone considering the situation of women anywhere because it gives voice to a concern that so many people feel. In seeking absolute equality, are feminists seeking the elimination of differences? This is not just a worry on the part of men with vested interests. Many people of both genders feel as if their gender were a deep fact about their identities, as if being male or female were something important to them, and therefore as if feminism might be asking them to give up something important.

I do not believe that gender has to be or should be a deep fact about the identity of a human being. To see why, we need to consider what is involved in having a gender. As far as I can see, there are five aspects to gender-identity as it has traditionally been conceived. (1) One is supposed to share certain qualities or attributes with the other members, or at least most of the other members, of one's gender. (2) The members of a gender are assigned certain tasks, for which these attributes supposedly make them especially well suited. (3) The members of a gender are subject to a certain gender ideal. Gender ideals are supposed to be associated with gender-correlated attributes: a perfect woman is a woman who exhibits the special attributes of women (or at least the positive ones) to a high degree. It will follow that she is especially well suited for the tasks assigned to women. (4) Gender is supposed to be a determinant of sexual orientation, and also to define what it is

---

[1] © The United Nations University 1995. Reprinted from *Women, Culture, and Development: A Study of Human Capabilities* edited by Martha Nussbaum and Jonathan Glover (1995) by permission of Oxford University Press.

that one is oriented towards. And (5) because of all these things, the members of a gender have a shared history and shared experiences, creating special bonds among them.

It all starts with the presumption of shared attributes. Many differences in physical, mental, psychological, and moral attributes have been correlated with differences in gender. Popular discussions of feminism have focused very heavily on the question whether any of these correlations actually exist, and, if they do, whether they are natural or the product of socialization. Although I think that many of the claims about natural correlations are nonsense, I also think that for most purposes it is not important to establish this point. Even if there are differences naturally correlated with gender, they are so correlated only statistically and on the average. No one can deny *or ever has denied* that there are *some* women who are physically large and strong, talented at mathematics or political leadership, hopeless at dealing with children, or tasteless in matters of appearance. No one can deny or ever has denied that there are some men who are sensitive to the feelings of others, naturally inclined to nurture, mechanically inept, or devoid of physical courage. The rough statistical character of the correlation of other attributes with gender holds even for the one kind of correlation that we know exists naturally, the correlation between gender and other physical differences. There are after all flat-chested women, and men with ample hips; there are women with moustaches, and men without body hair; there are very tall women and very short men. Even if there are norms of gender, there are individuals who deviate from those norms.

According to an old quip, Christianity has not been tried and found too difficult, but rather has been found too difficult and so not tried. Despite some currently popular claims about the bankruptcy of the Enlightenment, I believe that this is true of Enlightenment ideals. Communitarians, champions of the family, and the promoters of ethnic and gender-identification may suppose that they have somehow discovered that the ideal of the sovereign individual is inadequate for human flourishing. But the truth is that many of them have simply balked when they realized how different a world that respects that ideal would have to be from the one we live in now. The centrality of gender is one of the things that would have to go.

Even if members of genders do tend to be alike, there are individuals who are different. If the genders are treated differently, these individuals will be treated wrongly. By Kantian standards the argument is over: it does not matter whether these individuals are many or few. No important attributes other than the biologically definitive ones are universally shared by the members of a gender: the tasks of life therefore cannot properly be distributed along gender lines. Tasks can be distributed according to taste and ability directly; there is no need for gender membership to mediate that process. And whenever individuals deviate very far from gender norms, gender ideals become especially arbitrary and cruel. Human beings are fertile inventors of ways to hurt ourselves and each other, and gender ideals are one of our keenest instruments for the infliction of completely factitious pain. People are made to feel self-conscious, inadequate, or absolutely bad about having attributes that in themselves are innocuous or even admirable. Of course this is by no means all that is wrong with gender ideals. As they stand they contain elements that are not just difficult for some to live up to but impossible for anyone to meet. Women are supposed to have an almost magical ability to comfort the afflicted, to say the right words or make the right gesture. Men are expected to possess a high degree of completely instinctive sexual know-how. The absurd idea that people are supposed to be born knowing how to handle some of the most delicate and complex matters of human life creates a lot of unnecessary anxiety. It also stands in the way of people making the needed efforts to learn.

Shared history and the sense of a shared fate is another matter. This is the feature of gender-identification that many people find most attractive. Indeed, human beings will always both identify with and value the company of those whose lives are like their own. Perhaps the experiences of pregnancy, giving birth, and early child-care will always be a bond among women who have children, as Nancy Chodorow suggested in our discussion. But these are bonds among mothers, not among women, and not every woman is a mother. The shared history of women is largely a product of growing up under the same oppressive gender ideals, being assigned the same tasks, and having the same presumptive sexual orientation. The identification produced by this shared history will disappear to the extent that more arbitrary features of gender-identification are abolished from our lives.

I say 'to the extent' because I do not want to make assumptions about whether all of the features of gender-identification can or should be abolished. One feature of gender-identification about which I have said little so far is the familiar pair of assumptions that there is such a thing as sexual orientation towards one of the genders and that it is determined by the gender that one has. Homosexuals accept the first of these assumptions but challenge the second; theoretically it is possible to challenge them both. What would our social world look like without them? Lately we have made some progress in our treatment of homosexuals, in the sense that enlightened people are now committed to putting an end to the grosser forms of discrimination against them. But certainly their condition is still treated by society as deeply exceptional. To speak rather abstractly, our social world has mechanisms intended both to facilitate erotic life and to keep erotic forces from breaking out in the wrong place. The public culture of romance, the practices of dating, engagement, and marriage, our gender-based traditions in clothing and cosmetics, and the restrictions on who can share washrooms, public dressing rooms, and dormitory rooms are all institutions designed to handle eroticism, with the double aim of making it possible while regulating its form. And all of our institutions for handling eroticism do so on the assumption that people, or most people, are heterosexual, and that therefore that is the form of eroticism which is to be facilitated and where necessary contained. One worry that is sometimes rather apologetically voiced by heterosexual men is that if gender plays a diminished role in human life, eroticism may play a diminished role as well. It is hard to believe that there is any serious danger of that, but there is a related worry which is real. One might well wonder whether and how we can create a public culture of eroticism that depends less than the one we have now on rigid assumptions about gender itself, and perhaps also about the relationship between gender and sexual orientation. No one yet has a concrete picture of institutions which could provide erotic life with a public surface that does not depend heavily on gender, and this blank spot in the imagined scene may well induce a certain fearfulness. But after all, it is not as if our old institutions have been doing a *good* job either at curbing unwanted erotic aggression or at facilitating erotic flourishing. At present we know little about these matters. That may well be a reason for optimism.

The sense of a shared history with the members of one's gender will disappear only if and when other features of gender-identification are long gone. It is the remoteness of this prospect that makes the diminishment of gender-identification seem so science-fictional. As long as the recent history of the two genders is different, gender will of course remain an important part of our identities. And feminism itself is a central part of our own recent history. What woman, living now in the parts of the world where feminism is taking hold, could say that it is unimportant to her sense of herself that she is a woman? The adventure of making changes, breaking down barriers, being the first to penetrate various inner sancta, creates a strong bond among contemporary women. This may make it *especially* hard for us to imagine a world in which gender is not deeply constitutive of identity. But this is a fact about where we stand in history, not about our nature. There are other tasks for human beings to perform and so to share. With luck we will move on.

Permissions

Ake, Claude, "The African Context of Human Rights," pages 5-13 from *Africa Today*, Vol. 34, No. 142 by Claude Ake. Copyright ©1987 by Indiana University Press. Reprinted by permission.

Camacho, Luis N., "Consumption as a Theme in the North-South Dialogue," pages 32-34. From *Report from the Institute for Philosophy & Public Policy*, Vol. 15, No. 4, Fall 1995 by Luis Camacho. Copyright © 1995 by Institute for Philosophy and Public Policy. Reprinted by permission.

Chomsky, Noam, "What Makes Mainstream Media Mainstream," from *ZMagazine*, October 1997. Copyright © 1997 by Noam Chomsky. Reprinted by permission.

Daly, Herman E., "Globalization and its Discontents," pages 17-21 from *Philosophy & Public Policy Quarterly*, Vol. 21, No. 2-3, Spring/Summer 2001, by Herman Daly. Copyright © 2001 by Institute for Philosophy and Public Policy. Reprinted by permission.

Ebert, Teresa L., "Excerpt from Excess-ive Bodies" from *Ludic Feminism and After* pages 238-239 by Teresa Ebert. Copyright © 1995 by University of Michigan Press. Ann Arbor, pp 238, 239. Reprinted by permission of the publisher, University of Michigan Press.

Engel, Mylan, Jr., "The Consistency Argument for Ethical Vegetarianism: Why You are Committed to the Immorality of Eating Meat and Other Animal Products" (abridged by the author). Copyright © by Mylan Engel, Jr. Reprinted by permission of the author.

Falk, Richard, "Defining a Just War." Reprinted with permission from the October 29, 2001 issue of *The Nation*.

Filice, Carlo, "On the Obligation to Keep Informed About Distant Atrocities" *Human Rights Quarterly*, 12:3 (1990), 397-414. © The Johns Hopkins University Press. Reprinted with the permission of the John Hopkins University Press.

Foster, John Bellamy, "'Let Them Eat Pollution': Capitalism and the World Environment," *Monthly Review Press* January 1993 pages 10-20. Copyright © 1993 by Monthly Review Press. Reprinted by permission of Monthly Review Foundation.

Glover, Jonathan, "Nations, Identity and Conflict," pages 11-30 (abridged), from *The Morality of Nationalism*, edited by Robert McKim and Jeff McMahan, copyright © 1997 by Oxford University Press, Inc. Used by permission of Oxford University Press, Inc.

Harvey, David, "Guest Editorial: An Anniversary of Consequence and Relevance" from *Environment and Planning D: Society and Space*, Vol. 16, pages 379-385 by D. Harvey. Copyright © 1998. Reprinted by permission of Pion Ltd, London.

Korsgaard, Christine M., "A Note on the Value of Gender-Identification," in Martha C. Nussbaum and Jonathan Glover, editors, *Women, Culture, and Development: A Study of Human Capabilities*, 1995, Clarendon Press, Oxford, pp. 401-404. Reprinted by permission of Oxford University Press. © The United Nations University 1995. Reprinted by permission of Oxford University Press.

Lobel, Jules, and Ratner, Michael, "Humanitarian Military Intervention", from *Foreign Policy in Focus*, Vol. 5, No. 1, January 2000 by Jules Lobel and Michael Ratner, Copyright © 2000 by Jules Lobel and Michael Ratner. Reprinted by permission.

Mann, Michael, "Globalization and September 11." From *New Left Review* 12 (Nov-Dec 2001), pages 51-72. Copyright © 2001 *New Left Review*. Reprinted by permission.

Marx, Leo, "Post-Modernism and the Environmental Crisis," *Report from the Institute for Philosophy & Public Policy*, Volume 10, Number 3-4, Summer/Fall 1990, pages 13-15. Copyright © 1990 by Institute for Philosophy and Public Policy.

Rifkin, Jeremy, "The Biotech Century: Playing Ecological Roulette with Mother Nature's Designs, *emagazine.com* May, 1998. Reprinted with permission from *E/The Environmental Magazine*. Subscription department: PO Box 247, Marion, OH 43306. Telephone: (815)734-1242 (Subscriptions are $20 per year). On the Internet: www.emagazine.com. Email: info@emagazine.com.

Sagoff, Mark, "Nature Versus the Environment," from *Report from the Institute for Philosophy & Public Policy*, Vol. 11, No. 3, Summer, 1991 pp. 5-8. Copyright © 1991 by Institute for Philosophy and Public Policy. Reprinted by permission.

Sagoff, Mark, "Animals as Inventions: Biotechnology and Intellectual Property Rights," from *Report from the Institute for Philosophy & Public Policy*, Volume 16, Number 1, Winter 1996, pp 15-19. Copyright © 1996 by Institute for Philosophy and Public Policy. Reprinted by permission.

Shiva, Vandana, "Development, Ecology & Women" from *Staying Alive: Women, Ecology and Development*, London, Zed Books Ltd., 1989., pages. 1-13 only. Copyright © 1989 Zed Books Ltd. Reprinted by permission.

Singer, Peter, "The Biological Basis of Ethics" from *The Expanding Circle: Ethics and Sociobiology*, Farrar, Straus & Giroux, New York, 1981, chapter 2 only. Copyright © 1981 by Peter Singer. Reprinted by permission of the author.

Singer, Peter, "The Singer Solution to World Poverty" *New York Times Magazine*, September 5, 1999, pp. 60-63. Copyright © 1999 by The New York Times Co. Reprinted by permission.

United Nations, "Universal Declaration of Human Rights," Copyright © 1948 by United Nations. Reprinted by permission.

West, Cornel, "The Limits of Neopragmatism," in *Keeping Faith: Philosophy and Race in America*, Routledge, New York, 1993, pp. 135-141. Reprinted by permission of Cornell West.

Wresch, William, "Information Rich, Information Poor," from *Disconnected: Haves and Have Nots in the Information Age*. New Brunswick, NJ: Rutgers University Press, 1996, pages 1-19. Copyright © 1996 by William Wresch. Reprinted by permission of Rutgers University Press.